MONUMENTS AND MATERIAL CULTURE

Isobel Smith in 1957 with W.E.V. Young (Curator of Avebury Museum), flanked by two custodians of the museum (*Photograph: Alexander Keiller Museum (Denis Grant King)*)

Monuments and Material Culture

Papers in honour of an Avebury archaeologist: Isobel Smith

EDITED BY

ROSAMUND CLEAL AND JOSHUA POLLARD

Hobnob Press

First published in the United Kingdom in 2004 by
The Hobnob Press, PO Box 1838, East Knoyle, Salisbury SP3 6FA

The editors and publisher gratefully acknowledge the generous support of the Neolithic Studies Group, the Prehistoric Society, English Heritage (for 'William Cunnington and the Long Barrows of the River Wylye') and The National Trust (for 'Dating Avebury').

British Library Cataloguing in Publication Data
A catalogue record for this book is available from the British Library.

ISBN 0-946418-19-5

Typeset in 9/11 pt Souvenir Light
Typesetting and origination by John Chandler
Printed in Great Britain by Salisbury Printing Company Ltd, Salisbury

Contents

PART 2 ~ MATERIAL CULTURE

Foreword

It is a great privilege and pleasure to introduce this volume of essays for Isobel Smith. Her work, especially on the Neolithic, has been an inspiration to me, and to many others. What she had achieved stood as a clear signpost to what more could be done, at a time in the 1970s when studies of the Neolithic had not yet reached their current popularity. That they have since become so varied and dynamic owes much to the scholars of her generation, among whom Isobel was preeminent. It is hard to think of even approaching the study of the southern British Neolithic without her work, from her wide-ranging thesis on Neolithic pottery to her work on sites and monuments in the Avebury area and elsewhere. I think above all of *Windmill Hill and Avebury*, but not only that, since the list of achievements includes the Beckhampton and South Street long barrows and the still intriguing and important occupation site of Cherhill (the latter two in collaboration with John Evans), to say nothing of round barrows and their buried surfaces and Neolithic contents. And her 1974 synthesis of the early Neolithic reminds us that she was never a narrow specialist.

The contents of this volume nicely reflect her central contributions, in the study of monuments, especially around Avebury, and of material culture, especially of pottery and stone tools. When we prepared our own volume on the Windmill Hill causewayed enclosure, her work there proved to be of lasting value and a real help to our understanding. It will continue to be so. With Alex Bayliss, Frances Healy and many others, I am beginning a major programme of radiocarbon dating of causewayed enclosures in southern Britain, sponsored jointly by the Arts and Humanities Research Board and English Heritage. The papers here by Roger Mercer and Frances Healy show brilliantly from their work on Hambledon Hill what more can be done with sites of this kind, and Windmill Hill will be among the major sites to be dated in detail. That it has this importance, and that we have such an ordered account of its early investigation by Keiller and then by herself, are just two of the very many reasons to honour the work of Isobel Smith.

Alasdair Whittle
School of History & Archaeology
Cardiff University

Addresses of Contributors

Paul Ashbee
The Old Rectory
Chedgrave
Norwich, NR14 6ND

Humphrey Case
Pitt's Cottage
187 Thame Road
Warborough, Wallingford
Oxfordshire, OX10 7DH

Rosamund Cleal
Alexander Keiller Museum
High Street, Avebury
Marlborough
Wiltshire, SN8 1RF

Timothy Darvill
School of Conservation Sciences
Bournemouth University
Fern Barrow
Poole, BH12 5BB

Bruce Eagles & **David Field**
English Heritage
Great Western Village
Kemble Drive
Swindon, SN2 2GZ

J.G. Evans
15 Fairleigh Road
Cardiff, CF11 9JT

Peter Fowler
11 Amwell Street
London, EC1R 1UL

Alex Gibson
Department of Archaeological Sciences
University of Bradford
Bradford
West Yorkshire, BD7 1DP

Mark Gillings
School of Archaeology & Ancient History
University of Leicester
Leicester, LE1 7RH

Frances Healy
School of History & Archaeology
Cardiff University
P.O. Box 909
Cardiff, CF10 3XU

Roger Mercer
RCAHMS
John Sinclair House
16 Bernard Terrace
Edinburgh, EH8 9NX

Rick Peterson
School of Humanities & Science,
UWCN, Caerleon Campus,
P.O. Box 179,
Newport, NP18 3YG

Joshua Pollard
Department of Archaeology & Anthropology,
University of Bristol,
43 Woodland Road
Bristol, BS8 1UU

Alan Saville
Department of Archaeology
National Museums of Scotland
Chambers Street
Edinburgh, EH1 1JF

D.D.A. Simpson
School of Archaeology & Palaeoecology
Queen's University Belfast
Belfast, BT7 1NN

Julian Thomas
School of Art History & Archaeology
University of Manchester
Oxford Road
Manchester, M13 9PL

Aaron Watson
Department of Archaeology
University of Reading
Whiteknights, Box 227
Reading, RG6 6AB

Alasdair Whittle
School of History & Archaeology
Cardiff University
P.O. Box 909
Cardiff, CF10 3XU

Isobel Smith visiting Longstones Field, Beckhampton, during the excavation of the Beckhampton Avenue and Longstones enclosure in 1999: from left, Rosamund Cleal, Julian Richards, Isobel Smith, Joshua Pollard and Mark Gillings. (*Photograph: Gill Swanton (image), Colin Shell (processing)*)

Early Ditches: their forms and infills

Paul Ashbee

We owe it to Isobel Smith that the great potentialities in our prehistory of Neolithic pottery's progression and the nature of causewayed enclosures as well as many other things are now being realised. After a half-century of friendship, and occasional work together, it is with the greatest of pleasure and appreciation that the present writer is able to present this tentative excursus.

During prehistory, the construction of barrows and embankments entailed the digging of sometimes considerable ditches. From the first, their exposed sides were broken down by the action of rain, frost, wind and other elements, in short the physical and chemical weathering processes, which produced what is called *silt*. Such weathering was initially rapid and a ditch's original lineaments could have disappeared in a decade, while within a lifetime many, and their mounds and banks, would have been much as they are today. Ditches were either narrow and deep, or broad and shallow. Silt from the sides speedily infilled the former but in the latter it only accumulated against the sides. In such ditches the initial depth for long persisted. The object of this essay is to emphasise that raw chalk-cut ditches were a transient phenomenon, that the

nature of silting was known, and a particular ditch form could have been intentionally chosen.

Since Pitt Rivers (1898, Address, 24), prehistorians have been conscious that ditch infills result from weathering. His observations were given an extended time-scale by E. Cecil Curwen (1930; 1954, 74) who sectioned an abandoned military trench, dug into the chalk of Thundersbarrow Hill, near Shoreham, Sussex (Fig. 1). Thirteen years of weathering and infill, from 1915-16 to 1929, were seen in separate stages. Thereafter, it was thought that ditch sides were originally steeper than excavation might suggest, that pieces of chalk rubble were a rapid accumulation and that filling accrued within a few years of its digging. It became generally accepted that the *trumpet-mouth* profile, particularly of chalkland ditches, came from weathering, as did the notion of *rapid silt* (Wheeler 1943, 87, fig. 15; Piggott & Piggott 1944). Later, I.W. Cornwall (1958, 58) saw silting as exponential and defined stages, while having regard for plant life and burrowing animals.

By the late 1950s it was manifest that appraisals of the timescales of the weathering and denudation of banks and ditches were, despite enlightened observation, inexact, although it was

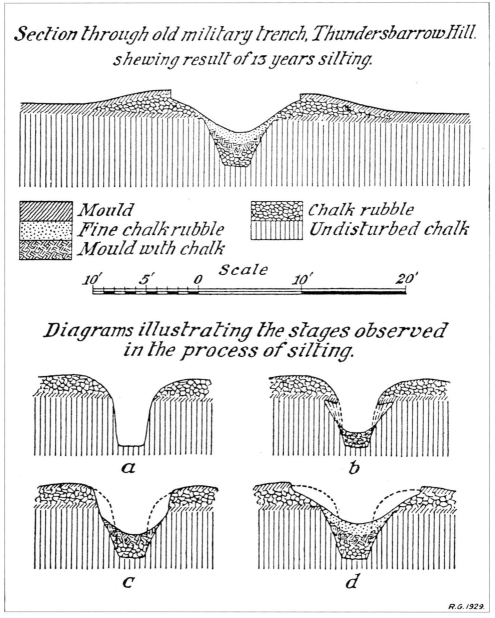

Fig. 1. The silting of First World War trenches on Thundersbarrow Hill, Sussex, observed by E.C.Curwen (1930) and drawn by Robert Gurd

tacitly agreed that initially the process may have been speedy. Experimental controls, or contrived replication, that would give precision to interpretation, were clearly a necessity. It is now a matter of archaeological history that Peter Jewell proposed, in a lecture at the 1958 Darwin Centenary Meeting of the British Association for the Advancement of Science, an experimental earthwork (Jewell 1958, 1993; Ashbee & Jewell 1998). In 1960 the Experimental Earthwork on the chalk of Overton Down, Wiltshire, came into being (Jewell 1963), followed by another on the sandy Eocene heathlands, near Wareham, Dorset, set up in 1963 (Evans & Limbrey 1974). Since those distant days the earthworks have been monitored (Jewell & Dimbleby 1966, Bell *et al.* 1996) and appreciations of the precisely measured results have been a feature of excavation reports treating various Neolithic and earlier Bronze Age monuments (Ashbee & Jewell 1998). These experimental earthworks have shown that dramatic changes can take place within about three decades (Bell *et al.* 1996, 234-5, figs14.1, 14.2). Thus a barrow with, initially, a raw, chalk-cut encircling ditch could have attained much the same form as is seen today within that span.

As in Cranborne Chase (Pitt Rivers 1898, Address, 24) and on Thundersbarrow Hill (Curwen 1930; 1954, 74), a ditch's chalk infill, the early silt, is a product of its sides, quantity being dictated by area, a dimension dependent upon depth. This principle obtains in all chalk-cut ditches, whether encircling a modest barrow or a huge henge. Narrow ditches, as shown so graphically by the Sussex chalkland military trenches, would have become rapidly infilled, while those broad, and sometimes shallow, only accumulated screes below their sides, their centre being relatively clear. The 1992 Overton Down Experimental Earthwork's ditch section (Bell *et al.* 1996, 71, fig. 7.5) illustrates this, the original depth of the ditch having been less than its base's breadth. These broad ditches would have retained their appearance of depth and demarcation for longer, because of their breadth, despite the weathering and denudation of their

sides. In both ditch forms, the narrower and the broader, something of the original ditch's sides, as was seen on Overton Down (Bell *et al.* 1996, 71, fig. 7.5), is regularly preserved beneath the first rubble falls. For the most part our earlier prehistoric ditches were dug with vertical, or near-vertical, sides. Given depth and breadth as the regulatory factors for ditch silting and ultimately appearance, it is not unlikely that those involved in the design, realisation, ministration and modification of monuments derived from ditches were well aware of the inherent proportionate principles.

Ditch silting: examples and contexts

Narrow and deep or broad and shallow ditches were employed for various long and round barrows. At Fussell's Lodge the proximal ends of the flanking ditches (Fig. 2) were, when dug, about 3.7m in depth, but only 2.1m in breadth and at an early stage some 2.1m of chalk rubble accumulated in them (Ashbee 1966, pls XIV, XXII). The West Kennet long barrow ditch, however, to judge from the single section, was originally about 3.7m in depth and breadth, although irregular, and had less than 1.5m of rapid silt (Piggott 1962, 12, fig. 3). Those of the Horslip long barrow (Fig. 3), on the Lower Chalk of Windmill Hill, initially about 2.1-2.4m in depth, although irregular and shallower in places, and 4.6m in breadth, had for the most part less than 0.6m of chalky rapid silt (Ashbee *et al.* 1979, figs 4-6). Winterbourne Monkton's massive Mill-barrow, a progressively modified monument, had an initial inner ditch, also dug into the Lower Chalk, which was of greater width than depth and more regular than that of the Horslip long barrow. Its chalky rapid silt was shallow, as might have been anticipated from its proportions. The ditches which defined the barrow's enlargement appear to have been narrower at their base than their initial depth, although these proportions may have varied. By and large the initial rapid chalky silt was deeper than might have been expected

Fig. 2. A 'narrow' deep silted ditch: proximal end of the Fussell's Lodge long barrow, 1957, on the southern side

(Whittle 1994, figs 3-7). The Badshot long barrow, on the Upper Chalk of Surrey's Hog's Back, employed, apparently, a deeper ditch on its northern side than its southern (Keiller & Piggott 1939, 137, fig. 53). Both silted rapidly.

Similar contrasting ditch examples can be culled from the carefully excavated round barrows. On Crichel and Launceston Downs, Dorset, barrows 2, 3 and 10 had narrow ditches while those of barrows 8 and 9 were broad and shallow (Piggott & Piggott 1944). Of four barrows excavated on New Barn and Earl's Farm Downs, east of Amesbury, the broad ditches of a bell- and disc barrow, and also an exceptional double barrow, were clearly different to the narrow ditch of the Beaker bowl-barrow, and here shallow and rapid chalk rubble was observed (Ashbee 1985).

Similarly, a barrow ditch on Snail Down (Thomas & Thomas 1958), originally 1.8m wide and 0.9m deep, had in its centre less than 0.15m of chalk rubble silt (Cornwall 1958, 53, fig. 2).

For the most part, considerations of ditch silting have been confined to barrows. However, the larger earthen monuments, cursus and henges, thought to have been the products of public labour (Renfrew 1973), also employed ditches, many of considerable size. In this context causewayed enclosures have been excluded as their ditches were sometimes deliberately backfilled (Smith 1965, 15-7). The ditches of the Stonehenge Cursus were broad and shallow, rapid chalky silt being confined to the sides (Stone 1948, fig. 3). Those of the huge Dorset Cursus were yet broader and deeper, although the chalky primary silt accumulations are for the most part shallow (Barrett *et al.* 1991a, 22, fig. 3.2; 1991b, 43-7). However, the ditches of the Dorchester-on-Thames cursus, sited upon level-bedded gravels, were perhaps modest at the outset and may have been periodically scoured (Whittle *et al.* 1992, 149, fig. 4, 150, fig. 5). The ditch of the great Avebury henge is, by its southern entrance, about 5.2m in breadth at its base and was more than 9.1m deep. Its squared bottom points to it having been dug with near vertical sides, for there is an accumulation of chalk rubble silt more than 3.0m deep within its confines (Gray 1935, pl. XXXIX, figs 1 & 2). It is thus of the deep, narrow, type of ditch (Fig. 4) and, although of huge size, is

comparable in character with those of the Fussell's Lodge long barrow (Ashbee 1966, pls XIV, XXII). In contrast, the ditches of the other great Wessex henges, Marden (Wainwright 1971, fig. 4), Durrington Walls (Wainwright & Longworth 1971, 19, figs 4 & 6), Woodhenge (Cunnington 1929, 6, pls 6-8; Wainwright 1979, 73, fig. 43) and Mount Pleasant (Wainwright 1979, 35-47, figs 22-25) are broad, shallow (Fig. 5), and not unlike those of the West Kennet and Horslip long barrows (Piggott 1962, 12, fig. 3; Ashbee *et al.* 1979, 214, figs 4-6).

It is unlikely that those charged with the design, realisation and modification of barrows and other earthworks were not aware of the

Fig. 3. A 'broad', shallow, ditch section on the eastern side of the Horslip long barrow, 1959. 0.84m of the fill is ancient silting. The remainder is from its razing and progressive cultivation

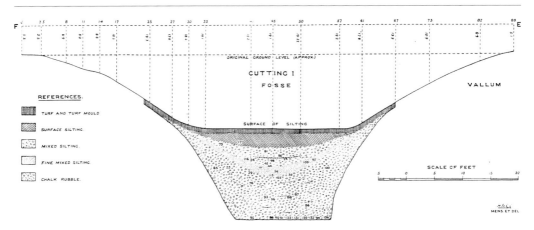

Fig. 4. Avebury's deep, narrow, ditch, which displays a considerable depth (4.0m) of chalk rubble silting (after Gray 1935, pl. XXXVI, fig. 1). Reproduced by kind permission of the Society of Antiquaries of London

characteristics of particular ditch forms and their silting patterns. At Wayland's Smithy the sarsen stone bounding of the later long barrow followed one of the silted ditches of the earlier construction (Whittle 1991, 65, fig. 2). The ditches of the initial Winterbourne Monkton Millbarrow had silted and were further infilled so that the second phase's sarsen stones could be set along their outer edges (Whittle 1994, 47). Varying ditch forms were a feature of the Stonehenge Cursus. At the western end a deep ditch, reminiscent of that of a long barrow, was employed, which contrasted markedly with the use of the modest, broad, shallow ditches for the sides (Stone 1948, Christie 1963). The great Dorset Cursus had also a broad, shallow, ditch, although at the Thickthorn Down termination the considerable bank suggests also a more massive ditch (Barrett *et al.* 1991b, 43-53, fig. 2.16). A succession of ditches was encountered beneath the considerable bowl-barrow, Amesbury 71, and, among other things, was evidence of progressive enlargement. The second phase ditch was broad and shallow and was followed by one of similar breadth and greater

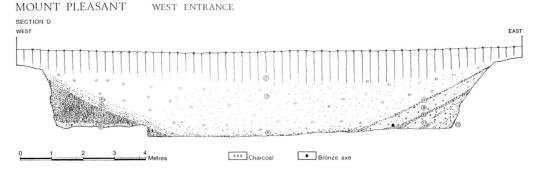

Fig. 5. The broad, shallow, ditch of the Mount Pleasant henge. Chalk rubble silting is no more than a scree at the base of the sides. As a boundary, its nature would have been clear for a considerable time (after Wainwright 1979, fig. 24). Reproduced by kind permission of the Society of Antiquaries of London

depth which had silted deeply and rapidly (Christie 1967). On Crichel Down, Barrow 11, a Beaker barrow, initially modest, with a deep ditch surrounding a near shaft-grave, was enlarged by a further shallow ditch, initially of about the same breadth as the first deeper one (Piggott & Piggott 1944, 73, pl. XIV). Clearly there was conscious choice and ditches, deep and narrow or broad and shallow, were matched to the desired qualities and functions of particular monuments.

Were the essentials inherent in an earthen monument to have determined the nature of its ditch or ditches there are feasible reasons for the employment of particular lineaments and proportions. The qualities of a narrow, deep, ditch, as for instance at Fussell's Lodge (Ashbee 1966, pls XIV, XII), are that the bottom of the sides would have been covered after about two years, a further infill, perhaps as much as 0.9m, after eight years and, after 16 years, more silt and a measure of stabilisation and vegetation. Within a lifetime such a ditch could be much as that of an unmutilated long barrow today. That silting was of significance is illustrated by the various ditch-incorporated deposits, for example the ox remains at Fussell's Lodge (Ashbee 1966, 16) and elsewhere (Ashbee 1970, 77). Indeed, it is arguable that ditch silting, a patent product of weather and time, may have been thought of as access to, and contact with, a perceived past. The back-filling, from the banks, of the ditches, after appropriate deposits, on Windmill Hill, and at other causewayed enclosures (Smith 1965, 15-17, 41-2), could have been a ritual mimicry of the observed natural process! Were this so, it can be no accident that Avebury's great ditch was, despite its huge size, relatively narrow, and would have rapidly infilled with silt, as it is the successor monument to Windmill Hill. The broad shallow ditches at the latter, comparable with those of the Horslip long barrow (Ashbee *et al.* 1979), have the quality of retaining a marked concavity for a considerable time. For long there would have been no more than an accumulation of chalky rubble at the sides, while the central area would have remained the naked chalk. The initial

digging of the ditches could have involved the removal of much the same volume of chalk as the narrower, deeper, ditches but, because of the fetch and lift factors (Ashbee 1966, 34) would have been a less demanding task. Were there, for a while, scouring, this would also have been a relatively easy undertaking. Indeed, consideration of the circumstances points unerringly to conscious choice of ditch form for particular earthen barrows and banks.

Avebury, Silbury Hill and the Wessex henge

An aspect of the ditch of the Overton Down Experimental Earthwork in its early stages was the apparently seasonal alternation of fine and coarse rubble layers, the finer containing soil and dust (Jewell & Dimbleby 1966, 316, 340, pls XXIII, 3; XXIV, 3). In the event, this banding was still visible after 32 years, although blurred by earthworm activity and groundwater percolation (Bell *et al.* 1996, 72). Banding of this nature was observed within the chalk rubble infill of the narrow, but deep, Fussell's Lodge long barrow ditch (Ashbee 1966, pls XIV, XVIb) and, in retrospect, it seems likely that the chalk rubble fill had accumulated within about seven years. A similar fill may have accumulated in much the same time within the wider West Kennet ditch (Piggott 1962, fig. 3). Despite the differences of the Lincolnshire chalk, similar banding was seen in the Skendleby long barrow ditches (Phillips 1936, pl. XXII, fig. 1; Evans & Simpson 1991, figs 17-20). Incidental banding has been seen in various chalk-cut, modestly sized, round-barrow ditches (Ashbee 1978, 1981, 1985) but they were almost all too imprecise for more than an impressionistic count to be made. In the not unsubstantial ditches of the two large Milton Lilbourne bell-barrows, however, the banding suggested rapid silt accumulation within about eight years (Ashbee 1986, 52). Because of its great size, the massive Avebury ditch silts contained, within their lower register, clear, well-defined banding (Gray 1935, 120, pl. XXXIX; Malone 1989, 106, fig. 84). It appears that some 3.0-3.7m of chalk rubble, derived from the near-vertical sides, could have accumulated in about seven or eight years. Within a lifetime the ditch, and its huge bank, could have been near-static and clothed with vegetation. The bones and other materials would have been deposited during the early stages.

Unless apparent settlement debris was kept and used over a period, it is not unreasonable to suppose that the ditches of Windmill Hill were all open at the same time (Smith 1965, 14). Thus one could consider that the similarly planned, only approximately circular, causeway-divided, Avebury ditch of greater magnitude was executed as an entity. Although liberal estimates for the digging of Avebury's ditch and the raising of its bank have been made, the original formula, extrapolated from the Experimental Earthwork and subsequently modified by R.J.C. Atkinson (Ashbee & Cornwall 1961, 133; Atkinson 1961, 295) is not unrealistic. Its great circumference, nearly 1.2km, involved the removal of some 96,220 cubic metres of chalk. Expressed in terms of 10 hour man-days, 68,000 would be the total, which could be expressed as 1000 people working for 68 days or 100 people for 680 days. It should not be overlooked that there is evidence for a primary bank, a precursor of that seen at the present time (Pitts & Whittle 1992, 206). Were this a guiding device it might follow that work on the great ditch could have been concurrent and not progressive, although this is by no means certain. At Avebury, however, the crest of the bank originally rose about 16.8m above the bottom of the ditch, as against the mere 3.4m of Overton Down, a ratio of 5:1. Thus, with these considerations in mind, if the time for 100 people, arrived at by application of the Overton Down rates, be multiplied merely by five, a time of some nine and a half years is reached. Because of the silting factor, which, if an initial clear ditch and dumped bank was the objective, there would have to have been a task-force of about 250 at work to ensure completion within about four years. Richard Atkinson (1961, 295) felt that because of the uncertainties involved in the deployment of

human endeavour the linear scaling-up of the Overton Down outputs was over-simplistic. He stressed that, in all earthworks, constructional processes would have involved two kinds of operations, digging and filling containers *in the ditch*, and the transport and dumping of those containers *onto the bank*. The first would vary with the hardness of the material dug into (Avebury's ditch is into the Lower Chalk, in places through the Middle Chalk capping (Smith 1965, 194)), the second is related to the scale of the earthwork desired. His estimate for the endeavours required were 156,000 man-days, or 100 people for three and a quarter years. This it should be observed is well within the time-limit of noticeable, inhibiting, weathering and silting. These principles, expressed as a mathematical formula (Atkinson 1961, 295, fn. 7) were applied to the ditch-digging, chalk-rubble transport and dumping involved in the construction of the Fussell's Lodge long barrow and realistic results emerged (Ashbee 1966, 34-5).

Avebury's great ditch, which encircled 11.5ha, was dug vertically, as can be seen from the bottom 1.2m. Furthermore, in plan it is far from a circle and excavation has shown that it was irregular, with marked variations in width and depth (Gray 1935, 161; Smith 1965, 193). The external bank of chalk from this huge ditch displays also, apart from modern mutilations, conspicuous irregularities. An attempt at chalk-block walling for retention was observed but there were also loose piles of large chalk lumps. Indeed, it is difficult to avoid a comparison with the Windmill Hill causewayed enclosure's circles of ditches (Smith 1965, fig. 3), for Avebury's ditch is likely to have been an aggrandised and stylised version of them. Fragmentary human remains were within the chalk rubble, while the irregularities of the bank might well reflect material thrown back to emulate and augment the natural silting processes (Gray 1935, pl. XLIV). All in all, it can be contended that the huge, deep, narrow, ditch was for silting rather than to be seen!

An integral part of the Avebury monument combination is Silbury Hill, raised from an enormous version of a broad, and relatively shallow, ditch, thought to have been designed to hold water (Whittle 1997, 22-4, pl. 2, figs 4, 5 & 23). Presumably it was progressively dug to an eventual regular form, as its extension may also have been. Richard Atkinson, the excavator, thought of a work-span of 10 years and an even longer time has been envisaged. Truncated layers within the ditch may have resulted from material deposited to check erosion considered to have been threatening the stability of the mound. Its sides, almost 35 degrees (much less than chalk's angle of rest which is about 45 degrees), are comparable with those of the steeper Wessex bell-barrows, while the inside of the ditch displays a sloping berm (Ashbee 1960, 58, fig. 19), the result of differential weathering, the adjustment between a barrow's buried ancient soil, its ditch and the modern soil surround. Despite silting, it would appear as likely that Silbury Hill's essentially broad ditch was designed to endure and to be a positive, observable, feature, enhancing the great mound into the future. Indeed, it has fulfilled this function into our own time.

The Wessex henges (Wainwright 1989) are of two kinds, although for the most part they are characterised by broad, relatively shallow ditches. Three of them, the first phase of Stonehenge, the Coneybury henge (at no great distance) and the substantial hilltop Mount Pleasant henge, may have been concerned primarily with formulistic, or prescriptive, ends. Maumbury Rings may also have been in this category but the shafts and subsequent modifications have destroyed the character of its initial ditch (Bradley 1976, 14). Marden, Durrington Walls and Woodhenge had within them the remains of substantial timber buildings.

Stonehenge's circular ditch, Phase 1 of that remarkable monument (Cleal *et al.* 1995, 63-94), of which a considerable number of profiles were recorded, is clearly of the broad and relatively shallow class. It was, however, dug as a series of interconnecting segments, in the mode of a causewayed enclosure. There is a low internal bank and a lower counterscarp bank resulting from scouring or, perhaps, modification. This bank, a series of disconnected arcs, seems modest for the magnitude of the ditch, although the counterscarp bank could have been more substantial than is commonly thought. Despite its near-geometric circularity, it may have been dug for back-filling but was only infrequently so used. Presumably its precursor was Robin Hood's Ball, two ovate ditches on an east-facing slope, the outer having a not dissimilar profile (Thomas 1964, 6, fig. 9.1). The modest ovate henge on Coneybury Hill, within sight of Stonehenge, had, for the most part, deep, narrow, ditches which would have speedily accumulated silt. Indeed, as at Avebury, it appears that an insilted ditch was the objective (RCHME 1979, 13, pl. 10; Richards 1990, 123-58).

Mount Pleasant, the spacious hilltop henge in Dorset, is, basically, a slightly less than half-size replica of Avebury (Wainwright 1979, 232). Its broad, relatively shallow, ditch, dug into the Upper Chalk, with external bank, breached by four entrances, would, like others of its kind, have been slow to silt and would have been a positive, perceptible, feature for a considerable time. Initially, a circular timber, ditched, Woodhenge-like structure was sited towards its southwestern quarter. This was replaced by a rectangular sarsen stone setting and some pits. Termed a *cove*, it is rather more reminiscent of the setting within Avebury's southern circle. At a later juncture, a massive and spectacular timber palisade was erected shadowing the ditch, while a large barrow, with a broad ditch, was set-up on its bank.

Marden (Wainwright *et al.* 1971), with its ditch dug through Chalky Drift into Greensand, and encroached upon by an Avon tributary, which would originally have been faster flowing, may at the outset have been a four-entranced oval of north-south orientation. A simple, circular, timber structure stood by its north entrance, the great Hatfield Barrow in a similar situation by its east entrance and another barrow faced the erstwhile south entrance. Its ditch, before weathering and denudation, would have been 9.1m in breadth and about 2.4m deep. Such shallow sides, together with this considerable breadth, would have resulted in no more than a relatively modest accumulation of silt at the sides and thus unambiguous demarcation for a considerable time. The bank may have been about the same height as the depth of its ditch (Wainwright *et al.* 1971, 190, fig. 6). Marden's giant Hatfield Barrow may have been, after Silbury Hill, the largest in Wessex (Whittle 1997, 149-50), and, like other massive mounds, have had non-material qualities as well as being a yardstick for emulation (Ashbee 1978, 129).

Woodhenge (Cunnington 1929; Wainwright, 1979, 71-4) and Durrington Walls (Wainwright & Longworth 1971) are both on the Upper Chalk, which fringes the west side of the Avon valley, and are integral parts of the Stonehenge ensemble of monuments. Woodhenge, the post-hole circles of a substantial circular structure, was closely contained within its broad, but relatively shallow, ditch (Cunnington 1929, pls. 6-8; Wainwright 1979, 73, figs 42-3). In this respect it resembled the ditch-circumscribed circular structure within Mount Pleasant (Wainwright 1979, 13, fig. 7) and the Arminghall henge, Norfolk (Clark 1936, p1. IV). At this last site the inner ditch, the greater, and the outer, the lesser, had been dug into glacial sands and gravels. Although weathered and silted (Clark 1936, pl. VI), it is clear that they had, like those of Woodhenge, been of the broad and relatively shallow kind. Durrington Walls, adjacent to Woodhenge (Wainwright & Longworth 1971), a massive double-entranced henge enclosure, bestrides a dry valley. Excavation revealed the postholes of two circular timber structures, the larger by the eastern entrance, at the lowest point of this dry valley. The considerable ditch, originally and largely of the broad, relatively shallow variety, describes an irregular ovate course. Care was taken to site the bank on level land and, at one point, there is a considerable berm. Regarding the ditch silting, the excavators (1971, 20) invoked the Overton Down Experimental Earthwork. (Jewell & Dimbleby 1966, 340-1). Its sides weathered and chalk rubble would have accumulated at their

foot. The wide ditch would have been a massive, prominently perceptible, circumscription for many more years than its narrow, deep, counterpart at Avebury (Gray 1935, pl. XXXIX).

Beyond Wessex

Beyond Wessex there is a considerable, well-recorded, repertoire of ditches dug into gravels, glacial deposits and rock formations, in various parts of Britain. So far as could be seen from a sample of these, narrow, deep, ditches were few and confined to barrows, whereas henges were mostly demarcated by broad, shallow versions.

A number of narrow ditches characterised the razed barrows and other earthworks on the gravels of the Upper Thames, near Dorchester, Oxfordshire (Atkinson *et al.* 1951, Whittle *et al.* 1992). Here Sites I, II, IV, V, VI, XII, 2, 4 had ditches which were deep and narrow, sometimes pronouncedly, and had been dug with vertical sides. For some 13 weeks before Christmas in 1947, Richard Atkinson left such a ditch open in which time there was a 0.8m accumulation of silt (Atkinson *et al.* 1951, 42). Some sites (XI, XIV), however, had ditches that were neither broad nor narrow, although those of the Big Rings Henge (XIII) were pronouncedly broad and shallow. This complex, at the north-eastern fringe of Wessex, displayed similarities with that area, as have other such monuments sited upon gravels. Of note also are the Holdenhurst long barrow, sited upon sands and gravels, near Bournemouth, which had broad, shallow, ditches (Piggott 1937, pl. III) and the Arminghall henge, on a low river-gravel shoulder, near Norwich (Clark 1936, 7, pl. VI).

The ditch of Arbor Low (Gray 1908; Burl 1976, 276), cut into Derbyshire's limestone, was only modestly silted, by mould and fragments of chert, and it was questioned as to whether its debris would have been sufficient for the bank. Even today, it clearly demarcates and is thought to resemble that of Cairnpapple, West Lothian, which had been quarried into the basalt lava flows interbedded with sandstone, shales and limestones, in which clayey and stony silts had slowly accumulated (Piggott 1947-8, 82-3, fig. 6). In form they are both of the broad, shallow, kind, although not as pronouncedly as many. The broad ditch of the Balfarg henge, described as of splayed 'U' profile, had been dug into mixed glacial till and boulder clay. Its fill was eroded and windborne materials, and it was thought possible that it had periodically been cleared out. So far as can be seen this substantial ditch had been initially dug with near-vertical sides and its appearance resulted from weathering and silting (Mercer 1981, 66-70, figs 4-5).

Dalladies, Fettercairn, Kincardineshire, an earthen long barrow (Piggott 1971-2), had features comparable with those of the Wessex chalklands. Insubstantial flanking ditches, dug into a gravel terrace, delimited the trapezoidal area within which the barrow stood. They could have made only a slight contribution to its bulk. There was no coarse primary silt, the infill being dark soil, containing small stones, seemingly a deliberate infill. There is the possibility that these token ditches were deliberately backfilled in emulation of the rapid silting of a larger, narrow, ditch.

Among the prominent monuments of the Orkney Islands there are ditches which must have been clearly illustrative of their particular inherent qualities. At Maeshowe the ditch, cut into the natural basal clays, proved to have been almost 9.1m in breadth and about 1.8m deep. Peat had developed on one side, because of minimal silting, and a loam on the other (Renfrew 1979, 31-8). The rock-cut ditch of the Ring of Brodgar was broad and shallow on the north side of the circle, yet on the south side it was only half that width, although it had been cut to much the same depth. Here there was marked rocky infill, betokening frost weathering (Renfrew 1979, 39- 43, fig. 15). By way of contrast, the rock-cut ditch of Stenness (Ritchie 1975-6, 17, fig. 3) was neither excessively broad nor pronouncedly narrow. It appears to have had, initially, near-vertical sides and its silting was derived from the mantling soils and deposits of the site. Animal bones and pieces of wood were found, as in Wessex, in what eventually became a waterlogged infill. It was conjectured that the cutting of the ditch, which involved the removal of large blocks of Orcadian sandstone, and the throwing-up of the bank, may have entailed 50,000 man-hours, an estimate based upon the work-rates formulated on Overton Down (Jewell 1963). Also taken into account were some computations for the raising of the Rodmarton stone-built long barrow (Clifford 1950, 35), where it was suggested that construction gangs may have been wayfaring specialists.

Envoi

These examples of ditches, from well-recorded Wessex, and other sites, make no pretension to completeness. They show, however, that in Neolithic and earlier Bronze Age times two fundamental forms were prescribed, planned and executed when appropriate. Narrow, deep, ditches, within which a considerable depth of silt speedily accumulated, appear as continuing the practices observed on Windmill Hill and elsewhere (Smith 1971, 97-100). Indeed, such rapid infills may have been of more consequence than the ditch from the sides of which they were derived. Broad, shallow, ditches were clearly different in that silting was relegated to the sides and thus they would have for long been an evident demarcation. Each form of ditch attracted deposits (Wainwright 1979, 40) and burials (Ashbee 1978, 16; Evans *et al.* 1983).

Beyond seasonal change (Cornwall 1964, 64) and cyclic practices (Barrett 1994, 70-2) there is little indicative of prehistoric time perception. Ditch silting, together with the weathering and denudation of earthen monuments was, however, an inexorable continuing process, apart from, although related to, seasonal succession. Because of the selection of particular ditch forms, it follows that their silting could have provided vision of the effluxion of time. Indeed, the barrow groups such as Snail Down (Thomas & Thomas 1958) or Winterbourne Stoke (Grinsell 1958, 108) would have been a monumental perspective of time passing as, for long, there would have been mounds and ditches at *every* stage of weathering, denudation, silting and vegetational colonisation. Whatever their significance, narrow, deep, ditches, in which a considerable depth of silt speedily accumulated, would have been in contrast with those which were broad and shallow, with no more than a seemingly modest amassment at the bases of their sides.

Change and decay may have led to endeavours to achieve permanence for particular long barrows. Wayland's Smithy I had a modest irregular mound and the sarsen stone kerb could have been an attempt to arrest its denudation and spread. Ultimately it was superseded by a regular stone-built structure (Whittle 1991). Other earthen mounds within the Avebury area (Barker 1985) may have been restated in stone and there is evidence that it was, perhaps, a regular practice where the stone was suitable (Masters 1983, 103-4). In regions such as Caithness and the Orkney Islands, cairns and circles, encompassed by broad, rock-cut, ditches, attained a permanence difficult elsewhere, except in favoured and local circumstances.

It is appreciated by few, but it must be emphasised, that ditch silts, of long barrows, cursus, round barrows and henges are the repositories of a wealth of environmental information, predominantly local. Nonetheless, were systematic studies embarked upon, regional trends and circumstances could emerge. Three long barrow ditches, in Dorset, Wiltshire and Lincolnshire, have already been examined (Evans 1990) and significant inferences have been made. Land use and landscape have emerged as dynamic dimensions of our prehistoric studies. Investigations such as that of the Cherhill, Wiltshire, deposits (Evans & Smith 1983) or the South Downs valley sediments (Bell 1983) graphically illustrate the changes wrought in Neolithic and earlier Bronze Age times, as have ditch infills. It is manifest that such infills are often far more informative than the ditches from which they are all too often relentlessly removed and even their nature, narrow and deep or broad and shallow, is rarely pursued!

Postscript

This examination of early ditches emanates from the Experimental Earthwork, built in 1960, under the leadership of Peter Jewell (1963), on Overton Down. Now definitively published, after the assigned 32 years (Bell *et al.* 1996), it was Peter's chef-d'oeuvre. Working with the present writer, various issues were retrospectively recorded (1998) but, sadly, he did not live to see them in print. Hence, this essay is an individual perspective.

Bibliography

Ashbee, P. 1960. *The Bronze Age Round Barrow in Britain*. London: Phoenix House

Ashbee, P. 1966. The Fussell's Lodge long barrow: excavations 1957. *Archaeologia* 100, 1-80

Ashbee, P. 1984. *The Earthen Long Barrow in Britain*. 2nd edition. London: Dent

Ashbee, P. 1978. Amesbury barrow 51: excavations 1960. *Wiltshire Archaeological & Natural History Magazine* 70/71, 1-60

Ashbee, P. 1981. Amesbury barrow 39: excavations 1960. *Wiltshire Archaeological & Natural History Magazine* 74/75, 1-34

Ashbee, P. 1985. The excavation of Amesbury barrows 58, 61a, 61, 72. *Wiltshire Archaeological & Natural History Magazine* 79, 39-91

Ashbee, P. 1986. The excavation of Milton Lilbourne barrows 1-5. *Wiltshire Archaeological & Natural History Magazine* 80, 24-96

Ashbee, P. & Cornwall, I.W. 1961. An experiment in field archaeology. *Antiquity* 35, 129-34

Ashbee, P., Smith, I.F. & Evans, J.G. 1979. Excavation of three long barrows near Avebury. *Proceedings of the Prehistoric Society* 45, 207-300

Ashbee, P. & Jewell, P. 1998. The experimental earthworks revisited. *Antiquity* 72, 485-504

Atkinson, R.J.C. 1961. Neolithic engineering. *Antiquity* 35, 292-9

Atkinson, R.J.C., Piggott, C.M. & Sandars, N.K. 1951. *Excavations at Dorchester, Oxon., First Report*. Oxford: Ashmolean Museum

Barker, C.T. 1985. The long mounds of the Avebury region. *Wiltshire Archaeological & Natural History Magazine* 79, 7-38

Barrett, J.C. 1994. *Fragments from Antiquity.* Oxford: Blackwell

Barrett, J.C., Bradley, R. & Hall, M. 1991a. *Papers on the Prehistoric Archaeology of Cranborne Chase.* Oxford: Oxbow Books

Barrett, J.C., Bradley, R. & Green, M. 1991b. *Landscape, Monuments and Society: the prehistory of Cranborne Chase.* Cambridge: Cambridge University Press

Bell, M. 1983. Valley sediments as evidence of prehistoric land-use on the South Downs. *Proceedings of the Prehistoric Society* 49, 119-50

Bell, M., Fowler, P.J. & Hillson, S.W. 1996. *The Experimental Earthwork Project, 1960-1992.* London: Council for British Archaeology

Bradley, R. 1976. Maumbury Rings, Dorchester. *Archaeologia* 105, 1-97

Christie, P.M. 1963. The Stonehenge Cursus. *Wiltshire Archaeological & Natural History Magazine* 58, 370-82

Christie, P.M. 1967. A barrow-cemetery of the second millennium BC in Wiltshire, England. *Proceedings of the Prehistoric Society* 33, 336-66

Clark, J.G.D. 1936. The timber monument at Arminghall and its affinities. *Proceedings of the Prehistoric Society* 2, 1-51

Cleal, R.M.J., Walker, K.E. & Montague, R. 1995. *Stonehenge in its Landscape: twentieth-century excavations.* London: English Heritage

Clifford, E.M. 1950. The Cotswold megalithic culture: the grave goods and their background. In C. Fox & B. Dickens (eds), *The Early Cultures of North-West Europe* (H.A. Chadwick Memorial Studies), 23-40. Cambridge: Cambridge University Press

Cornwall, I.W. 1958. *Soils for the Archaeologist.* London: Phoenix House

Cornwall, I.W. 1964. *The World of Ancient Man.* London: Mentor Books

Cunnington, M.E. 1929. *Woodhenge.* Devizes: Simpson

Curwen, E.C. 1930. The silting of ditches in chalk. *Antiquity* 4, 97-100

Curwen, E.C. 1954. *The Archaeology of Sussex.* 2nd edition. London: Methuen

Evans, J.G. Atkinson, R., O'Connor, T. & Green, S. 1984. Stonehenge - the environment in the late Neolithic and early Bronze Age and a Beaker-age burial. *Wiltshire Archaeological & Natural History Magazine* 78, 7-30

Evans, J.G., 1990. Notes on some Late Neolithic and Bronze Age events in long barrow ditches in southern and eastern England. *Proceedings of the Prehistoric Society* 56, 111-16

Evans, J.G. & Limbrey, S. 1974. The experimental earthwork in Morden Bog, Wareham, Dorset. *Proceedings of the Prehistoric Society* 40, 170-202

Evans, J.G. & Simpson, D.D.A. 1991. Giants' Hills 2 long barrow, Skendleby, Lincolnshire. *Archaeologia* 109, 1-45

Evans, J.G. & Smith, I.F. 1983. Excavations at Cherhill, north Wiltshire, 1967. *Proceedings of the Prehistoric Society* 49, 45-117

Gray, H.St.G. 1903. On the excavations at Arbor Low, 1901-2. *Archaeologia* 58, 461-98

Gray, H.St.G. 1935. The Avebury excavations, 1908-1922. *Archaeologia* 84, 99-162

Grinsell, L.V. 1958. *The Archaeology of Wessex.* London: Methuen

Jewell, P.A. 1958. Natural history and experiment in archaeology. *Proceedings of the British Association for the Advancement of Science* 59, 165-72

Jewell, P.A. (ed.) 1963. *The Experimental Earthwork on Overton Down, Wiltshire, 1960.* London: British Association for the Advancement of Science

Jewell, P.A. 1993. Natural history and experiment in archaeology revisited. In A. Clason, S. Payne & H.-P. Uerpmann (eds.), *Skeletons in her Cupboard*, 109-16. Oxford: Oxbow Books

Jewell, P.A. & Dimbleby, G.W. 1966. The Experimental Earthwork on Overton Down, Wiltshire, England: the first four years. *Proceedings of the Prehistoric Society* 32, 313-42

Keiller, A. & Piggott, S. 1939. Badshot long barrow. In *Survey of the Prehistory of the Farnham District*, 133-49. Guildford: Surrey Archaeological Society

Malone, C. 1989. *Avebury.* London, English Heritage

Masters, L. 1983. Chambered tombs and non-megalithic barrows in Britain. In C. Renfrew (ed.), *The Megalithic Monuments of Western Europe*, 97-112. London: Thames & Hudson

Mercer, R.J. 1981. The excavation of a late Neolithic henge-type enclosure at Balfarg, Markinch, Fife, Scotland. *Proceedings of the Society of Antiquaries of Scotland* 111, 63-171

Phillips, C.W. 1936. The excavation of the Giants' Hills long barrow, Skendleby, Lincolnshire. *Archaeologia* 85, 37-106

Piggott, S. 1937. The excavation of a long barrow in Holdenhurst parish, near Christchurch. *Proceedings of the Prehistoric Society* 3, 1-14

Piggott, S. 1948. The excavations at Cairnpapple Hill, West Lothian, 1947-48. *Proceedings of the Society of Antiquaries of Scotland* 82, 68-123

Piggott, S. 1962. *The West Kennet Long Barrow: excavations 1955-56*. London: HMSO

Piggott, S. 1971-2. Excavation of the Dalladies long barrow, Fettercairn, Kincardineshire. *Proceedings of the Society of Antiquaries of Scotland*, 104, 23-47

Piggott, S. & Piggott, C.M. 1944. Excavation of barrows on Crichel and Launceston Downs. *Archaeologia* 90, 47-80

Pitt Rivers, A.H.L.F. 1898. *Excavations in Cranborne Chase*. Volume 4. Privately printed

Pitts, M. & Whittle, A. 1992. The Development and Date of Avebury. *Proceedings of the Prehistoric Society* 58, 203-12

Renfrew, C. 1973. Monuments, mobilisation and social organisation in Neolithic Wessex. In C. Renfrew (ed.), *The Explanation of Culture Change: models in prehistory*, 539-58. London: Duckworth

Renfrew, C. 1979. *Investigations in Orkney*. London: Society of Antiquaries of London

Richards, J. 1990. *The Stonehenge Environs Project*. London: English Heritage

Ritchie, J.N.G. 1975-6. The Stones of Stenness, Orkney. *Proceedings of the Society of Antiquaries of Scotland*, 107, 1-60

RCHME, 1979. *Stonehenge and its Environs*. Edinburgh: Edinburgh University Press

Smith, I.F. 1965. *Windmill Hill and Avebury: excavations by Alexander Keiller, 1925-39*. Oxford: Clarendon Press

Smith, I.F. 1971. Causewayed enclosures. In D.D.A. Simpson (ed.), *Economy and Settlement in Neolithic and Early Bronze Age Britain and Europe*, 89-112. Leicester: Leicester University Press

Stone, J.F.S. 1948. The Stonehenge Cursus and its affinities. *Archaeological Journal* 104, 7-19

Thomas, N. 1964. The Neolithic causewayed camp at Robin Hood's Ball, Shrewton. *Wiltshire Archaeological & Natural History Magazine* 59, 1-27

Thomas, N. & Thomas, C. 1958. Excavations at Snail Down, Everleigh. *Wiltshire Archaeological & Natural History Magazine* 56, 127-48

Wainwright, G.J. 1971. The excavation of a later Neolithic Enclosure at Marden, Wiltshire. *Antiquaries Journal* 51, 177-239

Wainwright, G.J. 1979. *Mount Pleasant, Dorset: excavations 1970-1971*. London: Society of Antiquaries of London

Wainwright, G.J. 1989. *The Henge Monuments*. London: Thames & Hudson

Wainwright, G.J. & Longworth, I.H. 1971. *Durrington Walls: excavations 1966-1968*. London: Society of Antiquaries of London

Wheeler, R.E.M. 1943. *Maiden Castle, Dorset*. London: Society of Antiquaries of London

Whittle, A. 1991. Wayland's Smithy, Oxfordshire: excavations at the Neolithic tomb in 1962-3 by R.J.C. Atkinson & S. Piggott. *Proceedings of the Prehistoric Society* 57(2), 61-101

Whittle, A. 1994. Excavations at Millbarrow Neolithic chambered tomb, Winterbourne Monkton, north Wiltshire. *Wiltshire Archaeological & Natural History Magazine* 87, 1-53

Whittle, A. 1997. *Sacred Mound, Holy Rings. Silbury Hill and the West Kennet palisade enclosures: a Later Neolithic complex in north Wiltshire*. Oxford, Oxbow Books

Whittle, A., Atkinson, R.J.C., Chambers, R. & Thomas, N. 1992. Excavations in the Neolithic and Bronze Age complex at Dorchester-on-Thames, Oxfordshire. *Proceedings of the Prehistoric Society* 58, 143-201

Hambledon Hill and its Implications

Frances Healy

The starting point

Isobel Smith's interpretation of the uses of Windmill Hill (1965, 19) rings as true today as it did when it was first published:

'. . . the pottery evidence at Windmill Hill . . . points to visits by groups of people coming from other regions . . . as well as by those who may be assumed to have lived in the immediate vicinity, so that the enclosure may be seen to have served as a centre or rallying-point for the population of a fairly wide area.

> Such rallying-points play an essential role in the lives of some contemporary communities living in a comparable stage of economic and technological development . . . Assembly of the scattered families of tribal units takes place at one or more intervals during the year, at the slack periods in the agricultural and/or stock-tending cycle, and affords opportunities for the transaction of the necessary business of tribal life. In addition to those matters which may come within the political field in its broadest sense, such other matters can be attended to as the holding of initiation ceremonies, match-makings and weddings, the exchange of stock and seed corn and perhaps of more durable goods. Rites and ceremonies are performed to ensure the fertility of the flocks and herds and the growing of the corn, and finally to celebrate the harvest. Communal feasts are an inevitable

accompaniment of such occasions, and some industrial activities may be undertaken, either because they are less tedious when performed to the accompaniment of a lively exchange of news and gossip, or because there is insufficient time at other seasons.'

This picture is instantly recognisable in interpretations of more recently excavated enclosures like Etton in Cambridgeshire (Pryor 1998), in the reworking of the Windmill Hill record by Whittle, Pollard and Grigson (1999), and in the vivid semi-fictional narrative of Edmonds (1999, 106–108, 130–132).

Hambledon Hill

Hambledon Hill in Dorset, centred at NGR ST 849 122, was excavated between 1974 and 1986 by Roger Mercer, on behalf of English Heritage and its predecessors. From the first, the project has benefited from Isobel Smith's participation, experience and insight. Its contributions to an understanding of causewayed enclosures and of the wider archaeology of the earlier fourth millennium stem mainly from the large scale on which it was investigated (some 4.25 ha were excavated); from the size of the assemblages recovered; from its chronology, based on Alex Bayliss' Bayesian modelling of 161 radiocarbon dates, in which other evidence, primarily the stratigraphic relationships of the samples, was used to constrain the probability distributions of the measurements (Bayliss *et al.* forthcoming); and from its location at the south-east edge of Cranborne Chase, which makes it possible to relate the Hambledon record to that of an area much used in prehistory and much researched in recent times (Barrett *et al.* 1991; Green 2000).

The hill consists of a central dome from which there extend three main spurs, the hillfort spur to the north, the Shroton spur to the east, and the Stepleton spur to the south (with the Hanford spur jutting from its western side Fig. 1). The tip and sides of the hillfort spur are steep. The other spur tips slope gently to the valley floors and provide the easiest access to the hill. The known Neolithic earthworks are as follows:

• The main causewayed enclosure on the central dome of the hill.
• Two pairs of cross-dykes, set across the necks of the Shroton and Stepleton spurs of the hill immediately outside the main enclosure. These are likely to equate to the outer circuits of other enclosures and are probably matched by a third pair now concealed by the southern ramparts of the Iron Age hillfort.
• The small south long barrow between the main enclosure and the south cross-dykes.
• A massive north long barrow on the axis of the hillfort spur, cut by an undocumented antiquarian trench, but otherwise uninvestigated
• The western outwork, skirting the west end of the south cross-dykes, running downslope from the main enclosure, and continuing around the hillfort spur under the western ramparts of the Iron Age hillfort.
• The Shroton spur outwork to the east of the main enclosure, set at the break of slope of the Shroton spur.
• The Stepleton enclosure, much smaller than the main enclosure, on the Stepleton spur to the south.
• Three outworks (the inner, middle and outer Stepleton outworks) skirting the Stepleton enclosure, two of them carrying on around the south-west of the hill to the Hanford spur.
• Numerous pits.

Quarries on the Hanford spur, once thought to be flint mines coeval with the construction of the earthworks (Mercer 1987), have been found to date to the third millennium cal BC (Table 1: OxA-7833); the north cross-rampart within the hillfort, once thought to be part of a third Neolithic enclosure (Mercer 1988), is now dated to the first millennium cal BC (Table 1: OxA-7776).

Before the enclosure was built

One implication of the Hambledon record is that early Mesolithic activity extended over areas where few or no contemporary artefacts are known, a conclusion which has also emerged at Stonehenge and elsewhere (Allen & Gardiner 2002). An excavated collection of some 89,000 pieces of struck flint from the hill includes one, possibly two, Mesolithic cores (Saville forthcoming), in contrast to an abundance of Mesolithic lithics on the Clay-with-Flints in Cranborne Chase to the east (Barrett *et al.* 1991, 29–30; Arnold *et al.* 1988; Green 2000, 20–28). Yet pine charcoal from two posthole-like features on the hill is dated to the eighth millennium cal BC (Table 1: OxA-7816, OxA-7845–6). The hill seems to have been a vantage point rather than a living place. Both features were in break-of-slope positions, where posts set in them or fires lit close to them would have been conspicuous. They would not, however, have been visible from the occupied chalk downland of Cranborne Chase, since both were on the west side of the hill (Fig. 2), which, vegetation permitting, commands and is visible from a very different terrain, the low-lying Vale of Blackmoor, based mainly on Kimmeridge and Oxford Clays, which in turn gives way to the Jurassic ridge, the Somerset Levels and the Mendips. Hambledon lies at the boundary of the chalk of central southern England and the physically – and in historical times culturally – distinct south-west. Those who generated the eighth millennium pine charcoal on the hill seem to have focussed their attention on this region, where contemporary activity is evidenced on the Mendips and Quantocks and in the Somerset

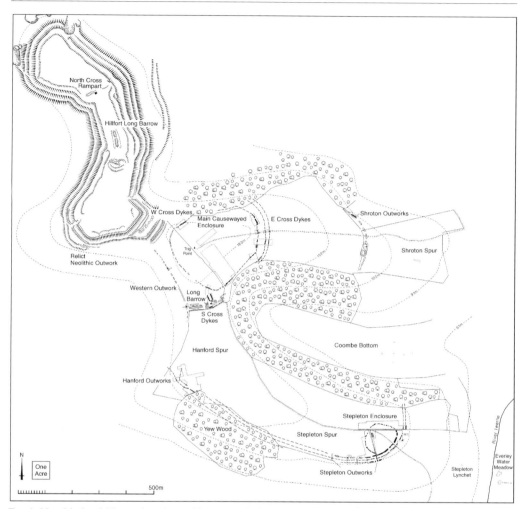

Fig. 1. Hambledon Hill. earthworks and location of 1974–86 excavations

Levels (Jacobi 1982) rather than in the adjacent Blackmoor Vale.

In Cranborne Chase to the east, Mesolithic activity continued to the turn of the fifth and fourth millennia cal BC. In the upper fill of a natural sink-hole, the Fir Tree Field shaft, was a group of seven microliths in fresh condition, clustered as if they had formed part of a spearhead or other composite implement, and bracketed by radiocarbon determinations on short-life charcoal samples of 4340–4040 cal BC (stratified below them) and 4050–3800 and 3970–3700 cal BC (stratified above them, and associated with a hearth and Neolithic Bowl pottery; Table 1: OxA-8009–11; Allen & Green 1998). The sequence is most readily interpreted as reflecting a fairly rapid transition from one tradition to the next. The earliest elements of the Hambledon complex are

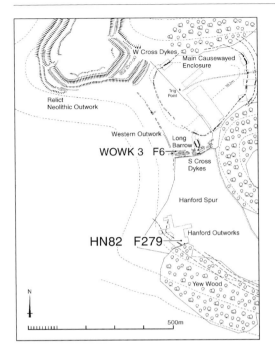

Fig. 2. Hambledon Hill. Location of features containing pine charcoal of Boreal age

estimated to have been built in *3680–3630 cal BC (95% probability)*, at most six hundred years after the loss or deposition of the Mesolithic hunting weapon, and possibly as little as three hundred years (Fig. 3). Elsewhere in Britain, dates reliably associated with Mesolithic artefacts extend into the early fourth millennium cal BC (Spikins 2002); and some Neolithic monuments, including long barrows and cairns, were being built from *c* 3800 cal BC, on the evidence of radiocarbon measurements on the contained human remains, including some of those listed by Richards and Hedges (1999). The potential for the adoption of Neolithic lifeways within a couple of generations becomes a real one, with connotations of the persuasive power of new beliefs as well as new practices (Thomas 2003; Healy & Harding forthcoming).

Building and using the complex

Some of the most labour-consuming constructional episodes at Hambledon came early in the history of the complex, and may provide some indication of the scale of the community that gathered to build and use it. It has been estimated that the main enclosure could have been built in two years by a workforce of 100 working for two months in late summer/early autumn (Mercer forthcoming). Neolithic earthworks eventually encompassed the hill, with a maximum extent of 2 km from north-west to south-east. Construction of new elements in the complex, and the modification of existing ones, especially by the recutting of ditches, was episodic over a period of 300–400 years, to *c* 3300 cal BC. The construction of the last dated earthworks (Table 1: UB-4267, UB-4271, UB-4272) seems to have taken place at much the same time as the last dated interventions in the main enclosure ditch (Table 1: OxA-7039, OxA-7040, UB-4269). This episodic history reinforces two points made by Chris Evans: that construction and reworking were an inherent part of the use of causewayed enclosures and that their multiple circuits cannot be assumed to have been contemporary (1988). This author would add that no two segments in a single ditch can be assumed to have been built at the same time.

Numerous strands of evidence combine to indicate that use of the complex was intermittent, as envisaged by Isobel Smith for Windmill Hill. She herself has pointed out that the Hambledon pottery shows a prevalence of small bowls and cups, suitable for cooking and eating, and a scarcity of larger vessels suitable for storage (Smith forthcoming a). The cattle butchered on the hill were predominantly females between one and a half and four years of age (i.e. subadults and young adults), with notably lower proportions of younger and older animals and of males. This does not reflect the complete cull of a sustainable herd, which, whether reared primarily for dairy products or for meat, would include more calves and more mature, breeding-age females. The

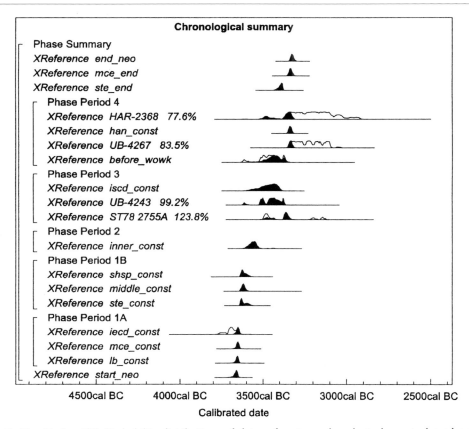

Fig. 3. Hambledon Hill. Probability distributions of dates of major archaeological events, based on the chronological modelling of 161 radiocarbon measurements and the stratigraphic sequence. Each distribution represents the relative probability that an event occurred at some particular time. *Lb_const* = the estimated date for the construction of the southern long barrow, *mce_const* = the estimated date for the construction of the main causewayed enclosure, *iecd_const* = the estimated date for the construction of the inner east cross-dyke, *ste_const* = the estimated date for the construction of the Stepleton enclosure, *middle_const* = the estimated date for the construction of the middle Stepleton outwork, *shsp_const* = the estimated date for the construction of the Shroton spur outwork, *inner_const* = the estimated date for the construction of the inner Stepleton outwork, *ST78 2755A* = the estimated date for the death of a young man whose articulated skeleton was found in the rubble fills of the inner Stepleton outwork with a leaf arrowhead among his ribs, *UB-4243* = the estimated date for the death of a young man whose articulated skeleton was found on the base of the outer Stepleton outwork with a leaf arrowhead among his ribs, *iscd_const* = the estimated date for the construction of the inner south cross-dyke, *before_wowk* = a terminus post quem for the construction of the western outwork, *UB-4267* = the estimated date of the construction of the outer east cross-dyke, *han_const* = the estimated date for the construction of segment 3 of the outer Hanford outwork, *HAR-2368* = the estimated date of a remodelling or repair of the Shroton spur outwork bank or gateway, *ste_end* = the estimated date for the last Neolithic interventions in the Stepleton enclosure ditch (there was a dearth of suitable samples, activity here may have continued as late as in the main enclosure), *mce_end* = the estimated date for the last Neolithic interventions in the main enclosure ditch.

Laboratory Number	Sample	Radiocarbon Age (BP)	Weighted mean (BP)	Calibrated date range (95% confidence)	*Estimated date range (95% probability)*
	Hambledon				
OxA–7845	HN82 F279, layer 4A. HN82 C123. Single fragment of *Pinus sylvestris* charcoal	8400±60	–	7580–7200 cal BC	
OxA–7846	HN82 F279, layer 3A. HN82 C115. Single fragment of *Pinus sylvestris* charcoal	8480±55	–	7600–7380 cal BC	
OxA–7816	WOWK area 3 F4. WOWK82 C31. Single fragment of *Pinus sylvestris* charcoal (from the first of two successive sockets in a possible posthole within the protected chalk of the inner south cross dyke bank	8725±55	–	8160–7590 cal BC	
OxA–7768	Main enclosure. Segment 18. HH76 1948. Femur from articulated burial of human juvenile cut into base of segment, possibly through primary silts, possibly before they had accumulated, covered by flint cairn	4810±45	4803±33 (T'=0.0; T (5%)=3.8; ν=1)	3650–3520 cal BC	*3660–3540 cal BC*
OxA–7769	Replicate of OxA–7768	4795±50			
OxA–7039	Main enclosure. Segment 17. HH76 3046. Grave cut into probably silted segment butt. R femur from articulated burial of young juvenile	4550±60	4557±42 T'=0.0; T (5%)=3.8; ν=1	3500–3090 cal BC	*3380–3320 cal BC*
OxA–7040	Replicate of OxA–7039.	4565±60			
UB–4269	Main enclosure. Segment 18, layer 10. HH76 2970. Articulated cattle distal tibia fragment, calcaneum, astragalus, navicular–cuboid, cuneiform, and lateral malledus, interpreted as having lain in an undetected recut	4562±27	–	3370–3100 cal BC	*3370–3330 cal BC*
OxA–8893	Inner east cross–dyke. Segment 1 layer 5A Top of silted ditch. HH76 680. Two cattle vertebrae found in articulation in compact butchery deposit	4255±50		2920–2700 cal BC	
UB–4267	Outer east cross–dyke. Segment 4, layer 10. From slight hollow in the base of segment butt. HH75 2171. Red deer antler beam and trez tine, worn, perhaps a pick	4497±26	–	3350–3040 cal BC	*3360–3310 cal BC*
OxA–7037	Shroton spur outwork. Site K/L baulk, base of ditch. HH76 2864. Articulated dog skeleton.	4710±55	4737±40 T'=0.5; T (5%)=3.8; ν=1	3640–3370 cal BC	*3640–3490 cal BC*
OxA–7038	Shroton spur outwork. Replicate of OxA–7037	4770±60			
UB–4148	Shroton spur outwork. Site K/L, base of ditch .HH76 2895. Worn red deer antler pick	4753±27	–	3640–3380 cal BC	*3640–3510 cal BC*
UB–4149	Shroton spur outwork Site K/L, layer 9. Primary silt. HH76 2650. Worn red deer antler pick	4756±20	–	3640–3380 cal BC	*3640–3550 cal BC (73%) or3545–3515 cal BC (22%)*
UB–4150	Shroton spur outwork. 'Virtually on ditch bottom' (label) in primary silt, site K/L, layer 9. HH76 1387. Worn red deer antler pick with burning to the base of the beam	4736±21	–	3640–3380 cal BC	*3635–3555 cal BC (71%) or 3540–3505 cal BC (24%)*
OxA–7102	Shroton spur outwork. Site K/L, layer 7, in cluster of jumbled bones in chalk rubble ditch fill, stratigraphically later than samples for OxA–7037–8 and UB–4148–50. HH76 1968. Articulating first metatarsal and first phalanx of mature human adult, found together, apparently in articulation	4890±35	–	3710–3640 cal BC	*3760–3630 cal BC*

Laboratory Number	Sample	Radiocarbon Age (BP)	Weighted mean (BP)	Calibrated date range (95% confidence)	*Estimated date range (95% probability)*
OxA–7835	Inner Stepleton outwork bank area. Area 2A F200. ST79 2025. R femur of articulated older adult human, possibly male, tightly crouched in ploughed–down scoop	4855±45	–	3710–3530 cal BC	*3780–3630 cal BC*
OxA–7044	Inner Stepleton outwork. Segment 7, layer 4. ST78 2755A. L femur of articulated older subadult/young adult human male, prone in chalk rubble with leaf arrowhead in chest area.	4560±55	4598±40 T'=1.1; T' (5%)=3.8; ν=1	3500–3120 cal BC	*3500–3420 cal BC (31%) or 3390–3320 cal BC (64%)*
OxA–7045	Replicate of OxA–7044.	4645±60			
UB–4243	Outer Stepleton outwork. Segment 3, unit 1, ditch base. ST80 1875. R femur of articulated young adult human male, flexed in recess in angle of ditch butt, with arrowhead among ribs.	4679±27	–	3630–3360 cal BC	*3620–3600 cal BC (3%) or 3530–3360 cal BC (92%)*
UB–4272	Outer Hanford outwork, segment 3. Base of ditch. HN82 154. Articulated cattle pelvis and femur with cut marks	4476±26	–	3340–3020 cal BC	*3350–3310 cal BC*
UB–4271	Outer Hanford outwork, segment 3. Base of ditch. HN82 153. Articulated cattle lower vertebrae and sacrum	4492±27	–	3350–3030 cal BC	*3360–3310 cal BC*
OxA–7833	Hanford 'flint mines'. HN82 F644, layer 2HN82 744. Red deer antler with significant evidence of wear, probably used to excavate the feature in which it was found. From undercut at base of quarry pit..	3810±45	–	2460–2060 cal BC	
OxA–7776	North Cross Rampart. HH86 118. Unidentified long bone fragment from a lower fill of the earliest earthwork on the northern (hillfort) spur	2450±35	–	770–400 cal BC	
	Fir Tree Field shaft (Allen and Green 1998)				
OxA–8011	L8. *Corylus* charcoal below cluster of seven microliths	5355±45		4340–4040 cal BC	
OxA–7987	L7. Red deer scapula	5275±50		4250–3970 cal BC	
OxA–8000	L7. *Bos ?primigenius* scapula at level of microliths	5300±70		4230–3960 cal BC	
OxA–8010	L6b. *Fraxinus* charcoal from hearth associated with Neolithic Bowl pottery	5150±45		4050–3800 cal BC	
OxA–8009	L6b. Charred clematis roots from near hearth associated with Neolithic Bowl pottery	5045±45		3970–3700 cal BC	
OxA–7981	L6a. Pig femur from same layer as Neolithic Bowl sherds	5250±50		4230–3960 cal BC	

Table 1. Selected radiocarbon dates from Hambledon Hill and the Fir Tree Field Shaft

The Hambledon dates listed here are only some of a series of 161 measurements (Bayliss *et al.* forthcoming) which are incorporated in the model represented in Figure 3. They have been chosen to illustrate particular points made in the text. Calibrations have been calculated using the datasets published by Stuiver *et al.* (1998) and the computer program OxCal (v3.3) (Bronk Ramsey 1994; 1995; 1998). The ranges in normal type have been calculated according to the maximum intercept method (Stuiver and Reimer 1986). They are quoted in the form recommended by Mook (1986), with the end points rounded outwards to 10 years if the error term is greater than or equal to 25 radiocarbon years, or to 5 years if it is less. The estimated ranges printed in italics are derived from the mathematical modelling of archaeological problems.

animals killed at Hambledon were thus selected from their herds for a combination of cultural preferences and practical considerations and brought there to be consumed (Legge forthcoming). Legge's preferred interpretation is that the young females are the surplus adults from dairy herds, a conclusion reinforced by the frequency of milk lipids in a sample of sherds from the site (Copley *et al.* 2003; Copley *et al.* forthcoming). The charred cereal consists almost entirely of cleaned grain, with very little chaff or weed seeds, and may have been brought to the hill already processed, with the exception of a single large deposit of charred emmer spikelets (Jones & Legge forthcoming).

Mollusc samples from various locations on the hill reflect the vicinity of mature shady habitats in an environment dominated by varying degrees of woodland, not the vegetation that would be expected in an area habitually used by people and livestock. Differences in the level of woodland cover reflected in Neolithic pits suggest that not all of them were filled in at the same time. This is particularly persuasive in the case of two adjacent pits on the Stepleton spur, in which respectively 27% and less than half that proportion of the molluscs were open country taxa (Bell *et al.* forthcoming). This contrasts with rather more open conditions in Cranborne Chase, where there were local clearances around the early 4th millennium hearth in the Fir Tree Field shaft (Allen in prep.), the Handley Down mortuary enclosure, and the Thickthorn Down long barrow (Allen 2000, 43–44). By the time the Hambledon complex went out of use in the later fourth millennium, molluscs from the upper Neolithic fills of its ditches were still dominated by shade-loving species. To the east, however, the Dorset cursus was built *3360–3030 cal BC (91% probability)* (Barclay & Bayliss 1999, 22–23), in what now seems to have been a mosaic of scrub and lightly-grazed grassland, and the Monkton-up-Wimborne 'temple' nearby, also built during the second half of the 4th millennium, stood in a large tract of grassland (Allen 2002, 61–63).

There is a similar contrast between the vegetation of the Maiden Castle causewayed enclosure, where, as at Hambledon, scattered mollusc samples reflected predominantly but variably, wooded surroundings (J.G. Evans & Rouse 1991), and the more open settings of early 4th millennium pits next to the Flagstones enclosure to the north, while the late 4th millennium monuments of the Flagstones enclosure itself and the Alington Avenue long mound stood in grassland (Allen 1997). This picture is replicated at Windmill Hill, where the environment of the enclosure was predominantly wooded, while nearby long barrows were built in clearings (Fishpool 1999). It seems that, at least on the southern chalk, causewayed enclosures were built at the edges of more habitually used areas, and visited only occasionally (J.G. Evans *et al.* 1988), while late 4th/early 3rd millennium monuments were built in occupied areas.

If people visited causewayed enclosures occasionally, in what numbers did they do so? The larger episodes of construction obviously called for large numbers. But the digging and filling of a pit or the recutting of a ditch segment could have been the work of a handful of people. At least some non-constructional events, however, took place on a larger scale. One of the young cows which dominate the faunal remains would have provided some 300 kg of meat, offal and fat, the consumption of which would call for a gathering of many more than a handful. Yet some of the later, slot-like recuts, which seem to have been cut and filled in single events, contained the remains of two or three animals (Legge forthcoming). It is, of course, possible that these events may have included the construction of some of the later earthworks. The seasons in which Hambledon was visited remain elusive. A hint comes from a small sample of immature caprine mandibles, which fall into two groups, one of less than three months of age and another of 6–9 months of age. Assuming spring-time birth, this could reflect a human presence in spring and late summer (Legge forthcoming).

Among the ancestors

The question of who frequented the complex can only be entertained through the imperfect proxy of those whose largely disarticulated remains were deposited there. These seem to have been drawn from an entire population. They were demographically balanced, unlike the livestock, the excavated sample comprising a minimum of 35–36 children and 40–41 adults of whom only 10 females and 17 males could be sexed (McKinley forthcoming). They furthermore ranged from those who may have obtained almost all their dietary protein from animal sources to those whose diet had included both animal and plant protein (Richards 2000; Richards forthcoming). This last observation might reflect variations in status (especially as those from the south long barrow had all consumed comparably high levels of animal protein) or the deposition of the remains of members of several communities, with different dietary habits.

Alternating frequentation and abandonment would have had a particular impact on the condition of the human and animal bone at the site. Both were exposed to canids and rodents, the former of which may have been largely responsible for the under-representation of the less robust bones of all species. Human remains, however, tend to be more severely weathered and otherwise degraded than those of animals (McKinley forthcoming; E.-J. Evans 2000), suggesting that the process of excarnation which almost all had undergone had entailed prolonged exposure. Bones normally entered ditches or pits after total excarnation and disarticulation, as when femurs from two individuals were placed crossed over each other in a ditch butt beside an entrance to the main enclosure. In these cases the bones could have been brought from elsewhere. Evidence for intermediate stages in the process, however, shows that at least some excarnation took place on the hill. It is possible to envisage that corpses were left in the open and their bones buried at a later date in enclosures, pits, cross-dykes and outworks. There is one case where c

50% of the disarticulated bones of a juvenile were placed in the middle Stepleton outwork ditch together, and another where c 40% of the bones of an older juvenile were built into a flint cairn on the base of the main enclosure ditch, in both cases as if they had been gathered up while still undispersed. There were also two still-articulated half skeletons, one of them dog-gnawed (Mercer 1980, fig. 21). Excarnation was not, however, left entirely to time, carnivores and the elements. Cut marks have been identified on the remains of 23 individuals and, given the weathered condition of the bone and the faintness of the cuts, this is likely to be a minimum. The cuts contrast with the butchery practised on the animal bone from the site and seem to have resulted from not very systematic excarnation. They range from over a hundred more-or-less transverse cuts on the anterior surface of one femur to two parallel cuts on a mandible. Some had been made with a scraping rather than a cutting motion. They were found on articulated skeletons as well as on disarticulated bone (McKinley forthcoming; E.-J. Evans 2000). Comparable cuts have been noted on the human remains from the Haddenham long barrow, Cambridgeshire (Hodder & Evans forthcoming), and there are traces of dismemberment with lithic implements at the chambered tombs of Coldrum in Kent and Eyford in Gloucestershire (Wysocki & Whittle 2000). Manipulation of the fleshed human corpse, as well as of defleshed bones, may have been far more prevalent than it has so far appeared.

Once disarticulated, human bone could have been retained among the living or moved from one burial context to another (Smith 1965, 137). While burial contexts can to some extent be identified, most obviously in pits and long barrows in Cranborne Chase (Pitt Rivers 1898, 42–101; Piggott, 1936), above-ground contexts may have figured significantly. Diverse histories for the disarticulated remains on Hambledon are evidenced by small numbers of fragments (mainly skull) which were charred when already dry; others which, though not charred, showed dark staining not always attributable to their final burial environment; and others marked by a distinctive pattern of fissuring, characteristic of rapid drying, perhaps in intense sunlight following soaking (McKinley forthcoming). Human foot and toe bones, found in apparent articulation in the rubble fills of the Shroton spur outwork ditch (Table 1: OxA-7102) were older than antler picks and an articulated dog which lay beneath them on the base of the same segment (Table 1: OxA-7037, OxA-7038, UB-4148, UB-4149, UB-4150). This may apply to all of the larger group of jumbled bones from at least two individuals, of which the foot and toe bones formed a part, and in which a radius and a fibula had been placed side-by-side, giving the impression of a complete forearm. It would be no surprise if the defleshed skulls placed on the bases of several of the ditches were already old when deposited. None has yet been dated, because the dating programme focussed on articulated samples likely to be coeval with their contexts. Skulls, however, tend to be particularly weathered and worn, and Jacqueline McKinley concludes that most of them were subject to greater exposure to the elements than the rest of the assemblage (forthcoming). Given the probable late fourth millennium construction date of the Dorset cursus, Tilley's suggestion that movement along that monument played a part in the circulation of human remains to and from the hill (1994, 200) becomes less plausible, although the cursus may have formalised, even closed off, an older route, as Johnston suggests (1999).

Hambledon confirms that a minority of individuals were buried fully articulated in the earlier 4th millennium. Three were in single graves, which Isobel Smith long ago picked out as a feature of some causewayed enclosures (1971, 96). The earliest (Table 1: OxA-7835) was a possible male of 45 or more, very tightly contracted in a small pit in the protected chalk of the ploughed-down inner Stepleton outwork bank. The burial had taken place before the construction of the outwork bank, and possibly before that of the preceding enclosure bank. The location and maturity of the subject, although not other aspects of the burial, recall the interment of

an adult male beneath the outer bank of Windmill Hill (Whittle et al. 1999, 79–81, 344–6). An almost equally early child burial, on or near the base of the main enclosure ditch (Table 1: OxA-7768, OxA-7769), includes personal accoutrements, in the form of three bone beads in the head area (Mercer 1980, fig. 20). Barring cremation, the gamut of earlier 4th millennium funerary practice is represented on the hill. The treatment of human remains was at least as diverse as the roles which individuals may have filled in life. One possible interpretation, of this and of the varying sources of dietary protein, is the existence of hierarchy in what has often been seen as an egalitarian society.

Actions, artefacts and food remains

Intermittent human presence at the site is reflected in the interplay between natural silting and human intervention in the ditch fills (Fig. 5). Isobel Smith was among the first to recognise how thoroughly reworked were the fills of causewayed enclosure ditches, whether this was reflected in the lack of meaningful stratification of finds in the primary levels at Windmill Hill (1966, 473), in retrospectively recognised finds-rich recuts in largely silted ditches (1971, 97–8), or in the deliberate burial of deposits placed in ditches (1966, 473), deposits which may have had 'a special, even sacramental, significance' (1965, 20). Pattern is everywhere at Hambledon, reinforcing her conclusion that '. . . there is no doubt whatever that the mass of this material was deliberately thrown or placed in the hollows.' (1965, 7). At a gross level, the two enclosures and the areas around them were used in myriad different ways, some of which are summarised in Table 2. But there are also variations over time and, on a far more intimate scale, between individual pits and ditch segments. In the central area the frequency of ditch recutting and, generally, the density of cultural material were at their highest in the main enclosure, lower in the cross-dykes, and at their lowest in the western

Main enclosure and central area	Stepleton enclosure and surrounding area
Recutting frequent and complex, with a measure of regularity around enclosure, many pits also recut	Recutting of ditch less frequent and less regular, pits rarely recut at all
Upper, linear recuts ('slots') in enclosure and cross-dyke ditches, and recuts in pits both often packed with unworked flint nodules and fragments	Only one flint-packed recut in an enclosure segment, close to entrance giving onto route to main enclosure.
Human remains placed in ditches from first	Human remains placed in ditches only after some fill had accumulated
Deer bone (as distinct from antler) rare	Deer bone (as distinct from antler) less rare
Articulated animal bone most abundant in final linear recuts ('slots') made in almost fully silted ditch, which were the ditch contexts richest in bone and other cultural material	Articulated animal bone rarer than in main enclosure and virtually absent from final midden-like deposits made in almost fully silted ditch, although these were the ditch contexts richest in bone
Material in 'slots' often placed in discrete piles	Little obvious placement of material in midden-like upper deposits
Antler implements concentrated in pits in interior	Antler implements concentrated in enclosure ditch
Almost no refitting knapping debris	Clusters of refitting knapping debris on ditch floors and higher up sequence
Almost all of the 39 chert artefacts from the site, including 6 leaf arrowheads; also 1 leaf arrowhead of variegated red/white flint	Almost none of the 39 chert artefacts from the site; no chert or coloured flint arrowheads
Hammerstones include beach pebbles	No beach pebbles
Many axeheads and fragments of rocks from remote sources	Almost all axeheads and fragments of flint
Most frequent non-local quern material Old Red Sandstone from Mendips	Most frequent non-local quern material heathstone from between Wareham and Poole, in south-east Dorset
Gabbroic vessels concentrated in pits in interior	Gabbroic ware extremely rare
Most abundant non-local pottery well made and finished and derived from limestone ridge to north-west and west	Most abundant non-local pottery roughly made and finished and possibly derived from same area as heathstone

Table 2. Hambledon Hill. Some of the distinctions between the Neolithic uses of the central area and the Stepleton spur.

outwork. The ditches of the south Long Barrow, however, were recut, and its location at an entrance to that enclosure is reflected in preferential deposition in the west ditch, the side along which those walking between the two enclosures would pass (Fig. 1). The south butt of that ditch contained a number of fragmentary stone artefacts, and 'It is important to note that these items were not all deposited at one time; they represent a gradual accumulation, spread throughout the entire sequence of fills from phase I upwards. This would appear to attest a deliberate practice, maintained over a considerable period of time' (Smith forthcoming b). These artefacts include a fragment from a group I axehead from the south-west peninsula, and the primary silts of the same ditch contained a sherd of Gabbroic ware from the same region, others of clays characterised by iron-rich red pellets, possibly originating in south-east Dorset, and others of clays containing fossil shell from the limestone to

the west and north-west, more of which was in the primary silts of the main enclosure and in a treethrow hole under its bank.

The long barrow was one of the earliest elements of the complex, perhaps as early as the main enclosure (Figs 3–4), so that non-local axeheads and pottery, some from remote sources, were brought to the hill from the first, as they continued to be over the following centuries. What changed was the frequency with which they and other cultural material were placed in the ditches. At both Hambledon enclosures, by far the largest assemblages came from the later 4th millennium Neolithic deposits. In the central area these were shallow 'slots' cut, sometimes repeatedly, into the largely silted ditches of the main enclosure, its cross-dykes and the long barrow, like the finds-rich recuts retrospectively recognised by Isobel Smith at several enclosures (1971, 98), the 'midden' in the inner ditch at Abingdon, Oxfordshire (Avery 1982, 16–17), or the phase

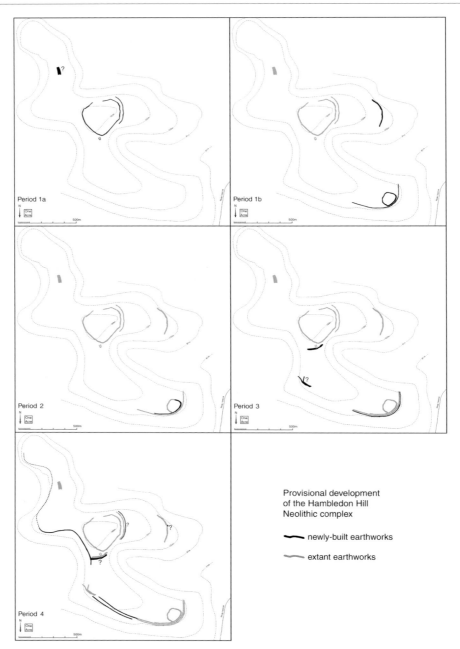

Fig. 4. Hambledon Hill. Development of the Neolithic complex

1C recuts at Etton (Pryor 1998, 13–51). In the Stepleton enclosure at the same stratigraphic horizon there were less structured but equally rich deposits, rarely in recuts, and comparable with successive 'midden' layers in the inner ditch at Maiden Castle (Sharples 1991, 50–51). This is unlikely to reflect the gathering of more people than before, since large numbers must have been needed for construction, when little was deposited. It must reflect a change in practice. The artefacts and food remains in these deposits seem to have been freshly introduced rather than reworked from superficial deposits. Decoration and heavier rims are more frequent in them than in the underlying layers, (Smith forthcoming a), as are the main non-local pottery fabrics. In the central area theses deposits often include articulated animal bone. Indeed, the numerous unworked flint nodules and fragments which characterise these deposits, and seem originally to have been heaped up, may have protected them against predators (Fig. 5).

The overall incidence of the main fabric groups more-or-less corresponds to that documented for Neolithic Bowl pottery in Wessex by Cleal (1995), with presumably local flint- or flint- and sand-tempered wares accounting for just over half the total, and shell and other calcareous tempers for a substantial proportion of the rest. But the distribution of fabric groups is far from even across the components of the site (Smith forthcoming a). There seems to have been a sense for what kinds of vessel should be deposited where. Flint or flint- and sand-tempered fabrics were most frequent in cross-dykes and outworks, rising to almost 90%, and least frequent, at 40–50%, in the two enclosures, their associated pits and the long barrow (Fig. 6). The non-local wares varied according to location. Gabbroic wares, a tiny minority of the total, were concentrated in pits in the interior of the main enclosure. Most of the non-local wares in the central area were tempered with a range of Jurassic material, generally including fossil shell. On the Stepleton spur, the Jurassic inclusions were equally diverse, but more often included ooliths, while the wares containing them were out-numbered by fabrics containing the red clay pellets described above. The ditches of the long barrow, outside the main enclosure and on the way to and from the Stepleton spur, are the only features in the central area to contain a substantial proportion of this fabric group (Fig. 6).

Apparently utilitarian distributions appear less so on closer inspection. In the central area, knapping debris is concentrated in areas with

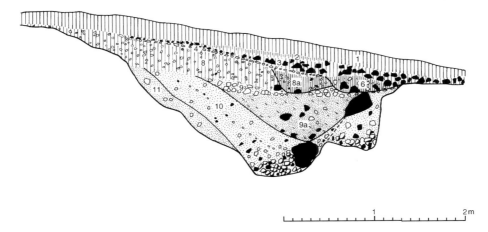

Fig. 5. Hambledon Hill. Section through a segment of the main causewayed enclosure

deposits of Clay-with-Flints, which provides flint superior to the degraded material from the Upper Chalk of the hill, which was not used in the Neolithic (Saville forthcoming). But the distribution of hammerstones bears little relation to this, concentrating instead around what was

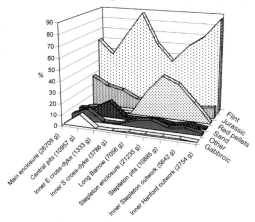

Fig. 6. Hambledon Hill. The incidence of the main fabric groups in subassemblages yielding >1 kg of Neolithic Bowl pottery. 'Jurassic' covers a range of fabrics incorporating varying combinations of ooliths (sometimes recrystalised), fossil shell, calcite, quartz, mica, limestone and flint. 'Red pellets' covers an equally diverse group characterised by small, roughly spherical, iron-rich, red-coloured clay pellets, which occur with varying combinations of flint, chalk, crushed land mollusc shell, fresh shell, sandstone and quartzite (Darvill forthcoming).

almost certainly an entrance in the east side of the main enclosure. This brings into focus the notion of a hammerstone as a curated, personal item (Saville forthcoming), perhaps to be deposited on entering or leaving the circuit. This view of hammerstones as personal equipment accords with the burial of a quartzite hammerstone near the left hand of an articulated male skeleton also accompanied by a flint core at Hazleton, Gloucestershire (Saville 1990, 103–4, fig. 115). The Middle Chalk of the Stepleton spur is not flint-bearing, and Clay-with-Flints there is confined to a single fissure, with no indication in the

composition of the feature fills of formerly more extensive deposits. Yet here there are numerous clusters of refitting knapping debris, sometimes including hammers of both flint and antler. Most were well removed from the Clay-with-Flints, and all of them were originally sizeable nodules of good quality, although not pristine, chalk flint (Fig. 7; Saville forthcoming). These were not extracted during the excavation of the ditch segments in which the results of their reduction were deposited. They would have been brought to these locations, whether from a few tens of metres or, perhaps more probably, from a few kilometres away. Just as causewayed enclosures may have been foci for the exchange of stone implements (although not the ones buried there), so they may have been foci for the exchange of flint (Smith 1971, 105). The extent to which flint from the chalk was transported westwards has been explored many times, with some disagreement as to the scale of the transport, but none as to its reality (Saville 1982; Healy 1988; Tingle 1998, 89–98). In this author's view, flint from the chalk may have moved in greater bulk than any other material in the fourth millennium. Hambledon's location at the interface of the chalk and the non-flint-bearing geology of the south-west and the probability that some of those who came to the hill came from the west (discussed below), argue for a role in flint exchange. Paradoxically, the burial of some of this material at the site may emphasise the significance of this.

The distribution of antler is uneven. While antler implements were probably used to excavate all of the ditches, they were found regularly in only some of them. In the central area, antler was concentrated in pits near the centre of the main enclosure, and was found only occasionally in the ditches, mainly those segments of the main enclosure and the inner east cross-dyke which flanked the eastern entrance. There was something of a concentration of antler fragments, but not implements, in the west ditch of the long barrow. Where antler implements did occur in ditches, they were often in upper fills with no direct relation to ditch-digging or recutting. If they are to be related to episodes of excavation, they may have entered the ditches after some time on the surface, or have been used in the excavation of cross-dykes, the western outwork, or pits. In the Shroton spur outwork there were four antler picks on the base of the only substantially excavated segment. On the Stepleton spur, antler implements were scarce in primary and subsequent levels in outwork ditches and in pits. They were instead concentrated in the segments of the enclosure, where they were far more frequent than in the larger outwork ditches. Here, many were indeed on the ditch floor, often carefully placed in pairs or larger groups. But they were spread very unevenly among the segments, with marked concentrations in the north and south-west of the circuit and none in many of the segments to the west. Here too, many were in the upper fills with no direct relation to ditch-digging or recutting. At least three implements had not been abandoned immediately after use, since they had undergone

Fig. 7. Nodule from the ditch of the outer Stepleton outwork, refitted by Alan Saville and reproduced from Saville (forthcoming). Maximum dimension 134 mm. Photo National Museums of Scotland

groove-and-splinter working (Legge forthcoming). The deposition of antler implements was a matter of choice, rather than the routine abandonment of worn or damaged implements at the end of a task. It may be that it was appropriate to leave the implements used to dig some segments of some ditches *in situ*. Given, however, that antlers were much used both as digging implements and as raw material for smaller artefacts, they are likely to have been exchanged and curated (Smith 1965, 20). As well as being brought to the site, many may have been carried away from it, a scenario frequently entertained for other kinds of artefact and raw material at enclosures. There is reason to question the frequent assumption of a functional link between antlers found on a ditch bottom and the excavation of that ditch.

How did the complex function?

At first sight, the numerous differences between the two enclosures and their related features might suggest the expression of the identities of two principal social groups, in terms of their practices, the areas from which they came, and the extent of their access to goods from remote sources (Table 2). But the picture is more complex. There are pointers to movement between the two enclosures at either end of the route between them, in the high frequency in the long barrow ditches of the main non-local ceramic of the Stepleton spur (Fig. 6), and in the cutting of a flint-packed slot in a segment at the north-west entrance to the Stepleton enclosure. The source areas of the materials deposited in the two parts of the complex do not fall into two groups, but overlap and interweave. The most abundant non-local quern materials from the Stepleton spur came from south Dorset, near the coast, and the most abundant non-local ceramics may have done the same (Table 2). A couple of scallop shells may have had a similar origin. Yet beach pebble hammerstones, possibly from the Chesil Beach in the same area (Roe forthcoming) are confined to the central area, which also has most of the 'Portland' chert, from the same general zone whether obtained from Portland itself or from the Carstens series soils of the Dorchester area (Woodward & Bellamy 1991, 31). Gabbroic pottery and stone axeheads from the south-west peninsula are strongly concentrated in the central area. But charred fragments of Cornish Heath (*Erica vagans*), now native in Britain only on the Lizard peninsula and in the north-west of Ireland, came from a pit on the Stepleton spur. Another pit on the Stepleton spur yielded a grape pip dated to the mid-4th millennium (Jones &Legge 1987; Jones & Legge forthcoming). Yet the only charred grape vine fragment so far identified is from the main enclosure (Austin *et al.* forthcoming). The presence of the grape is a reminder that the innovations of the 4th millennium may have included mind-altering substances as well as food crops, monuments and artefacts. The identification of opium poppy seeds in a waterlogged sample from near the base of an early 4th millennium long barrow ditch at Raunds, Northamptonshire (Campbell and Robinson forthcoming) is now echoed by a further identification in a previously unanalysed sample from the Etton causewayed enclosure in Cambridgeshire (Mark Robinson pers. comm.).

Etton in fact provides a model for the interpretation of the differences between the two enclosures at Hambledon. There, in a single circuit much the size of the Stepleton enclosure, there were contrasts of a comparable order but different nature between the east and west sides. Pryor's view of this dichotomy as reflecting spheres in which different kinds and scales of ceremony were enacted and different kinds of deposit were made (1998, 363–368) would fit the Hambledon record. It is even possible to envisage individuals or crowds proceeding from one to the other. The topography ensures that, for most of the gentle ascent from the Stepleton spur to the central dome of the hill, the main enclosure and the surrounding earthworks remain out of sight, bursting into view quite suddenly at a late stage of the approach. This effect would have been heightened by the largely wooded conditions inferred from the molluscs. Its impact on those who knew the

significance of the earthworks and knew at least the general nature of what was to take place inside them can only be guessed at.

Comparable levels of diversity may have marked the use of the rest of the hill. The unexcavated areas, including the ditches of the north long barrow, could have equally distinctive signatures. The whole hilltop was encompassed in Neolithic activity as well as by Neolithic earthworks. There were pits outside the Stepleton enclosure, between the cross-dykes surrounding the main enclosure, and on the Hanford spur away from both enclosures. There were early Neolithic flint scatters north-west of the Stepleton enclosure (on the route between the two enclosures), and outside the Shroton spur outwork (Palmer & Oswald forthcoming). The struck flint found during the excavation of a section across the 1st millennium north cross rampart within the hillfort was overwhelmingly early Neolithic in character (Saville forthcoming). Sherds of Neolithic Bowl pottery have been found in a rabbit scrape in the hillfort (RCHME 1996, 95–96).

Looking out

Although artefacts and materials do not serve to link particular parts of the complex to specific regions, they may be a rough index of the overall territory from which people gathered there, if the more abundant kinds of quern material and non-local ceramics are regarded as domestic equipment (Smith 1965, 42). The hypothetical range would extend to the Dorset coast, 30–45 km to the south. Hambledon and the coast are linked by the river Stour, on the lower reaches of which evidence for earlier Neolithic settlement is markedly more abundant than in Cranborne Chase (Gardiner 1991). This is slightly to the east of the area indicated by some of the coastal artefacts and materials, but may reflect an acceleration of discovery in the course of gravel quarrying around Bournemouth and construction within it. The catchment would also extend to various locations along the Jurassic ridge, 25–60 km to the west and north-west, and, at its farthest, to the Mendips, 40–80 km to the north-west. This approximation may be skewed by the recognisability of materials from these areas — the flint-tempered pottery and flint nodules of the Wessex chalk cannot be pinned down with even this level of imprecision. Travel by individuals over distances of this order, however, is made all the more plausible by the history of a woman buried in the Monkton-up-Wimborne 'temple' towards or after the end of the use of the Hambledon complex. The level of lead in her bones was such that the Mendips were the nearest area in which she could have lived a substantial part of her life (Green 2000, 77–84). These distances, at most a couple or three days walk, may provide an inkling of the kind of territory from which people gathered at the Hambledon complex. Weathered skulls found at Hambledon may have been kept in a Mendip cave.

The proximity of other enclosures (Whitesheet Hill at 22 km, Maiden Castle at 30) raises the question of the relationships between population and monuments. The recurrent clustering of causewayed enclosures (Oswald et al. 2001, fig. 1.1) raises the possibility of significant areas in which different communities each maintained a ceremonial focus, some foci being larger and more important than others. The scale of the Hambledon complex is so far unparalleled. The only obvious comparison is with Whitesheet Hill. Here, although only the causewayed enclosure is dated, there may be a second, smaller enclosure and associated cross-dykes (Rawlings et al. forthcoming). It may be no coincidence that Whitesheet, like Hambledon, lies at the edge of the Chalk. This highly visible ecotone may have had particular meaning.

A vivid example of distinct traditions in two enclosures within a single cluster is the contrast between the pottery assemblages from Briar Hill, Northamptonshire, and Etton, 60 km away, both in use for centuries in the early to mid 4th millennium. While both assemblages are predominantly shell-tempered, that from Briar Hill is light-rimmed and sparsely decorated (Bamford 1985, 101–103, figs 52–55) and that

from Etton heavy-rimmed and profusely decorated (Pryor 1998, 209–212, figs 175–201). Such a marked distinction suggests that, throughout their lives, the two enclosures were frequented by people with different traditions and preferences.

As Isobel Smith has pointed out, causewayed enclosures tend to be located across the contours rather than on hilltops, and most seem designed to face in a particular direction (1971, 92). This observation has been persuasively elaborated by Oswald et al, who propose connections between enclosures and the areas to which they are 'tilted' and with which they are intervisible (2001, 91–106). The Stepleton enclosure lies on a gentle slope and overlooks low-lying ground to the south and east (Fig. 1). The main enclosure also tilts slightly to the south-east. But it has another kind of orientation too. To the east, visibility into Cranborne Chase is cut off by the height and abruptness of the slopes on the opposite side of the Iwerne valley. To the south and west, however, cloud cover and vegetation permitting, the rather lower chalk downland of south-west Dorset provides uninterrupted visibility as far as the sea; while the low-lying topography to the west and north-west affords views extending to the Somerset Levels and even to the Mendips. The hill itself, higher than the surrounding downs and of distinctive form, is correspondingly visible from long distances in these directions. The terrain visible from the hill encompasses the source areas of the more abundant non-local materials brought to it. What if this is the terrain to which the complex was most closely related?

A westerly orientation in human terms as well as in terms of visibility might account for a dearth of carved chalk and for the simplicity of the few pieces that were found. Despite the extent of the excavations, the tally stands at two balls, three perforated fragments, a striated fragment, a subcylindrical object apparently made of puddled chalk, and two shallowly grooved chalk lumps found behind the head of a later fourth millennium child burial (Table 1: OxA-7039). This meagre collection contrasts with the quantity and diversity of carved chalk from Windmill Hill (Smith 1965, 130–135) and other chalkland enclosures, including Maiden Castle, in both Wessex and Sussex (Piggott 1954, fig. 14). Some of the repeatedly encountered products of this tradition are represented only 11 km to the east by two phalli and a chalk cup recovered with two perforated fragments and eight grooved and scored fragments from the Thickthorn Down long barrow (Drew and Piggott 1936, 86–87). The practice of chalk carving and the beliefs which it expressed seems to have been less important at Hambledon. A scarcity of sarsen, often the main quern material on chalkland sites, may also be significant here. The hill may have been oriented to the west in the 4th millennium, as in the eighth.

Fire and arrows

Although the Hambledon outworks seem to have been built sequentially rather than as part of a single system (Fig. 4), some of them nonetheless have defensive qualities, which have often been emphasised (Mercer 1988; 1999). This holds particularly for the most massive of them, the inner Stepleton outwork (Fig. 4: period 2), the excavation of which confirmed the existence of a timber substructure, like those which Isobel Smith had inferred for some enclosure banks (1971, 95). This outwork showed signs of hasty construction and of abandonment in an incomplete state. The ditch was the most irregular on the hill, and was cut in such as way as to maximise speed and minimise effort. Unlike the more regular pre-existing middle outwork, which ran outside the Stepleton enclosure, part of the inner outwork followed the south-east side of the enclosure ditch, where the existing bank could be incorporated in the larger new one and the ditch fills would have been easier and quicker to excavate than solid chalk. Where the outwork was cut in solid chalk, some of the irregularity seems to have been due to the use of natural fissures as starting points for excavation. On the north-east side of the enclosure, its surviving depth dropped abruptly from 1.2 m to less than 0.20 m, its line continuing

as a slight depression outside the enclosure ditch for a further 60 m, suggesting that this part of it was never finished. To the west of the enclosure, depth and width diminished, although not to the same extent, and there is a 22 m-wide causeway less than 50 m west of a timber-lined gateway where the ditch was at its widest and deepest. If it was intended as a defensive work, it has an unfinished aspect. After primary silt had accumulated and, in some segments, been cleaned out, the earthwork was burnt for 200 m, in an episode which probably entailed the deaths of two men, one of them buried with burnt chalk and clay in a grave 80 m away, the other placed in the base of the ditch.

Its destruction was far from the end of activity on the spur. Shortly afterwards, a setting of sherds and animal bone was placed on the surface of the burnt material in the ditch base at one side of the gateway; the overlying fills of the outwork ditch contained artefacts, including compact clusters of knapping debris, and animal bone, some of it articulated; a recut in the butt of one segment contained a particularly rich deposit of artefacts and animal bone which had come into the ditch from the outside; the richest deposits in the enclosure ditch were yet to be made. The gateway seems to have been rebuilt, on the evidence of the replacement of at least one burnt post with an unburnt one. This may have occurred at the same time as the construction of the third and final outwork on the spur. This too coincided with a violent event: the body of a young man with a leaf arrowhead among his ribs was placed in a natural cavity in the butt of one segment as soon as it was excavated (Fig. 3, Table 1: UB-4243). It is impossible to tell if his death formed part of larger-scale hostilities, but it at least broadly coincided with that of a second young man, also with an arrowhead among the ribs, found prone in the fill of the partly silted inner outwork (Fig. 3: ST78 2755A; Table 1: OxA-7044, OxA-7045). These deaths by arrowshot are not unique in the area: in Cranborne Chase individuals with leaf arrowheads among the ribs were buried in the Wor Barrow (Pitt Rivers 1898, 63) and at Crichel

Down 13 (Piggott & Piggott 1944, 51, 74, fig. 23:3).

Charcoal from the postholes of the inner outwork bank was almost exclusively oak, and, where charcoal from burnt deposits on or near the ditch bottoms has been identified, it is predominantly of oak and hazel, with small quantities of other species (Austin *et al.* forthcoming). This accords with other evidence which suggests that the outwork had an oak frame and a breastwork of hurdling, probably of hazel (Mercer 1988, 101). It contrasts with the more diverse composition of the charcoal from most other Neolithic contexts on the hill, whether ditches or pits. The only other place where the charcoal is so dominated by oak and hazel is the Shroton spur outwork. Excavation here was more restricted than on the Stepleton spur, but the combined results from work in 1976 and from trenches cut by Desmond Bonney in 1960 indicate that there had been posts, some of them burnt, in the bank area, and that charcoal and other burnt material had entered the ditch from the inner edge along a distance, if the process was continuous, of 140 m. Burnt material was densest on the surface of the primary silt, although it also occurred at higher levels. Here too, a rampart may have burnt and the ash and charcoal silted into the ditch. It may be relevant that the Shroton and Stepleton spurs provide the easiest approaches to the hill (Fig. 1).

Whatever the nature of these events at Hambledon, they were different from other apparent hostile encounters at Crickley Hill, Gloucestershire, and Carn Brea, Cornwall, where hundreds of flint-tipped arrows were fired (Dixon 1988; Mercer 1981; Saville 2002, 96–98). Arrowheads were scarce at Hambledon. They total 42 (0.05% of a flint and chert assemblage of 89287) and were thinly spread in time and space. It is worth remembering too that other kinds of early Neolithic structure were burnt, apparently in the course of ceremony rather than conflict, although the practice was rare in the south of England, where the firing of the forecourt structure of the Nutbane long barrow on the Hampshire

chalk (Morgan 1959) echoes more frequent such events in the north and east (Kinnes 1992, 93).

The two burnt ramparts at Hambledon probably reflect two episodes of conflict, however; and two deaths by arrowshot may reflect one or two more. But these would have been three or four episodes in as many centuries. The gathering of otherwise scattered populations could provide opportunities for hostilities on a scale otherwise impossible, and could prompt the construction of defences. The scale of the Hambledon complex and, by implication, its importance and the numbers of people which it could accommodate, could have made its users particularly conspicuous and vulnerable. The ecotonal — even frontier — location of the site may have made it more of a theatre for conflict than many other enclosures. But this does not make its prime function a defensive one. It rather encapsulated numerous aspects of contemporary life of which conflict, on whatever scale, was one.

Change and abandonment

The abandonment of Hambledon in the later 4th millennium appears more abrupt than that of other enclosures. Peterborough Ware, current c 3400–2500 cal BC (Gibson & Kinnes 1997), is confined to one semi-complete vessel and a few scattered sherds, all from the Stepleton spur. Grooved Ware is absent and there is a single oblique arrowhead. It is difficult not to link this to events in Cranborne Chase. The ideological, perhaps cosmological, transformations of the period, expressed in the construction of new kinds of monument, reached its apogee in the building of the Dorset cursus. Like Hambledon, this is the largest known monument of its kind in Britain. With its construction, the monumental and ceremonial focus was shifted from the boundary of the Chalk and the land to the south-west into the heart of the chalk downland of Cranborne Chase, where numerous smaller monuments were built in the late 4th and the early 3rd millennium (Barrett *et al.* 1991; Green 2000). It was only after Beaker pottery, current c 2600–1800 cal BC (Kinnes *et al.* 1991), came into use that artefacts were again deposited on Hambledon Hill; this time in open conditions, round barrows were built there, and the Hanford 'flint mines' were excavated. Yet one of the largest animal bone deposits, a compact heap in the top of a cross-dyke ditch including the remains of two adult cattle, one caprine and some bones of infantile cattle and of pig, is dated to 2920–2700 cal BC (Table 1: OxA-8893). The kinds of meat yield quoted above suggest that hundreds of people could have consumed the results of this slaughter. But it took place in a period when, on all the other available evidence, the hill was disused. Just as in the 8th millennium, the absence of artefacts does not mean the absence of activity. Furthermore, the date is within the currency of Grooved Ware, *c* 2900–2100 cal BC in southern Britain (Garwood 1999), a ceramic almost monotonously associated with pig remains. The consumption of cattle on Hambledon at this time emphasises how specialised were the pit deposits and henge monuments which have yielded most of the pig-dominated late Neolithic assemblages.

Acknowledgements

I am profoundly grateful to Isobel Smith for help, support and personal kindness over the years. Contributing to this volume has been a pleasure, and I thank Rosamund Cleal and Joshua Pollard for their invitation to do so. Without Alex Bayliss there would have been less of a story to tell, and a different one. The same holds for all the contributors to the forthcoming Hambledon Hill monograph. She, Roger Mercer and Alan Saville have kindly commented on this paper, and Roger Mercer has generously permitted the use of illustrations from the monograph. Sylvia Stevenson and John Borland were responsible for the original illustrations on which Figures 1–2 and 4–5 are based.

Bibliography

Allen, M.J. 1997. Land-use History: Land Molluscan Evidence. In R.J.C. Smith, F. Healy, M.J. Allen, E.L. Morris, I. Barnes & P.J. Woodward, *Excavations along the Route of the Dorchester By-pass, Dorset, 1986-8* (Wessex Archaeological Report 11), 166–83, 260–67

Allen, M.J. 2000. Soils, Pollen and Lots of Snails. In M.G. Green, *A Landscape Revealed — 10,000 Years on a Chalkland Farm,* 36–49. Stroud: Tempus

Allen, M.J. 2002. The chalkland landscape of Cranborne Chase: a prehistoric human ecology. *Landscapes* 13, 55–69

Allen, M.J. & Gardiner, J. 2002. A Sense of Time — Cultural Markers in the Mesolithic of Southern England? In B. David & M. Wilson (eds), *Inscribed Landscapes. Marking and Making Place,* 139–53. Honolulu: University of Hawaii Press

Allen, M.J. & Green, M. 1998. The Fir Tree Field shaft; the date and archaeological and palaeo-environmental potential of a chalk swallowhole feature. *Proceedings of the Dorset Natural History and Archaeology Society* 120, 25–37

Arnold, J., Green, M., Lewis, B. & Bradley, R. 1988. The Mesolithic of Cranborne Chase, *Proceedings of the Dorset Natural History and Archaeology Society* 110, 117–25

Austin P., Hather, J. & Chisham, C. forthcoming. The Wood Charcoal. In R. Mercer & F. Healy, *Hambledon Hill, Dorset, England. Excavation and Survey of a Neolithic Monument Complex and its Surrounding Landscape* (English Heritage Archaeological Report)

Avery, M. 1982. The Neolithic Causewayed Enclosure, Abingdon. In H.J. Case & A.W.R. Whittle (eds), *Settlement Patterns in the Oxford Region: Excavations at the Abingdon Causewayed Enclosure and Other Sites* (Council for British Archaeology Research Report 44), 10–50. London: Council for British Archaeology

Barclay, A. & Bayliss, A. 1999. Cursus Monuments and the Radiocarbon Problem. In A. Barclay & J. Harding (eds) *Pathways and Ceremonies. The Cursus Monuments of Britain and Ireland* (Neolithic Studies Group Seminar Papers 4) , 11–29. Oxford: Oxbow Books

Bamford, H.M. 1985 *Briar Hill. Excavation 1974–1978* (Northampton Development Corporation Archaeological Monograph 3). Northampton: Northampton Development Corporation

Barrett, J.C. Bradley, R. & Green, M. 1991 *Landscape, Monuments and Society. The*

Prehistory of Cranborne Chase. Cambridge: Cambridge University Press

Bayliss, A., Healy, F., Bronk Ramsey, C., McCormac, F.G. & Mercer, R. forthcoming. Interpreting Chronology. In R. Mercer & F. Healy, *Hambledon Hill, Dorset, England. Excavation and Survey of a Neolithic Monument Complex and its Surrounding Landscape* (English Heritage Archaeological Report)

Bell, M. Allen, M.J., Johnson, S. & Smith, R. W. forthcoming. Mollusc and Sedimentary Evidence for the Palaeoenvironmental History of Hambledon Hill and its Surroundings. In R. Mercer & F. Healy, *Hambledon Hill, Dorset, England. Excavation and Survey of a Neolithic Monument Complex and its Surrounding Landscape* (English Heritage Archaeological Report)

Bronk Ramsey, C. 1994. Oxcal (v2.0): A radiocarbon calibration and analysis program, Oxford: Oxford Radiocarbon Accelerator Unit

Bronk Ramsey, C. 1995. Radiocarbon calibration and analysis of stratigraphy. *Radiocarbon* 36, 425–30

Bronk Ramsey, C. 1998 Probability and dating. *Radiocarbon* 40, 461–74

Campbell, G. & Robinson, M. forthcoming. Environment and Land Use in the Valley Bottom. In F. Healy & J. Harding, *Raunds Area Project. The Neolithic and Bronze Age Landscapes of West Cotton, Stanwick and Irthlingborough, Northamptonshire* (English Heritage Archaeological Report)

Cleal, R.M.J. 1995. Pottery Fabrics in Wessex in the Fourth to Second Millennia BC. In I. Kinnes & G. Varndell (eds), *'Unbaked Urns of Rudely Shape'. Essays on British and Irish Pottery for Ian Longworth* (Oxbow Monograph 55). Oxford: Oxbow Books, 185–94

Copley, M.S., Berstan, R. Dudd, S.N., Docherty, G., Mukherjee, A.J., Straker, V., Payne, S. & Evershed, R.P. 2003. Direct chemical evidence for widespread dairying in prehistoric Britain, *Proceedings of the National Academy of Sciences* 100(4), 1524–9

Copley, M. Berstan, R. Stott, A, & Evershed, R. forthcoming. Organic Residue Analysis of Pottery Vessels: Determination of Vessel Use and Radiocarbon Dates. In R. Mercer & F. Healy, *Hambledon Hill, Dorset, England. Excavation and Survey of a Neolithic Monument Complex and its Surrounding Landscape* (English Heritage Archaeological Report)

Darvill, T.C. forthcoming. Petrological Analysis of Neolithic Pottery Fabrics. In R. Mercer & F. Healy, *Hambledon Hill, Dorset, England. Excavation and Survey of a Neolithic Monument Complex and its Surrounding Landscape* (English Heritage Archaeological Report)

Dixon, P. 1988. The Neolithic Settlements on Crickley Hill. In C. Burgess, P. Topping, C. Mordant & M. Maddison (eds), *Enclosures and Defences in the Neolithic of Western Europe* (British Archaeological Reports International Series 403), 75–87. Oxford: British Archaeological Reports

Drew, C.D. & Piggott, S. 1936. The excavation of long barrow 163a on Thickthorn Down, Dorset. *Proceedings of the Prehistoric Society* 2, 77–96

Edmonds, M. 1999. *Ancestral Geographies of the Neolithic. Landscapes, Monuments and Memory*. London and New York: Routledge

Evans, C. 1988. Acts of Enclosure: a Consideration of Concentrically-organised Causewayed Enclosures. In J.C. Barrett & I.A. Kinnes (eds), *The Archaeology of Context in the Neolithic and Bronze Age: Recent Trends*, 85–95. Sheffield: Department of Archaeology and Prehistory

Evans, E.-J. 2000. Neolithic Burial Practices at Hambledon Hill, unpublished dissertation submitted in partial fulfilment of the requirements of MA in Osteoarchaeology by instructional course, University of Southampton

Evans, J.G. & Rouse, A. 1991. The Land Mollusca. In N.M. Sharples, *Maiden Castle. Excavations and Field Survey 1985–6* (English Heritage Archaeological Report 19), 118–125. London: English Heritage

Evans, J.G., Rouse, A. & Sharples, N. 1988. The Landscape Setting of Causewayed Camps: Recent Work on the Maiden Castle Enclosure. In J.C. Barrett & I. Kinnes (eds), *The Archaeology of Context in the Neolithic and Bronze Age: Recent Trends* (Recent Trends Series 3), 73–78, Sheffield: Department of Archaeology and Prehistory

Fishpool, M. 1999. Land Mollusca. In A. Whittle, J. Pollard & C. Grigson, *The Harmony of Symbols: the Windmill Hill Causewayed Enclosure, Wiltshire* (Cardiff Studies in Archaeology), 127–38. Oxford: Oxbow Books

Gardiner, J.P. 1991. The [earlier Neolithic] flint

industries in the study area. In J.C. Barrett, R. Bradley & M. Green, *Landscape, Monuments and Society. The Prehistory of Cranborne Chase*, 31. Cambridge: Cambridge University Press

Garwood, P. 1999. Grooved Ware in Southern Britain: Chronology and Interpretation. In R. Cleal & A. MacSween (eds), *Grooved Ware in Britain and Ireland* (Neolithic Studies Group Seminar Papers 3), 145–76. Oxford and Oakville: Oxbow Books

Gibson, A. & Kinnes, I. 1997. On the urns of a dilemma: radiocarbon and the Peterborough prob-lem. *Oxford Journal of Archaeology* 16(1), 65–72

Green, M., 2000. *A Landscape Revealed: 10,000 Years on a Chalkland Farm*, Stroud: Tempus

Healy, F. 1988. Reports on prehistoric pottery and lithic material. In P.M. Christie, A barrow cemetery on Davidstow Moor, Cornwall. Wartime excavations by C.K. Croft Andrew. *Cornish Archaeology* 27, 27–169

Healy, F. & Harding, J. forthcoming. *Raunds Area Project. The Neolithic and Bronze Age landscapes of West Cotton, Stanwick and Irthlingborough, Northamptonshire* (English Heritage Archaeological Report)

Hodder, I. & Evans, C. forthcoming. *A Woodland Archaeology. The Haddenham Project*, vol. 1. Cambridge: MacDonald Institute Research Papers

Jacobi, R. 1982. Mesolithic Hunter-gatherers 9000–4000 BC. In M. Aston & I. Burrow (eds), *The Archaeology of Somerset. A Review to 1500 AD*, 11–21. Taunton: Somerset County Council

Johnston, R. 1999. An Empty Path? Processions, Memories and the Dorset Cursus. In A. Barclay & J. Harding (eds) *Pathways and Ceremonies. The Cursus Monuments of Britain and Ireland* (Neolithic Studies Group Seminar Papers 4), 39–48. Oxford: Oxbow Books

Jones, G. & Legge, A. 1987. The grape (*Vitis vinifera* L.) in the Neolithic of Britain. *Antiquity* 61, 452–5

Jones, G. & Legge, A. J. forthcoming. Evaluating the Role of Cereal Cultivation in the Neolithic: Charred Plant Remains from Hambledon Hill. In R. Mercer & F. Healy, *Hambledon Hill, Dorset, England. Excavation and Survey of a Neolithic Monument Complex and its Surrounding Landscape* (English Heritage Archaeological Report)

Kinnes, I. 1992. *Non-Megalithic Long Barrows and Allied Structures in the British Neolithic* (British Museum Occasional Paper 52). London: British Museum

Kinnes, I., Gibson, A., Ambers, J., Bowman, S., Leese, M. & Boast, R. 1991. Radiocarbon dating and British Beakers: the British Museum programme. *Scottish Archaeological Review* 8, 35–68

Legge, A.J. forthcoming. Livestock and Neolithic Society at Hambledon Hill. In R. Mercer & F. Healy, *Hambledon Hill, Dorset, England. Excavation and Survey of a Neolithic Monument Complex and its Surrounding Landscape* (English Heritage Archaeological Report)

McKinley, J.I. forthcoming. Human Remains. In R. Mercer & F. Healy, *Hambledon Hill, Dorset, England. Excavation and Survey of a Neolithic Monument Complex and its Surrounding Landscape* (English Heritage Archaeological Report)

Mercer, R. 1980. *Hambledon Hill. A Neolithic Landscape*. Edinburgh University Press

Mercer, R.J. 1981. Excavations at Carn Brea, Illogan, Cornwall, 1970–1973: a Neolithic fortified complex of the third millennium bc. *Cornish Archaeology* 20

Mercer, R.J. 1987. A Flint Quarry in the Hambledon Hill Neolithic Enclosure Complex. In G. de G. Sieveking & M.H. Newcomer (eds), *The Human Uses of Flint and Chert: Papers from the Fourth International Flint Symposium*, 160–3. Cambridge: Cambridge University Press

Mercer, R.J. 1988. Hambledon Hill, Dorset, England. In C. Burgess, P. Topping, C. Mordant & M. Maddison (eds), *Enclosures and Defences in the Neolithic of Western Europe* (British Archaeological Reports International Series S403), 89–106. Oxford: British Archaeological Reports

Mercer, R.J. 1999. The Origins of Warfare in the British Isles. In J. Carman & A. Harding (eds), *Ancient Warfare*, 143–156. Stroud: Sutton Publishing

Mercer, R.J. forthcoming. The Nature of Enclosure Construction at Hambledon Hill. In R. Mercer & F. Healy, *Hambledon Hill, Dorset, England. Excavation and Survey of a Neolithic Monument Complex and its Surrounding Landscape* (English Heritage Archaeological Report)

Mook, W.G. 1986. Business meeting: recommendations /resolutions adopted by the twelfth international radiocarbon conference. *Radiocarbon* 28, 799

Morgan, F. de M. 1959. The excavation of a long barrow at Nutbane, Hants. *Proceedings of the Prehistoric Society* 25, 15–51

Oswald, A., Dyer, C. & Barber, M. 2001. *The Creation of Monuments. Neolithic Causewayed Enclosures in the British Isles.* Swindon: English Heritage

Palmer, R. & Oswald, A. forthcoming. The Field Survey. In R. Mercer & F. Healy, *Hambledon Hill, Dorset, England. Excavation and Survey of a Neolithic Monument Complex and its Surrounding Landscape* (English Heritage Archaeological Report)

Piggott, S. 1936. Handley Hill, Dorset — a Neolithic bowl and the date of the entrenchment. *Proceedings of the Prehistoric Society* 2(2), 229–230

Piggott, S. 1954. *Neolithic Cultures of the British Isles,* Cambridge: Cambridge University Press

Piggott, S. & Piggott, C.M. 1944. Excavation of barrows on Crichel and Launceston Downs, Dorset. *Archaeologia* 90, 47–80

Pitt Rivers, A.H.L.-F. 1898. *Excavations in Cranborne Chase near Rushmore, on the Borders of Dorset and Wiltshire 1893–1896.* Volume IV. Privately printed

Pryor, F. 1998. *Etton: Excavations at a Neolithic Causewayed Enclosure near Maxey, Cambridge-shire, 1982–87* (English Heritage Archaeological Report 18). London: English Heritage

Rawlings, M.N., Allen, M.J., Cleal, R.M.J. & Healy, F. forthcoming. Investigation of the Whitesheet environs: the Neolithic causewayed enclosure on Whitesheet Hill and Iron Age settlement at Whitesheet Quarry, *Wiltshire Archaeological & Natural History Magazine*

Richards, M.P. 2000. Human Consumption of Plant Foods in the British Neolithic. In A. Fairbairn (ed.), *Plants in Neolithic Britain and beyond* (Neolithic Studies Group Seminar Papers 5), 123–135. Oxford: Oxbow Books

Richards, M.P. forthcoming. Stable Isotope Values. In R. Mercer & F. Healy, *Hambledon Hill, Dorset, England. Excavation and Survey of a Neolithic Monument Complex and its Surrounding Landscape* (English Heritage Archaeological Report)

Richards, M.P. and Hedges, R.E.M. 1999. A Neolithic revolution? New evidence of diet in the British Neolithic. *Antiquity* 73(282), 891–7

Roe, F.E.S. forthcoming. Worked Stone other than Axes. In R. Mercer & F. Healy, *Hambledon Hill, Dorset, England. Excavation and Survey of a Neolithic Monument Complex and its Surrounding Landscape* (English Heritage Archaeological Report)

Robertson-Mackay, R. 1987. The Neolithic causewayed enclosure at Staines, Surrey: excavations 1961–63. *Proceedings of the Prehistoric Society* 53, 23–128

RCHME 1996. *Hambledon Hill, Child Okeford, Hanford and Iwerne Courtney or Shroton, Dorset. NMR numbers ST 81, SW 10 and 17. Request Survey June–September 1996.* Cambridge: RCHME

Saville, A. 1982. Carrying cores to Gloucestershire: some thoughts on lithic resource exploitation, *Lithics* 3, 25–28

Saville, A. 1990. *Hazleton North, Gloucestershire, 1979–82: the Excavation of a Neolithic Long Cairn of the Cotswold-Severn Group* (English Heritage Archaeological Report 13). London: English Heritage

Saville, A., 2002. Lithic Artefacts from Neolithic Causewayed Enclosures: Character and Meaning. In G. Varndell & P. Topping (eds), *Enclosures in Neolithic Europe. Essays on Causewayed and Non-causewayed Sites,* 91–105. Oxford: Oxbow Books

Saville, A. forthcoming. The Flint and Chert Artefacts. In R. Mercer & F. Healy, *Hambledon Hill, Dorset, England. Excavation and Survey of a Neolithic Monument Complex and its Surrounding Landscape* (English Heritage Archaeological Report)

Sharples, N.M. 1991. *Maiden Castle. Excavations and Field Survey 1985–6* (English Heritage Archaeological Report 19). London: English Heritage

Schulting R.J. 2000. New AMS dates from the Lambourn long barrow and the question of the earliest Neolithic in southern England: repacking the Neolithic package? *Oxford Journal of Archaeology* 19(1), 25–35

Smith, I.F. 1965. *Windmill Hill and Avebury: Excavations by Alexander Keiller, 1925–1939.* Oxford: Clarendon Press

Smith, I.F. 1966. Windmill Hill and its implications. *Palaeohistoria* 12, 469–81

Smith, I.F. 1971. Causewayed Enclosures. In D.D.A. Simpson (ed.), *Economy and Settlement in Neolithic and Early Bronze Age Britain and Europe*, 89–112. Leicester: Leicester University Press

Smith, I.F. forthcoming a. The Pottery from the Hilltop Excavations of 1974–82. In R. Mercer & F. Healy, *Hambledon Hill, Dorset, England. Excavation and Survey of a Neolithic Monument Complex and its Surrounding Landscape* (English Heritage Archaeological Report)

Smith, I.F. forthcoming b. Stone axes and adzes. In R. Mercer & F. Healy, *Hambledon Hill, Dorset, England. Excavation and Survey of a Neolithic Monument Complex and its Surrounding Landscape* (English Heritage Archaeological Report)

Spikins, P.A. 2002 *Prehistoric People of the Pennines*. Leeds: West Yorkshire Archaeology Service

Stuiver, M. & Reimer, P.J. 1986. A computer program for radiocarbon age calculation, *Radiocarbon* 28, 1022–30

Stuiver, M., Reimer, P.J., Bard, E., Beck, J.W., Burr, G.S., Hughen, K.A., Kromer, B., McCormac, F.G.

van der Plicht, J. & Spurk, M. 1998. INTCAL98 radiocarbon age calibration, 24,000–0 cal BP. *Radiocarbon* 40, 1041–84

Thomas, J. 2003. Thoughts on the 'repacked' Neolithic revolution. *Antiquity* 77(295), 67–74

Tilley, C. 1994. *A phenomenology of Landscape: Places, Paths and Monuments*. Oxford and Providence: Berg

Tingle, M 1998. *The Prehistory of Beer Head. Field Survey and Excavations at an Isolated Flint Source on the South Devon Coast* (British Archaeological Reports British Series 270). Oxford: British Archaeological Reports

Whittle, A., Pollard, J. & Grigson, C. 1999. *The Harmony of Symbols: the Windmill Hill Causewayed Enclosure, Wiltshire* (Cardiff Studies in Archaeology). Oxford: Oxbow Books

Woodward, P.J. & Bellamy, P. 1991. Artefact Distribution. In N.M. Sharples, *Maiden Castle. Excavations and Field Survey 1985–6* (English Heritage Archaeological Report 19), 21–32. London: English Heritage

Wysocki, M. & Whittle, A. 2000. Diversity, lifestyles and rites: new biological and archaeological evidence from British earlier Neolithic mortuary assemblages. *Antiquity* 74(285), 591–601

Enclosure and Monumentality, and the Mesolithic – Neolithic Continuum

Roger Mercer

In 1971 Isobel Smith published her much needed 'stock-taking' of the current state of knowledge relating to causewayed enclosures in Britain (Smith 1971). This paper, certainly, was a prime mover in the extraordinary development of studies relating to these complex, often badly damaged and ill-understood monuments that dominate, today as they did then, the study of Neolithic culture and society wherever they are found. Since 1971 their known distribution has been mightily extended, into Wales and Ireland and substantially to the north in England – although, so far, there is no certain evidence for their presence in Scotland. We also know now that their chronology extends well over a millennium from the early centuries of the presence of farming society in Britain until their identity can be seen to fuse with later insular monumental traditions before the mid point of the 3rd millennium cal BC (Mercer 1991). Dr Smith's seminal paper provides us with a necessary datum against which to measure how far we have come, and, indeed, how far we have *not* come in the subsequent three decades.

Causewayed enclosures are, of course, very ancient, generally well over five thousand years old, and, where they have survived, have done so in a landscape that has been intensively developed and re-developed over more or less the entirety of that interval. Today most are visible only as faint traces from the air with only a tiny proportion of the one hundred or so that are now known (cf. 17 in Smith 1971) being visible as standing earthworks. Yet recent large-scale excavations at Crickley Hill, Gloucestershire (Dixon 1988), Hambledon Hill, Dorset (Mercer & Healy forthcoming), as well as at Etton, Cambridgeshire (Pryor 1998), and Briar Hill, Northamptonshire (Bamford 1985) – including, thus, both upland and lowland settings - have shown that in their initial conception these sites were monumental (in all instances their construction, however cumulative, must have taken hundreds if not thousands of man days) and that their function was truly enclosive.

The writer would like to pause momentarily to consider these two words – monumental and enclosive. 'Monumental' would appear to have at least two attributive components, both of which may be projected towards the same social and psychological ends. One is undoubtedly the sheer scale of human effort and economic input required in construction which, in the impact that it has upon the social interaction and economic production of its originating community, generates a corporate focus in the very act of that construction. The other principal component lies in the creation through that constructive effort of a 'marker' of some longevity which may serve to prolong that sense of corporate focus, usually by the enactment of corporate (or individual) observance at the location. Such observances will, of course, change through time both in their physical aspect and their significance. There may be *lacunae* in observance after which the marker is 're-invented' to form a different social focus (just as Stonehenge has been, and is being, 're-invented' in the 20th and 21st centuries!). Of course natural features can become the focus of recurrent observance reinforcing corporate focus. Are these monuments, are they monumental? Likewise great constructions may, after their initial input of effort, excite no further 'recurrent observance' activity. Yet even passive wonderment or superstition aroused in surrounding consciousness may serve as the 'focus' of which we have spoken. 'Monumental' is therefore, not an entirely simple conception and is one that occurs both in time and through time with prolonged and varied social impacts.

'Enclosive' would on first impression seem an altogether easier adjective to define but it may transpire that this is not necessarily the case for once again it, like 'monumental', has initial physical connotations that in themselves depend upon subsequent social interaction. 'Enclosive' is nothing if it is not 'exclusive' and 'inclusive' and some of our modern uses of the latter words will indicate how 'fuzzy' definitions may easily become. 'Enclosive' is really the description of a boundary, a marker again, that controls access to an area limiting access to certain people or defining the conduct of people once they have crossed the boundary. Such boundaries may be monumental, but, equally, they may not be. The boundary of a football field is a white line painted upon grass, hardly a durable archaeological phenomenon, which controls (or should) the conduct, entirely, of people allowed within it.

Interestingly, only when it was found that this ideal was too optimistic were more durable and obstacle-like boundaries built around that initial, and only essential, boundary. 'Enclosive' then is a functional term relating to the nature of activity and not the nature of boundary. By the early Neolithic we are in the presence of monumental enclosures which, in the case of the large-scale excavated sites referred to above, have clearly taken on exclusive and inclusive components. From their earliest phases all of these sites would appear to have had continuous banks within their causewayed ditches with well-defined entrance points to their interior. In all four cases where archaeological examination has been of an adequate scale the activity within the enclosed area would appear to be quite distinct, in its archaeological expression, from that without.

In the natural successor to Isobel Smith's 1971 paper, significantly entitled 'The Creation of Monuments' (Oswald *et al.* 2001), the result of work conducted by her parent institution (the Royal Commission on the Historical Monuments of England – RCHME), the splendid series of plans rectified from aerial photographs and amended on the ground creates, thirty years on, a new datum. In some 40% of these plans more or less formal 'gate' arrangements can be intuitively distinguished, and if this is a risky statement then the writer will be forgiven for making no presumption whatever about their internal arrangements. Nevertheless the *leit-motif* of excavations great and small within these monuments is that, at least in their initial stages, internal activities would seem to be associated with non-domestic, 'ceremonial' activities while the boundary, or at least the archaeologically accessible quarries associated with that boundary appear to be consistently re-marked and re-defined by recutting and re-deposition (see Mercer 1991).

If we feel a little more confident now of the initial nature and functions (perhaps) of causewayed enclosures, our perception of their place within and relationship to the landscape has undergone some fairly wild oscillations during the 30 odd years since 1971. During this period causewayed enclosures have been seen to be more or less everything from 'central places' (Renfrew 1973), through 'sites at ecotonal boundaries' (Barker & Webley 1978), to sites located at the very extremity of the influence of any one society in an attempt to establish communication with other groups, even, perhaps, deliberately isolated (Gardiner 1984).

These arguments, are to some extent deliberately simplistic in so far as they suggest a common function (a socio-historical reality) for an archaeological site type (a morpho-taphonomic creation). Is it likely that the function of Crickley Hill, set on the Jurassic Limestone, Hambledon set at the boundary of an entirely different landscape, Abingdon on a terrace of the Thames Valley, and Etton set on an outlet to the Fens, all of them spread over a distance of 200km, had an identical function or functional history in the 4th millennium cal BC?

So at this point the writer deliberately narrows his perspective to Hambledon Hill, the site he naturally knows best, and its close parallels. Frances Healy will review the significance of this site elsewhere in this volume so the writer will concentrate on some thoughts directed towards the exploration of the *origins* of such sites. How do they appear so consistently and rapidly in the British Neolithic record within an, apparently, relatively insular cultural context? For the chalk ridge sites the evidence is relatively consistent (and different from, e.g. Etton). They were set within a landscape that hardly had felt the impact of the farmer. The advice from palaeo-environmentalists is reasonably consistent. These hilltop sites, whether in Dorset/Wiltshire or Sussex, were set in woodland, in clearings admittedly, but in a landscape that had not yet been totally altered by farmers, whereas Etton's environment had been. Elsewhere the evidence is not so good but at Hambledon, Windmill Hill (Whittle *et al.* 1999), Offham (Drewett 1977) and others the causewayed enclosure was set in a clearing, if that, and visited relatively seldom.

Yet when they were visited they were witness to the full recognised panoply of farming culture.

Any assessment of the relationship between 'British' Mesolithic populations and the development of farming is vitiated to some extent by the extraordinary, if one doesn't take into account the issues related to probability, exclusion of radiocarbon dates from one group to the other. Such a void *is* now, however, beginning to fill particularly in Yorkshire and in Scotland (see Telford 2002). In Scotland continuations of Mesolithic practice, midden accumulation (dare one say building?), microlith production sometimes apparently directly associated with plain bowl pottery and with polished stone axes occur well within an orthodox Neolithic time-span. We will return to middens in due course but perhaps, logically, we ought first to examine a larger scale phenomenon of Mesolithic economic development visible throughout the British Isles, and indeed elsewhere in north and west Europe, during the period of some two to three thousand years prior to the development of farming cultures. The burning of tracts of woodland to create open ground whereupon, the evidence would suggest (see Simmons 1996), first coloniser species would provide an attraction for ungulate animals (deer, aurochs) to enter the area and, caught in the ensuing enfilade, lead to their entrapment. Evidence exists for the repeated hunting of individual animals at the period and indeed for the hunting to extinction of aurochs in Denmark at this time (Noe-Nygaard 1974, 1975). Rackham (1986, 79) has been at pains to point out just how difficult such fires may have been to start and we should perhaps not underestimate the amount of organisation and coordination required to carry out such exercises successfully – to create a clearing of the right size in the right place and at the right time. Jenny Moore (1996) has shown how complex this matter may really be depending upon a series of issues relating to the nature and extent of the fire. Her key is that 'British woodlands without a high pine component were flammable in the past is evidenced by the presence of macro- and microscopic charcoal. The dilemma now faced is: natural or anthropogenic fire?' Her answer to this question lies in a series of ethnographic and forest ecological comparisons that indicate that such fires, the outcomes of complex sequences of events, were entirely feasible. Simmons perceives the process as that of:

> a largely sedentary group which spends much of the year near the coastline . . . but which moves inland up the river valleys as a unit at the end of the summer. Once out of the terrain that can be hunted over on a daily basis from the main settlement, smaller subgroups of hunters are spun off and some of these make for upland hunting grounds for red deer. In order to increase the chances of success, areas in the woodlands and at the forest/scrub edge have been fired in order to encourage plants known to be favoured by the deer. (Simmons 1996, 221)

But Simmons also then immediately notes that 'fire may also act as a territorial marker, in effect it appropriates the land to a particular group . . . Hence, a small hunter gatherer population can produce a relatively large detectable environmental impact, especially in ecotonal vegetation' (1996, 221). We should perhaps note that such activity is in all likelihood to take place in settings peripheral to the societies involved and therefore, perhaps, in contexts where different groups will meet. Indeed the organisational effort noted above may well have led to a proprietorial sense established in one group against another – possibly even a source of conflict.

We will return to these issues in due course but let us note immediately that, however ephemeral such a clearing, with the economic and, perhaps, proprietorial overtones that it is likely to have possessed, set as it is in otherwise unaffected woodland margin, with sufficient distinction to perform its suggested function, *is* a form of enclosure in all but the 'detail' of exclusive definition by some form of barrier, which, of course, in the circumstances, would have been counter-productive.

Perhaps we should now move to another 'fact' of Mesolithic existence - the 'shell midden'. So much have these been viewed as 'a fact' since the early 19th century and the early comprehension of their age and 'function', that the writer has found it difficult to locate any discussion in recent or early debate as to *why* hunter gatherers should create such often 'monumental' mounds ('structures', 'accumulations'). The subject is, of course, the collection of limpets and other shellfish carried out along a fairly long stretch of foreshore, particularly where harvesting has been consistent. The rewards are pretty meagre both in dietary and nutritional terms. Why, therefore, is it regarded as appropriate to carry the dead weight of shells uphill to a point clear of the high tide mark to an established central point in order to divest the 30% weight of flesh from the 70% of shell when, in all likelihood, the requirement for much of the flesh is as bait in the very element from which the resource has just been derived? Why, if this is a 'landscape-tidy' exercise, is the balance of domestic refuse so relatively impoverished? Even if (Stiner *et al.* 2003, 78) the requirement is to apply heat to the molluscs to facilitate removal of meat from shell, there is no compelling reason why such activity should be centralized, and little archaeological indication of this degree of importance of fire-setting within well excavated midden deposits. At Cnoc Coig, Oronsay (Mellars 1987, 234-7), a number of small hearths occur within the midden but exhibit little indication of the 'industrial' processing of shell fish by heating, nor apparently do the bulk of shells present indicate traces of such processing.

The question therefore remains as to the functional basis upon which many tons of shell are piled into mounds (Mellars 1987 gives sparse attention to the extent, volume and 'tonnage' of the mounds, but Cnoc Coig would appear to be at least 2m high and 20 x 20m on plan representing at least 400m³ of debris, mostly shell, weighing some 80-100 tons). The writer suggests that such 'accumulation' requires to be explained in functional terms that are not readily visible in 'economic' or 'industrial' reality. Are such 'accumulations' social statements of 'right' or 'social solidarity'? It is unlikely that the explanation will be the same along the entirety of the distribution of such 'accumulations' along the whole north and west littoral of Continental Europe and throughout the British and Irish archipelago. Yet consistently whether in Portugal (Stiner *et al.* 2003) or in Denmark (see Whittle 1985, 123) or in Britain (Mellars 1987) these sites produce radiocarbon dates that indicate persistence up to, and within, the period of local farming activity and frequently exhibit evidence of the presence of farming culture (identity?) on, at least, their upper levels. Pollard points out that:

> The shell midden therefore represents a place of transformation where terrestrial resources were transformed into tools prior to their deployment in the marine environment and marine resources transformed into food prior to its consumption or movement into the terrestrial zone... the shell midden represents a place of mediation between land and sea. (Pollard 1996, 203)

The bones of hands and feet of humans are common on these sites and while some have clearly been shown to be later intrusions (Saville & Hallen 1994) there may exist here traces of some process linked to the excarnation of human remains in this boundary setting. Tidal linkage to lunar state may well have been observed by early man. Were these therefore cosmically linked 'boundary zones' used for excarnation as Pollard suggests?

It is also possible to demonstrate a direct linkage between the siting of chambered cairns and earlier shell middens. At Glecknabae, Isle of Bute, deposits of marine shells were found beneath the cairn by Bryce (1904), and Scott (1961, 16) observed a simple superimposition at Crarae, Argyll. It is interesting perhaps to note that these superimpositions mark an apparent

end to midden development on the site which can only excite interest in the light of Richards' (2000) observations relating to the isotopic analysis of human bone from Neolithic contexts in coastal South Wales that indicate an abandonment of marine food sources at this time. Indeed a location of mediation may have become one of spatial and socio-economic limitation.

Such ideas may be reflected, however hazily, in the superimposition recorded by Alan Saville at Hazleton North, Gloucestershire (Saville 1989, 259; 1990), where the long cairn of quite clearly Neolithic date and cultural attribution was built upon a former land surface upon which discreet and well defined Mesolithic assemblages of stone tools had been accumulated. Saville indicates an assemblage of material underlying the chambered long cairn, where a 'midden deposit' broadly circular in form and completely delimited by excavation was sited quite precisely on the axis of the barrow, with a further concentration of typologically Mesolithic flintwork material also occurring in the area of the later cairn forecourt. A distribution of diagnostically early Neolithic flintwork on the pre-cairn surface seems unrelated to these concentrations. Such concentrations of typo-logically Mesolithic material have also occurred under the only other chambered cairns to be totally excavated under modern conditions, at Ascott under Wychwood, Oxfordshire (Selkirk 1971), and Gwernvale, Brecknockshire (Britnell & Savory 1984). At Gwernvale Healy and Green (in Britnell & Savory 1984) suggest that the 'predecessor' artefactual assemblage may reach back through the later and earlier Mesolithic into the Upper Palaeolithic.

Once again as with forest clearance exercises we may be looking at a by-product of an 'economic' process that by an act of 'accumulation' and 'contra-natural statement' creates a symbolic statement of human presence which may, given time and circumstance, come to control the nature of human activity and interaction that is later to occur there.

A third seam in this particular exploration, again, originates in the writer's awareness of issues at Hambledon Hill, but began elsewhere. In 1966 excavations undertaken in advance of the extension of the Stonehenge parking area recovered traces of pits that had incontrovertibly acted as the receptacles for vertical posts of considerable stature (0.5-0.75m in diameter). The pits were, at the point of excavation, 1.0-1.25m deep suggesting, if the 'average' loss of the surface of chalk subsoil applies (Atkinson 1957), that they may have approached 2m in original depth. This might suggest, if we follow Mercer (1981), that posts some 5-6m in height were erected within them. In terms of the diameter such posts may well have weighed well over a ton and would have had to be at least trimmed neat in their lower regions if the result of treefall, or, of course, directly felled before manouevring and erection. The surprise was, of course, the identification of the charcoal of these posts as *pinus* and a series of radiocarbon dates that suggest initial placement during the 9th-8th millennia BC. It was a paper published by Michael Allen and Julie Gardiner (2002) that suggested to the writer the scope of the conjectures contained in the current paper and the comparison that they made with the situation at Hambledon Hill where two subsoil features, in no way as 'convincing' as their Stonehenge 'counterparts', but nevertheless apparently anthropogenic, and containing charcoal of *pinus sylvestris*, yielded radiocarbon dates also in the 8th millennium BC. Similar pits with apparent post-pipes, no associated artefacts, but with comparable environmental 'dates' of Boreal complexion have occurred at Boscombe Down, Wiltshire (Allen & Gardiner 2002).

Much of the evidence brought together above is tentative and the linkages suggest tenuous. It is, however, the case that direct archaeological evidence for such remote valencies between the relatively well-understood structures of our Neolithic and a possible 'local' ancestry are likely to be hard to come by. Nevertheless in a prevailing climate of study

where the Mesolithic contribution to the early farming cultures of north and west Europe is perceived as increasingly important in both ethnic and economic terms, and where that contribution in archaeologically cultural terms is receiving increasing recognition, a preliminary rehearsal of a possible anterior contribution to that most distinctive of 'Neolithic' cultural developments, the monumental enclosive structure, is useful and stimulating, if only in its rebuttal. This essay has endeavoured to show that in Britain, and indeed across a broader swathe of north and west Europe, hunter-gatherer populations had been familiar with issues of monumental 'marking' whether by deliberate erection or accumulation and that such developments were sometimes the object of later 'Neolithic' activity of a broadly similar character. Furthermore, hunter-gatherers were familiar with the differential marking of areas of landscape for quite specific functions over which the effort of prior organisation and execution may have given them a sense of proprietorial right.

This may in turn suggest that the archaeologically clearer 'monumental' arrangements of the Neolithic were not so much a new way of thinking (Thomas 1988, 1991) but, less ambitiously, a new way of doing old things, several millennia old, in the context of a more crowded and varied landscape. Such 'new ways of doing old things' must have been as, if not more, familiar to hunters living in the 5th millennium BC as they are to us living in the 3rd AD. This familiarity may, in turn, help to explain the apparent rapidity, both in space and time, with which these innovations were adopted.

Bibliography

Allen, M.J. & Gardiner, J. 2002. 'A sense of time: cultural markers in the Mesolithic of Southern England?' In B. David & M. Wilson (eds), *Inscribed Landscapes: Marking and Making Place*, 139-53. Honolulu: University of Hawaii Press

Atkinson, R.J.C. 1957. 'Worms and weathering' *Antiquity* 31, 219-33

Bamford, H.M. 1985. *Briar Hill Excavation 1974-78*. Northampton: Northampton Development Corporation Archaeological Monograph 3

Barber, G. & Webley, D. 1978. Causewayed camps and Earlier Neolithic economies in Central Southern England. *Proceedings of the Prehistoric Society* 44, 161-86

Britnell, W. & Savory, H. 1984. *Gwernvale and Penywyrlod: two Neolithic long cairns in the Black Mountains of Brecknock*. Cardiff: Cambrian Archaeological Association

Bryce, T.H. 1904. On the cairns and tumuli of the Island of Bute. *Proceedings of the Society of Antiquaries of Scotland* 38, 17-81

Dixon, P. 1988. The Neolithic settlements on Crickley Hill. In C. Burgess, P. Topping, C. Mordent & M. Maddison (eds), *Enclosures and Defences in the Neolithic of Western Europe*, 75-88. Oxford: British Archaeological Reports, International Series 403

Drewett, P. 1977. The excavation of a Neolithic causewayed enclosure on Offham Hill, East Sussex, 1976. *Proceedings of the Prehistoric Society* 43, 201-41

Gardiner, J.P. 1984. Lithic distributions and Neolithic settlement patterns in Central Southern England. In R. Bradley & J. Gardiner (eds), *Neolithic Studies*, 15-40, Oxford: British Archaeological Reports, British Series 133

Mellars, P. 1987. *Excavations on Oronsay*. Edinburgh: Edinburgh University Press

Mercer, R.J. 1981. The excavation of a late Neolithic henge-type enclosure at Balfarg, Fife, Scotland. *Proceedings of the Society of Antiquaries of Scotland* 111, 63-171

Mercer, R.J. 1991. *Causewayed Enclosures*. Princes Risborough: Shire Publications

Mercer, R.J. & Healy, F.M. Forthcoming. *The excavation of a Neolithic Enclosure Complex at Hambledon Hill, Dorset 1974-86*. London: English Heritage

Moore, J. 1996. Damp squib: how to fire a major deciduous forest in an inclement climate. In T. Pollard & A. Morrison (eds), *The Early Prehistory of Scotland*, 62-73. Edinburgh: Edinburgh University Press

Noe-Nygaard, N. 1974. Mesolithic hunting in Denmark illustrated by bone injuries caused by human weapons. *Journal of Archaeological Science* 1, 217-48

Noe-Nygaard, N. 1975. Two shoulder blades with healed lesions from Star Carr. *Proceedings of the Prehistoric Society* 41, 10-16

Oswald, A., Dyer, C. & Barber, M. 2001. *The Creation of Monuments: Neolithic Causewayed Enclosures in the British Isles*. London: English Heritage

Pollard, T. 1996. Coastal environments, cosmology and ritual practice. In T. Pollard & A. Morrison (eds), *The Early Prehistory of Scotland*, 198-210. Edinburgh: Edinburgh University Press

Pryor, F. 1998. *Etton: Excavations at a Neolithic Causewayed Enclosure near Maxey, Cambridgeshire, 1982-87*. London: English Heritage Archaeological Report 18

Rackham, O. 1986. *The History of the Countryside*. London: Dent

Renfrew, C. 1973. Monuments, mobilisation and social organisation in Neolithic Wessex. In C. Renfrew (ed), *The Explanation of Culture Change: Models in Prehistory*, 539-58. London: Duckworth

Richards, M.P. 2000. Human consumption of plant foods in the British Neolithic: direct evidence from bone stable isotopes. In A. Fairbairn (ed.), *Plants in Neolithic Britain and Beyond*, 123-35. Oxford: Oxbow Books

Saville, A. 1989. A Mesolithic flint assemblage from Hazleton, Gloucestershire, England, and its implications. In C. Bonsall (ed), *The Mesolithic in Europe*, 258-63. Edinburgh: John Donald

Saville, A. 1990. *Hazleton North: The excavation of a Neolithic long cairn of the Cotswold-Severn group*. London: English Heritage

Saville, A. & Hallen, Y. 1994. The 'Obanian Iron Age': human remains from the Oban cave sites, Argyll, Scotland. *Antiquity* 68, 715-23

Scott, J. 1961, The excavation of the chambered cairn at Crarae, Loch Fyneside, Mid Argyll. *Proceedings of the Society of Antiquaries of Scotland* 94, 1-27

Selkirk, A. 1971. Ascott-under-Wychwood. *Current Archaeology* 24, 7-10

Simmons, I.G. 1996. *The Environmental Impact of Later Mesolithic Cultures*. Edinburgh: Edinburgh University Press

Smith, I.F. 1971. Causewayed enclosures. In D.D.A. Simpson (ed), *Economy and Settlement in Neolithic and Early Bronze Age Britain and Europe*, 89-112. Leicester: Leicester University Press

Stiner, M.C., Bicho, N., Lindly, J. & Ferring, R. 2003. Mesolithic to Neolithic transitions: new results from shell middens in the Western Algarve, Portugal. *Antiquity* 77, 75-86

Telford, D. 2002. The Mesolithic inheritance: contrasting Neolithic monumentality in eastern and western Scotland. *Proceedings of the Prehistoric Society* 68, 289-315

Thomas, J. 1988. Neolithic explanations revisited: the Mesolithic-Neolithic transition in Britain and south Scandinavia. *Proceedings of the Prehistoric Society* 54, 59-66

Thomas, J. 1991. *Rethinking the Neolithic*. Cambridge: Cambridge University Press

Whittle, A. 1985. *Neolithic Europe, A Survey*. Cambridge: Cambridge University Press

Whittle, A., Pollard, J. & Grigson, C. 1999. *The Harmony of Symbols: The Windmill Hill Causewayed Enclosure, Wiltshire*. Oxford: Oxbow Books

William Cunnington and the Long Barrows of the River Wylye

Bruce Eagles & David Field

One of the more important contributions in the field of Neolithic studies was that of the survey of the long barrows in Hampshire (RCHME 1979), which was carried out while Isobel Smith was an Investigator for the Royal Commission on the Historical Monuments of England (RCHME) during the 1970s. That project, in which Isobel played the major role, not only compared long barrow types as observed and measured in the field, but also considered their landscape position and took long barrow studies on the kind of major leap forward rarely seen since the pioneering work of William Cunnington at the beginning of the 19th century. Cunnington's work too was painstaking and imaginative. Nobody had dug into a long barrow before, or at least in a recorded way, and until then the only model in terms of excavating tumuli was that of the Reverend Douglas in Kent. Both Cunnington's study and that of the RCHME were innovative and both remain significant. This paper is offered as a tribute to Isobel as a scholar, colleague and friend.

William Cunnington

Having been told by his doctors to 'ride out or die', William Cunnington, a draper and cloth merchant of Heytesbury, Wiltshire, embarked on what must then have been seen as an unusual pursuit of investigating the earthen mounds that were to be found liberally scattered on the local chalk Downs. Records of these interventions are preserved in letters to his benefactors and supporters, initially H.P. Wyndham, MP for Salisbury; and later R.C. Hoare of Stourhead, who used the work in his *Ancient Wiltshire*, the first folio of which was published in 1810. These letters often describe the stratigraphy that was encountered, along with the discovery of skeletons and other finds. Though dictated by Cunnington, they were written by his daughters, a copy being retained in each case (R.H. Cunnington 1975, 7-8: 1954). Hoare's copy bound into five volumes was eventually purchased by the Society of Antiquaries (Soc. of Ants. London ms.217), while Cunnington's copy sorted into 13 books and bound in three volumes, went to the library of the Wiltshire Archaeological and Natural History Society (referred to below as Cunnington mss Devizes). From these it is clear that Cunnington made some tentative explorations, initially to satisfy the question posed by Wyndham as to whether, in contrast to the round mounds, the long examples covered bodies slain in battle. Cunnington knew little about long barrows, but then neither did anyone else, and given the medical advice he had received

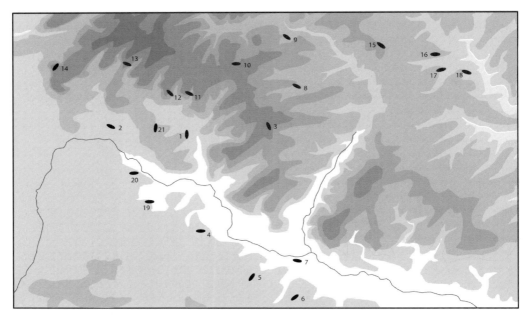

Fig. 1. Map of the distribution of Long Barrows along the River Wylye and the south eastern part of Salisbury Plain: 1 Heytesbury North Field, 2 King Barrow, 3 Knook, 4 Corton, 5 Boyton, 6 Stockton, 7 Sherrington, 8 Knook Down, 9 Imber, 10 Boles Barrow, 11 Norton Bavant, 12 Middleton Down, 13 Oxendean Down, 14 Arn Hill, 15 Kill Barrow, 16 Tilshead Lodge, 17 Old Ditch, 18 White Barrow, 19 St Leonard's Church, 20 Dairy Plantation, 21 Scratchbury

concerning the importance to his health of exposure to the downs air, the pursuit seemed as good as any and was one that gripped him with increasing fascination.

Between 1800 and 1809 Cunnington excavated 18 of the 53 or so long barrows subsequently recorded on Salisbury Plain and in South Wiltshire, that is 25% of the present total, having discovered many of them himself during trips on to the downs. These formed part of the Salisbury Plain West group defined by Ashbee (1970) and many were investigated by the RCHME during the late 1980s and early 1990s, those situated on military land being published as part of a survey of that area (McOmish et al. 2002). Most were only at a little distance from Cunnington's home and in particular they focus on the upper reaches of the River Wylye (Fig. 1). Some he excavated more than once, returning to

both Heytesbury North Field (Heytesbury 4: National Monuments Record (NMR) Number ST 94 SW 6) and King Barrow (Warminster 14: NMR ST 84 SE 8), for example, to ask questions refined by the experience of his later excavations.

Heytesbury North Field

Initial efforts were modest enough. In 1800, at the invitation of Sir William A'Court, of Heytesbury House, he dug a small trench into the centre of the low long barrow that lay just outside the park and within Heytesbury North Field, little more than a kilometre north of Cunnington's home. The result was inconclusive, though Wyndham was content with the human bones found in association with a deposit of black earth (R.H. Cunnington 1975, 12) that seemed to help to support his theory concerning battle casualties.

Lying within the Heytesbury arable it is of no surprise that the mound has been reduced. It now reaches barely 1m in height, but it is likely to have been little different in Cunnington's day and the bulk of the mound might indicate that it was always low. At c.38m long, by a maximum of c.15m wide, it lies towards the shorter end of the range and its orientation along the contours, with its axis towards the south, was not then seen as unusual or noteworthy. No ditches are visible now, but according to the Ordnance Survey Record Card (incorporated into NMR records) they were noted as formerly being present from traces on an air photograph (Crawford Coll. No. 3071 15-5-33).

Not unreasonably Cunnington's attention focused on the centre of the mound with the expectation of that being the 'business' area and it was there that he cut a not inconsiderable trench some 5m in length by c.2.5m wide. Four years later, with the experience of having dug several other barrows in the vicinity, he returned to the site and placed two further trenches towards the broad end, a position where he had since made discoveries in some of the other mounds. He wrote to Wyndham in February of that year describing his finds (Cunnington mss Devizes, Book 3, 45) and in order to assist his description, he annexed a plan of the excavations (McOmish *et al.* 2002, fig 1:11), one of the earliest of excavation plans and certainly the first of a long barrow.

At the base of the first trench, Cunnington discovered the 'black earth' and traced it through to the second, where it was observed to increase in height and rise to form a circular barrow, the black earth being mixed with large flint nodules, sarsens and chalk marl. The third trench was cut into this 'conical' mound and excavated down through it until a circular pit was encountered (Cunnington thought that it was a cist), c.1.5m in diameter and 0.7m deep, that was neatly cut into the underlying natural chalk. The pit contained no artefacts, but was filled with the same material as that of the overlying circular mound. Between this pit and the southern edge of the trench lay a great number of human bones evidently in disarray and many in a state of decay 'crossing each other in every direction'. Cunnington thought that more than ten individuals were represented and perhaps as many as twenty.

King Barrow

Late in October 1800, with his first exploration into a long barrow behind him, he made his way to Boreham, near Warminster, 3km from his home in Heytesbury, where, with the help of some labourers, he cut into the enormous mound known as King Barrow. The contrast with the mound in Heytesbury North Field could not be more marked. However, now armed with only a little background knowledge, he clearly felt up to the task. The mound (Fig. 2), a massive 62m in length, 17m wide and 4.5m in height, is situated on the edge of a small bluff overlooking what is now the floodplain of the River Wylye at Bishopstrow and viewed from the west this position enhances its profile considerably. Reference to the hachured plan makes it clear that its wider end lies to the southeast, though Cunnington, perhaps influenced by the manner in which the natural ground surface dramatically falls away here, considered it to be in the north. Strangely, the only contemporary measured plan that survives indicates the same width, 16.4m, at either end (Cunnington mss Devizes, Book 11). Only a few metres away from the south end, and on the same axis, is a round mound and a little to the southwest another, both now landscaped as part of the garden of Bishopstrow House (see below NMR ST 84 SE 48 and ST 84 SE 10). Notwithstanding this and site landscaping, and the effects of former cultivation, the surviving earthworks associated with the long barrow allow the identification of several components that appear to be ancient, each separated by a break of slope or ledge along the length of the mound.

At the base lies a raised platform (Fig. 2a), less marked on the northeast side, where it is composed of a shallow scarp no more than 0.2m in height, though in the west it forms a substantial lynchet-like feature. In the southwest the scarp bifurcates, its ultimate extent being unclear as it is overlain by recognisable garden features associated with Bishopstrow House, but it may once have been unitary with scarps around or beneath the round barrow 20m southeast of the long mound. A more substantial platform (Fig. 2b), appearing as a ledge or berm particularly on the western flank, where it is over 1m wide and up to 2m in height, lies over it and on this the main part of the superstructure has been built. The upper portion (Fig. 2d), though prominent at the southeast end, noticeably broadens and

becomes indistinguishable from the lower in the north (Fig. 2c) and given the Bronze Age and Saxon finds discovered by Cunnington (below) could even, in part, be a secondary structure. No side ditches are evident, indeed on the western side there is no room for one unless it lay at the foot of the natural scarp. However, there may be some artificial scarping here that would not only have provided material for the construction of the mound, but also would have enhanced its perceived height. Any ditch in the northeast could potentially be filled in and cultivated, though for a mound of this size one might expect such a feature to be of considerable proportions and some trace, however shallow, visible on the surface.

On the summit a large depression, 9 x 6m by 1m deep, situated towards the northwest end may

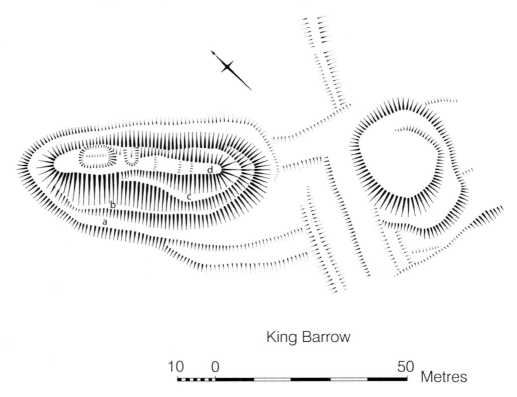

King Barrow

10   0   50
                                                              Metres

Fig. 2. Hachured plan of King Barrow, Bishopstrow, Wiltshire

represent the episode of destruction ascribed to Mr Morgan, the farmer, who according to Hoare (1810, 73) intended to level the mound, having already ploughed away part of it. There is no other scar on the mound that matches the description of this event and it appears unlikely that such a trench would have been backfilled.

A little north of centre, a cut into the mound from the northeast, 4m in width, may mark the site of Cunnington's initial exploration. Hoare (ibid., 72) remarked that Cunnington had opened 'a section of twenty eight feet (8.5m) in length from the northeast edge to the centre....', while Cunnington himself (Cunnington mss Devizes, Book 11, 22) records that work began in the northeast of the cutting near the edge of the mound and worked towards the centre, before moving northwest and then southwest, resulting in a T-shaped trench. Presumably work proceeded by digging straight down to the ground surface at the edge of the mound, placing the first spoilheap away from the mound, before moving on to repeat the process and perhaps moving fresh spoil into the area vacated.

Confirmation of the location of these events is provided by a sketch (Fig. 3) of the profile of the mound on the reverse of one of the later Cunnington papers (Soc. of Ants. London ms.217/ Volume IV, folio 76: Devizes, Book 11, 22). This clearly indicates the position of Cunnington's first T-shaped trench at about the mid-point in the side of the mound, with the damage caused by the farmer depicted towards the northwest end. Other illustrations were evidently prepared but are lost, there being references in the letters to 'Fig 1 The South West side of the Barrow' and 'Sir. You will receive with this a drawing of King Barrow by my Brother...' and 'My Brother has been very much from our home and could not finish the drawings before this Evening'. Evidently these referred to an illustration, lettered A-M, marking the position of features of interest found in the mound, including the position of bones and charred wood found beneath the barrow (Cunnington mss Devizes, Book 11, 21). Some of the finds were illustrated too, though unfortunately the figures

described do not tie in with the illustration of artefacts made later by Crocker (below). Cunnington's early notes, amounting to a daily record, were later copied by Hoare during his preparations for *Ancient Wiltshire*. Entries for October 31st, November 2nd, 5th, 8th and 21st 1800 occur, though sometimes appear a little confused (Cunnington mss Devizes, Book 11, 22): 'we began by making a section 6 feet wide and 28 feet from the present edge C to the interior part of the barrow D'. Immediately below the turf the excavators encountered a deposit of chalk, 'white Marl stones', beneath which the mound as a whole was found to comprise 'white Marley Earth, and often vegetable mould, also Nodules of Pyritical kind' (*ibid.* 21). On October 31st, he 'found more bones of horses, swine - a piece of ivory 8 1/2" long, like the point of an elephant tooth (tusk), a piece of black urn... when the bottom (was) found (to be)... almost red by the action of fire...'. On November 2nd '... found (the) same... bones, fragments of horn and (I) suppose the barrow was larger'. He may have been digging at the south end, for on several occasions he indicates that he believed the mound to have been larger and that it may have originally joined the round mound to the south. On November 5th he came across '... a pavement of burr stones...' and on November 8th, '... a kind of Skeleton near the same place and a piece of Stags Horn near it...'. A note in a letter written on 1st December 1800 adds that 'at H [on the lost plan] was found some irregular common Stones such as the Farmers in this neighbourhood pave their Stables with'. This was probably deliberately broken sarsen, similar to that later encountered in Knook Barrow.

According to Cunnington, fragments of coarse pottery and animal bones, including antler and boar tusks, were frequently encountered throughout the fabric of the mound. He commented that the antlers were remarkably large and the tips of some firm and white like ivory (*ibid.* 21).

Beneath the mound, 'a floor of yellow clay' was met with and Cunnington was led to conclude

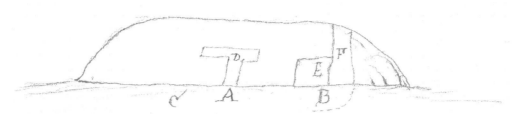

Fig. 3. Sketch of King Barrow showing the position of excavation trenches (from Soc. of Ants. London ms.217/ Volume IV, f 76)

that when the barrow was constructed all of the adjacent land might have supported a deposit of clay. He noted, however, that the base of the barrow was over half a metre lower than the adjacent ground, the floor being easily distinguished from the mound that covered it (*ibid.* 21). Hoare (1810, 72) too, indicated that the floor lay 'more than two feet below the present surface'. Cunnington further remarked that, in places, the yellow floor was stained a dull rusty red colour 'rather as blood appears on the roads a few days after it has been shed' and that 'flakes' of similar colour to corroded iron were observed and that it was also covered with charred wood and ashes, with animal bones, both 'beasts and birds', fragments of human bones and potsherds all present. Bones amounting to almost 4.5 litres (½ peck) were recovered (Cunnington mss Devizes, Book 11, 21).

The nature of this deposit is quite uncertain. The floor evidently extended a distance of 12.5m from Cunnington's trench D at least as far as A (Fig. 3): i.e. from the centre towards the edge of the mound, from where it rose steadily to within less than 0.5m of the surface. In tracing it, Cunnington found that in the northeast it extended for 'many feet' beyond the strict confines of the mound and indeed as far as the round mound to the southeast, while Hoare too felt it was 'remarkable that this floor should extend several feet from the barrow on the northeast side' (Hoare 1810, 72). It is possible that the platform identified in the earthwork survey provided a covering for this, as it extends for several metres beyond the mound proper in every direction.

Nine years later, this time with the support of Richard Colt Hoare, Cunnington returned to the mound at the point at which Mr Morgan, the farmer, had 'cut through' it. Cunnington's account (Soc. of Ants. London ms.217/ Volume IV, f76) states clearly that the farmer had 'carried away a great deal of the barrow' near the point marked 'B' on his sketch plan, that is, towards the northern end of the mound. Conveniently it presented a ready-made section that could be utilised and this is marked 'E' on this sketch plan.

Certainly Cunnington investigated the northwest end of the mound, for he revealed secondary skeletons close to the surface at that end. The stratigraphy matched that found in the earlier trench. Here Hoare quoted Cunnington's notes almost verbatim, recording that:

we also found the floor of it full 2 feet and a half lower than the adjoining ground, and covered with black ashes, as in the first section; and the soil as before in some places had the appearance of iron when decomposed. In uncovering this floor we were surprised to find that as we approached the edge of the barrow, the clay and earth which covered the floor rose 3 feet in height like another tumulus, and ten or twelve feet in diameter; amongst this clay was an immense quantity of animal bones, some of oxen, but mostly of swine; among these bones and ashes were several pieces of burned human bones and fragments of an urn and other British pottery, some specimens of which are curiously ornamented. After exploring a great many feet of this barrow within a barrow, we made a large section from top to bottom, but found nothing but a few animal bones and a little charred wood. (Hoare 1810, 73)

This section was at 'F' on Cunnington's plan.

Cunnington was concerned at the lack of a primary interment and concluded that the enormous quantity of ashes may have represented cremations, but was particularly struck by the profusion of animal bone here in contrast to the other excavated long mounds. The floor was evidently 'covered with animal bones of almost every description', including those of birds, along with fragments of charred wood, some of which still adhered to bones. Just above the floor in the northeast of the trench was the complete skeleton of a horse. Cunnington noted the distinction in position and in his later note observes that it was found near point 'A' on the sketch plan, i.e. close to the edge of the mound. The latter would appear to have been incorporated within the structure of the mound, or perhaps more likely inserted later.

No trace remains of the 'curiously ornamented' pottery from the clay floor and while a water colour by Philip Crocker (Crocker folio Devizes Pl. XLIII, figs 3-5) illustrates several sherds, it is not clear whether these were among those found at the base of the mound. Crocker depicts three sherds, all of which appear to display Grooved Ware characteristics, and if these can be identified as those mentioned as 'curiously ornamented' from the clay beneath the mound, they would be a unique find from such a position. It may perhaps be safest to assume that they came from deposits around the edges of the mound and represent later activity.

At the base of the final trench 'F', a portion of what appears to be a ground axe was recovered. Hoare (1810, 73) describes it as a violet colour and it may perhaps be from one of the Cumbrian or Welsh grouped rock sources. Cunnington's watercolour (ibid. fig. 6) indicates that it may be a mid-portion of a ground axe of lenticular cross-section and therefore unlikely to be of Group VI rock. If indeed recovered from the position indicated by Cunnington this also is a rare find

indeed. Though edge ground axes are frequently associated with Neolithic round barrows (e.g. Kinnes 1979), no other examples of ground axes from long barrows are known (e.g. Kinnes 1992, 108-110) and, like the pottery, it may be prudent to suggest that it derived from the edge of the mound where secondary activity may not have been easily distinguished.

The sequence here appears to begin with the clay floor. This represents a considerable amount of activity involving animal bones, fragments of pottery and episodes of burning represented by charred wood, ashes and perhaps by the reddened ground, though whether burning comprised the main part of the activity is unclear. Over this at one point, a circular mound, c.3-4m in diameter by c.1m in height, was constructed of clay and earth, within which human and animal bones and potsherds were all incorporated, suggesting that the material may have been composed of debris from the floor. Around and over the floor, perhaps sealing the event, the base platform identified during the earthwork survey (Fig. 2) must have been constructed – its composition and purpose unknown – and this in turn must have provided a platform for the superstructure of the mound proper. However, the problem with this interpretation is that it allows no room for what appear to be later Neolithic deposits, even around the edges of the mound, and for the moment they remain unsatisfactorily unexplained.

In whatever form that it appeared at the end of the Neolithic, the mound appears to have attracted subsequent activities. In 1800 Cunnington had opened a trench at 'E' on the sketch plan, close to the area later disturbed by the farmer and found a 'prettily ornamented' urn that he thought might have contained a secondary cremation burial, but which had in turn been disturbed by Saxon insertions. His text suggests that this was found 'on top of the barrow E', though this could mean it was close to the surface on the slope down to the barrow edge rather than actually at the summit. However, only a small percentage of the mound was investigated and this may be only one of a number of such insertions. Crocker's illustration of finds from the mound (Philip Crocker folio Devizes Museum Pl. XLIII, fig. 2, 109) depicts what appears to be a large, buff coloured, potsherd from a Collared Urn, with six horizontal lines of twisted cord decoration on the collar and four further lines on the neck. Below this, rows of short diagonal twisted cord (maggots) are arranged either side of the shoulder. Horizontal lines of twisted cord are frequently found on the neck and collar of both primary and secondary Collared Urns, examples being widespread from Wales to Yorkshire (Longworth 1984): Wiltshire examples including Longworth's numbers 1631 from Amesbury; 1664 from Bower Chalke; 1681 from Durrington; and 1694 from Ogbourne St Andrew.

Twenty metres to the southeast of King Barrow lies a round mound of considerable size (NMR ST 84 SE 48). In its present form it measures almost 40m by 30m and reaches no more than 1.5m in height, but it has been deformed by the construction of a spiral path and its summit and incorporation into a landscaped garden. Today no surface indication of the presence of a ditch can be detected. The mound was evidently excavated by Cunnington in 1801 (Cunnington 1975, 164), though other than the fact that no burial was found (Soc. of Ants. London ms.217/ Volume IV, f76), no details are known. However, he cautiously referred to the long barrow floor as extending as far as the round barrow and indeed felt that the mound itself once formed part of the long barrow. He acknowledged that were this so it would form one of the largest mounds on Salisbury Plain, though no longer than the massive Old Ditch long barrow at Tilshead (Tilshead 2: NMR SU 04 NW 9) that he had excavated in 1802 and which he had shown to cover a round mound (Cunnington mss Devizes, Book 3, 39).

Little more than 150m to the southeast a further large round barrow (NMR ST 84 SE 10) is situated on the same terrace edge. Measuring 52m by 50m by 2.2m high in the north and 4m high in the south, with a flat summit 7m in diameter containing an old excavation hollow, it

is no wonder that Grinsell (1957, 160) thought that it may be a motte. Included on Hoare's map as a barrow (1810, fp50) and also considered a barrow by the Ordnance Survey Archaeological Investigator, Norman Quinnell in 1967, the bowl-shaped profile, although large, can be compared to other local large round barrows, in particular Westbury 7 (NMR ST 84 NE 30). This was excavated by Hoare (Hoare 1810, 54) and is almost certainly Neolithic in date. The Compton Barrow (NMR SU 15 SW 17), which reaches some 46m in diameter (McOmish et al. 2002, 39), has also been suggested to be Neolithic on account of its great size.

Although by no means a critical indicator of date, there are a number of other excessively large mounds in the area. Further southeast, 500m from King Barrow, a large round mound to the east of Bishopstrow Farm (NMR ST 94 SW 17: ST 94 SW 93) was also formerly considered to be a motte (Cunnington M, 1930, 137). Bob Smith (1985) independently came to the same conclusion on the basis of a very wide ditch around the mound visible on an air photograph. However, the ditch at Compton is of similar proportions and given the local context of other large round barrows there seems to be no reason why this should not be another example, together forming a small cemetery of Neolithic barrows.

A further example, a large ring ditch of 50m in diameter, thought to be a plough-levelled barrow, has recently been discovered from the air south of the River Wylye at Heytesbury (M Barber pers. comm.: NMR 1382371), and this in turn lies close to a pair of conjoined ring ditches each c.44m in diameter (NMR 1382373). These appear to form part of a cemetery of ten further round barrows at Tytherington that focus on a small relict tributary that fed into the River Wylye at Mill Farm (NMR AP Nos 4526/101), at least four of which had ditches in excess of 50m in diameter. Two further ring ditches of exceptional size occur amongst a levelled cemetery at Upton Lovell (NMR No 78865/10 series). However, the Knoll (NMR ST 94 SW 38), a round barrow situated within a cemetery of six ring ditches (NMR AP Nos 4436/04-07) at Sutton Veny, a kilometre to the southwest, urges caution as its ditch of between 60-70m in diameter surrounds a mound of no more than 30m in diameter.

Knook Barrow

In 1801 Cunnington turned his attention away from the Wylye and cut a trench into the centre of Knook Barrow (Knook 2: NMR ST 94 SE 21), a mound of parabolic profile with side ditches, situated on the Down between Knook and Imber on Salisbury Plain. He found only four headless skeletons, just beneath the turf, that he considered secondary. However, following the pattern already established, in Autumn 1802 he returned and with the assistance of two workmen made a large cut from the centre towards the east end. Here he encountered a cairn of flint and 'man made stones', presumably deliberately broken sarsen, piled upon a flint pavement c.4.5m long by c.2.0m wide and narrowing towards the east. The cairn rose to c.1.3m in height, reducing in extent as it did so towards a ridge first encountered at just c.0.3m below the topsoil. Lying over the cairn, 'immediately under the turf', were part of the head and horn cores of a large ox, one horn being burnt. Cunnington showed it to his butcher who said that it was larger than any ox that he had seen. It may have been *Bos primigenius* and given the shallow deposits between the turf and the ridge of the cairn this may originally have been formally placed on the ridge itself.

The pavement was 'covered' with small fragments of burnt bones, both animal and human, together with fragments of charred wood. Amongst them Cunnington singled out birds, 'some of which appeared like the bones of an Heron'. Cunnington estimated that there might have been eight humans represented but emphasised the conjectural nature of that figure given the great number of small intermixed bones. Close to the centre of the mound, at the west end of the platform, was a neatly cut semi-circular pit, similar to that encountered beneath Heytesbury

North Field long barrow, filled with earth and containing two fragments of bone and pieces of charred wood. The clean nature of the pit appears to imply that it was backfilled deliberately, its relationship to the pavement being uncertain.

Having investigated other long barrows – Boles Barrow (Heytesbury 1: NMR ST 94 NW 20), Arn Hill (Warminster 1: NMR ST 84 NE 5), Old Ditch (Tilshead 2: NMR SU 04 NW 9), White Barrow (Tilshead 4: NMR SU 04 NW 3), Tilshead Lodge (Tilshead 5: NMR ST 04 NW 12) and Knook Down (Knook 5: NMR ST 94 NE 18), all situated further into the interior of Salisbury Plain (McOmish *et al.* 2002) – Cunnington returned to the Wylye and turned his attention to long mounds south of the river.

Corton Long Barrow

In 1804 he returned to Corton to re-investigate the nearby Corton long barrow (Boyton 1: NMR ST 94 SW 37), situated on the chalk valley slopes and with good views along the Wylye, which he had initially trenched in 1801. In Cunnington's day it measured some 65m in length (although this would be of greater than average length for a long barrow and may be an error) by 7.5 wide at the east end and was said to reach almost 3m in height, though even then it had been damaged by cultivation and its appearance as confluent round barrows was considered to have resulted from quarrying by local farmers (Lambert 1806b, 339). By 1914 it had been reduced to almost half that length (M. Cunnington 1914, 386) and today, covered with 14 beech trees and elder shrubs, it is 36m and some 16m wide, though still retaining considerable height, at a maximum of just over 3m. Its current ovoid shape (Fig. 4) is due to cultivation and the remaining outline of the mound and the bulk of ploughed down soil suggests that it may originally have been longer, perhaps a little short of 40m in length, by about 22m wide and probably wedged shape in plan, a little like Ellbarrow (Wilsford N 3: NMR SU 05 SE 22: McOmish *et al.* 2002, 25a). Recent augering (Allen & Gardiner 2004) has indicated

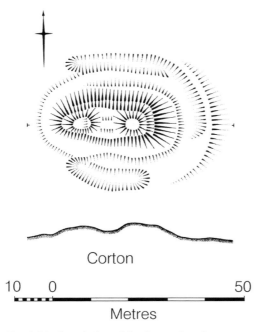

Corton

10   0   50

Metres

Fig. 4. Hachured plan of the Corton long barrow

that while the surrounding chalk has been
truncated, a perched chalk bench had been
preserved immediately about the barrow. Side
ditches are in part just visible and appear to curve
slightly, though presumably curtailed at either
end – which the augering would appear to
confirm.

Cunnington cut a trench at the east end and
in this encountered features similar to those in
mounds to the north of the river. At the base of
the mound, two oval pits, each just over a metre
in length and c.0.7m deep, were neatly cut into
the underlying chalk; but they contained nothing
of note in their fill. Between these, eight human
skeletons, like those in other mounds, lying in no
particular order and in different directions, were
encountered. Over these a ridged cairn of flints
and chalk, measuring 6m by 3m at the base, rose
to about 2m in height, where it was surmounted
or capped by a massive boulder, probably of
sarsen, that 'required three men to lift it out'.

Recent air photographs taken by Damien
Grady, indicate that little more than 30m east of
the long barrow, two parallel ditches, some 55m
apart, can be traced for 180m northwards towards
the river (NMR 1382383). Unfortunately there is
no indication of function or date, but they are
mentioned here as they may represent a mortuary
enclosure or cursus.

Boyton

Little more than 1km to the east of this, Boyton
(Sherrington 4: NMR ST 93 NE 23) long barrow
is situated in a superb position on a bluff
overlooking the Wylye. Its location appears to
have been deliberately chosen opposite the Imber
stream, which meets the Wylye at right angles at
this point and provides a magnificent view down
the Chitterne valley opposite. Holdenhurst long
barrow, in Hampshire (Piggott 1937), is similarly
sited alongside the River Stour and facing the
Moors River valley. In 1914, Boyton long barrow
measured 45.5m in length by a maximum width
of 19.5m (M. Cunnington 1914, 399) and there
appears to have been little change as, in 1975,
the Ordnance Survey recorded it as 45m by 17m
by 3m in height. Most of its centre has been
quarried away and Mrs Cunnington was informed
that the centre of the mound was occasionally
used to mend the adjacent trackway (ibid. 399).
When visited by the RCHME in 1992 dense
vegetation prevented reasonable measurements
being obtained. No ditches are visible, cultivation
taking place right up to the southern flank, while
a track traverses the northern side.

Stockton

South of Sherrington Clump, Stockton 1 (NMR
ST 93 NE 26) long barrow is a further large,
wedge-shaped, mound measuring 29m by 12m
by 1.4m maximum height, oriented to the
northeast, and now situated within a clump of
trees around which cultivation has created a
plough lynchet. Side ditches were visible in 1914
(M. Cunnington 1914, 399), but have since been

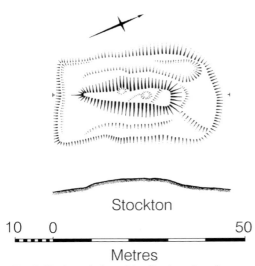

Stockton

10   0   50

Metres

Fig. 5. Hachured plan of the Stockton long barrow

almost levelled (Fig. 5). A shallow remnant of the westernmost ditch and a slight trace of the eastern one is all that can now be seen. The mound was excavated by Cunnington and Hoare and a series of at least five human skeletons discovered beneath a conical flint cairn. A rectangular pit, filled with flint and chalk, was found to be cut in the chalk to a depth of 1.2m (Cunnington mss Devizes, Book 3, 49). Hoare provides little information and no further details have been discovered among Cunnington's notes, which simply indicate that when opened it proved similar to other long barrows (Hoare 1810, 107).

Sherrington

On Friday 2nd November 1804 Cunnington investigated a mound situated just metres away from the bank of the river at Sherrington (Sherrington 1: NMR ST 93 NE 1). He described it as an 'egg cut in two lengthways... the large end to the westnorthwest', a description that he had used to describe Boles Barrow as well as Silver Barrow at Tilshead. In a sketch of the profile of the mound (Hoare mss, 68, Devizes Musem) however, its form appears more like half a pear

than an egg, and the illustration to accompany Lambert's article suggests so too (Lambert 1806b, pl. XVIII). Then it measured 33m in length by a maximum of 24m wide and 4.2m in height (Cunnington mss Devizes, Book 1, 51: Hoare 1810, 100-1). Sadly, like other mounds by the Wylye, it has since been much reduced by cultivation, being recorded as 26m in length in 1914 (M. Cunnington 1914, 399) and although now still standing to a considerable height the ends have been severely curtailed and it is almost circular. Its original form can only be gauged from Cunnington's descriptions and illustrations, the latter prepared by Philip Crocker (Lambert 1806b pl. XVIII: presented here as Fig. 6). While the perspective in Crocker's engraving produces uncertainty about the orientation, the tower of Codford St Mary church (which has since lost its pinnacles) depicted in the middle distance, provides a reference point. The large end of the mound clearly lies to the west, though whether aligned generally north or south is less evident. Cunnington's letter, however, is clear enough and for him, having considered the northwest end of King Barrow to be the business end, it would not seem out of place. The Ordnance Survey Archaeological Investigator indicated that the mound was thus oriented in 1975, with the higher portion at the southwest, with a small hollow, an indication of digging, at the highest point. However, air photographs (NMR 18867/17-18: 18821/33-5) depict curvilinear soil marks alongside and southwest of the existing mound. Some caution is necessary here as the detail of the photographs is blurred by cultivation, but the alignment, general shape and position of the marks indicate the possibility that they may relate to the long barrow. If so, they may indicate that the mound was formerly much larger, perhaps as long as 50m, flanked by the 'ghosts' of curving ditches a maximum of 30m apart and narrowing to 5m in the southwest. Such a length is reasonably standard for long barrows within the region, and the orientation of the soil marks would indicate that the axis of the mound lay with broad end towards the northeast. If so, the remaining

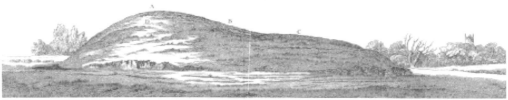

Fig. 6 Crocker's illustration of the Sherrington 1 long barrow, with Saxon spearhead below, originally published in *Archaeologia* (Lambert 1806b)

portion of the mound, i.e. that excavated, formed part of the wider end.

The first trench was made in what in 1804 was the broader end, and the mound found to be composed of gravel. No ditches were visible and Cunnington only mentions that the gravel was dug from 'near the Wylye'. At a depth of 4.2m he found that, like King Barrow, the floor of the mound was covered with charred wood and ashes (Cunnington mss Devizes, Book 1, 51). A skeleton of a pig and a large unidentified bird and other bones were recovered, probably from the floor, though the precise stratigraphical position is not entirely clear. As in other mounds, a neatly cut circular pit was encountered at the base. In this one, an ox skull and a small antler had been deposited. A further trench cut to the south of the pit added no further details. Subsequently, in 1856, John Thurnam and the Reverend A. Fane excavated part of the mound, but there are no recorded details, nor is there any mention of the event in Thurnam's catalogue of skulls (copy WANHS library Devizes) or amongst items from Thurnam's excavations deposited at the British Museum (BM Acc. Reg. 1873, 12-19).

Internal features

The features encountered by Cunnington during excavation of these mounds are consistent enough to suggest that they form some common cultural thread in at least this western portion of the Salisbury Plain chalk. Some of the elements can be traced across wider areas. Pits beneath the mounds appear to begin the process and aside from those examples mentioned here and elsewhere on Salisbury Plain – e.g. beneath Fussell's Lodge (Ashbee 1966) where a C14 date of 4330-3700 cal BC (BM 134) was obtained from material sealing the pits (Schulting 2000), and at Knook 2 and 5, Tilshead 2, Arn Hill, Warminster and Winterbourne Stoke (McOmish *et al.* 2002, 28-9: Hoare 1810, 65, 71-2, 83, 86, 91, 102, 107, 117) – they occur too in Dorset at Wor Barrow (Pitt-Rivers 1898, 66) and Thickthorn Down (Drew & Piggott 1936, 81), and also in Hampshire at Moody's Down Northwest (Grimes 1960, 248-9). At further distance, traces of hurdling around a pit at Skendleby 1, Lincolnshire, has indicated that it was unlikely to have served as a posthole (Phillips 1936). However, in contrast, at Skendleby 2 nearby, two oval pits were thought to contain posts and there were human bones positioned between them in a manner similar to that at Fussell's Lodge. The C14 dates imply that a time span, perhaps of several centuries, could separate the use of the pits from any covering event (Evans & Simpson 1991, 42). A sarsen standing stone was encountered at one end of a pavement in Arn Hill long barrow (Warminster 1: NMR ST 84 NE 5: McOmish *et al.* 2002, 29) in a position similar to that where pits occur in other mounds, and it was suggested that others also may have been stone sockets that once supported monoliths.

The discovery of a pavement, probably of broken sarsen at King Barrow, is notable in that similarities can be observed with the deliberately broken sarsen that comprises the cairn at Knook long barrow. Here, it was suggested that the fragmented sarsen had derived from a broken standing stone that had formerly stood in the pit at the base of the mound (McOmish *et al.* 2002). If this interpretation is accepted it draws interesting parallels with activities involving the deliberate destruction of standing stones and subsequent incorporation of their fragments into tombs in Brittany (Bradley 2002, 34-41).

The pavement itself, at King Barrow, is a feature found in five other local barrows, most of which provided a platform on which human bones, either articulated or burnt or both, were found. The descriptions of skeletons placed on platforms vary and it is by no means clear that they are articulated. Sometimes burnt bone fragments are present and occasionally burnt animal bones too. At several sites, King Barrow, Sherrington, Old Ditch and Knook Barrow, charred wood and ashes are specifically mentioned, usually lying on a pavement. At Knook Barrow, the pavement was covered with charred wood and burnt bones (both animal and human), mostly as small fragments. However, among these were clearly identifiable bird bones that had either remarkably escaped the fire or had been placed there afterwards. The different condition of human bone was noted by Cunnington on the platform at the west end of Old Ditch (Tilshead 2), where two skeletons were described as lying side by side

and a third at the heads of these. They were associated with a great amount of charred wood and ashes, along with fragments of bones that had been half burnt. However, Cunnington was led to comment on the lack of ashes and burnt bone or indication of fire at Boles Barrow. In contrast to the great number of (perhaps disarticulated) skeletons found there, just one piece of burnt bone was recovered. Similarly, no burnt bones were recovered at Heytesbury North Field, even though there were many skeletons present. A similar situation occurred at Knook Down where four skeletons were found lying in the same direction, but no evidence of fire or burnt bones.

It may be that many of these sites represent crematoria (Kinnes 1992, 85), with the pits playing a role in assisting draught onto or under the platform. The frequent accounts of surfaces reddened by fire, charred wood and burnt bone provide some support, and stone platforms and pits used in the firing process have been recorded beneath round mounds in northern England (Kinnes 1979). Some of the charred wood at King Barrow 'adhered to the bones half cremated', although the presence of animal bone in some quantities might suggest that this was not a process restricted to human funerary rites. Sites such as Kill Barrow (Tilshead 1: NMR SU 04 NW 11) and Winterbourne Stoke 53 (NMR SU 14 SW 92), where material had fused together and the chalk burned to a lime-like substance (Thurnam mss catalogue copy Devizes: but also M. Cunnington 1914, 400-1 and 407), has greater potential in this respect. However, there is no need to explain the process here as a single event (e.g. the burning of a mortuary house) and instead the pavement may provide a platform for a series of events.

Mounds or cairns covering these platforms are of frequent occurrence. Sometimes they are evidently ridged, as at Corton (Boyton 1), but in a number of cases they appear to be circular. Heytesbury 4 (Heytesbury North Field), Stockton 1, Tilshead 2 (Old Ditch) (McOmish *et al.* 2002, 28) and in one account, Boles Barrow, are said to have circular or conical internal mounds and

	Black earth	Pit	Pavement	Fire	Humans	Animals	Cairn
King Barrow			*	*	*	*	earthen circular
Sherrington		*		*		ox head	
Corton		*			8		pyramid-ridge
Boyton							
Stockton		*			5		circular
Old Ditch	*	*	*	*	3	*	circular
Tilshead Lodge		*					
White	*						
Boles		*	*	No	*	oxen	ridge
Arn Hill		Stone	*		*		
Silver Barrow			*		*		
Knook Down		*	No				
Knook	*	*	*	*	* burnt	* burnt	ridge
Heytesbury	*	*			*		circular

to that we can add the clay/earthen mound beneath King Barrow. This might be less of a surprise if we consider the number of circular elements, cairns or chambers contained within megalithic structures, for example, Camster Long (Masters 1983, 107), Clyde Cairns, e.g. Mid Gleniron I and II (Scott 1969, fig. 73), tombs in Wales such as Capel Garmen and Dyffryn Ardudwy (Lynch 1969, figs 45 and 51), or Cotswold cairns such as Ty Isaf (Corcoran 1969, fig. 22). The multi-phase construction involved in such sites is evident and it clearly occurs in earthen long mounds too, as at Wayland's Smithy, where one mound with side ditches was constructed on top of an earlier example (Whittle 1991). Cairns within earthen long barrows are usually thought to cover mortuary chambers, the ridging echoing the form of the roof. However, at Fussell's Lodge, one of the best excavated examples, the cairn appeared to be ovoid (Ashbee 1966) and as recorded may even have been anthropomorphic in form, with head and leg-like projections: the association of head and hooves deposits adds, perhaps, a little support to this suggestion. In this respect it is worth considering, too, the similar deposits found on top of the cairn at Knook.

The nature of the floor at King Barrow is intriguing. Described as set beneath the present land surface it is unclear whether this was a surface excavated in antiquity, or a mistake in identification by Cunnington. The factor evidently so concerned him that he returned for a second look, but in doing so simply confirmed his earlier observations. The position of the mound on the lip of the terrace may have something to do with it, where deposits may be more liable, for example, to landslip or soil creep. The process of mounding up the earth from the material of the floor (ashes, bones and potsherds) appears to be of some importance, and the conical mound so described formed a component at the distal rather than the wider end. Cunnington's excavations at King Barrow do, in fact, appear to have concentrated at the smaller end and it may be that features, such as mortuary deposits similar to those encountered in other barrows, exist elsewhere in the mound. The hachured plan suggests it, as does the contrast in the excavated material with other local long barrows. If so, in addition to the various phases of pre-mound activity, it may be that activities continued on and around the mound and even that the mound itself was extended. Both its length and height are above average for long barrows within the area (McOmish *et al.* 2002). Its great size has similarities with Old Ditch long barrow, which at 101m is even longer, though it too may have been extended (cf. the butt end of the mound at Skendleby 2 was extended at some point (Evans & Simpson 1991)). The implication is of common though slowly changing practice, well established by tradition on the western part of Salisbury Plain, but with comparable elements from elsewhere in Britain.

Position in the landscape

The siting of long barrows on Salisbury Plain appears to be remarkably riverine, with examples set on the slopes above the River Avon and by and near the winterbournes and springs of the River Till and elsewhere (McOmish *et al.* 2002). The association with water is paramount, though whether this is purely a practical consideration, or whether the sites are positioned with more sacred factors in mind is not clear. The location of at least some mounds close to the River Wylye and along the slopes and flanks of the valley imply some association with the river and, given their spacing, access to the river frontage. Nearest neighbours Corton/Boyton/Sherrington and Stockton indicate intervals of about 2km, depending on details of the topography. Towards King Barrow, this leaves a gap of some 5km, but if the long ditched features noted on air photographs between Bishopstrow and Codford are taken into account this discrepancy may be explained.

Cunnington's original account of the 'Golden' barrow (NMR ST 94 SW 13), situated on the river bank at Upton Lovell (Cunnington mss Devizes Book 10, 16: Lambert 1806a, 126-8), provides more detail than that of Hoare (1810, 98-100) and indicates that it may even have been a short long barrow. It is clear from Hoare's account of the excavation that the 'Wessex' material comes from a secondary deposit set into an earlier mound. Hoare says little of the barrow itself, the assumption being that it was circular and it was subsequently described as a bowl barrow by the

Ordnance Survey. Cunnington's account, however, introduces caution. Having trenched the mound at the end of July 1803, he wrote to A. B. Lambert, the landowner, on 1st August:

> The tumulus... is situated a few yards north of the river Wylye. It is of pyramidical form [the term pyriform having been used by Stukeley in connection with long barrows on the Marlborough Downs (Stukeley 1743, 45)], the base length 58 feet by 38 feet wide (the length on the top 21 feet) and 22 feet in the slope, and stands from east to west. (Lambert 1806a, 128)

He goes on to say that whereas the north side of the barrow was extremely neat, presumably that to which Hoare referred, the south side (that facing the river), was mutilated. A trench cut lengthways along the barrow revealed a cist at a depth of just over 0.5m with 'Wessex' material recovered adjacent to it. At 17.5m by 11.5m, this might be an oval or small long barrow. However, Cunnington returned to the mound in July 1807 and made a point of stating that his earlier description was incorrect, as 'I have since been informed that it was originally circular and the sides were cut through by the plough when the land (now a water meadow) was in tillage'. He went on to estimate its diameter as 21m and height as 3m (Cunnington mss Devizes, Book 10, 16). Excavation to the floor of the mound revealed a rectangular pit nearly 0.5m deep that contained a small deposit of burnt human bones, though no accompanying grave goods.

At times both Leman and Hoare appear to have pointed to errors in Cunnington's interpretations (R.H. Cunnington 1954, 234-5), though it may be that on this occasion his original observation, uninfluenced by archaeological literature, was valid. Unfortunately it is now difficult to confirm matters either way. The exact site of the mound appears to have been lost. It is depicted as, perhaps 200-300m, north of the river by Hoare in his map of the Wylye Station (1810, 97) and early Ordnance Survey editions place it at NGR ST 94444010. The mound had been cultivated in Cunnington's day and the process of preparing the land for water meadows must have levelled it completely (land levels being critical in the operation of water meadow systems). Certainly by 1920 there was no trace of the mound and its location was known only from the testimony of the Rector of Upton Lovell who indicated that it was in a field named 'Barrow Newtons' (Goddard 1922). Grinsell (1957, 193) acknowledged the mound as destroyed, but nevertheless gave a description of it as measuring 19 by 13 paces, perhaps estimating it from Cunnington's description, and as being 'high'. It is clear from air photographs, however, that more than one barrow was present in the field and the 'Golden Barrow' must have been part of a cemetery of at least seven round mounds, visible as ring ditches on air photographs situated alongside this stretch of river (NMR 18865/10 series), all thus introducing greater uncertainty.

A mound (NMR ST 94 SW 24) situated 300m to the east of St Leonards Church, Sutton Veny, near Warminster, has also been claimed as a long barrow (Grinsell 1957, 143). Situated just above what is now the floodplain of the Wylye and measuring 32m in length by 27.5m, and reaching 1.4m in height, it has been partially destroyed by a trackway and its original form and extent obscured. M. Fletcher, the Ordnance Survey Archaeological Investigator, considered it to be a round barrow in 1969. Air photographs provide the merest hint that it may indeed have some length, with soil marks extending into the cultivated field to the west (NMR AP Nos 4526/85, 89, 93). Nearby, 100m to the southwest, soil marks indicate the presence of a further oval ditched feature some 50m in length. Another mound at Sutton Veny (NMR ST 94 SW 16) situated in a field c.300m to the north-northwest of St Leonards Church, has also been claimed to be a long barrow. It was reported as being circular in 1914, but of great size and motte-like with a flat top (Cunnington 1914, 400), though as it was marked as a long mound on Hoare's map of the area (Hoare 1810, 97) it was accepted that it may then have been observed when in better condition. South of the river at Dairy Plantation,

opposite Norton Bavant, cropmarks of two almost parallel ditches, oriented to the northeast and slightly expanding at the northeast end may represent a another levelled example (NMR AP No ST 2042/99). Occupying a shallow saddle in the terrace above the river, they reach almost 100m in length, the southernmost ditch curving inwards at the terminal.

If this, along with any one of the potential examples at Sutton Veny is eventually shown to be genuine, the even spacing is retained: Corton to Norton Bavant at 2.3km, Norton Bavant to King Barrow, 2km. To the north of King Barrow a series of long barrows also lie along the bluff overlooking a re-entrant and almost hidden valley which lies parallel to the mainstream of the Wylye, its minor tributary stream issuing into the Wylye at Heytesbury. They occur at Norton Bavant 13 (NMR ST 94 NW 28), Middleton Down (Norton Bavant 14: NMR ST 94 NW 16), Heytesbury North Field, Oxendean (Warminster 6: NMR ST 94 NW 17), Knook and an oval or short example situated within Scratchbury hillfort (McOmish et al. 2002, 36). Their spacing too, generally matches that along the Wylye itself, though some, Norton Bavant to Middleton Down at 1km and Middleton to Heytesbury North Field at 1.6km, lie a little closer together. The landscape itself appears to have been sub-divided into units based on access to water. Only Boles Barrow and Ell Barrow stand out from this general pattern, both having been placed high on interfluves at a distance from springs or streams.

Later prehistoric burial activity at long barrows

While King Barrow alone appears to provide a focus for the positioning of what are probably Neolithic round barrows, others appear to have attracted later round barrows. The well-known Winterbourne Stoke Crossroads group is perhaps the best example, although such associations with cemeteries are not that commonplace. No such known grouping occurs around the Tilshead long barrows, or Boles Barrow, or the Norton Bavant examples, nor those at Sherrington and Corton. At Oxendean, there is one round barrow nearby and similarly one at Boyton. At neither do levelled examples appear on air photographs. In contrast, there is a slight indication that oval barrows or short long barrows in the area provide a focus for round barrow cemeteries, for example at Tytherington and perhaps at Sutton Veny and Upton Lovell, as they do elsewhere (e.g. Radley (Bradley 1992, Barclay & Halpin 1999)). However, the degree to which long mounds were used for secondary insertions during the Bronze Age is unknown. At King Barrow one secondary burial was certainly disturbed by later ones, and Cunnington refers to the presence of two cremations found on top of Old Ditch long barrow (Cunnington mss Devizes, Book 3, 39). One of these was unfortunately dispersed before he could inspect it. The second, however, with several teeth and fragments of skull recognisable, was placed in a small depression or cist 'not larger than the crown of a small hat'. Accompanying these were several very large antlers and fragments of charred wood.

Some of these mounds continued to be observed as important features in the landscape millennia after their initial use. For example, some were used as markers when linear ditches were aligned on them during the Late Bronze Age, as were Oxendean, Old Ditch, Kill Barrow and White Barrow (McOmish et al. 2002). Some of the barrows on lower ground may have served the same function, though if so cultivation has removed any surface evidence. Finally, reuse of some of these mounds for inhumation again in Saxon times implies their further, or at least renewed, importance both as landscape features and as burial places.

Inhumations of the early Anglo-Saxon period intrusive in long barrows in the Wylye Valley

William Cunnington recorded several intrusive accompanied burials of early Anglo-Saxon date, together with others, which were

unaccompanied and may be of similar origin, from his excavations of long barrows in south Wiltshire. Indeed, in the subsequent two hundred years there has been little additional information to add to his list. Only one of his Anglo-Saxon finds, the sword from King Barrow appears to survive. In interpreting what he found we are, therefore, almost wholly dependent upon Cunnington's own brief manuscript record, some of it published, and illustrations prepared by Philip Crocker.

At King Barrow, 'at the depth of eighteen inches, three human skeletons were found, lying from south-west to north-east; and on the thigh of one of them was an iron sword, which originally had a handle of oak wood; the blade is about eighteen inches long, two wide, and single-edged' (Hoare 1810, 72). The seax was recorded in a watercolour by Crocker (Philip Crocker folio Devizes, pl. XLIII, fig.1), and the weapon itself has now been identified by Paul Robinson with an unprovenanced one in the Wiltshire Heritage Museum, Devizes (Robinson 1979/80). On the Continent, seaxes have been classified into three groups: narrow, broad and long, although this subdivision is less clear in England (Böhner 1958, I, 130-45; Geake 1997, 72-3). The overall proportions, together with the length (443mm) and width (50mm) of the blade, show the one from King Barrow to be of the broad variety. It exhibits the typical long, shallow groove along either side of the blade and has a single-handed tang, 130mm long. Although the broad seax is dated to the 7th century AD on the Continent, it is far less common in England than the other types and it may have appeared here only later in that century (Evison 1961, 229-30; Geake 1997, 74). It has been pointed out that the lightness of the construction of the seax, in contrast to the sword, makes it more suitable as a hunting knife than a fighting weapon (Gale 1989, 80).

Cunnington recovered another, more elaborately furnished, 'Anglo-Saxon' sword burial in his excavations in the long barrow at Sherrington, discussed above (Lambert 1806b, 344-5). There, in trench C:

at the depth of 18 inches... [he] discovered the skeleton of a stout man, (the extreme length of the thigh bone was nineteen inches) lying from west to east. On the right side of this skeleton, close by the thighs, lay a two-edged sword, the blade two feet in length, with rather an obtuse point, but no guarded hilt; it had been enclosed in a scabbard of wood, a considerable quantity of which now adheres to it. On the right side of the head lay an iron spear and on the left, and close to the head... the *umbo* of a shield. With the latter... an iron buckle, a piece of leather, a strip of brass perforated in several places... also a thin piece of silver... near the *umbo* was found the knife. (*ibid.*)

In addition, there were two other skeletons, with the same orientation, to the east of this one: 'one of an adult, the other of a child four or five years of age; with these were found a small knife, and a piece of corroded lead' (*ibid.*). A further west-east burial, with a spearhead to its right, had already been recovered, again at eighteen inches depth, from trench B.

Black-and-white illustrations (Figs. 6 and 7) of all of these weapons, together with the knife, appear in the plates which accompany Lambert's paper. They are derived from watercolours by Philip Crocker which are preserved, together with much other material by other antiquarians, in folio volumes in the library of the Society of Antiquaries of London. The sword (Fig. 7) lacks fittings and is undatable (Soc. of Ants. London, *Primaeval Antiquities*, vol. 1, folio 4, no. 2). The spearhead (Fig. 6) from the same grave (*ibid.* no. 1) appears to belong to Swanton Type H3 (pers. comm. H. Härke; *contra* Swanton 1974, 80) datable between the late 5th and the end of the 6th century (Swanton 1973, 114). The shield-boss (*ibid.* no. 4: Fig. 7) is difficult to classify from the drawing but seems to be a 'low straight cone' of the late 6th to mid-7th centuries (Evison 1963, 41-2). Finally, the knife (Soc. of Ants. London, *Albums of Drawings, Wiltshire Red Portfolio*, vol. 2, folio 10, no. 5: Fig. 7) looks to be of the large variety which is rare before the 7th century (Härke 1989). The perforated strip of brass may be from a bucket. Overall, the burial is likely to date no

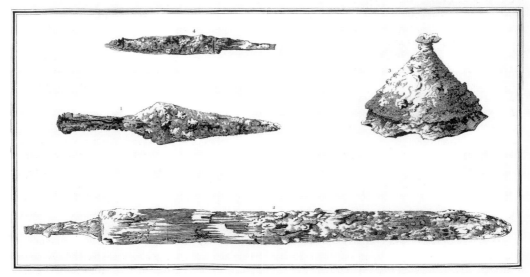

Fig. 7. Illustration of Saxon artefacts from the Sherrington long barrow taken from Crocker's watercolour and originally published in *Archaeologia* (Lambert 1806b)

earlier than the late 6th century and may belong to the first half of the 7th century. The spearhead (Fig. 7) from trench B (Soc. of Ants. London, *Primaeval Antiquities*, vol. 1, folio 4, no. 3) is of Swanton Type E2 (H. Härke pers. comm..; *contra* Swanton 1974, 80), not closely datable, but most examples are of the 6th or 7th centuries (Swanton 1973, 81).

A further 'Anglo-Saxon' weapon grave was uncovered by Thurnam in 1865 in the Tilshead Lodge long barrow, in the valley of the Till, a northern tributary of the Wylye, where Cunnington had found an unaccompanied intrusive burial towards its east end (Hoare 1810, 92): 'within a foot of the summit a skeleton stretched at length from east to west, with an iron *umbo* and other mountings of a shield on the breast, and the remains of a small brass-bound bucket of wood at the head' (Thurnam 1869, 196). The bucket, the only one of these finds to survive, is in the British Museum (accession no. 1873, 1219.204). The bucket has been reconstructed with four copper-alloy hoops and there are fragmentary uprights and indications of the handle (Cook forthcoming). The burial may date to the 6th century.

Another, probable, 'Anglo-Saxon' interment in a long barrow investigated by Cunnington is one with a copper-alloy buckle in Bowl's Barrow. Hoare (1810, 87) records that 'near the east end, and at the depth of two feet nine inches [Cunnington, in 1801] found a human skeleton lying south-west and north-east, and with it a brass buckle, and two thin pieces of the same metal'.

Early Anglo-Saxon presence in the Wylye valley and southern Wiltshire

In the 6th century much of the Wylye valley lay within those parts of Wiltshire to which Anglo-Saxon material culture, seen particularly through burials accompanied by grave-goods, had spread from its 5th-century nucleus round Old Sarum. A notable feature of some of these graves is their insertion in prehistoric burial mounds, an assoc-iation which has been considered to have been deliberate, one aspect of the exercise and display of power by new leaders through appeal to a mythical past (Williams 1998). The degree to which this novel culture was due to Saxon and other immigrants from the Continent or to native inhabitants who identified with them is a matter of lively and ongoing debate. Widely divergent views are held on the numbers who arrived from overseas, some arguing for no more than a small elite.

It is only in the first half of the 7th century, however, that Anglo-Saxon style male and female burials make their appearance along the upper Wylye, or Deverill, and generally in south-western Wiltshire west of Teffont and south of Cold Kitchen Hill (Fig. 8). These graves include a weapon burial on the top of Barrow Hill at Ebbesborne Wake and others under primary barrows at Alvediston, West Knoyle and Maiden Bradley. The burial with the seax at Sherrington may now be added to this notable group of graves. In the Roman period, it has been argued, south-west Wiltshire lay within the *civitas Durotrigum*, bounded in part on the east by Bokerley Dyke (today on the Dorset/Hampshire county boundary). To the north of the Dyke a probable Roman temple site at Teffont, an Old English name meaning 'the **funta* (perhaps borrowed direct from Latin *fontana*, 'a spring') on the boundary', may reasonably be argued to lie on the same *civitas* limit. Such shrines were often associated with both natural springs and boundaries. The location of the Sherrington burial is of particular interest in this context in providing further suggestive evidence for the recognition of another point on the boundary of this Roman canton. The siting of this grave at such a prominent spot immediately south of the Wylye suggests that here the river itself formed the *civitas* edge. From Teffont, therefore, the limit, it may be argued, continued northwards as far as the river – long considered to mark the northern limit of the Durotriges (Cunliffe 1973, 435) – and thence westwards along it to its source by Cold Kitchen Hill. The source of the river affords a typical location for the extensive Iron Age and Roman religious complex on the hilltop above, where the

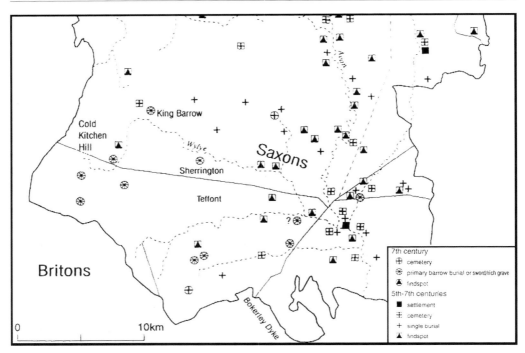

Fig. 8. The distribution of 'Anglo-Saxon' and other sites of the 5th – 7th centuries

civitas Durotrigum may have met those of the
Dobunni and the Belgae. The seax in the
Sherrington grave indicates its high status. Seaxes
were prized possessions of the elite (Gale 1989,
80). The primary Saxon barrows also point to
the high status of other burials in this group, and
the location of the grave at Ebbesborne Wake is
similarly suggestive. These distinctive early 7th-
century interments may well mark, through their
explicit burial ritual, the Saxon takeover of new
territory.

In this same south-western part of Wiltshire
there are also two richly furnished female burials
of the second half of the 7th century. They occur
at Mere (a flat grave) and at Swallowcliffe, inserted
through the primary burial in a Bronze Age round
barrow. These remarkable interments are part of
a pattern of burials, widespread in Wiltshire and
elsewhere, which indicate an increasingly
competitive burial display among the elite. A

contemporary male grave with weapons is that
on Ford Down, to the east of Old Sarum, under a
primary barrow and of the very end of the 7th
century or the early 8th (Musty 1969). The seax
burial at King Barrow is of a similar date. Part of
the ostentation here would seem to be the
deliberate choice of the insertion of the Saxon
burial into such a massive mound (Eagles 2001,
passim., for further discussion of themes referred
to in this section).

Later Anglo-Saxon burials

At Knook long barrow, Cunnington:

> in digging near the centre, about eighteen inches
> below the surface, discovered four headless
> skeletons lying from south to north, which
> appeared to have been deposited with very little
> ceremony, as two of them had their legs laid

across each other. Not having sufficient time to prosecute his researches, he reinterred the bones, and closed up the barrow. (Hoare 1810, 83)

The burials at Knook Barrow might be thought to belong to an Anglo-Saxon execution site. Such places are of widespread occurrence from the 8th century onwards, though some apparently have slightly earlier origins. They are almost always located on hundred boundaries (Reynolds forthcoming). Knook Barrow, however, is not so placed. Furthermore, it is intriguing to note that a headless skeleton, with an iron buckle at the waist, together with several skulls, three of them said to exhibit sword cuts, nearby, have been recorded from New Town Plantation, Heytesbury (Salisbury Museum Annual Report (1954-5), 11; NMR ST 94 SW 14). The oval buckle is in Salisbury Museum and is typical of the 6th century, though such a simple type is difficult to date closely and the burial may be later. It is reasonable to hold doubts whether this brief record really does describe the victims of executions, but it may be noted that the site lies on the boundary which not only divided Heytesbury (the adjacent parish to Knook on the west) from Norton Bavant, but also separated Heytesbury hundred from that of Warminster (Gover *et al.* 1939, map of 'Wiltshire hundreds and parishes' in end pocket). Another explanation may therefore have to be sought for the exceptional burials inserted into Knook Barrow.

Conclusion

It is perhaps astonishing that in Wiltshire, at the heart of Wessex, barrow study continues to rely, at least in part, on a data set that is now 200 years old. While to some degree a comment on the nature of modern archaeology, it emphasises the great and continuing importance of the pioneering work by William Cunnington.

In form the long barrows discussed here fall into similar categories to those defined on Salisbury Plain Training Area (McOmish *et al.* 2002). However, while that study was concerned

with a block of higher downland – marginal land throughout the historic period – the monuments considered here focus on well-watered, more sheltered land (where, in particular, settlement might be expected to occur). Furthermore, the large number of round barrows identified on air photographs alongside the river indicates that this upper stretch of the Wylye was of continued significance right through the Early Bronze Age. Indeed in a footnote Hoare (1810, 98) compared the area with the chalk plains of Wiltshire and stated that nowhere were the barrows so large or numerous as in this part of the Wylye valley.

While Roman and earlier construction and cultivation had changed the face of the land immeasurably since the long barrows had first been introduced, in the Anglo-Saxon period they were nevertheless again being perceived as of some spiritual significance. Now encountered by new arrivals, they were regarded as appropriate locations or monuments for warriors and heroes, among others, to be interred. As such they were powerful places that perhaps provided a link with the supernatural, an interface with a world of timeless spirits built upon traditions, and ancestral tales of themselves now part of the creation of a new mythology.

Acknowledgements

The long barrows of the River Wylye were surveyed by staff of the Royal Commission on the Historical Monuments of England during the early 1990s as part of a project that investigated the earthworks of southern Wiltshire. Aside from the authors, staff who participated in this survey were Hazel Riley and David McOmish, while Deborah Cunliffe penned the final drawings. We should like to thank Drs Mike Allen and Julie Gardiner for a copy of their forthcoming report on their work on the Corton long barrow. Dr Heinrich Härke kindly provided comments on the Anglo-Saxon weapons in the graves at King Barrow, Warminster and Sherrington. We are also grateful to Barry Ager who gave us information about the Anglo-Saxon burial at Tilshead Lodge, Dr Birte Brugmann for allowing us to see a draft copy of the late Jean

Cook's Corpus of Anglo-Saxon Buckets and Dr Andrew Reynolds for similar access to material on Anglo-Saxon deviant burials in his forthcoming book. Gary Calland of the Stourhead Estate (National Trust), Bernard Nurse at the Society of Antiquaries of London, and Dr Lorna Haycock at the Wiltshire Archaeological and Natural History Society, Devizes, were very helpful in seeking out documents in those respective libraries, as was Dr Paul Robinson of the WANHS Museum, Devizes. Dr Mike Allen, Mark Bowden and Graham Brown helpfully commented on earlier drafts of text. All are gratefully thanked for their assistance. Figure 8 was drawn by Alejandra Gutierez.

Bibliography

Allen, M.J. & Gardiner, J. 2004. Neolithic of the Wylye Valley 1: Millennium Reinvestigation of the Corton Long Barrow, ST 9308 4034. *Wiltshire Archaeological & Natural History Magazine* 97, 63-77

Anon 1965. Excavation and fieldwork in Wiltshire 1964. *Wiltshire Archaeological & Natural History Magazine* 60, 132

Ashbee, P. 1966. The Fussell's Lodge long barrow excavations 1957. *Archaeologia* 100, 1-80

Ashbee, P. 1970. *The Earthen Long Barrow in Britain*. London: Dent

Barclay, A. & Halpin, C. 1999. *Excavation at Barrow Hills, Radley, Oxfordshire. Vol. 1, The Neolithic and Bronze Age Monument Complex*. Oxford: Oxford Archaeological Unit

Böhner, K. 1958. *Die fränkischen Altertümer des Trierer Landes*, Teil 1 and 2. Berlin: Mann

Bradley, R. 1992. The excavation of an oval barrow beside Abingdon causewayed enclosure, Oxfordshire. *Proceedings of the Prehistoric Society* 58, 127-42

Bradley, R. 2002. *The Past in Prehistoric Societies*. London: Routledge

Cook, J.M. Forthcoming. Early Anglo-Saxon buckets. In B. Brugmann (ed.), *A Corpus of Copper Alloy and Iron Bound Stave-built Vessels*

Corcoran, J.X.W.P. 1969. The Cotswold-Severn group 2. Discussion. In T.G. Powell (ed.), *Megalithic Enquiries in the West of Britain*, 73-104. Liverpool: Liverpool University Press

Cunliffe, B.W. 1973. The late pre-Roman Iron Age, c.100BC-AD43. In *Victoria County History of Wiltshire*, vol. 1, part 2, 426-39. London: Oxford University Press

Cunnington, M.E. 1914. List of the long barrows of Wiltshire. *Wiltshire Archaeological & Natural History Magazine* 38, 379-414

Cunnington, M.E. 1930. Some Norman Castle sites in Wiltshire. *Wiltshire Archaeological & Natural History Magazine* 45, 137

Cunnington, M.E. 1933. Wiltshire in Pagan Saxon times. *Wiltshire Archaeological & Natural History Magazine* 46, 147-75

Cunnington, R.H. 1954. The Cunningtons of Wiltshire. *Wiltshire Archaeological & Natural History Magazine* 55, 211-36

Cunnington, R.H. 1975. *From Antiquary to Archaeologist*. Princes Risborough: Shire Publications

Drew, C. & Piggott, S. 1936. Excavation of long barrow 163a on Thickthorn Down, Dorset. *Proceedings of the Prehistoric Society* 3, 77-96

Eagles, B.N. 2001. Anglo-Saxon presence and culture in Wiltshire AD c.450-c.675. In P. Ellis (ed.), *Roman Wiltshire and After*, 199-233. Devizes: Wiltshire Archaeological & Natural History Society

Evans, J.G. & Simpson, D.D.A. 1991. Giants Hills 2 Long Barrow, Skendleby, Lincolnshire. *Archaeologia* 109, 1-46

Evison, V.I. 1961. The Saxon objects. In J.G. Hurst, 'The kitchen area of Northolt Manor, Middlesex'. *Medieval Archaeology* 5, 226-30

Evison, V.I. 1963. Sugar-loaf shield-bosses. *Antiquaries Journal* 43, 38-96

Gale, D.A. 1989. The seax. In S.C. Hawkes (ed.), *Weapons and Warfare in Anglo-Saxon England*, 71-83. Oxford: Oxford University Committee for Archaeology

Geake, H. 1997. *The Use of Grave-Goods in Conversion-Period England, c.600-c.850*. Oxford: British Archaeological Reports, British Series 261

Goddard, H. 1922. The Site of the 'Golden Barrow' at Upton Lovell. *Wiltshire Archaeological & Natural History Magazine* 42, 77

Gover, J.E.B., Mawer, A. & Stenton, F.M. 1939. *The Place-names of Wiltshire*. Cambridge: Cambridge University Press

Grimes, W.F. 1960. *Excavations on Defence Sites, 1939-1945, 1: Mainly Neolithic–Bronze Age.*

London: HMSO

Grinsell, L.V. 1957. Archaeological Gazetteer. In R.B. Pugh & E. Crittall (eds), *Victoria County History of Wiltshire*, vol. 1, part 1. London: Oxford University Press

Härke, H. 1989. Knives in early Saxon burials: blade length and age at death. *Medieval Archaeology* 33, 144-48

Hoare, R. Colt 1810 *The Ancient History of Wiltshire* vol 1 London : Miller

Kinnes, I 1979 *Round Barrows and Ring Ditches in the British Neolithic* British Mus Occasional Paper 7 London: British Museum

Kinnes, I. 1992. *Non-megalithic Long Barrows and Allied Structures in the British Neolithic* British Mus Occasional Paper 52 London: British Museum

Lambert, A.B. 1806a. Account of Tumuli opened in Wiltshire, in three letters from Mr William Cunnington to Aylmer Bourke Lambert. *Archaeologia* 15, 122-129

Lambert, A.B. 1806b. Further account of Tumuli opened in Wiltshire, in a letter from Mr William Cunnington to Aylmer Bourke Lambert. *Archaeologia* 15, 338-346

Longworth, I.H. 1984. *Collared Urns of the Bronze Age in Great Britain and Ireland*. Cambridge: Cambridge University Press

Lynch, F. 1969. The megalithic tombs of North Wales. In T.G. Powell (ed.), *Megalithic Enquiries in the West of Britain*, 108-148. Liverpool: Liverpool University Press

Masters, L. 1983. Chambered tombs and non-megalithic barrows in Britain. In C. Renfrew (ed.), *The Megalithic Monuments of Western Europe*, 97-112. London: Thames & Hudson

McOmish, D., Field, D., & Brown, G. 2002. *The Field Archaeology of Salisbury Plain Training Area*. London: English Heritage

Musty, J. 1969. The excavation of two barrows, one of Saxon date, at Ford, Laverstock, near Salisbury, Wiltshire. *Antiquaries Journal* 49, 98-117

Phillips, C.W. 1936. The excavation of the Giants' Hills Long Barrow, Skendleby, Lincolnshire. *Archaeologia* 85, 37-106

Piggott, S. 1937. The excavation of a long barrow in Holdenhurst Parish, near Christchurch, Hants. *Proceedings of the Prehistoric Society* 3, 1-14

Pitt-Rivers, A.H.L.F. 1898. *Excavations in Cranborne Chase near Rushmore on the borders of Dorset and Wiltshire 1893-1896*, vol. 4. Privately printed

RCHME 1979. *Long Barrows in Hampshire and the Isle of Wight*. London: HMSO

Reynolds, A. Forthcoming. *Anglo-Saxon Law in the Landscape*. Oxford: Oxford University Press

Robinson, P. 1979/80. The single edged sword from King Barrow, Warminster. *Wiltshire Archaeological & Natural History Magazine* 74/75, 194

Schulting, R. 2000. New AMS dates from the Lambourn long barrow and the question of the earliest Neolithic in southern England: repacking the Neolithic package? *Oxford Journal of Archaeology* 19(1), 25-35

Scott, J.G. 1969. The Clyde cairns of Scotland. In T.G. Powell (ed), *Megalithic Enquiries in the West of Britain*, 175-222. Liverpool: Liverpool University Press

Smith, R. 1985. *Prehistoric Human Ecology in the Wessex Chalklands: with special reference to evidence from valleys*. PhD thesis: University of Southampton

Stukeley, W. 1743. *Abury: a temple of the British Druids*. London

Swanton, M.J. 1973. *The Spearheads of the Anglo-Saxon Settlements*. London: Royal Archaeological Institute

Swanton, M.J. 1974. *A Corpus of Pagan Anglo-Saxon Spear-Types*. Oxford: British Archaeological Reports

Thurnam, J. 1869. On Ancient British Barrows: part 1, long barrows. *Archaeologia* 42, 161-244

Whittle, A. 1991. Waylands Smithy, Oxfordshire: excavations at the Neolithic tomb in 1962-63 by R J C Atkinson and S Piggott. *Proceedings of the Prehistoric Society* 57, 61-101

Williams, H. 1998. Monuments and the past in early Anglo-Saxon England. *World Archaeology* 30(1), 90-108

Round in Circles. Timber Circles, Henges and Stone Circles: some possible relationships and transformations

Alex Gibson

Since Isobel Smith's publication of the model excavation report *Windmill Hill and Avebury* in 1965, Neolithic henges and things circular have been the focus of a great deal of archaeological attention. Aubrey Burl identified regional styles in 1969 at which time Geoff Wainwright was concentrating on the other large Wessex enclosures. Roger Mercer and Gordon Barclay redressed the English bias in these studies by publishing respectively the Balfarg and North Mains sites while Anthony Harding concentrated on the more modest sites of the Milfield Basin in Northumberland. In 1987, Anthony Harding, with Graham Lee, published a landmark corpus of henge monuments which clearly illustrated the range of forms and sizes that existed within the 'class'. A new scheme for the classification of henges had already been published by Tom Clare in 1986 which similarly illustrated the diversity of monuments to which the label 'henge' was usually attached. Meanwhile Aubrey Burl's corpus of stone circles was first published in 1976 and later up-dated in 2000. The same writer's *Prehistoric Avebury* appeared in 1979. Timber circles were brought together by the present writer in 1994 and 2000[1].

In all these works the links between the various circular or sub-circular monuments are generally acknowledged and comparatively little attention was or has been paid to their differences. Little consideration has also been given as to why these sites are circular or generally rounded.

•   Do they represent the solar and lunar orbs upon which they are often orientated?

•   Do they represent a type of environmentalist view (Ingold 1993) where the immediate environment of a group is bounded by its 360° horizon and therefore represented by a circle?

•   Does the shape represent a perception of the rotational nature of time and the enduring seasonal cycle?

•   Did the ring then, as it does today, represent the unending, eternity and the everlasting?

•   Is it unresolvable, unbreakable and therefore magical (with or without the recent resurgence of Tolkienian mythology)?

•   Or was the ring, quite simply a practical form? It is, after all, the easiest geometric shape to lay out accurately, with a peg and a rope, and it is the most economical shape to use in terms of the ratio between the length of perimeter to area enclosed.

In a prehistoric environment these questions must remain largely rhetorical but immediately it can be seen that reasons for the circularity of these monuments may be varied and numerous. Even in our own culture, the ring is omnipresent and the concept of circularity is a powerful one. We talk of cycles of events, running rings (never squares or ovals) around the opposition, we 'go round in circles', we have biological cycles, we have temporal cycles, we say that the year has come 'full circle' or 'Christmas has come *round* again' confusing the cyclical nature of the seasons with calendrical linear progression and we recycle (in reality transform) our rubbish. Even the square boxing arena is known as the 'ring' albeit in memory of the origins of the sport.

However it has long been realised that not all prehistoric 'circles' need be circular. Timber circles occur in circular (Sarn-y-bryn-caled) or oval (Woodhenge) variants. Stone circles may have complex geometries according to some (Thom *inter alia* 1967) or more restricted forms as rationalised by Burl (2000, 49). Either way true circles (Brodgar) and oval (Twelve Apostles, Dumfries) or flattened circles (New-grange) exist within this monument class. Furthermore henge monuments also have circular (Arminghall) and distinctly oval (Cairn-papple) forms and the large henge enclosures of Wessex (particularly Marden) are more irregular still. Although it may have been the case at many sites, I do not believe that all these monuments were intended to be circular (see, for example, Barnatt & Moir 1984). For example the recurring oval shape of class II henges with their longer and shorter ditch/bank arcs is remarkable and there is a distinct grammar here. Whether the henge is large (Cairnpapple) or tiny in the extreme (Billown (Darvill 2002)) the layout is the same. None is perfectly circular.

Ring cairns and ring ditches also need not be truly circular and many exhibit a polygonal outline (*inter alia* Burl 2000, 49). This may be a result of human nature always tending towards the economy of effort. By this I mean that if the perimeter of a circle was laid out on a number of points, rather than as a continuous line, the ditch diggers or bank builders would tend to join these points by the shortest route – a straight line – even if this was a subconscious act. Indeed it might be argued that stone circles are not circles at all but polygons because although each stone may be on the perimeter of a circle, it is related to its neighbour by a straight (if imaginary) line. But before this strays down a semantic corridor it is worth noting that Richard Bradley's excavations at Tomnaverie (Bradley 2002a, 2002b) have indeed shown that straight or near-straight lines can also be *deliberately* incorporated into otherwise circular monuments and the oval monuments (particularly class 2 henges such as Cairnpapple) and flattened circles mentioned above clearly indicate that true circularity was not always important.

But this general 'roundedness' has linked these monuments in the archaeological literature. Thus timber circles and henges might be described as proto-types for stone circles (see for example Burl 2000, 33-4), henges may be envisaged as enclosing co-existent circles of timber (Woodhenge) and stone (Arbor Low) and the earthwork henges may be interpreted as the lowland equivalent of stone circles, the lack of available stone necessitating their earthen perimeters (Burl 1969). While the generally upland distribution of stone circles and lowland distribution of henges is clearly undeniable, this dichotomy is nevertheless an oversimplification. The rock cut postholes of the timber circle at Oddendale, the rock cut ditches at Stenness and Arbor Low (and even Avebury albeit in chalk) and the Welsh and English stones at Stonehenge on the stoneless Salisbury Plain all serve to demonstrate that what was wanted could be achieved by and large irrespective of geology. However there is also considerable variation within each of these monument classes and these variations must be briefly considered.

In terms of size alone, henges vary from 400m to less than 10m across. Even discounting the Wessex enclosures such as Avebury and Durrington Walls, this size range still reaches in

excess of 100m (Stanton Drew, Brodgar) though
the single-entranced monuments tend to be
slightly smaller. This huge variation in size
prompted Wainwright (1969) to coin the phrase
'hengiform' to describe the smaller monuments
thus acknowledging both the discrepancy in size
yet morphological similarities with the large sites.
In addition to a variation in size, 'henges' may
have internal and external banks (Stonehenge),
double ditches with central banks (Arminghall),
single entrances (Moncrieff), double entrances
(Arbor Low) or as many entrances as four
(Mount Pleasant). Ditches and banks may be
slight (Sarn-y-bryn-caled site 2 (Gibson 1994))
or monumental (Avebury), scraped up (Mayburgh), rock cut (Stenness) or the banks may be
non-existent (Brodgar). In short, the term
'henge' covers a huge range of monuments
whose single consistent feature appears to have
been a ditch.

Timber circles can also vary from a few
metres across (Poole) to some 90m (Stanton
Drew). It has already been stated that there may
be circular and oval variants and there may even
be penannular arrangements (Arminghall). They
may be single (Cairnpapple), double (Oddendale) or multiple (Woodhenge) and they may
have internal arrangements (Knowth) or be
apparently empty (North Mains). Posthole
depths can also vary suggesting different post
dimensions even when allowing for different
degrees of erosion. Some may have readily
identifiable entrances (Sarn-y-bryn-caled, Ballynahatty), some may be approached by avenues
(Ogden Down, Poole) while at others the
perimeter seems to be a uniform ring.

Stone circles vary in layout as has already
been discussed. They also vary in size from
c.110m (Stanton Drew) to some 3.5m (Four
Stones, Powys) as well as in appearance or
monumentality. The large stones of Avebury,
Stenness or Brodgar, for example contrast with
small monuments such as The Rollright Stones,
Rhos-y-beddau or Y Capel where the stones are
low (at the last-named site protruding barely
30cm above the turf). This is not just a

topographical issue for large stones can also be
found in these areas.

Stone circles differ significantly from timber
circles and henges. For example, a case has been
made elsewhere for timber circles involving a
degree of exclusion of individuals, formalised
approach and perambulation (see Gibson
2000a, 83-91 for a summary). Screens and
avenues at Durrington Walls, Stonehenge phase
2 and avenues at Poole and Ogden Down
suggest formalised approach and prescribed
entry as do the formal entrances recognisable at
some timber circles such as Sarn-y-bryn-caled or
Knowth. Perambulation within monuments has
been proposed by Josh Pollard (1992) at Mount
Pleasant and this is perhaps also the case at
other multiple circles and may even be the
reason for the spiralling nature of the Y & Z holes
at Stonehenge leading to a possible entrance in
the south of the monument coinciding roughly
with the north end of the phase 2 timber avenue
and the very much shorter Stone 11, due south,
in the Sarsen ring. This stone is generally
described as having been broken in antiquity
(Cleal et al. 1995, 194) but as it is still standing,
this seems unlikely. If its current state reflects its
original appearance, then the lintel ring must
have also been broken at this point. Mike Pitts
(2000), however, suggests that the spiralling
nature of the Y and Z holes may be because
sarsens 8 and 9 had already fallen.

At multiple sites, whether they were roofed or
screened or not, direct vision into the interior
would have been severely restricted by the sheer
number of posts (Fig. 1). Indeed the Bluestones
at Stonehenge produce a similar visual block.
Even at the single timber circles, the finding of
planking at Dorchester (Atkinson et al. 1951),
North Mains (Barclay 1983), Bleasdale (Varley
1938) and Ballynahatty (Hartwell 1998) further
suggest that at least some were closed
monuments. If such is the case, they must have
been closed, both physically and visually, to
certain members of the community at certain
times. Perhaps the ceremonies were even based
on mystery cults with several degrees of

initiation. The important point is that what was happening in the interior could not be seen from outside and at Durrington Walls in particular even the 'keyhole' view through the entrance was protected by a screen. Screening may also have been the function of the enigmatic yet monumental Gate Palisade at Stonehenge, the Heel Stone and its neighbour within the Stonehenge Avenue and the posthole complex within the phase 2 entrance of the same site.

The evidence for exclusion at henges is more ambiguous. Certainly the banks of the monumental enclosures would have been sufficient to hide the inside while the ditches would have formed an additional barrier. The increased bank heights at the entrances of some henges (e.g. Mayburgh (Topping 1992)) as well as some possible gate structures at the entrances (Burl 1969) may also have been excluding devices. However, the banks, particularly of the larger enclosures, may also have acted as viewing platforms with the internal ditch acting as a physical boundary, though proving this would be difficult. The smaller hengiform sites are less easy

Fig. 1. Exclusion. The interior of Arbor Low (top) is hidden despite the obvious visibility of the bank. At Sarn-y-bryn-caled (centre), screens or planking may have closed the gaps but even without, the centre is largely obscured by the uprights. At Stonehenge, the sarsen and bluestone rings would have hidden the interior.

Fig. 2. The stone circles of Y Capel (top), Scorhill (centre) and Glassel. None of these monuments can hide the interior in the same way as do henges and timber circles.

to see as either visual or physical barriers in any
way other than symbolic. However this is largely
due to our interpretation of these sites based on
their present survival or inferred reconstruction.
Had the banks been surmounted by hurdling or
hedges for example, the barrier may have been
far more physical. Again this may be difficult to
prove either way. But, as mentioned above, it
may well have been the ditch that was the more
important element.

Stone circles, by contrast, cannot exclude in
any way other than symbolically. The avenues at
some sites (Rhos-y-beddau, Broomend of
Crichie) may still hint at formalised approach,
and the entrance portals at some other sites
(Long Meg, Ballynoe) may indicate prescribed
routes of access but the gaps between the stones
cannot exclude visual access in the same way as
can timber circles or henges (Fig. 2). Indeed the
small stones of some Welsh sites in particular
(Rhos-y-beddau, Y Capel), standing as they do
to less than knee-height, must have formed the
most symbolic of barriers (but see below).

There is another fundamental difference
between timber circles (and to an extent henges)
and stone circles. So far we have been viewing
the circles from outside, trying to look in. From
the inside looking out the experience must have
been very different. The envisualisation of the
contrasts depends on how one sees the
reconstructions of timber circles: free-standing
posts, roofed buildings or lintelled and screened
structures. Each would have provided a different
experience. But even if we choose the minimalist
reconstruction, free-standing posts, the experience within a multiple site such as
Woodhenge would still have been one of
claustrophobia (Fig. 3). Confronted by such
large, close-set timbers, the subject would have
become quickly disorientated and seeing out
would have been as difficult as seeing in. Indeed,
seeing out may not have been important as
those inside, the initiated, would probably have
been concentrating on the rituals they were
performing. External views may have been very
focused, for example on specific lunar or solar

Fig. 3. The confused and cluttered interiors of
Woodhenge (top), Stonehenge (centre) and Sarn-y-
bryn-caled (bottom)

events or landscape features. In this regard Stonehenge can help us experience timber circles. Visitors that I have taken to Stonehenge have all commented on how claustrophobic and disorientating it can be, particularly in the north, west and south sectors between the sarsen ring and the trilithons. The bluestone ring adds to this confusion. To a certain extent, this is also conveyed at the reconstruction at Woodhenge, though one has to lie down on the ground to appreciate it fully.

This mild claustrophobia can also be the case at some henges. One is enclosed at Arbor Low and the immediate outside environs are hidden. Similarly the Giant's Ring at Ballynahatty and Mayburgh in Cumbria convey the sense of being enclosed. Once again the small hengiform enclosures pose problems with this hypothesis unless they were hedged or fenced. However we may be falling into the trap of assuming that all sites that *we* characterise as the same or comparable were indeed regarded similarly by

Fig. 4. Inside the henges of Arbor Low (upper) and the Giant's Ring (lower)

their builders over the millennium or so of the currency of the monument tradition(s).

At stone circles, the experience was (and is) very different. Not only are they visually accessible from the outside, but equally the outside and landscape is freely accessible from within (Fig. 5). One cannot become disorientated in the majority of stone circles. This is not to deny that, as at timber circles, some lines of vision may have been focused, for example the moon and landscape at recumbent stone circles, but rather to point out the obvious fact that one can see *over* the stones of many stone circles and the claustrophobia referred to earlier is not experienced at these sites. Once more there are exceptions and the large stones at Brodgar and Callanish do tend to hem one in. Does the openness of stone circles mark a change in practices or even beliefs?

The relative chronologies of timber circles, henges and stone circles have already been discussed elsewhere (Gibson 2000a) but some reiteration is necessary here. Where timber circles are found on the same site as henges, the timber circle is always primary. At Woodhenge, for example, Grooved Ware was found below the bank and therefore its presence on site predates the henge and the postholes of the outer ring are so close to the ditch that they must surely pre-date it. At North Mains there are two timber circles. Ring B may have predated the henge given the eccentricity of this monument with any other structural feature. Ring A certainly did predate the henge as the post ramps almost encroach on the henge ditch and the posts could not have been erected with the ditch in place. The length of time that elapsed between the construction of the circle and the henge is an unknown quantity. It is often assumed that, because the henge respects the circle, the circle may have still been in use (or at least intact) when the henge was constructed. However this need not necessarily be the case and if the circle had been allowed to collapse (or had been pulled down) the resulting ground disturbance would have been sufficient to ensure that the

Fig. 5. The Twelve Apostles stone circle, West Yorkshire

henge respected the place. Equally, the collapsed structure may have resulted in a low mound (as Richard Bradley (1998) has suggested for LBK longhouses and long barrows), which may also have been respected by the henge diggers. In short, the length of time between the timber circle and the henge need not necessarily have been minimal.

Gordon Barclay has made a similar case for a comparable sequence at Cairnpapple and Balfarg (Barclay forthcoming) and it is certainly also the case at Arminghall where the radiocarbon date of *c*.3000 cal BC from one of the timbers may predate the rusticated Beaker in the ditch by as much as a millennium. At Milfield North the larger of the two timber circles *underlay* the presumed bank of the henge and the two monuments do not share the same centre so there is also a potentially large gap here.

Where timber circles and stone circles coincide, stone circles are always secondary. Croft Moraig clearly demonstrates this observation as does Temple Wood (Fig. 6). Once again, the assumption tends to be that one followed quickly on the heels of the other and the Sanctuary on Overton Hill is invoked as proof. Here the stones respect the postholes (as recorded by Cunnington) and therefore it is assumed that either the posts were still standing

or at least that the postholes were still visible when the stones were erected. The irregularity of the possible small stone circle surrounding the Knowth timber circle might also suggest that the timbers were in place before the stones were set (Roche & Eogan 2001, fig. 2). At other sites however, the evidence does not always support this hypothesis and at Machrie Moor, for example, there was an episode of fence construction and ploughing before the stone circles were erected (Haggarty 1991). By and large, the ploughing avoided the actual areas of the timber rings and Richard Bradley has interpreted this as a deliberate avoidance of the area of the circles (Bradley 2002c, 91). It may also have been because the detritus from the decayed structures was mounded up in the centres of the original sites. If this is the case, then the accuracy with which the stone circles coincide with the timber ones is more easy to understand and the circles having been erected around slight mounds or sites of mounds may echo the case at Tomnaverie discussed below.

The sequence at circle-henges, if indeed there was one, is more difficult to determine. Unlike the post ramps at North Mains or the position of the bank at Milfield North, there is rarely a tangible stratigraphical relationship between the two monuments. Aubrey Burl has stated that 'what is becoming clear is that these

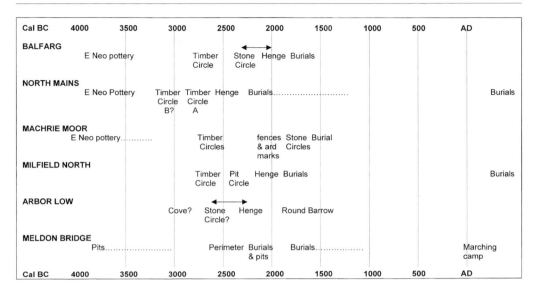

Fig. 6. Possible sequences at selected sites: Arbor Low is speculative and relationship between the round barrow and henge is uncertain. Bateman records that the barrow is 'wholly' detatched (from the bank) except at the base' (1848, 111, my brackets). It now appears to lie over the bank as a result of the spoil from past excavations.

composite circle-henges were usually of several phases, often a ring of stones being added to an old henge, not unlikely if, as supposed, the earliest stone circles had henges as their prototypes' (2000, 285). The key words in that sentence are 'as supposed'. While the stone circles are later than the enclosure at Stonehenge, this is such an unusual site and the ditch is quite 'un-henge-like' it may be dangerous to over-cite this example. Also the stones are well removed from the ditch unlike the norm at circle-henges. Other sites that Burl uses to illustrate his case are Broomend of Crichie and Balfarg. However, at neither site can the stone circle be said to postdate the henge with any degree of certainty. Indeed, at Balfarg, while the stone circle does post-date the timber rings, there was no dating evidence from any of the stone holes. Even at Arbor Low what stoneholes have been recognised have proved unproductive. However the proximity of some of the stones to the edge of the ditch may support an argument like that

proposed for North Mains and timber circles, namely that they are so close to the ditch that their erection may have been difficult had the ditch already been in existence. We cannot be certain either way and re-excavation of some sites and the re-assessment of some existing archives is timely.

Recent work by Richard Bradley (2002b) at the recumbent stone circles of Aberdeenshire has demonstrated that at Tomnaverie, Cothiemuir and Aikey Brae the stone circle is the last monumental phase. Far from the previously accepted view that the cairns filled the centre of an existing circle, the sequence has proved to be that the circle 'closed' an existing cairn. Moreover Bradley argues that the monument was planned from the start and was not so much a case of one monument type replacing another, but rather planned stages taking place in a pre-determined sequence, presumably at pre-determined times. If this is the case, then our working chronologies must of necessity be largely relative as absolute dating methods are unlikely to be refined enough to be useful within a few generations. Chronologies must also be site-specific, at most regional, and are unlikely to be refined enough to be nationally instructive. In other words, the earliness of henges in, say, Wessex or Orkney cannot mean that they are equally early in Derbyshire or County Down. Their place in *local* sequences must be considered.

At present, our absolute chronologies for timber circles span over two millennia (*c.*3300-900 cal BC) and this can be extended if the Irish material is built into the sequence. Made of wood and often with timbers carbonised below ground (either deliberately as waterproofing or as a result of the site's destruction) timber circles can be relatively easy to date. Henges are more difficult because the open ditches can trap unrelated material. For example, the Grooved Ware in the ditch at Woodhenge could easily be derived from the spread of sherds located beneath the bank of the henge and which became incorporated into the primary silts as a result of the initial weathering. Notwithstanding, the available radiocarbon dates suggest that henges appear at about the same time as timber circles but are generally assumed to be going out of vogue by 2000 cal BC. Some smaller sites such as City Farm, Hanborough, or Balneaves, Angus (Russell-White *et al.* 1992) may suggest that some hengiforms persist further into the early Bronze Age. Stone circles are even more difficult to date given the inorganic nature of the uprights and the general lack of a demonstrable stratigraphic sequence between the pillars and the activity they surround. Secure dates must rely on contemporary deposited material within the stoneholes and such material is very rare. But the available dates suggest a currency with timber circles rather than henges. That is to say emerging just before 3000 cal BC and continuing through the Bronze Age, particularly (though not exclusively) in Ireland.

Such longevity provides ample scope for chronologically separated site sequences at different locations and at different times. Thus a timber circle in one part of the country may have been replaced in stone and then 'en-henged' all within the early 3rd millennium. The same sequence may have taken place elsewhere all within the early 2nd millennium. Timber circles and stone circles may have continued to be built after the decline of the henge tradition. It is therefore little wonder that no meaningful national sequence can be detected amongst these three monument classes.

As mentioned above, the importance of place as evidenced by continued activity may be detected at many sites such as North Mains which see deposition from the early Neolithic until the early Christian period. Similar longevity, certainly until the Bronze Age, has been noted at Balfarg and Croft Moraig. There is earlier Neolithic pottery from Durrington Walls, Woodhenge and Mount Pleasant and Iron Age pottery from a later pit within Site IV (the timber circle) at Mount Pleasant (Wainwright 1979, 125). The 'Grooved Ware' from the Yeavering henge has been reinterpreted as middle Bronze Age (Gibson 2002) and, of course, the longevity of Stonehenge is well documented. There are, of course, numerous other examples beyond the scope of this essay.

Linked with this concept of important places, at some other long-lived ritual sites, such as round barrows and cairns, there seems to have been one or several episodic attempts to 'close' the site. Like episodes in a narrative, this closure does not always seal the site permanently and subsequent activities may still take place. For example, the very construction of a mound renders inaccessible the pre-mound activity (Woodward 2000), which might include timber circles, and some cairns can be 'capped' with flat stones as if to make a statement of closure (Gibson 1993). It suggests episodic construction and modification, each episode in the serial making its own stand-alone statement. Secondary burials may still be made, in a later episode, even up to the Saxon period in the case of Tandderwen (Brassil *et al.* 1991).

Might this also be the case at some other ritual sites as Richard Bradley (2002b; 2002c) has suggested for recumbent stone circles? Might in fact the henge be a form of closure or indeed an 'episode' in the ritual life of a location? Thus the henge might 'close' the timber circle activities at Woodhenge and North Mains or the timber and stone activities at Balfarg or the stone activities at Arbor Low. This hypothesis depends on a timber-stone-earthwork sequence at a site-specific level and need not have any widespread chronological implications. In other words, the sequence may have happened at different times at different sites; early 3rd millennium at site X and early 2nd millennium at Site Y as already discussed. After all, the sequence of a timber circle later covered by a cairn has been dated to the earlier Bronze Age at Oddendale but to the Iron Age at Navan. Timber circles have been dated from the early 3rd millennium to the later Bronze Age (Ogden Down in Britain and Raffin in Ireland) and Bronze Age and Iron Age 'henges' are also known, particularly in Ireland (Condit & Simpson 1998, Warner 2000). The site-specific recurrences may be more significant than national monument chronologies. At some sites, the episodes within the site narrative may have been intentionally different or the episodes may have been capable of standing alone (as part of a series rather than a serial) and thus many timber and stone circles may lack henges while some henges represent the only monumental activity at a place. Some embanked stone circles (Castlerigg, Castleruddery) may indicate a similar if less monumental form of earthwork 'closure'.

Two important papers have been published that might be relevant to this hypothesis. The first, by Mike Parker Pearson and Ramilisonina (1998), has interpreted stone monuments as representative of death and ancestors while timber represents the living and the continuous. This is derived from a specific ethnographic parallel and its relevance to British prehistory is open to question, but nevertheless it has its attractions and certainly does fit the British

stratigraphy with timber monuments of the present being replaced by stone to 'commemorate' the past. The second paper may extend this hypothesis.

Mention has been made above of the grammar involved in henge construction, particularly class 2 henges, and the various positions and numbers of the bank(s). As mentioned above, this suggests that the ditch is the only true common feature to many of these sites and it is the ditch that is defining the space with the bank being purely the up-cast. It is the ditch that adheres to the outline of the earlier timber or stone setting. The shape of the internal area may be defined by the earlier monument. With this possibility in mind, Richard Warner's paper may be instructive. Warner (2000), using the mythology preserved in the Irish texts to support his case, has argued that the internal ditches (and external banks) of later prehistoric 'hengiform' sites in Ireland may actually have been defensive but not as barriers to keep people out, but as devices to keep the spirits in: to protect the outside world by confining the potentially damaging forces of the spirit world. Entrances may have facilitated communication between the two worlds by specific individuals and at specific times of the year. Warner is also at pains to point out that he is expressly discussing the later Irish material. However he states 'that is not to say that... the explanation proposed... for the Iron Age earthworks may not apply independently to the far earlier monuments, but I am making no such claim here.' Whether one believes in the potential of continuity or the reinvention of tradition (Gibson 2000b), I believe that Warner's arguments may well be relevant to the Neolithic monuments though unfortunately we do not benefit from the literary evidence.

In this light, the longevity of ritual activity at particular places may therefore imply that these locations were important in providing points of access or gateways between worlds or dimensions. They may have continued to be venerated in later periods, the sites of sacred groves for example. In this respect we may remind ourselves of the Romano-British altars to *genii loci* as well as the discovery of Neolithic sites at places with *Nemeton* placenames (Griffith 2001). The traces of later prehistoric metalworking in the central pit at Sarn-y-bryn-caled and at other sites such as Moncrieff, Loanhead of Daviot and Four Crosses (Warrilow *et al.* 1986) might imply that these places had continued importance, perhaps even sanctuary, for itinerant smiths amongst others. Furthermore, the slighting of Neolithic palisade enclosures by Roman marching camps (Walton, Hindwell, Meldon Bridge) may also suggest the continued importance of place to local populations long after the demise of the original, archaeologically visible, monuments. The Post-Roman burials at North Mains, Cairnpapple, Mount Pleasant and Tandderwen suggest that some locations at least retained their importance well after the Roman occupation.

As Richard Bradley (2002b) has argued, the transformations at these monuments may have been intentional. The archaeological 'phasings' may have been episodes within site narratives, planned events in a predetermined sequence (in this respect it is noteworthy that some timber circles such as Sarn-y-bryn-caled or Dorchester 3 had been deliberately destroyed). If so, then we see not just references to the present and past, but also perceptions of the future: the present will be the past and the ancestors will become spirits. This is the way of life, mortality and the supernatural as has happened in the past, is happening in the present and will happen in the future. This is a never-ending, *circular*, process and therefore its associated monumentality may well have been metaphorical and is, furthermore, unlikely to have been synchronous throughout Britain and Ireland. Thus organic timber may have been replaced by the colder more durable stone which in turn is defended, 'en-henged', against what lies within. In this case the circle itself may be a defence: it is continuous and unbroken even if symbolically represented by stone pillars. It may have been unbreakable,

magical even, and therefore secure against the spirit world. In the same way that present folklore tells us that witches cannot cross water, perhaps the *genii loci* could not break a circle. That the timber circle-stone circle-henge sequence cannot be demonstrated at all sites does not detract from the argument: each 'circle' site may have been able to function independently. Sites with sequences may represent more potent places, more affluent groups with more available labour or simply local preference for an extended narrative. The prolonged and monumental activity at Stonehenge clearly indicates that some sites received more attention than others.

We are, however, in danger of falling into the uncharted depths of supposition, and conjecture but we are left with some very real observations, that 'sacred' places continued in use for considerable periods of time and that the chronologies of some accepted sequences are far from understood.

Note

1. In order to cut down on a list of bibliographical references that would potentially be longer than the article, Burl 2000 has been used as the source for stone circles, Harding & Lee 1987 for henges and Gibson 2000a for timber circles. Other sites have been referenced in the usual way.

Acknowledgements

I am grateful to Gordon Barclay for commenting on an earlier draft of this paper and to Richard Bradley for discussing some of the ideas raised.

Bibliography

Atkinson, R.J.C., Piggott, C.M. & Sandars, N.K. 1951. *Excavations at Dorchester, Oxon.* Oxford: Ashmolean Museum

Barclay, G. J. 1983. Sites of the third millennium bc to the first millennium ad at North Mains, Strathallan, Perthshire. *Proceedings of the Society of Antiquaries of Scotland* 113, 122-281

Barclay, G.J. forthcoming. The 'henge' and 'hengiform' in Scotland

Barnatt, J. & Moir, G. 1984. Stone circles and megalithic mathematics. *Proceedings of the Prehistoric Society* 50, 197-216

Bateman, T. 1848. *Vestiges of the Antiquities of Derbyshire*. London: John Russell Smith

Bradley, R. 1998. *The Significance of Monuments*. London: Routledge.

Bradley, R. 2002a. The land, the sky and the Scottish stone circle. In. C. Scarre (ed) *Monuments and Landscapes in Atlantic Europe. Perception and Society During the Neolithic and Early Bronze Age*, 122-138. London & New York: Routledge

Bradley, R. 2002b. The stone circles of Northeast Scotland in the light of excavation. *Antiquity* 76, 840-48

Bradley, R. 2002c. *The Past in Prehistoric Societies*. London: Routledge

Brassil, K., Owen, W.G.. & Britnell, W.J. 1991. Prehistoric and early Medieval cemeteries at Tandderwen, near Denbigh, Clwyd. *Archaeological Journal* 148, 46-97

Burl, A. 1969. Henges: internal features and regional groups. *Archaeological Journal* 126, 1-28

Burl, A. 2000. *The Stone Circles of Britain, Ireland and Brittany*. London & Newhaven: Yale

Clare, T. 1986. Towards a reappraisal of henge monuments. *Proceedings of the Prehistoric Society* 52, 281-316

Cleal, R.M.J., Walker, K.E. & Montague, R. 1995. *Stonehenge in its Landscape: Twentieth Century Excavations*. Archaeological Report 10, London: English Heritage

Condit, T. & Simpson, D. 1998. Irish hengiform enclosures and related monuments: a review. In A. Gibson & D. Simpson (eds), *Prehistoric Ritual and Religion*, 45-61. Stroud: Alan Sutton

Darvill, T. 2002. Billown Neolithic enclosures, Isle of Man. In G. Varndell & P. Topping (eds), *Enclosures in Neolithic Europe*, 83-9. Oxford: Oxbow Books

Gibson, A.M. 1993. The excavation of two cairns and associated features at Carneddau, Carno, Powys, 1989-90. *Archaeological Journal* 150, 1-45.

Gibson, A.M. 1994.Excavations at the Sarn-y-bryn-caled cursus complex, Welshpool, Powys and the timber circles of Britain and Ireland.

Proceedings of the Prehistoric Society 60, 143-223

Gibson, A.M. 2000a. *Stonehenge and Timber Circles*. 2nd Edn. Stroud: Tempus

Gibson, A.M. 2000b. Circles and henges: re-incarnations of past traditions? *Archaeology Ireland* 14(1), 11-14

Gibson, A.M. 2002. A matter of pegs and labels: a review of some of the Prehistoric pottery from the Milfield Basin. *Archaeologia Aeliana*, 5th series, 30, 175-180

Griffith, F.M. 2001. Recent work on Neolithic enclosures in Devon. In T. Darvill & J. Thomas (eds), *Neolithic Enclosures in Atlantic North-west Europe*, 66-77, Oxford: Oxbow Books

Haggarty, A. 1991. Machrie Moor, Arran: recent excavations at two stone circles. *Proceedings of the Society of Antiquaries of Scotland* 121, 51-94

Harding, A.F. & Lee, G.E. 1987. *Henge Monuments and Related Sites of Great Britain*. BAR 175. Oxford: British Archaeological Reports

Hartwell, B. 1988. The Ballynahatty complex. In A. Gibson & D.D.A. Simpson (eds) *Prehistoric Ritual and Religion*, 32-44. Stroud: Alan Sutton

Ingold, T. 1993. Globes and spheres. The topology of Environmentalism. In K. Milton (ed), *Environmentalism: The View from Anthropology*, 31-42. ASA Monograph 32. London: Routledge

Parker Pearson, M. & Ramilisonina, 1998. Stonehenge for the ancestors: the stones pass on the message. *Antiquity* 72, 308-326

Pitts, M. 2000. *Hengeworld*. London: Century.

Pollard, J. 1992. The Sanctuary, Overton Hill, Wiltshire: a re-examination. *Proceedings of the Prehistoric Society* 58, 213-26

Roche, H. & Eogan, G. 2001. Late Neolithic activity in the Boyne Valley, County Meath, Ireland. *Revue Archéologique de l'Ouest, Supplément No.9, 125-40*

Russell-White, C.J., Lowe, C.E. & McCullagh, R.P.J., 1992. Excavations at three early Bronze Age burial monuments in Scotland. *Proceedings of the Prehistoric Society* 58, 285-323

Thom, A.S. 1967. *Megalithic Sites in Britain*. Oxford: Clarendon Press

Topping, P. 1992. The Penrith Henges: a survey by the Royal Commission on the Historical Monuments of England. *Proceedings of the Prehistoric Society* 58, 249-264

Varley, W.J. 1938. The Bleasdale Circle. *Antiquaries Journal* 18, 154-71

Wainwright, G.J. 1969. A review of henge monuments in the light of recent research. *Proceedings of the Prehistoric Society* 35, 112-33

Wainwright, G.J. 1979. *Mount Pleasant, Dorset: Excavations 1970-1971*. Research Report 37, London: Society of Antiquaries of London

Warrilow, W., Owen, G. & Britnell, W. 1986. Eight ring-ditches at Four Crosses, Llandysilio, Powys, 1981-85. *Proceedings of the Prehistoric Society* 52, 53-88

Warner, R. 2000. Keeping out the Otherworld: the internal ditch at Navan and other Iron Age 'hengiform' enclosures. *Emania* 18, 39-44

Woodward, A. 2000. *British Barrows: A Matter of Life & Death*. Stroud: Tempus Publishing

Monuments that Made the World: performing the henge

Aaron Watson

Introduction

Isobel Smith's publication of Alexander Keiller's excavations at Windmill Hill and Avebury remains an invaluable resource for anyone studying Neolithic Britain (Smith 1965). The volume communicates a subtlety of observation and recording that has often been absent from more recent treatments of monuments, and it was this attention to detail that inspired my own initial explorations of the Avebury region. In this paper I would like to consider whether the term 'henge' is useful to our understanding of Avebury, along with other related monuments such as the Ring of Brodgar and Maumbury Rings. Dating to the later Neolithic (c. 3100 – 2000 BC), **henges** have traditionally been classified according to their architecture. Here, I would like to reflect upon recent research that has observed close relationships between these enclosures and the landscapes in which they are situated. This is reflected not only in their location in relation to rivers and hills, but also the presence of other archaeological sites. Overall, I will suggest that it may be insufficient to characterise prehistoric sites by their architecture alone, raising important questions for both the **henge** and the study of Neolithic monuments in general.

What is a *henge*?

The **henge** has evolved throughout its history. First coined to describe the earthworks surrounding Stone**henge** and Avebury (Kendrick & Hawkes 1932), the term was soon expanded to encompass other sites that displayed similar features. The key components of a **henge** were deemed to be a near-circular earthwork with an internal ditch and external bank, entrances with causeways and internal settings of pits, timbers or stones (Clark 1936, 23-5). Subsequently, the group was further divided between sites with single entrances and those with two (Piggott & Piggott 1939), often labelled as Class I and Class II (Atkinson 1951). By 1969, new discoveries had almost doubled the number of sites, requiring the category to be further expanded (Wainwright 1969). Indeed, had the criteria originally applied by Clark in 1936 been retained, only 19 of these 78 monuments would have been considered **henges** (Burl 1969, 3). Further approaches were taken to define the class. Catherall (1971) favoured a distinction between sites featuring pits, timbers or stones, while Clare considered the format of the perimeters in com-bination with internal features. Clare was especially concerned that existing classification was inadequate, and developed an elaborate scheme of sub-types to capture greater variability (1986).

It is evident that the classification of the **henge** has been a process of definition followed by re-definition in the light of new evidence. Indeed, one of the greatest problems of cat-egorising the archaeological record is that it becomes difficult to account for variability: 'the more archaeologists pay attention to empirical detail the more the analysis shatters the category that it sets out to investigate' (Tilley 1999, 97). Create a classification based upon entrances, Class I and Class II, and there are sites that do not fit: Milfield North has three, Avebury four. If we attempt to define a **henge** as a ditch con-tained by a bank, are we to include sites like Mayburgh that may never have possessed a ditch (Topping 1992), or the Thornborough sites which have two? How should we classify Marden, where excavations (Wainwright *et al.* 1971) revealed that part of the **henge** perimeter was defined by a river rather than an earthwork? Even the archetype, Stone**henge**, has its bank and ditch the wrong way around and therefore should not be a **henge** at all. The scale of analysis also seems important. While the number of entrances might be self-evident, minor variations in geometry are less apparent. Which architectural features should be included, and which are to be ignored? How is categorisation to account for chronological phasing, especially at sites like Stone**henge** that were repeatedly re-built through contrasting phases? While it is possible to devise ever more elaborate schemes to empirically label and document these sites in all their diversity, such exercises are ultimately unable to satisfactorily account for all configurations (Barclay 1989). Taken to an extreme, there might ultimately be as many categories of **henge** as there are sites in the landscape.

Experiencing *henges*

Archaeologists have become preoccupied with describing what **henges** should be, not with what they do. In part this is because evidence for their original purpose is ambiguous. There is little to suggest that they had a specific function as settlements or burial grounds, nor do their boundaries appear defensible. Gray suggested that the interiors might have been sacred arenas overlooked by spectators from the bank (1935, 161), a perspective that might have been inspired by his research at a Roman amphi-theatre (Gray 1909). Drawing upon Gray's premise, Clark surmised that a distinct group of people must have overseen these activities while being observed by a larger congregation (1936, 26). Harding & Lee (1987, 34) have noted that elements such as the number of entrances might be relevant because they reflect how monuments were used and experienced. This has been further elaborated by suggestions that some double-entrance **henges** might be orientated along routeways through the landscape (Loveday 1998). There have also been discussions of the ways in which **henges** can create a diversity of experiences for people who encounter them. Their circular format was an efficient way to enclose an area, and constituted an ideal meeting place (Fleming 1972, 59). It is possible that access might have been controlled in some way, and that the **henge** format can limit those who view or participate (Bradley 1998a). The size and complexity of Avebury is confusing to modern visitors because it is not possible to view the whole of the interior at the same time, and by approaching this monument along the Kennet Avenue features of the interior are sequentially and theatrically revealed (Thomas 1993; Barrett 1994). These perspectives do not, however, address the ways in which monument class-ification might itself limit interpretation. The **henge** is now treated as a fundamental category of monument that has even been afforded its own place in the archaeological literature (e.g. Harding & Lee

1987, Wainwright 1989). This presupposes that architecture alone is the defining criteria when considering **henges**, rather than a broader perspective that ackno-ledges their place in the wider landscape. In order to begin to approach these issues, it may be necessary to see beyond their boundaries.

Henges in the landscape...

Writing in 1951, Richard Atkinson suggested that the topographic context of **henges** might be significant. In particular, he noted a tendency towards low-lying settings and proximity to water that was not shared by other kinds of Neolithic monument (Atkinson 1951). The situation of **henges** within valleys has since been confirmed by other studies (Roese 1980) and it has been calculated that 90% of 'classic' **henges** lie below 125m (Harding & Lee 1987, 34). The recognition of these patterns emphasises that there might be significant aspects of **henge** monuments that architectural classification does not take into account. It appears that their location in the landscape was not random, requiring further investigations into the relationships be-tween **henges** and their surroundings.

The landscape is not just a neutral background against which people live their lives, but is fundamentally bound within the ways in which people think about, and engage with the world. Landscape can therefore be understood and experienced in many different ways (Cosgrove & Daniels 1988; Hirsch & O'Hanlon 1995). Likewise, the meanings of monuments are rarely fixed but have to be socially negotiated (Bender 1998). Therefore, it seems unrealistic for archaeologists to apply inflexible and overly simplistic interpretations to explain the format of prehistoric sites. Rather than classifying architecture according to rigid schemes, perhaps we should consider the possibility that **henges** materialised the subtle relations between people and landscape. Not only might this encourage archaeologists to engage in rather more subtle and self-reflective ways with their material, but it

also emphasises that it might be unrealistic to consider monuments in isolation to the wider environ-ment in which they are situated (Bender 1993; Tilley 1994, 1999; Bradley 1998a; Ingold 2000).

. . . from Orkney . . .

It was in this context that Colin Richards first observed how the Ring of Brodgar and Stones of Stenness in Orkney appeared to embody qualities of their wider social and topographic setting (Richards 1996a, 1996b). The two **henges** are centrally situated within a broad basin and set upon a narrow isthmus between two lochs. Both consist of outer walls or banks, which are now poorly preserved, and substantial rock-cut inner ditches that were probably water-logged in prehistory. Inside are circles of standing stones. Critically, there appeared to be a resonance between the topography of the basin and the **henges** at its centre. The water-filled ditches and containing banks recall how the surrounding lochs are themselves enclosed by hills, and the view out from the monument juxtaposes these elements, rendering the relationships between them visible (Fig. 1). Furthermore, some features within the **henges** are reminiscent of other sites in Orkney, and in particular the spatial arrangement of Neolithic houses and passage graves nearby (Richards 1993). Indeed, the integration of these diverse facets of the wider world might suggest that each **henge** was a microcosm, a representation of social and physical elements that were present in the surrounding environment (Richards 1996b). Might such perspectives be applied to **henges** elsewhere?

. . . to Avebury

At first sight, Avebury creates a quite different impression to the Ring of Brodgar and the Stones of Stenness. The Wessex **henge** is considerably larger, the banks monumental, and there are complex arrangements of sarsen stones

Fig. 1. The Ring of Brodgar; ditches, banks(?), water, hills.

within its interior. Similar to the Orcadian sites, however, Avebury is situated within a basin defined by low hills so that an observer within its boundaries is enclosed, at very different scales, by both the monument and the landscape (Watson 2001a). Even allowing for the erosion of the bank, there exists a symmetry between the banks and the chalk ridges beyond (Fig. 2). Considered together, the two Orcadian sites and Avebury appear to share fundamental ordering principles relating to their setting in the landscape, yet each retains highly individual qualities. How might these differences and similarities be understood?

In contrast to the Ring of Brodgar and Stones of Stenness, Avebury was not situated within a large open basin containing lochs. Rather, the upper Kennet consists of a series of discrete valley environments. Indeed, the contemporary monuments of Silbury Hill and the palisaded enclosures were also situated within the valley,

but visitors to these sites perceive themselves to be at the centre of isolated and rather more confined basins (Watson 2001a). This complex topography might be reflected by the internal configuration of Avebury itself, which is divided into smaller stone circles (Fig. 3). Might this subdivided space reflect the division of the wider landscape into smaller basins that are collectively contained by higher ground, just as the circles inside the **henge** are set within enormous earthworks? This is not to suggest that Avebury maps the landscape as if it were being viewed from above, but rather is a reflection of how these discrete basins are experienced by people moving through them. Might the configuration of Avebury reproduce and reinforce a sense of space which is already present in the natural landscape that surrounds it?

The Ring of Brodgar, Stones of Stenness and Avebury have traditionally been categorised as **henges** because of their architecture, yet to give primacy to these features neglects their relations with the local topography. Perhaps Avebury does not precisely resemble the Ring of Brodgar because, unlike that monument, it was not attempting to materialise qualities of Orkney. Rather, features within Avebury resonated with the topography and archaeology of the local chalkland landscape. I have already noted that the smaller stone circles inside the earthwork divided the interior into discrete spaces that echoed smaller basins in the wider topography. While there are no lochs around Avebury, the

Fig. 2. Avebury; symmetry between banks and hills.

standing stones can be sourced to extensive natural clusters of sarsens on the downs, and a number of monoliths stood within pits lined with clay that had been brought from nearby streams (Pollard & Gillings 1998). The choice of stones might have reflected pre-existing myths that were

attached to these boulders, a number of which seem to have had long histories as axe polishing stones (Smith 1965, 223; Gillings & Pollard 1999). Furthermore, just as the Stones of Stenness and Ring of Brodgar shared features with tombs and settlements nearby, perhaps

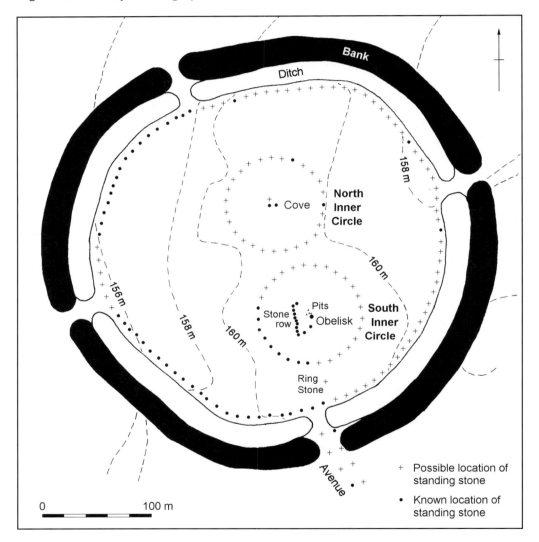

Fig. 3. A plan of Avebury (after Watson 2001a, Figure 2). In the absence of a published metric plan, the contour lines have been derived from Smith (1965)

Avebury responded to local buildings; the Cove within the Northern Inner Circle is a feature that Aubrey Burl has suggested might echo the chambers of older monuments such as the West Kennet long barrow (Burl 1988). During the construction of Avebury, the addition of each individual stone may have been an event that was imbued with its own meanings and significance derived from both landscape and society, so that the act of construction was also an act of composing narratives about places and people. In short, Avebury was *not* conceived in isolation to the environment, but built to integrate facets of the local landscape in its own unique way. Can similar observations be extended to other sites?

The south Dorset landscape contains one of the densest distributions of distinctive natural hollows, termed dolines, in southern England (Sperling *et al.* 1977). These striking circular depressions have formed throughout the Holocene as a result of cave collapses in the underlying limestone, and often cluster to give the ground a cratered appearance (House 1991). In this context it is intriguing that early twentieth century excavations at the **henge** of Maumbury Rings revealed a circular arrangement of exceptionally deep pits (Bradley 1975). Conical in profile and with no known parallel at sites elsewhere, these features are strikingly reminiscent of the geological formations in the nearby landscape (Watson 2001b, 211). This does not seem unreasonable given that many of the dolines are of considerable antiquity. Indeed, a significant number of round barrows on the South Dorset Ridgeway appear to have been constructed in association with them, including examples where natural hollows take the place of ditches (RCHME 1970, 466; Tilley 1999, 225-228). Given that the dolines are widely distributed across the local landscape, it is feasible that the large pits within Maumbury Rings were intended to resemble these distinctive features in the local terrain. Again, it seems that this **henge** was responding to the unique character of the region.

Similar to Avebury, the Knowlton **henges** might have been constructed in the image of basins along the course of the River Allen (Fig. 4). In contrast to the Kennet, however, these basins are arranged along a more linear valley. Likewise, the **henges** are individual enclosures that could have been approached in a sequence that mirrored journeys along the valley. A similar situation is encountered at Stanton Drew, where the **henge** and circles might also reflect movement along a river valley. Landscapes were sometimes incorporated in different ways. Clark (1936, 23) was unsure whether Durrington Walls should be a **henge** at all because of its sloping interior, yet it could be argued that this vast enclosure was an embodiment of the landscape. Its perimeter earthworks were carefully fitted into a confined valley, reinforcing a distinctive sense of place that was already present (Bradley 1998a, 122). The integration of a river into the perimeter of Marden can be understood in a similar way, and once again the view from this site is framed by hills.

The *Henge*™

In this paper I have questioned the rigid classification of the **henge** and suggested some alternative ways of perceiving these monuments, but I have not been able to abandon the terminology altogether. Discussions of archaeological evidence rely upon key words, and throughout this paper I have emboldened the word '**henge**' to highlight the frequency of its usage. Archaeological practice is bound up with the ways in which we use words and language (Hodder 1989; Tilley 1999, Chapter 3), but would our understanding of the past be advanced if we rejected familiar labels? Certainly, **henge** is problematic if used uncritically, but might it remain a useful reference as long as we are aware of its constraints? **Henge** is a modern invention, a 20th century 'brand' of Neolithic monument. This brand has gained power and influence by virtue of its frequent

Fig. 4. Knowlton; enclosure and river basin

citation in the literature, but I hope to have shown that this has often been a very specific way of telling. Architectural classification emphasises the similarities between sites but is unable to account for their diversity and variability, and has been conducted at the expense of embodied experience. The brand ultimately becomes imprinted upon the evidence itself, creating an impression that prehistoric monuments were kit-built from archetypal blueprints. As Harding & Lee have noted, the exclusion of Stone**henge** from the **henge** class 'discourages confidence in the validity of the term and suggests that the criterion may be unduly inflexible' (1987, 41). No one ever seemed to stop and question the relevance of classification to Neolithic people. What does it actually tell us? Obsessed by definitions, archaeological investigations avoid some of the more challenging and interesting questions: In

what ways could **henges** have been perceived in the Neolithic? How might they have been used?

While classification tends to assume that the monuments we see are complete in their final form, perhaps we might better understand them as projects (Bradley 1993, 1998a; Barrett 1994) which responded in diverse ways to the physical and social landscapes in which they were used. Indeed, the form and location of **henges** could even reflect a compromise between a series of diverse influences which were only partially realised. The location and form of a **henge** need not have been determined by any single reason, but was the result of negotiation between many different influences, including regional traditions (Burl 1976, 1979). Instead of thinking in terms of absolute types of monument, perhaps we should consider how **henges** integrated structural, ideological and symbolic principles in ways that were rather fluid.

Encircling landscapes

Traditional schemes of monument classification are reliant upon the objectification of architecture, exemplified by the illustrated plans common to archaeological texts (e.g. Fig. 3). Classification only works if we abstract architectural features and examine them in isolation, replacing an embodied experience of a place with the static and featureless margins of the page. Yet this is tantamount to suggesting that the Neolithic users of a monument like Avebury arrived within the **henge** without having first travelled through its hinterland and, once there, were unable to see anything except for the features of the monument. This perspective is contrary to even our own experiences of visiting Avebury in the modern world, and is problematic for our understanding of the Neolithic. The use of classification assumes that boundaries can be drawn around monuments in certain kinds of ways. These boundaries demarcate the features that identify a site, define what is to be represented through survey, and even determine the zone that is afforded state guardianship. Yet these boundaries might reflect assumptions that are unhelpful to our interpretation of the past as they presume that Neolithic people drew the same distinctions between natural and artificial landscapes that we do today. This seems unlikely, as the history of archaeology has been a history of learning to see the world in a specific way (Bradley 1997). Central to this has been the ability to distinguish landscapes made by people from those formed by natural processes. Even features within substantial monuments like Avebury appear to have been perceived as natural until the earliest antiquarians learnt to read the land in new ways (Ucko et al. 1991). Given that scientific pursuits such as geology and archaeology have largely been rationalised since the 17th century, it seems reasonable to suppose that Neolithic understandings of the landscape might have been rather different to our own. We could explore many interpretations, but one possibility is that

Neolithic people believed that what we describe as 'natural' landforms were actually the work of supernatural ancestors (Bradley 1998b), a perspective partly derived through ethnographic analogy with non-western societies today (Taçon 1991). This seriously questions our definitions of monuments because it breaks down the simple separation between natural and cultural. From the perspective of a world constructed by mythical ancestors, where does a 'monument' end and the 'landscape' begin? Each could be a reflection of the other and it becomes meaningless to isolate either. In other words, the land might be as much a part of the **henge** as banks and ditches, pits, timbers or standing stones.

Classification not only abstracts **henges** from the landscape, but compares and contrasts them in ways that are simply not possible when visiting these sites on the ground. This denies the embodied experiences of people dwelling within monuments. Considerations of materiality, colour, texture, sound or vision play little role in classification, yet it is these qualities that actually define the experience of a place (Jones 1998, 1999; Jones & MacGregor 2002; Cummings 2002; Watson & Keating 1999; Watson 2001a; Cummings et al. 2002). Some of these difficulties have been emphasised by studies of stone circles, which have often been classified according to the geometry of their groundplan: e.g. circular, oblate, egg shaped, etc (Thom 1967; Cowan 1970; Thom et al. 1980). Not only is it almost impossible to visually appreciate these subtle variations on the ground, but experimental research has suggested that precisely the same variety of shapes can be accidentally achieved by laying out the rings by eye (Barnatt & Herring 1986). The critical issue is that we should be careful not to impose specific ways of viewing monuments that are solely determined by abstract representations. In the case of **henges**, the precise form of the monument may not be as important as the overall experience that it generates. When viewed in plan (Fig. 3), the earthwork enclosure at Avebury is clearly not

Fig. 5. **Henge**-ing the land, dislocating Avebury

perfectly circular, yet an observer inside the inner stone circles is unable to perceive these irregularities. Rather, the enclosure appears to describe a circle around the viewer. Likewise, the upper Kennet valley is itself not arranged around a circle, but irregularities in the topography appear flattened to the observer within Avebury, creating the illusion that the **henge** is situated at the centre of a circular landscape. The same is true of other sites, from Wessex to Orkney. In this sense, **henge** monuments were not simply built in the image of the landscape, but simultaneously reworked the appearance of that land so that it appears to wrap in a circle around the monument (Watson 2000). This is reminiscent of sacred sites in many non-western societies that are situated in places believed to be at the centre of the cosmos (Eliade 1954, 12-4; Tuan 1977, 39, 91; Higuchi 1983, 110; Norberg-Schulz 1985). In these settings, sacred architecture may seek to 'visualise' qualities of that place in order to reveal its 'underlying' form (Norberg-Schulz 1979). In this sense, **henges** might have been conceptual centres in the Neolithic, places that materialised a microcosm of the wider landscape (Richards 1996b; Bradley 1998a, 121-4; Watson 2001a); monuments that made the world. This interpretation would not have been possible within the framework of classification as this is predicated upon a modern way of seeing that is fundamentally detached from the environment (Ingold 2000, 209-18).

But there remains a problem. While I have talked about some of the ways in which we might compromise overly rigid perceptions of the **henge**, it remains difficult to fundamentally challenge its authority. This paper has perpetuated a sense that the **henge** is a tradition of monument that extends across the British Isles, a class of site that was adapted to local circumstances. I have suggested that this could begin to explain why the classification of these monuments has been so problematic, but this does not make space for other readings of the evidence. Might **henge**™ have other voices?

Henge-ing the world

Since it is unlikely that there were rational scientific enterprises called geology or archaeology in the Neolithic, it is equally unlikely that there were rigid distinctions between landforms made by people and landforms made in other ways. How could we work with this possibility? Embodied experiences of places are dynamic and partial, never static and complete. Thus there could be no one, objective monument that is visible in a single glance, but rather a series of disparate and fluid experiences that can be reformulated in various ways. Perhaps we have underestimated the importance of the changing seasons, the time of day or night and the shifting weather in our tellings of the Neolithic (Watson 2003). Traditional conceptions of monuments do not account for these possibilities. In a world where **henge** and land are interchangeable, should our monuments and their legislated boundaries be allowed to ebb and flow with the changing light and weather? Might we have to question the scale and integrity of monuments that is implied by classification? Not far from Avebury, the stone and timber circles of the Sanctuary never had banks and ditches and therefore have not been included in discussions of **henges**. By virtue of its location, however, the Sanctuary effectively condenses the world in a way that creates enclosure. The circle is surrounded by a river valley (ditch) closed by chalk ridges beyond (bank). All of the elements that we call **henge** are present, but they only materialise at this place. Should we describe the Sanctuary as a **henge**, an orchestration of natural features, or something else altogether? Might these be dichotomies of our own creation? It is possible 'to **henge**' other sites. That is, to actively envisage 'natural' landforms as 'artifical' earthworks so that the experience of a **henge** might be revealed (Fig. 5). For example, viewers on the summit platform of Silbury Hill perceive themselves to be central to a space described by the margins of the hill *and* the valley basin that surrounds it. Again, the

Figure 6. **Henge**-ing monuments: the Sanctuary, Silbury Hill and Castlerigg.

spatial organisation that is ordinarily accredited to the **henge** is present at a mon-ument which archaeologists would ordinarily describe in entirely different ways. Likewise, the Cumbrian site of Castlerigg has traditionally been described as a classic open stone circle, yet the juxtaposition between mountains and stones again recalls the **henge** experience (Fig. 6). Importantly, this effect cannot be extended to all monuments; for example, long cairns dating to the earlier Neolithic create asymmetrical relations with their environment (Cummings *et al.* 2002).

If we acknowledge that banks, ditches, hills and valleys were interchangeable in the later Neolithic, then our definition of **henges** would have to be fundamentally reconsidered. In this way, the **henge** can be thought of not as a specific class of monument but rather a performance that creates a world with the audience at its centre. As I have suggested, the act of '**henge**-ing' is not necessarily restricted to the monuments that we call **henges** but can also be extended to other sites and even the wider landscape.

Conclusions

Classification does not reflect how landscape is experienced, but how it is objectified. Abstraction is therefore intrinsic to the creation of a category, a fixed point that permits comparisons between sites in ways that cannot be experienced in the landscape. **Henge** is an example of how the archaeological record has been rationalised and predetermined. For this reason it is critical to reconsider the foundations of classification and the rigidity that it imposes upon interpretation.

Henge is a contemporary idea; the challenge for archaeology is to make the boundaries of these monuments open and fluid. As an initial step, **henges** could be envisaged as places where elements and meanings from the wider landscape coalesce. Beyond this, perhaps **henges** were not architecture at all, but an active

transgression of 'natural' and 'built'. Rather than autonomous monuments, I have suggested the notion of '**henge**-ing' as a performance that places people at the centre of the cosmos. Thus freed from the fixity and finality of classification, a conception of **henges** as cosmological performances reveals an unfamiliar and dynamic Neolithic that was in a perpetual state of becoming.

Henges were not monuments built from landscapes, they were monuments that made the world.

Acknowledgements

An earlier draft of this paper was first presented at the Neolithic Studies Group meeting in 2002, and I would like to thank Gordon Barclay and Tim Darvill for their invitation to speak. Thanks also to Richard Bradley and Colin Richards for advice and discussion. I am most grateful to Ros Cleal and Chris Gingell for their assistance with access to the World Heritage site at Avebury. Fieldwork was conducted as part of a doctoral thesis supported by grants from the British Academy and the University of Reading.

Bibliography

Atkinson, R. 1951. The henge monuments of Great Britain. In R. Atkinson, C. Piggott & N. Sandars, *Excavations at Dorchester, Oxon,* 81-107. Oxford: Department of Antiquities, Ashmolean Museum

Barclay, G. 1989. Henge monuments: reappraisal or reductionism? *Proceedings of the Prehistoric Society* 55, 260-2

Barnatt, J. & Herring, P. 1986. Stone circles and megalithic geometry: an experiment to test alternative design practices. *Journal of Archaeological Science* 13, 431-49

Barrett, J. 1994. *Fragments from antiquity: an archaeology of social life in Britain, 2900-1200 BC.* Oxford: Blackwell

Bender, B. 1993. *Landscape: politics and perspectives.* Oxford: Berg

Bender, B. 1998. *Stonehenge: making space.* Oxford: Berg

Bradley, R. 1975. Maumbury Rings, Dorchester: the excavations of 1908-13. *Archaeologia* 105, 197

Bradley, R. 1993. *Altering the Earth*. Edinburgh: Societies of Antiquaries Monograph 8

Bradley, R. 1997. 'To see is to have seen'. Craft traditions in archaeology. In B.L.Molyneaux (ed.), *The cultural life of images: visual representation in archaeology*, 62-72. London: Routledge

Bradley, R. 1998a. *The significance of monuments*. London: Routledge

Bradley, R. 1998b. Ruined buildings, ruined stones: enclosures, tombs and natural places in the Neolithic of south-west England. *World Archaeology* 30 (1), 13-22

Burl, A. 1969. Henges: internal features and regional groups. *Archaeological Journal* 126, 1-28

Burl, A. 1976. *The stone circles of the British Isles*. London: Yale University Press

Burl, A. 1979. *Prehistoric Avebury*. London: Yale University Press

Burl, A. 1988. Coves: structural enigmas of the Neolithic. *Wiltshire Archaeological & Natural History Magazine* 82, 1-18

Catherall, P. 1971. Henges in perspective. *Archaeological Journal* 128, 147-53

Clare, T. 1986. Towards a reappraisal of henge monuments. *Proceedings of the Prehistoric Society* 52, 281-316

Clark, G. 1936. The timber monument at Arminghall and its affinities. *Proceedings of the Prehistoric Society* 2, 1-51

Cosgrove, D. & Daniels, S. 1988. *The iconography of landscape*. Cambridge: Cam-bridge University Press

Cowan, T. 1970. Megalithic rings: their design construction. *Science* 168, 321-5

Cummings, V. 2002. Experiencing texture and touch in the British Neolithic. *Oxford Journal of Archaeology* 21 (3), 249-61

Cummings, V., Jones, A., & Watson, A. 2002. Divided places: phenomenology and asymmetry in the monuments of the Black Mountains, Southeast Wales. *Cambridge Archaeological Journal* 12 (1), 57-70

Eliade, M. 1954. *The myth of the eternal return*. London: Arkana (Penguin Books)

Fleming, A. 1972. Vision and design: approaches to ceremonial monument typology. *Man* 7, 57-73

Gillings, M. & Pollard, J. 1999. Non-portable stone artefacts and contexts of meaning: the tale of the Grey Wether (www.museums.ncl.ac.uk/Avebury/stone4.htm). *World Archaeology* 31 (2), 179-93

Gray, H.St.G. 1909. Excavations at the amphitheatre, Charterhouse-on-Mendip, 1909. *Proceedings of the Somerset Archaeological & Natural History Society* 55, 118-37

Gray, H.St.G. 1935. The Avebury excavations, 1908-1922. *Archaeologia* 84, 99-162

Harding, A. & Lee, G. 1987. *Henge monuments and related sites of Great Britain*. Oxford: British Archaeological Reports, British Series 175

Higuchi, T. 1983. *The visual and spatial structure of landscapes*. London: Massachusetts Institute of Technology Press

Hirsch, E. & O'Hanlon, M. 1995. *The anthropology of landscape*. Oxford: Oxford University Press

Hodder, I. 1989. This is not an article about material culture as text. *Journal of Anthropological Archaeology* 8, 250-69

House, M. 1991. Dorset dolines: Part 2, Bronkham Hill. *Proceedings of the Dorset Natural History & Archaeological Society* 113, 149-55

Ingold, T. 2000. *The perception of the environment*. London: Routledge

Jones, A. 1998. Where eagles dare: landscape, animals and the Neolithic of Orkney. *Journal of Material Culture* 3, 301-24

Jones, A. 1999. Local colour: megalithic architecture and colour symbolism in Neolithic Arran, *Oxford Journal of Archaeology* 18 (4), 339-50

Jones, A. & MacGregor, G. (eds.) 2002. *Colouring the past: the significance of colour in archaeological research*. Berg: Oxford

Kendrick, T. & Hawkes, C. 1932. *Archaeology in England and Wales 1914-1931*. London: Methuen & Co Ltd

Loveday, R. 1998. Double entrance henges - routes to the past? In A. Gibson & D. Simpson (eds), *Prehistoric ritual and religion,* 14-31. Stroud: Sutton Publishing

Norberg-Schulz, C. 1979. *Genius Loci: towards a phenomenology of architecture*. London: Academy Editions

Norberg-Schulz, C. 1985. *The concept of dwelling: on the way to figurative architecture*. New York: Electra/Rizzoli

Piggott, S. & Piggott, C. 1939. Stone and earth

circles in Dorset. *Antiquity* 13, 138-58

Pollard, J. & Gillings, M. 1998. Romancing the stones: towards a virtual and elemental Avebury. *Archaeological Dialogues* 5 (2), 143-64

RCHME (Royal Commission on Historical Monuments, England). 1970. *An inventory of historical monuments in the county of Dorset, Vol. 2: south-east*. London: HMSO

Richards, C. 1993. Monumental choreography: architecture and spatial representation in Late Neolithic Orkney. In C. Tilley (ed.) *Interpretative Archaeology*, 143-78. Oxford: Berg

Richards, C. 1996a. Henges and water: towards an elemental understanding of monumentality and landscape in late Neolithic Britain. *Journal of Material Culture* 1 (3), 313-36

Richards, C. 1996b. Monuments as landscape: creating the centre of the world in late Neolithic Orkney. *World Archaeology* 28 (2), 190-208

Roese, H. 1980. Some aspects of the topographical locations of Neolithic and Bronze Age monuments in Wales. II. Henges and circles. *The Bulletin of the Board of Celtic Studies* 29 (1), 164-70

Smith, I. 1965. *Windmill Hill and Avebury: excavations by Alexander Keiller 1925-1939*. Oxford: Clarendon Press

Sperling, C., Goudie, A., Stoddart, D. & Poole, G. 1977. Dolines of the Dorset chalklands and other areas of southern Britain. *Transactions of the Institute of British Geographers* 2, 205-3

Taçon, P. 1991. The power of stone: symbolic aspects of stone use and tool development in western Arnhem Land, Australia. *Antiquity* 65, 192-207

Thom, A. 1967. *Megalithic sites in Britain*. Oxford: Oxford University Press

Thom, A., Thom, A. & Burl, A. 1980. *Megalithic rings*. Oxford: British Archaeological Reports, British Series, 81

Thomas, J. 1993. The politics of vision and the archaeologies of landscape. In B. Bender (ed.), *Landscape: politics and perspectives,* 19-48.

Oxford: Berg

Tilley, C. 1994. *A phenomenology of landscape*. Oxford: Berg

Tilley, C. 1999. *Metaphor and material culture*. Oxford: Blackwell

Topping, P. 1992. The Penrith henges: a survey by the Royal Commission on the Historical Monuments of England. *Proceedings of the Prehistoric Society* 58, 249-64

Tuan, Yi-Fu. 1977. *Space and place: the perspective of experience*. London: Edward Arnold

Ucko, P., Hunter, M., Clark, A. & David, A. 1991. *Avebury reconsidered: from the 1660s to the 1990s*. London: Unwin Hyman

Wainwright, G. 1969. A review of henge monuments in the light of recent research. *Proceedings of the Prehistoric Society* 35, 112-33

Wainwright, G. 1989. *The henge monuments*. London: Thames & Hudson

Wainwright, G., Evans, J., & Longworth, I. 1971. The excavation of a Late Neolithic enclosure at Marden, Wiltshire. *Antiquaries Journal* 51, 177-239

Watson, A. 2000. *Encircled space: the experience of stone circles and henges in the British Neolithic*. Unpublished PhD thesis, University of Reading

Watson, A. 2001a. Composing Avebury. *World Archaeology* 33 (2), 296-314

Watson, A. 2001b. Round barrows in a circular world: monumentalising landscapes in early Bronze Age Wessex. In J. Brück (ed.) *Bronze age landscapes: tradition and transformation*, 207-16. Oxford: Oxbow

Watson, A. 2004. Fluid horizons. In V. Cummings & C. Fowler (eds) *The Neolithic of the Irish Sea*. Oxford: Oxbow

Watson, A. & Keating, D. 1999. Architecture and sound: an acoustic analysis of megalithic monuments in prehistoric Britain. *Antiquity* 73, 325-36

The Later Neolithic Architectural Repertoire: the case of the Dunragit complex

Julian Thomas

One of Isobel Smith's many contributions to British prehistory lay in her evaluation of the relationship between causewayed enclosures and henge monuments (Smith 1971, 100). This arose out of her publication of Alexander Keiller's excavations at Windmill Hill and Avebury, which prompted reflection on the spatial juxtaposition of the two classes of monuments, both in north Wiltshire and further afield. Smith pointed out that the presence of certain classes of artefacts (particular styles of pottery, stone axes, carved chalk objects) at both kinds of site indicated 'a continuity of concepts and practices' between earlier and later Neolithic monuments (Smith 1965, 252). If in particular geographical areas both a causewayed enclosure and a henge monument could be identified, it was possible that something of the role of the one had been taken on by the other as time progressed (Smith 1966). This, of course, was later to provide one of the critical arguments in Colin Renfrew's study of monumentality and social organisation in Neolithic Wessex. Renfrew was to suggest that the spatial coincidence of causewayed enclosures and henges could be attributed to the endurance of particular political units throughout the Neolithic, within which

processes of the centralisation of authority and population increase could be identified. As larger structures, requiring the investment of greater quantities of labour in their construction, the henges of Wessex took on the functions of the causewayed enclosures, but for a larger and more structured community (Renfrew 1973). In this respect the crucial element of Smith's contribution was that she had addressed prehistoric monuments from the point of view of their use and function, rather than simply their morphology or cultural affinities. Smith considered the social role of earlier and later Neolithic enclosures in terms of the gathering of dispersed populations, the consumption of shared meals, the circulation of livestock, the exchange of goods, and the performance of religious and cult rituals. It was in this context of practice as opposed to form that causewayed enclosures could be considered ancestral to henges.

In the spirit of Smith's arguments, this contribution will be concerned with the monumental architecture of the later Neolithic, and with the problems that arise from understanding monuments as assemblages of typological traits rather than as constructed spaces occupied by human beings. In the first instance we will investigate the ways in which successive generations of archaeologists have sought to typify henges, although a consideration of the adequacy of this term will provide a means of broadening the discussion, while focusing on a particular site.

Classifying henges

The history of the category 'henge monument' is one of increasingly rigid classifications. When Kendrick first used the term in 1932 he did so in a very general way to refer to prehistoric 'sacred places', which might include stone circles as well as earthwork enclosures. These sites were not necessarily all of the same date, and were therefore not addressed under the heading of a particular period, and might have represented 'temples' or less emphatically religious 'meeting places' (Kendrick & Hawkes 1932, 83). Grahame Clark, in 1936, laid more emphasis on the presence of a circular central area, containing stone or timber uprights. The existence of a bank, providing spectators with a view of the interior, was also important to him, but clearly not essential, as he included the Sanctuary on Overton Hill, Wiltshire, as a henge monument. A ditch was still less fundamental to the henge class, and might have one or two entrances (Clark 1936, 23). A critical change in henge studies came with Piggott and Piggott's 1939 paper on the stone and earth circles of Dorset, which focused particularly on the role of the bank and ditch, perhaps because they provided the criteria for distinguishing between their Class I and II henges. The ditch was generally expected to have an external bank, and stones or posts might be found in the interior, but Class I monuments had a single entrance, and Class 2, two (Piggott & Piggott 1939, 140). Significantly, while Clark had described henges as a 'class' of monuments, the Piggotts introduced the notion of a henge 'idea', implying some kind of *underlying* unity. In this respect they followed the conventions of Old World culture-historic

archaeology by attributing regularities in material culture to the existence of a unifying 'spirit' or essence (Binford & Sabloff 1982, 142). Piggott and Piggott's arguments were codified by Atkinson in 1951, who, while he included Stonehenge in his list of henge monuments, made the bank with internal ditch the defining feature of henges. Atkinson explicitly excluded free-standing circles of posts or stones, such as the Sanctuary (Atkinson *et al.* 1951, 82). He also refined the typology by adding a Class IIA (monuments with a single bank within two concentric ditches), and noted that Class II henges were more likely to have a NW/SE orientation and contain stone uprights. This implied that the different categories of site had held a distinct significance for past societies, rather than simply being modern archaeological constructs.

A rationale for defining henges according to the presence of a series of traits was provided by Stuart Piggott in *Neolithic Cultures of the British Isles* (1954, 354). For him the henge 'idea' was grounded in the bank and ditch enclosure, but this had been elaborated in different ways by different cultural groups. Thus, henges with internal timber settings belonged to the Rinyo-Clacton culture, henges used as cremation cemeteries belonged to the Dorchester culture, and henges with two opposed entrances could be attributed to the Beaker culture. This provides a parallel with Piggott's more general discussion of 'Secondary Neolithic Cultures', each of which possessed a separate ceramic tradition, yet shared the same lithic assemblage. These were 'subcultures', distinct at one level, but linked infrastructurally. The henge idea was evidently pan-cultural and possibly long-lived, but adapted in various ways by different ethnic or social groups. What is not clear is whether Piggott understood this variation to be the consequence of customary practice (so that timber circles are simply a passive cultural marker of Grooved Ware users), or whether the henge form was consciously reworked in order to accommodate the various ceremonial activities of different communities. This latter possibility would effectively undermine the presuppositions on which the typology of henges is based, as we will see below.

Revisiting the categorisation of henge monuments in the following decade, Burl (1969, 3) re-emphasised the importance of the bank, which was present at all known sites save for the Ring of Brodgar in Orkney. Burl went on to point to the diversity of the internal features within henges, concluding that stone and timber uprights could not be seen as a diagnostic attribute of the class. More recently, some dissatisfaction with the accepted classification has begun to creep into the literature. Tom Clare, for instance, made the very important point that it is difficult to draw a sharp distinction between true henges and a very heterogeneous group of sites that he defines as 'hengiforms' (Clare 1986, 283). Any particular site might represent a permutation of a variety of different kinds of perimeter (ditches and banks, with or without interruptions) and internal features (pits, posts, stones, graves). On this basis, Clare established a new and more complex class-ification of henges and related sites, involving 12 distinct sub-groups. This system had the benefit of refraining from isolating a single variable which might serve as the basis for a binary distinction between henge and non-henge.

However, it may be that a more fine-grained classification is not the answer to the problem of understanding henges (Barclay 1989, 260). There is in archaeology a residual belief that cultural phenomena should resolve themselves into natural types, providing that we can identify the correct variables on which to base our typologies. This is somewhat akin to the ideas that underlay 17th and 18th century practices of classification, which imagined all of the things of the world as possessing a unique position on a massive classificatory table (Foucault 1970, 75). Where a particular phenomenon fitted in the overall scheme of things could be identified from its surface morphology, as in the case of Linnaeus' classification of plants on the basis of

their reproductive parts alone. Yet, by the start of the 19th century, biologists like Cuvier had demonstrated that organisms could not be understood exclusively from their appearance, and that issues of function, habit, behaviour and habitat also had to be taken into account (Foucault 1979, 128). This recognition of organ-isms as living creatures rather than static classificatory entities lay behind the kinds of multi-variate taxonomy that David Clarke applied to archaeology in the 1960s, inspiring a discussion of cultural phenomena as polythetic entities or 'fuzzy sets' (Clarke 1968, 372).

This I take to be the imperative behind Tom Clare's analysis: to demonstrate the inadequacy of a definition of henges on the basis of the single variable of the presence of a bank with internal ditch. However, it is arguable that the variability of later Neolithic monuments is organised in a fundamentally different way from that of the living things that taxonomic methods were originally devised to cope with. By the later Neolithic, a wide range of architectural devices was current in Britain, including banks, ditches, pits, upright timbers, standing stones, avenues, round mounds, coves, and so forth. Some of these elements had originally emerged in the various monumental constructions of the earlier Neolithic: earthen long mounds, ditch- and post-defined cursus monuments, causewayed enclosures. Extracted from these traditions, they could be deployed and combined in new ways. This architectural repertoire was drawn on, within a given topographical setting, in order to create certain effects: to provide spaces for the gathering of groups of people of different sizes, to create patterns of seclusion and disclosure, and to facilitate specific patterns of movement and encounter. The configuration that emerged was generally unique, and specific to local circumstances, but the key point is that it was the outcome of a series of *explicit choices* concerning the way in which a particular space was to be organised. These choices were clearly not just a matter of the unconsidered reproduction of tradition, and this is why conventional forms of classification cannot adequately account for the variability of later Neolithic monuments. These structures took the forms that they did because of the ways in which they were intended to be used and inhabited. In some cases, similar effects could be induced using quite different structural elements, while in others, similar architectural devices might have been used in entirely different ways.

A good example of this lies in the contrast between the two large Wessex henges of Durrington Walls and Mount Pleasant (Wainwright & Longworth 1971, Wainwright 1979). In abstract plan view on the page, these two monuments are very similar. While Mount Pleasant has four entrances and Durrington Walls only two, they are alike in shape, and not

far different in size. Both have a ditch with an external bank, both have internal features involving concentric rings of timber uprights, both produced large assemblages of Grooved Ware, and faunal assemblages dominated by pig. Yet these similarities of form and cultural associations potentially mask a fundamental difference. The enclosure at Durrington Walls surrounds a natural amphitheatre, while the Mount Pleasant ditch and bank run around a hilltop. This would result in quite different conditions of visibility or seclusion, both in terms of what could be seen from outside and within the monuments. This point is enhanced when one considers the internal structures within the two henges. At Mount Pleasant, Site IV was surrounded by its own bank and ditch, and

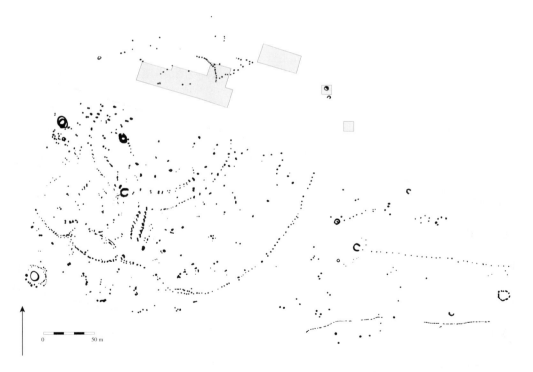

Fig. 1. Dunragit, Galloway: principal features of the monumental complex, based on the aerial photographic plots. Excavated areas north of the railway line shaded

positioned so that its entrance was precisely located on the crest of the hilltop. The innermost space of the complex was thereby rendered relatively invisible from the outside, within a larger enclosure that have been much more open to view. By contrast, the two internal timber circle complexes at Durrington were unenclosed, and their contents may have been open to view, at least from within the interior of the henge. What this demonstrates is that at Durrington Walls and Mount Pleasant, very similar structural configurations were subtly manipulated in relation to the natural topography in order to bring about entirely different effects.

Dunragit and later Neolithic architecture

Perhaps perversely, I want to pursue these arguments further by discussing a site which is not a henge at all. Between 1999 and 2002, excavations supported by Historic Scotland took place at Dunragit in Galloway. This site is immediately to the north of Luce Bay, adjacent to Luce Sands, where over the past century the discovery of hearths, burials and scatters of pottery has provided extensive evidence of Neolithic and Bronze Age occupation (Davidson

1952, McInnes 1964, Cowie 1996). In 1992 Marilyn Brown of the Scottish Royal Commission on Ancient and Historic Monuments identified a complex of crop-marks in fields south of Dunragit village, registering in grass and barley on either side of the modern railway line (Fig. 1). These included ring-ditches, hengiform enclosures, pit-circles and pit- or post-alignments, but the most striking element is a set of three concentric rings of cut features, the largest ring being roughly 300m in diameter. A monumental entrance avenue, facing to the south, is associated with the middle ring. This in particular suggests an affinity with a group of later Neolithic palisaded enclosures which includes Walton (Gibson 1999), Forteviot (St. Joseph 1978) and Meldon Bridge (Speak & Burgess 1999).

What is not immediately obvious from the air photographs is that the enclosure intersects with a post-defined cursus (presumably of considerably earlier date), the timbers of which appear to have been deliberately burnt. While a dense scatter of features is evident within the north-west quadrant of the enclosure, it was only on excavation that it became clear that many of them formed a coherent structure (Fig. 2). Only the north-east end of the cursus has been

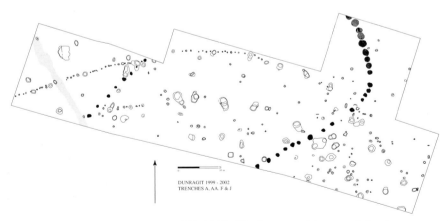

DUNRAGIT 1999 - 2002
TRENCHES A, AA, F & J

Fig. 2. Dunragit: main trenches excavated 1999-2002. The features of the post-defined cursus are shaded black, and cross over the two innermost rings of the later Neolithic enclosure

located: to the south and west the structure disappears under the modern road and into land unsuitable for air photographic reconnaissance. The uprights of the cursus appear to have been taller around its terminal, where the post-holes were larger, deeper, and contained more massive packing-stones. This suggests a parallel with some bank-and-ditch cursus monuments, such as the Stonehenge Cursus and the Dorset Cursus, in which the bank rose up around the terminals (Christie 1964). This was, after all, the reason why Greenwell imagined that he was digging a long barrow when he excavated a cursus terminal at Rudston (Greenwell & Rolleston 1877, 253-7). The burning of the up-right timbers at Dunragit suggests that the cursus was short-lived, yet at precisely the point where its western side was cut across by the middle post-ring of the enclosure, by far the largest post-hole in that ring was encountered. At the bottom of this post-hole was a stone axe, the cutting edge of which may have been deliberately broken. This is the *only* find of material culture of any kind from the middle ring, in contrast with the appreciable quantities of pottery and other cultural material from the innermost ring. This suggests that the large post-hole and its contents represented an explicit acknowledgement of the presence of the earlier monument. It also indicates that the earlier existence of the cursus may have been a factor influencing the location of the Dunragit enclosure. This kind of relation-ship with a cursus is shared by certain henges. At Thornborough and Maxey the henge lies directly over the cursus (Vatcher 1960, Harding 1998, Pryor 1984), but there are also close henge-and-cursus associations at Rudston, Dorchester and Llandegai (Atkinson *et al.* 1951, Houlder 1968).

One of the principal questions that the investigation at Dunragit was designed to answer was whether the enclosure was composed of true palisades, or whether it represented a series of circles of free-standing uprights. The aerial photographs had already demonstrated that the site did not possess a continuous palisade slot like those at West Kennet or Mount Pleasant

(Whittle 1997, 57). However, at Meldon Bridge the large uprights had been interspersed with pairs of smaller posts, which have been interpreted as retaining a post-and-panel structure of horizontal timbers (Speak & Burgess 1999, 20). At Dunragit it seems that the situation was different again: the innermost ring represented a colossal timber circle, around 120m in diameter, but the two outer rings were effectively fences, composed of large posts at roughly five-metre intervals, with smaller posts, much closer together, in between. The inner ring (the post circle) had had two distinct phases of construction. By contrast, each of the two outer rings was single-phase, and their entrances did not respect each other. This suggests that they were not contemporary, and that the monument as a whole was rebuilt on at least one occasion. In each phase it consisted of a timber circle surrounded by a single fence. The implication is that between the first and second phase the overall size of the enclosure changed, although it is not clear whether the larger or the smaller fence was the earlier.

The post-holes of the innermost ring were extremely large, perhaps conspicuously so, and ramped to allow the insertion of the uprights by toppling into the sockets. In contrast with the cursus, the enclosure posts had largely rotted away *in situ*. Around part of the arc of features in the excavated area the second-phase post-holes amounted to recuts of the first-phase posts. But further to the east the two lines diverged, and the second-phase sockets represented distinct features (Fig. 2). It is arguable that at this point little above-ground trace remained of the primary posts to allow them to be located and replaced, so that the second-phase circuit of uprights wandered off-line in places. In a minority of cases, predominantly attributable to the second phase, the posts had been pulled out from the post-holes, with considerable disruption of the profile of the fill as a result. In *every* example where this had taken place a distinctive placed deposit had been inserted into the crater left behind by the post. One of these was composed of the cremated remains of a woman and a sheep, placed immediately onto the surface left by the removal of the post; one was a deposit of black organic material containing sherds of Grooved Ware and flint tools including a fine triangular arrowhead; one was made up of Beaker pottery; and a final one was made up of a mass of oak charcoal containing small fragments of burnt animal bone poured over a small mound of sand which had been placed on the base of the cleaned-out post-hole (Thomas 2003).

In all respects, the major post-holes of the middle and outer rings contrast with those of the inner. We might say that they seemed more 'functional'. They were sometimes ramped, but they were no larger than required to hold a substantial timber, and consequentially smaller than the inner ring post-holes. As we have already seen, with the one exception of the stone axe they contained no structured deposits or other cultural material at all. The implication of this contrast is that the timber circle represented the symbolic focus of the monument, the uprights of which were significant in themselves, while the fence was the perimeter of the structure, and had the role of regulating access and vision into the interior. We might compare this arrangement to the relationship between the earthen bank and the internal features with a large henge monument. Indeed, one of the reasons why henge banks were generally external may have been to make the contents of the ditch accessible from the interior of the monument, but secluded from those outside.

That the Dunragit complex was organised in such a way as to establish particular relationships amongst people is especially clear when we consider its final element. The large mound at Droughduil had been recorded as a medieval motte, but looks quite unlike other mottes in coastal Galloway, having a rather more peaked profile and an ovoid plan. It is also located in a more low-lying position than most local mottes. The Droughduil mound lies about 400m to the south of the Dunragit enclosure, immediately on

the northern edge of the Luce Bay sand dunes. When the aerial photographs of the complex were overlaid on the map of the immediate area it became evident that the monumental entrance avenue that connects with the middle post-ring is almost precisely aligned on it. The mound is roughly 70 by 60m in extent, and 9m in height. Of course, similar large mounds are often found as elements of later Neolithic monumental complexes involving both henges and post-defined enclosures. Silbury Hill, for instance, lies close to both the Avebury henge and the West Kennet palisade enclosures (Whittle 1997, 5). At Knowlton in Dorset, a very large round barrow stands amongst a group of henges of varying sizes. The Hatfield Barrow, a colossal round mound, originally lay within the great henge at Marden in the Vale of Pewsey (Wainwright 1971). The Conquer Barrow stands on the bank of the Mount Pleasant henge, adjacent to the palisade enclosure that lies within the earthwork and seemingly post-dates it (Wainwright 1979). In the case of Silbury Hill, John Barrett (1994, 31) has argued that the mound is essentially a raised platform, which would allow a privileged group of people to stand in an elevated position in relation to a congregation gathered in an enclosure. If this were the case at Droughduil, such a group of people would have been silhouetted against the sky from the point of view of anyone inside the enclosure, looking out through the entrance.

In order to substantiate this idea, a limited investigation of the Droughduil mound was undertaken during the summer of 2002. A series of metre-square test-pits demonstrated that the mound had had no surrounding ditch, and the lack of a clear turf-line at the base of the mound suggests that it may have been built onto an existing sand-dune. There were no medieval finds whatever from a trench that was opened up the side of the mound (Fig. 3). The original surface of the structure proved to have been stepped, although these steps seemed to have filled relatively quickly with wind-blown sand. The stepped profile, of course, invites

Fig. 3. The Droughduil mound, Galloway, under excavation in summer 2002 (photo: author)

comparison with Silbury Hill and certain Breton passage-tombs, such as the Table des Marchands at Locmariaquer. A mound composed of a series of stepped drums with retaining and/or radial walls of stone or chalk blocks appears to have been a relatively common Neolithic constructional device in Atlantic Europe. However, in the case of the Droughduil mound it is less obvious that the form arose from structural considerations. Instead, it may have been that the mound was built in a certain way in order to evoke a series of comparisons with other monuments. That is to say, a stepped round mound may have been understood as an appropriate component of a later Neolithic monumental complex, which also referred to more distant structures.

No suitable dating material was recovered from the body of the mound, and indeed it was the need for dates that had originally inspired the search for a quarry ditch. However, a good indication of a Neolithic date was provided by the discovery of a round cairn on the summit of the mound, which produced fragments of burnt bone and flint scrapers. Very similar Bronze Age round cairns are known nearby at Mid Gleniron Farm. More reliable dating information will eventually be provided by a series of optically-stimulated luminescence samples taken at intervals down the profile of the mound. These should date the last occasion on which sand particles in the mound make-up were subject to direct sunlight.

As we have noted, there were no medieval finds from the mound, but there was one very interesting piece of post-medieval archaeology on the site. On the crest of the mound a small depression was identified in advance of excavation. It was conjectured that this might relate to an antiquarian shaft dug down through the monument, similar to that at Silbury Hill (Field 2000). For the purposes of monument management, a small trench was opened over this depression. What it revealed was the cellar of a very small mortared stone building, roughly 2 by 1.5m in extent. The building cut through the edge of the round cairn and into the body of the sand mound. Associated with the collapse of the building were a number of large glass bottle-bases, and it seems possible that the structure was some form of folly connected with one of the two historic gentry-houses in the immediate area. The removal of the rubble from the cellar produced a remarkable piece of dating information. On the wooden floor of the structure a stoppered glass bottle was located, and inside this was a piece of paper which bore a note written in pencil, which revealed that 'The Hut' had been demolished by Robert Broadfoot of Droughduil on October 14th 1908. Broadfoot's father had been the tenant farmer of the Droughduil estate, and both father and son are buried in Old Luce churchyard.

Conclusion

The Dunragit later Neolithic monumental complex contained a series of structural elements which provided spaces for people to gather, to process, and to stand in relation to one another. As such, it appears to have had a role that was very similar to some of the larger henge monuments. Some spaces were secluded, while others afforded enhanced visibility for numbers of people. This indicates that these structures were used for performances which involved some acts or events that were highly secretive, and others that were intended to be witnessed by many persons. Some of these spaces could accommodate large congregations, others would only admit a small minority of a population.

What distinguished Dunragit from the henges was the absence of a bank and ditch, although arguably the two (possibly successive) timber fences had much the same role. If we compare Dunragit with a site like Greyhound Yard in Dorchester (Fig. 4), where a massive ring of large posts was surrounded by a very minimal ditch (Woodward et al. 1984, 102), the problem of

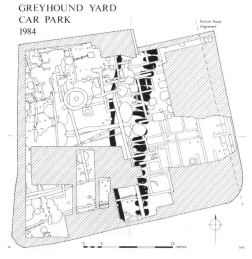

Fig. 4. Greyhound Yard, Dorchester, Dorset: the post-holes and ditch of the later Neolithic enclosure (in black), cut by Roman and later features (after Woodward, Davies & Graham 1984, with additions)

defining what is and what is not a henge comes into clearer focus. Equally, the binary sorting of henge and non-henge results in a situation where we have to say that Durrington Walls and Mount Pleasant have more in common with small henges like Gorsey Bigbury or the Bull Ring than they do with Dunragit. This is the drawback of using formal morphological criteria to define archaeological categories, rather than concentrating on practice, function and the role of entities in social life.

Late Neolithic monumental architecture was not composed of a series of ideal types. Each structure, and each local landscape, had its own particular history and development, played out in specific topographical circumstances in order to bring about a series of desired effects. Some monuments that we would define as henges were used in ways that were similar to some that were not, while the activities that took place in different henges may have been utterly unalike. This much is evident from the variation in the densities of cultural material recovered from these sites. I do not imagine that we will stop using the term 'henge' to describe a particular kind of construction: one that has a sub-circular plan with a ditch and external bank. Nor would I argue that this would be a positive development. The problem lies in believing that function can be derived from form, and that all monuments that can be grouped together using any particular set of formal criteria can be assumed to represent instances of a singular phenomenon. We need to be critical of the notion that henges amounted to a coherent and bounded tradition of construction, which was different in kind from those sites which happened not to be surrounded by a bank and ditch. The degree of overlap between henges, stone circles, timber circles and other monumental forms should alert us to the need for a contextual rather than a classificatory approach.

Bibliography

Atkinson, R.J.C., Piggott, C.M. & Sandars, N. 1951. *Excavations at Dorchester, Oxon.* Oxford: Ashmolean Museum

Barclay, G.J. 1989. Henge monuments: reappraisal or reductionism? *Proceedings of the Prehistoric Society* 55, 260-2

Barrett, J.C. 1994. *Fragments from Antiquity.* Oxford: Blackwell

Binford, L.R. & Sabloff, J.A. 1982. Paradigms, systematics and archaeology. *Journal of Anthropological Research* 38, 137-53

Burl, H.A.W. 1969. Henges: internal structures and regional groups. *Archaeological Journal* 126, 1-28

Christie, P. 1963. The Stonehenge Cursus. *Wiltshire Archaeological & Natural History Magazine* 58, 370-382

Clare, T. 1986. Towards a reappraisal of henge monuments. *Proceedings of the Prehistoric Society* 52, 281-316

Clark, J.G.D. 1936. The timber monument at Arminghall and its affinities. *Proceedings of the Prehistoric Society* 2, 1-51

Clarke, D.L. 1968. *Analytical Archaeology.* London: Methuen

Cowie, T. 1996. Torrs Warren Sands, Galloway: a report on archaeological and palaeoecological investigations undertaken in 1977 and 1979. *Transactions of the Dumfriesshire and Galloway Natural History and Antiquarian Society* 71, 11-105

Davidson, J.M. 1952. Report on some discoveries at Glenluce Sands, Wigtownshire. *Proceedings of the Society of Antiquaries of Scotland* 86, 43-69

Field, D. 2000. Archaeological investigations at Silbury Hill, Wiltshire. http://www.english-heritage.org.uk

Foucault, M. 1970. *The Order of Things: an archaeology of the human sciences.* London: Tavistock

Foucault, M. 1979. Cuvier's position in the history of biology. *Critique of Anthropology* 13/14, 125-30

Gibson, A. 1999. *The Walton Basin Project.* London: Council for British Archaeology Research Report 118

Greenwell, W. & Rolleston, G. 1877. *British Barrows.* Oxford: Clarendon Press

Harding, J. 1998. *Vale of York Neolithic Landscape Project. Interim Report 1998: Central Thornborough Henge.* Newcastle: Department of Archaeology

Hartwell, B. 1998. The Ballynahatty complex. In A. Gibson & D. Simpson (eds), *Prehistoric Ritual and Religion,* 32-44. London: Sutton

Kendrick, T.D. & Hawkes, C.F.C. 1932. *Archaeology in England and Wales, 1914-1931.* London: Methuen

McInnes, I.J. 1964. The Neolithic and Bronze Age pottery from Luce Sands, Wigtownshire. *Proceedings of the Society of Antiquaries of Scotland* 97, 40-81

Piggott, S. 1954. *The Neolithic Cultures of the British Isles.* Cambridge: Cambridge University Press

Piggott, S. & Piggott, C.M. 1939. Stone and earth circles of Dorset. *Antiquity* 13, 138-58

Pryor, F. 1984. Personalities of Britain: two examples of long-term regional contrast. *Scottish Archaeological Review* 3, 8-15

Renfrew, C. 1973. Monuments, mobilisation and social organisation in Neolithic Wessex. In C. Renfrew (ed.), *The Explanation of Culture Change*, 539-58. London: Duckworth

Smith, I.F. 1965. *Windmill Hill and Avebury*. Oxford: Clarendon Press

Smith, I.F. 1966. Windmill Hill and its implications. *Palaeohistoria* 12, 469-483

Smith, I.F. 1971. Causewayed enclosures. In D.D.A. Simpson (ed.), *Economy and Settlement in Neolithic and Early Bronze Age Britain and Europe*, 89-112. Leicester: Leicester University Press

Speak, S. & Burgess, C.B. 1999. Meldon Bridge: a centre of the third millennium BC in Peebleshire. *Proceedings of the Society of Antiquaries of Scotland* 129, 1-118

St. Joseph, J.K. 1978. Air reconnaissance: recent results 44. *Antiquity* 52, 47-50

Thomas, J.S. 2003. Materiality and traditions of practice in Neolithic south-west Scotland. In V. Cummings & C. Fowler (eds), *The Neolithic of the Irish Sea: Materiality and Traditions of Practice*. Oxford: Oxbow Books

Vatcher, F. 1960. Thornborough cursus, Yorks. *Yorkshire Archaeological Journal* 40, 169-82

Wainwright, G.J. 1971. The excavation of a late Neolithic enclosure at Marden, Wiltshire. *Antiquaries Journal* 51, 177-239

Wainwright, G.J. 1979. *Mount Pleasant, Dorset; excavations 1970-71*. London: Society of Antiquaries of London

Wainwright, G.J. & Longworth, I.H. 1971. *Durrington Walls: Excavations 1966-1968*. London: Society of Antiquaries of London

Whittle, A.W.R. 1997. *Sacred Mound, Holy Rings: Silbury Hill and the West Kennet Palisade Enclosures*. Oxford: Oxbow Books

Woodward, P.J., Davies, S.M. & Graham, A.H. 1984. Excavations on the Greyhound Yard Car Park, Dorchester, 1984. *Proceedings of the Dorset Natural History & Archaeological Society* 106, 99-106

Circles, Triangles, Squares and Hexagons

Humphrey Case

I first met Isobel in the late 1940s when she was Gordon Childe's secretary and pupil at the Institute of Archaeology, Regents Park, London, where I was among the students. Revered by us then for her knowledge of British Neolithic material culture, and for her authoritative interpretations of it in the manner of her mentor and for her generosity in sharing all this with us, we were not surprised to see her develop into a national supremo and international exponent - and not only of the Neolithic but also of the Bronze Age, especially concerning relations with the Netherlands (Smith 1961), in debate with the late Willem Glasbergen[1].

I salute her too in her role as a careful excavator and interpreter of other's work, and offer these notes to her, centred on the Wessex which she has illuminated so brightly, in reaffirmed respect and gratitude[2].

Circles and basic properties

Strong contrasts in the layout of circular monuments came to my attention, soon after leaving the Institute of Archaeology, through excavating two adjoining Bronze Age ditched and causewayed round barrows with stake- and postcircles at Poole, Dorset (Case 1952): *Barrow 1*, with a strongly symmetrical layout and regular circularity, which suggested some careful planning and execution, and *Barrow 2* which was contrastingly haphazard in layout (*loc. cit.*, figs. 2 and 4).

Dutch type 3 postcircles
Poole 1 has been seen as analogous to Dutch barrows with type 3 (single widely spaced) postcircles (*e.g.* Case 1952, 153; Glasbergen 1954 Part II, 152, 154, notes 163; Theunissen 1999, 65). Glasbergen published a corpus of 87 examples in the Netherlands (1954 part I, 13-42) and about a third as many more are now known in the Low Countries (Theunissen 1999, 67, table 3.4). These are by far the most numerous postcircle type in the north-east Netherlands, where they probably represent the greatest European concentration of such postcircle monuments. Unlike Poole 1 and 2 and most English examples, they are mostly barrows without quarry ditches.

No Late Neolithic type 3 postcircle barrows are known. They are mostly dated by radiocarbon to the Middle Bronze Age, from the second quarter of the 2nd millennium BC to the end of the millennium; but Toterfout - Halve Mijl 14 is Early Bronze Age, first quarter of the 2nd millennium (Theunissen 1999, Appendix 3.2). Poole 1 fits within this range (mid 2nd millennium: Gibson 1994, 202).

'Diameters' of type 3 postcircles range from about 6.75 to 16.3m, with one extreme measurement of 20m (Lohof 1991, fig. 86). Study of their geometrical layout has been based on Gerritsen's observations (first made in 1953: Gerritsen in van der Veen & Lanting 1989, 234) that their 'diameters' recurrently intersect at a central point (as seen for example here on Fig. 2: C Ring, The Sanctuary, Overton Hill, Avebury, Wiltshire). Lohof (1991, 167) found that such intersections were frequent: at 49 type 3 barrows out of a total sample of 72, with 15 more probable. The hypothetical method of layout (op. cit., especially 160-6) consisted in choosing a central point, lining up posts on either side to fix two diametrical points on the circuit, then proceeding around the centre lining up similar posts until the circuit was complete. Circular, oval, egg-shaped or irregular layouts could have been produced, depending on the distance chosen for each radial line. The spacing and

number of posts would be matters for judgement, with any excessive residual gap having to be filled with extra posts (e.g. op. cit., fig. 88f). Hardly surprisingly, the sightlines for the posts as constructed may show minor 'polygons of error' at the centre.

However, a quite significant minority of layouts with symmetry comparable to Poole 1 attract attention, with accurate or fairly accurate circles and evenly spaced 12, 16 or 18 post positions (e.g. 18 post: Hijken-'Hooghalen tumulus 1, period 3, van der Veen & Lanting 1989, fig. 4; Tumulus II, Mander, Tubbergen, Lohof 1991, fig. 87a). Possibly surveyors with exceptional spatial acuity could have laid them out by eye[3] using the method described; but I think it rather more likely that some geometrical expertise (or short cuts) were involved, of a kind which could have been readily acquired by those accustomed to working with circular layouts.

Accurate circles, as seen in the ditch at Poole 1, are achievable over the limited diameters involved in this contribution on unencumbered and fairly level ground by rotating a length of cord around a central peg[4]. In the course of fixing equidistant points on the circumference,

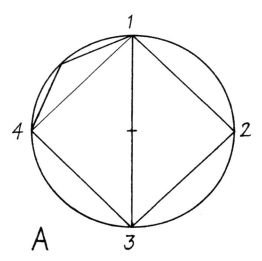
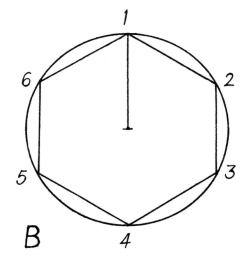

Fig. 1. A: Method 1. B : Method 2

only a little further experiment with cords, pegs, poles and sighting lines will reveal simple geometrical properties, which are repeatedly verifiable and open to rediscovery: first, that equal chords subtended by a diameter will produce two opposed isosceles triangles or a square of four equidistant points (Fig. 1, A: *Method 1*); and, secondly, that chords equal to the radius and projected serially around the circumference will produce a regular hexagon of six equidistant points (Fig. 1, B: *Method 2*). Isoceles triangles, squares or regular hexagons would thus establish accurate basic frameworks which could then be further subdivided equally by equidistant chords (e.g. Fig. 1, A) to produce regularly spaced layouts of 8, 16, 32... points in the case of Method 1 and 12, 24, 48... in the case of Method 2. (Some examples of such layouts are seen in Figs. 2 and 3). Alternatively, once the Method 1 or 2 frameworks were in place, satisfactorily regular intervening points could then be filled in partly or wholly *non-geometrically*, by eye and combinations of trial-and-error and sighting lines to produce numerical variations - say 2, 3, 4, 5... points per segment.

In order to estimate the frequency of regular layouts, Willem Glasbergen supplied me with plans at 1/40 scale of the majority of type 3 postcircles known in the Netherlands by 1953. Fifty-four plans were sufficiently complete for analysis, of which 11 appeared to have been laid out quite strictly by Methods 1 or 2 (Appendix 1)[5]. The majority of the remainder are treated here as more or less irregular layouts, mostly by the Gerritsen method.

British circular monuments

Conclusions from the Dutch evidence suggest that Methods 1 and 2 were applied to a significant minority of monuments, where special skills were available or considered appropriate for whatever reason. These conditions plainly applied to the Late Neolithic/Early Bronze Age English monuments of The Sanctuary, Overton Hill and Stonehenge. Before turning to them,

some selective comparisons with British monuments suggest that the late 3rd millennium BC Sarn-y-bryn-caled outer timber circle (Gibson 1994, 146-59) is an example of variation on Method 1 (20 posts: Appendix 2) and mid 2nd millennium Poole 1 (Case 1952) of variation on Method 2 (18 posts: Appendix 3). The inner and outer timber circles at Bleasdale, Lancashire (Varley 1938, pl. LXVI: respectively 11 and 36 posts; irregular layouts) are examples where the Gerritsen method appears to have been applied without any geometrical frame work, and with central 'polygons of error'; and the temporary inner circle of the Beaker-period outer stake settings at Amesbury 71, Wiltshire (Christie 1967, fig. 2, 341-2) seems similar.

The Sanctuary, Overton Hill, Avebury, Wiltshire
Excavated by Maud Cunnington (1931) and reassessed by Pollard (1992) and by Pitts (2001, following sample re-excavation), I see it as a monument essentially of concentric rings of freestanding posts and stones, with four radial aisles, built by users of Grooved Ware and resorted to over a prolonged period in the 3rd millennium BC, with its final phase of veneration conspicuously represented by a Beaker-associated grave. I regard its survey by R.H. Cunnington as reliable and within the standards of other surveys accepted in this contribution[6].

All seven rings (A - G) appear accurate or reasonably accurate circles, but the stones and posts of the two outer ones (A and B) are irregularly spaced. The outermost features to show regular spacing are the *C ring* posts. To achieve their 16 point Method 1 layout (Fig. 2: Appendix 4) would have required free space within their circumference, and I suggest that, apart possibly from a central peg, the C ring posts were the earliest features to be planned and built and were intended to enclose an *inner precinct* and establish the aisles as *internal* channels of communication, with an ambulatory inside their circumference.

Next in the interior would have come the *D* and then *E rings*, respectively Method 2 and

C RING POSTS

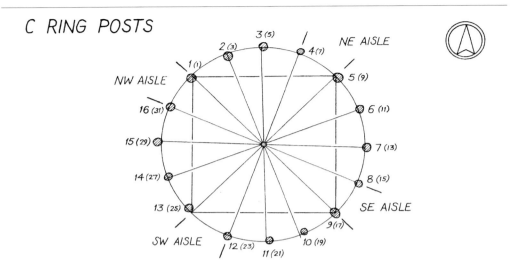

D RING POSTS

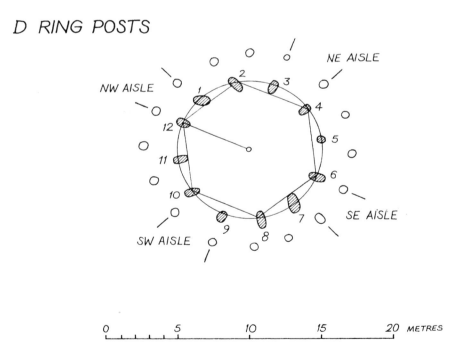

Fig. 2. The Sanctuary, Overton Hill: diagram settings, adapted from Cunnington 1931. *Above*: C Ring posts. *Below*: D Ring posts

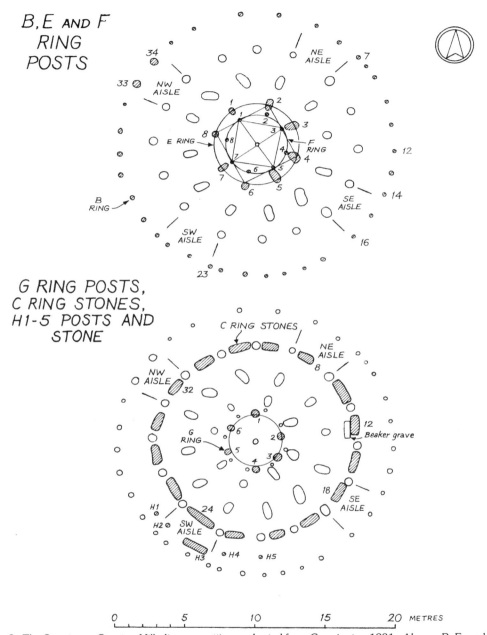

Fig. 3. The Sanctuary, Overton Hill: diagram settings, adapted from Cunnington 1931. *Above*: B, E, and F Ring posts. *Below*: G Ring posts, C Ring stones, and H 1 - 5 stone and posts

Method 1 layouts (Figs 2 and 3: Appendix 4), confirming the aisles and ambulatory and intended as the foci for *formal* ritual activity, with posts repeatedly renewed during the life of the site and with the densest deposits of material culture. Finally would have come the Method 1 *F ring* (Fig. 3: Appendix 4) respecting the aisles and forming an *innermost precinct* around the central post (itself on the site of the original surveying peg?) and with relatively little deposition of material culture.

Concurrently with this activity in the interior, would have come work on the *B ring posts* (Fig. 3: Appendix 4), a reasonably good circle more or less twice the diameter of the D ring, irregularly laid out by offsets from the C ring with the aid of such radial and diametrical sighting lines as would have been available before the E and F rings were in place. The B ring would have defined the *external access* to the monument from the northwest, the direction of Avebury and the headwaters of the Kennet. This would also have been the occasion (with relatively free access along the sighting lines) for the initial layout of the *A ring* (Cunnington 1931, pl. I; Appendix 4), if its original form was a timber circle, as the few recorded postholes might suggest. More or less twice the diameter of the B ring and similarly a reasonably good circle, it may have been planned by offsets from it and such diameters as survived. Space between rings A and B would have defined an *assembly point* outside the monument.

This sequence C - D - B - (A) - E - F can be seen as a single continuous purposefully planned layout, in which all major features were standing together in its completed state (Fig. 3). But I suggest that structural changes followed, with additions or modifications laid out by eye or by offsets from existing structures, restricting *internal access* (Fig. 3: Appendix 4) - with the posts of the *G ring* redefining the innermost space but blocking the northwest and southeast aisles; *H 1 - 5* forming a post and stone screen to the southwest; and the *C ring stones* blocking the gaps between its posts but leaving access from

the ambulatory to the interior at the northeast aisle. Finally the stones of the *A ring* emphasised the integrity of the Sanctuary with the main Avebury complex *via* the West Kennet Avenue.

The concluding stage of this earlier prehistoric sequence would have been the deposit of a little Beaker material culture in the eastern sector and the Beaker burial against the inner side of C ring stone 12 (Fig. 3. Pollard 1992, 217-8, 222).

Stonehenge: the Sarsen Circle and Trilithons; the Q and R hole complex

This account is based on the full description and appraisal by Cleal in Cleal *et al.* 1995, 188 - 206, and *op. cit.* fig. 79 and end-cover folder.

I assume the ground to have been unencumbered, with all earlier features levelled or removed before the planning of the Sarsen Circle and Trilithons began; and that a new axis had been determined and a new centre chosen (*op. cit.* fig. 79). Planning then proceeded with temporary pegs, sighting poles and cords. The intention of the surveyors was to plan a circle (radius about 15.44 m) of 30 equidistant points symmetrical to the new axis, but not blocking it at either end. The first step was to plan a second diameter at right angles, positioned stonehole 23 - stonehole 8, by Method 1 (Fig 4, A) and from those two points plan a regular hexagon by Method 2 (Fig. 4, A) of six points in positions of stoneholes 23 - 28 - 3 - 8 - 13 - and hypothetical position 18 in unexcavated ground west of Cutting C 17. Four equally spaced points within each segment would have been positioned by eye and sighting lines to produce 30 equidistant points.

Within this circle the five Trilithons would then have been planned symmetrically to the same axis, leaving unimpeded sighting lines to marker points 8, 13, 18 and 23 on the circumference of the Sarsen Circle. Trilithon uprights 53/54, 55?/56, 57/58 are on a circle concentric to that of the Sarsen Circle but half its radius (about 7.72m); and the axes of 52/51 and 59/60 are inclined tangentially more or less towards Sarsen Circle positions 29 and 2.

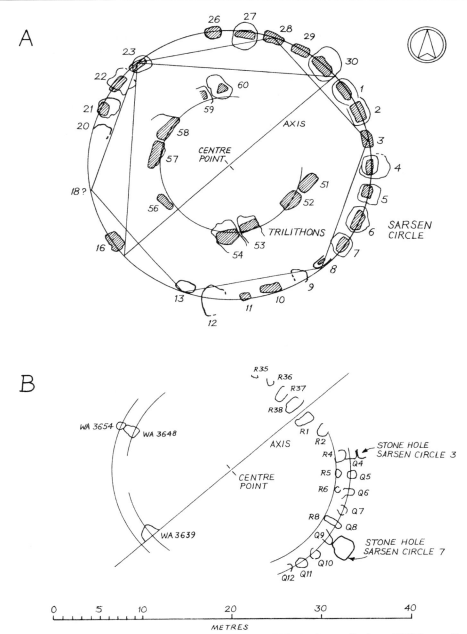

Fig. 4. Stonehenge: diagram settings, adapted from Cleal *et al.* 1995. A: Sarsen Circle and Trilithons. B: Q and R holes and some related features

In a similar way as at the Sanctuary or barrows such as Poole 1 (Appendix 3), this interpretation raises questions about the order of construction of the Sarsen Circle and Trilithons; and as to when the 'foreign stone' uprights presumably in the Q and R holes were erected and removed (Cleal in Cleal *et al.* 1995, 169-88).

Although the conception of the Sarsen Circle and Trilithons complex is likely to have been unitary, I take the surveying of the Circle to have come first. However, once the survey positions of both had been established and temporarily marked, with sighting lines remaining free, there seems no reason why both Circle and Trilithons may not have been erected in a single ongoing process. Of the 19 excavated stones of the Circle, nos 4, 5 and 22 had ramps or other features indicating erection from the outside, and erection from that direction seems likely for 29, 1, 2, 6, 7 and 12. Only 21 and possibly 27 seem likely to have been erected from the inside.

This would have left the inner space more or less free for erection of the Trilithons if their stones had been brought onto site at an early stage, and especially if the southern sector of the Circle was the last to be built[7]. Not surprisingly Trilithon uprights 51/52 and 53/54 seem to have been erected from the outside, and possibly also 57/58 and 60 - with 56 (Cleal in Cleal *et al.* 1995, 188) apparently erected from the northwest side.

However, the initial surveying process of the Sarsen Circle and Trilithons would not have been possible if there were uprights in the *Q and R hole complex* (described and assessed by Cleal in Cleal *et al.* 1995, 169-88). This could be taken to support my argument (Case 1997, 164-5, *contra* Cleal *et al.* 1995, e.g. 167) that these uprights postdated the Sarsen Circle and were part of a generally post-sarsen embellishment with 'foreign stones'. As Cleal emphasised (*op. cit.,* 188), more of the R hole setting may lie unexcavated to the northwest, which contributes to making its interpretation problematical; but, as it stands, the complex (Fig. 4 B) can be seen as two planned but uncompleted concentric circles

(radii about 13.2, 11.35m) sharing the same centre as the Sarsen Circle and Trilithons, comprised by: Q4-12 and R4-8 to the east, WA3654/WA3648 to the west, and WA3639 to the south on the main axis of the Sarsen constructions[8] and with a flattened segment to the north (R1, 2, 35-38) accurately straddling the same axis. The facts that this complex shows no independent geometrical layout, and no apparent siting except in relation to the Sarsen Circle and Trilithons, and that their respective diameters appear to show no clear ratios, would be consistent with my argument that the Q and R hole complex was fitted closely inside the Sarsen Circle and around the Trilithons when those two settings were nearly complete[9].

This interpretation has the merit of simplicity, but the conception of three major building operations overlapping with each other (competing?) in a constricted space may strain belief - especially for those whose views might be conditioned by chest-of-drawers sequences or the need for aesthetically tidy solutions. For such, the reported stratigraphical intersection of Q4 by Sarsen Circle stonehole 3 is crucial in providing evidence that a Q and R 'foreign stone' layout (Cleal in Cleal *et al.* 1995, sub-phase 3i) preceded the sarsen constructions in the interior of the monument. In which case, the Q and R layout would have been dismantled, its components stored around the monument, and the ground carefully levelled for surveying the Sarsen Circle and Trilithons. Presumably at least some of these early uprights would have been brought back for re-erection when the new layouts had been completed.

However, the crucial section which is taken to establish the priority of the Q and R complex appears ambiguous, as shown in the photograph reproduced as Cleal *et al.* 1995, fig. 92, with minimal overlap between Q4 and Sarsen Circle stonehole 3; and the scored (trowel?) lines which appear to mark it suggest that even very experienced excavators found it a problem difficult to resolve. In my view the problem continues.

Conclusions

I argue that surveyors of ritual monuments from the Late Neolithic to the Middle Bronze Age (3rd millennium BC to later 2nd) possessed at least some basic knowledge of plane geometry[10] and applied it selectively. But it may not be correct to speak of a continuing tradition, since such knowledge could have been repeatedly rediscovered by the experimentally minded.

Inferences about the layout of post circle monuments can throw light on the intentions of their builders. Among other things they lead to the conclusion that, in the case of barrows, the planning of the post circle and its erection or temporary marking were essential first or early steps in defining the precinct before the grave or any other feature was made (*e.g.* Poole 1, Appendix 3; Lohof 1991, 160-1 for Dutch monuments); and that the precinct was similarly defined at other circle monuments (*e.g.* The Sanctuary; Stonehenge Sarsen Circle).

The more or less perfect circle and accurate layouts appear together to have had a special role in this and other functions; and the occurrence of both *Method 1* and *2* at The Sanctuary and at Stonehenge may suggest that these methods had distinctive metaphysical significance, apart from convenience in surveying. The same may have been true of the numbers of uprights chosen.

Acknowledgements

I am grateful for exchanges of views with Mike Pitts, and especially for help with Dutch references from Zita van der Beek and Marcel Villingen; and to the late Willem Glasbergen for much information and also to the late H.H.Coghlan. Nick Griffiths drew the illustrations.

Notes

1. A mutual friend to whom I also now have the opportunity of repaying a long -standing debt (Appendix 1; also van der Veen & Lanting 1989, 193, 234).

2. Gratitude for being ever resourceful in information, opinion and advice; and not least for accepting my findings at the Neolithic site at Goodland, Co. Antrim (Case 1973), after they had been received with almost total disbelief at a meeting of the Prehistoric Society in the 1960s!

3. Giotto was reported to have been able to draw a perfect circle freehand without hesitation or correction (Vasari, *Lives of the Painters*). Apprentices at a steam locomotive workshop in the early 20th century were tested by being required to file rough castings by hand and without measurement to perfect cubes (information H.H. Coghlan).

4. A regular ellipse (forming the basis for oval layouts) can be similarly produced using two pegs, or one peg and an assistant: Case *et al.* 1964/5, 16-19, fig. 8.

5. A similar minority of regular layout seems represented at the more recently excavated Hijken -'Hooghalen' barrow cemetery, where tumulus 1, period 3 showed *Method 2* layout, and tumulus 6, periods 1 and 2, and tumulus 10, period 2, *irregular* layouts (van der Veen & Lanting 1989).

6. After sample re-excavation in 1999, Pitts concluded (2001, 8 and fig. 6) that the locations of the re-excavated post-pipes matched 'well' with Cunnington's larger scale survey (1931, plate II), although the post-excavation concrete marker posts showed variances up to 30cm. Keiller's scoffing accounts of R.H. Cunnington's survey equipment (Pitts 2001, 10; and more in Roberts 2002) may be attributable to vexation and jealousy. In contrast to Keiller, Cunnington as a Sapper officer was a trained and experienced surveyor and I think it unlikely that the regularities in layout in his plate II are post-excavation rationalisations on the drawing board - even though the excavations were filled in more or less immediately as they went along Pitts 2001, 18).

7. and perhaps never fully completed: Cleal in Cleal *et al.* 1995, 205.

8. which it seems reasonable to assume originally held the Altar Stone of Cosheston Beds sandstone: *op. cit.*, 188.

9. The direction of the ramp for Trilithon upright 56 suggests that the Altar Stone was in position before this upright was erected (*op. cit.*, 188). And the minimal reported intersection of Q4 by

the stonehole for Sarsen Circle upright 3 (*op. cit.*, 183, figs. 92 & 140) and the close proximity of Q9 and Sarsen Circle 7 suggest that the diggers of one setting were well aware of the other.

10. Knowledge which may well have dated from the earlier Neolithic in view of the recurrence of right angles at Cursus monuments.

APPENDICES 1- 4

Appendix 1: Dutch postcircles
Regularly laid out examples from a sample of 54 type 3 postcircles in the Netherlands are listed within the following corpus entries in Glasbergen 1954 Part II, 26 - 42.

Method 1: Drenthe 4, 25, 26, North Brabant 9 (all 16 post positions); Drenthe 11 (14 + 2).

Method 2: Drenthe 50, 54 (not in corpus); Gelderland 4; North Brabant 4, 7, 8. (North Brabant 4 and 8: 12 post positions; remainder 18 positions).

In addition: The layouts of North Brabant 16 (10 post positions) and possibly North Brabant 15 appear based on a regular pentagon, a figure somewhat more difficult to achieve on the ground. The rest of the sample of 54 show *irregular layouts* with numbers of posts ranging from 5 to 25, with the greatest frequencies ranging between 5 and 11, and 13 and 15.

Appendix 2: Sarn-y-bryn-caled outer timber circle
Sarn-y-bryn-caled, Welshpool, Powys: outer timber circle: 20 posts (Gibson 1994, figs. 5 & 9). *Method 1* layout. Taking the secondary Food Vessel to mark the centre point and posts 9-19 as both the diametrical axis (about 18.06m) and the axis of symmetry for the inner circle and two-poster, and entrance posthole 14 as the apex of the included isosceles triangle, then posts 8, 10-13, 15-19 and 20 were accurately filled in by eye and 1-7 somewhat less so - presumably by sighting lines from the western and southern sectors. Lohof (1991, 166) noted similar assymetrical irregularity in Bronze Age type 3 postcircles in the Netherlands.

Appendix 3: Poole 1
Poole 1, Dorset : postcircle (18 point layout), stakecircle, barrow ditch (Case 1952, fig. 2). *Method 2* layout. Take the centre point as that of the accurately dug ditch circle, diameter about 10.76 m,

and posthole 9 - the causeway centre point as the diametrical axis of the postcircle (diameter about 8.24 metres); then postholes 12, 16, 3 and destroyed posthole 6 were points on the included hexagon, with the remaining positions on the circumference filled in by sighting lines and by eye, and the positions of the surviving points of the inner stakecircle (diameter about 3.4m) 34-37, 39-42 and 44 similarly projected by sighting lines. Plainly the positions of both postcircle and stakecircle had been surveyed and marked before the grave, turf mound, gravel casing and ditch had been dug. Lohof (1991, 160-1) argued similarly for Dutch barrows.

Appendix 4: The Sanctuary, Overton Hill
C   *Ring postcircle* (Fig. 2, with posts numbered 1 to 16 and Cunnington's stone-and-post numbers in brackets): *Method 1*, diameter about 14.14m, 16 posts. Primary diametrical axis posts 1-9 spanning northwest - southeast aisles; secondary axis post 5 - centre point - 13 slightly skewed, spanning northeast - southwest aisles. Remaining positions filled in by chord bisection and sighting lines.

D   *Ring postcircle* (Fig. 2): *Method 2*, diameter about 10m, 12 posts. Primary radius for hexagon 12, 2, 4, 6, 8, 10 taken to be centre point - 12, and remaining positions fitted in as for C Ring and adjusted for aisles.

B   *Ring postcircle* (Fig. 3, after Cunnington 1931, pl. II; according to Pitts 2001, these points mark the positions of the posts themselves not the holes which contained them). 34 posts: circular layout by offset from C and from numerous radii available if E, F, and G Rings not yet in position. Diameter about 19.8-20m. Post spacing irregular: 7, 14, 16, and 23 appear conformable to aisle alignments, but others impede northeast, southeast, and southwest aisles. Posts 33 and 34 mark the external entrance.

A   *Ring Circle posts* (hypothetical: Cunnington 1931, 305 and pl. I). Laid out by offset from B Ring and available radii. At least one radius (to posthole 7a, about 19.5m) would appear to have remained unobstructed.

E   *Ring postcircle* (Fig. 3). *Method 1*, diameter about 6.1m, 8 posts. Primary and secondary axes: 8 - centre point - 4; 2 - centre point - 6; both continuing aisle alignments. Remaining posts fitted in by eye, and adjusted for aisle alignments.

F   *Ring postcircle* (Fig. 3; like the B Ring these appear to mark posts rather postholes). *Method 1*, diameter about 4.3m, 8 posts. Axes: 1 - centre point - 5; 3 - centre point - 7; both continuing aisle alignments. Remaining positions adjusted as in E Ring.

G   *Ring posts* (Fig. 3). 6 posts fitted in by eye between superseded(?) F Ring posts, with 1 and 2 and 4 and 5 respecting northeast and southwest aisles, but 3 and 6 blocking the northwest and southeast aisles.

H   *1 - 5* (Fig. 3). Laid out by eye between rings C and B, a screen of four posts and a stone upright impeding the southwest aisle.

C   *Ring stones* (Fig. 3; plotted as in Cunnington 1931, pl. II; cf. Pitts 2001 for accuracy of shapes). 16 stones fitted by eye between C Ring posts, impeding all the aisles. If stonehole 8, as recorded by Cunnington, corresponded more or less to the shape of the stone above ground, then the northeast aisle was the least impeded.

A   *Ring stones* (Cunnington 1931, pl. I). 42 stones on site of hypothetical A Ring posts (see above), with northwest extension joining the West Kennet Avenue.

Bibliography

Case, H.J. 1952. The Excavation of Two Round Barrows at Poole, Dorset. *Proceedings of the Prehistoric Society* 18, 148-55

Case, H.J. 1973. A Ritual Site in North-East Ireland. In G. Daniel & P.J. Kjærum (eds), *Megalithic Graves and Ritual: Papers at the III Atlantic Colloquim, Moesgard 1969*, 173-96. Copenhagen: Jutland Archaeological Society

Case H.J. 1997. Stonehenge Revisited. *Wiltshire Archaeological & Natural History Magazine* 90, 161-8

Case H.J., Bayne, N., Steele, S., Avery, G. & Sutermeister, H., 1964/5. Excavations at City Farm, Hanborough, Oxon. *Oxoniensia* 29/30, 1-98

Cleal, R.M.J., Walker, K.E. & Montague, R. 1995. *Stonehenge in its landscape: Twentieth-century excavations*. London: English Heritage

Christie, P.M. 1967. A Barrow-Cemetery of the Second Millennium B.C. in Wiltshire, England. *Proceedings of the Prehistoric Society* 33, 336-66

Cunnington, M.E. 1931. The 'Sanctuary' on Overton Hill, near Avebury. *Wiltshire Archaeological & Natural History Magazine* 45, 300-35

Gibson, A. 1994. Excavations at the Sarn-y-bryncaled Cursus Complex, Welshpool, Powys, and the timber circles of Great Britain and Ireland. *Proceedings of the Prehistoric Society* 60, 143-223

Glasbergen, W. 1954. *Barrow Excavations in the Eight Beatitudes: The Bronze Age Cemetery between Toterfout & Halve Mijl, North Brabant. I: The Excavations. II: The Implications*. Groningen: Wolters

Lohof, E. 1991. *Grafritueel en sociale verandering in de bronstijd van Noordoost - Nederland*. PhD thesis: University of Amsterdam

Pitts, M. 2001. Excavating the Sanctuary: New Investigations on Overton Hill, Avebury. *Wiltshire Archaeological & Natural History Magazine* 58, 1-23

Pollard, J. 1992. The Sanctuary, Overton Hill, Wiltshire: A Re-examination. *Proceedings of the Prehistoric Society* 58, 213-26

Roberts, J. 2002. 'That Terrible Woman': the Life, Work and Legacy of Maud Cunnington. *Wiltshire Archaeological & Natural History Magazine* 95, 46-62

Smith, I.F. 1961. An Essay towards the Reformation of the British Bronze Age. *Helinium* 1, 97-118

Theunissen, L. 1999. Midden- bronstijdsamenlevingen in het zuiden van de Lage Landen. Een evaluatie van het begrip 'Hilversum - cultuur'. Leiden: Liesbeth Theunissen

Veen, M. van der & Lanting, J.N. 1989. A group of tumuli on the 'Hooghalen' estate near Hijken (municipality of Beilen, province of Drenthe, the Netherlands), *Palaeohistoria* 31, 191-234

Varley, W.J. 1938. The Bleasdale Circle. *Antiquaries Journal* 18, 154-71

Dating Avebury

Joshua Pollard & Rosamund M. J. Cleal

The chronology of the Avebury henge remains problematic (Pitts 2001a, 278-80), not least because the monument is a complex construction, with two phases of earthwork and various internal and external megalithic settings of different scale and format (Smith 1965). In *Windmill Hill and Avebury*, Isobel Smith was the first scholar seriously to address the question of the monument's date and chronological position to other constructions in the region, here utilising ceramic sequences and Avebury's physical relationship, via the West Kennet Avenue, to the nearby site of the Sanctuary (Smith 1965, 244-9). The first move towards creating an absolute chronology came surprisingly late, with the radiocarbon programme undertaken by Pitts and Whittle in the 1980s (Pitts & Whittle 1992). This resulted in 13 dates, covering episodes of pre-henge activity, events at the henge itself, the outer stone circle and features on the West Kennet Avenue. However, while a significant step in its own right, comparison might be made with the data-base of 62 available dates from Stonehenge (Cleal *et al.* 1995). Clearly there is a need for further radiocarbon dating of both existing material from old excavations and newly acquired samples, and for the use of techniques such as Optically Stimulated Luminescence

(currently being applied to samples from the 2003 excavations at the Cove: Pollard 2003). To this end, here we report on four recently obtained radiocarbon dates from the henge ditch and stone 41 in the north-west sector of the outer circle. All samples were submitted to the University of Oxford Radiocarbon Accelerator Unit, and the results are presented in Table 1 and Figure 1.

The Ditch

All three dates are on shed red deer antler picks from the base and primary fills of the ditch

	Context	Sample	Result	Calibrated age range (cal BC) 68.2% probability	Calibrated age range (cal BC) 95.4% probability
Ditch					
OxA-12555	Base of ditch. Gray 136	Red deer antler	4036±34	2620-2610, 2580-2490	2830-2820, 2660-2640, 2630-2460
OxA-12556	Base of ditch. Gray 136	Red deer antler	4043±34	2620-2490	2840-2810, 2670-2640, 2630-2460
OxA-12557	Primary fill. Gray 234	Red deer antler	4038±34	2620-2610, 2590-2490	2840-2810, 2670-2640, 2630-2460
Outer Circle					
OxA-10109	Stone-hole 41	Human skull	3535±50	1940-1770	2020-1990, 1980-1730, 1710-1690

Table 1. Radiocarbon results. Calibration using OxCal v.3.5 (Bronk Ramsey 2000)

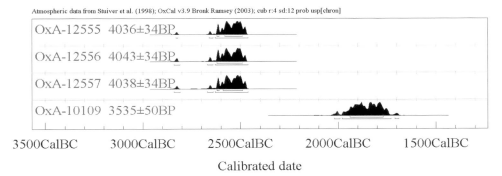

Fig. 1. Calibrated radiocarbon dates from the ditch and stone-hole 41

excavated by Harold St. Gray between 1908-22 (Gray 1935). OxA-12555 and 12556 are from a single antler recovered from Gray's Cutting I, in the south-west sector; while OxA-12557 is on an antler from low in the chalk rubble primary fills of Cutting IX, the eastern ditch terminal flanking the southern entrance (Fig. 2). Attempts at obtaining two additional dates from a third antler (Gray 90, also from the base of the ditch in Cutting I) have so far failed to produce consistent results (Tom Higham pers. comm.).

OxA-12555, 12556 and 12557 are remarkably consistent, and show no difference in result between antler found on the base of the ditch and low in the primary chalk rubble, as might be anticipated given the rapid formation of the initial ditch fills. The overall calibrated range spans 2840-2460 cal BC, but is weighted towards the 26th century BC. This must be taken as the date range in which the ditch and bank of the main henge earthwork were created. Earlier radiocarbon determinations would not contradict this. Gray's antler '136', here used for OxA-12555 and 12556, had earlier provided a result of 4300±90 (HAR-10502: Pitts & Whittle 1992), giving a calibrated age range at 95.4% probability of 3350-2600 cal BC, and therefore just overlapping the new determinations at the upper end of the calibrated range. In addition, there is a date of 2920-2490 cal BC (HAR-10326: Pitts & Whittle 1992) on antler from the

outermost portion of the bank of the henge in the north-west sector, excavated by Keiller in 1937.

Stone-hole 41

OxA-10109 (3535±50 BP) is on a fragment of human skull found in the basal packing of stone-hole 41 of the outer circle during Keiller's excavations of 1937 (Smith 1965, 226-7). This gives a calibrated range of 2020-1990, 1980-1730, 1710-1690 BC at 95.4% probability, placing it firmly within the Early Bronze Age. This is, in fact, the second date from stone-hole 41: an earlier determination on charcoal yielding a result of 2890-2470 cal BC at 95.4% probability (HAR-10062: Pitts & Whittle 1992). That the dates do not overlap is obviously problematic, though the charcoal from the latter could easily be derived or from old wood, and is therefore the least reliable of the two.

A further complication is provided by the unusual character of the fills in this stone-hole. The stone had been toppled and broken before 1720, and only the stump remained, not *in situ*, at the time of Keiller's excavations in 1937. In Keiller's typescript notes in the archive (Alexander Keiller Museum Accession No. 78510518) stone 41 is recorded as stone 6, which was largely covered by the field boundary which, before Keiller's work, ran along beside the line of the stones in this part of the Outer Circle. It

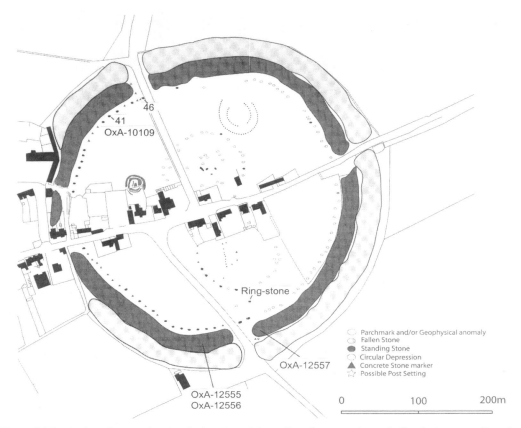

Figure 2. The Avebury henge, showing the location of the radiocarbon samples and other features mentioned in the text (base map produced by Mark Gillings)

is worth quoting Keiller's account in full as the setting for this stone was an unusual one:

> The stone-hole was again [i.e. like its neighbour stone 42] shallow, and although only two packing stones appeared at the level of the fallen base of the stone, a large quantity was found in the disturbed filling. On these being removed, a level surface of chalk was disclosed, the depth of which, below chalk level, was 1 ft [0.3m]. Upon this the stone had stood. This chalk, however, was found to have been artificially packed into position, and below this again further sarsens were found, all set on end, and apparently

forming supporting stones for the packed chalk platform [Fig. 3]. In this filling was found a quantity of variegated animal bones, a serrated flint flake, and some samples of charcoal, as well as decorticated pyrites. Actually on the bottom of what may be termed 'the lower stone-hole' were found two sherds of late Early Bronze Age pottery. The clay of this ware was of beaker type and the form flat-bottomed with a slight protuberant ridge squeezed out from the base, from which both sherds had been broken.

The only possible explanation for the curious formation of this stone-hole is that it was

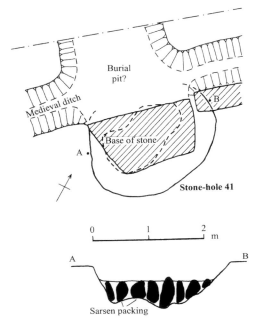

Figure 3. Plan and section of stone-hole 41 (taken from Keiller archive)

originally excavated to take a stone not only with a pointed base but which it was intended to 'insert' at a greater depth in the chalk than was feasible in the case of no. 6.

It may be worth noting that such a stone-hole would have fitted closely stone 7 [40] and one is tempted to wonder whether Stone-hole 6 [41] had not been originally prepared for that stone, which, however, through some confusion, had been erected in the stone-hole made 38.1 ft [11.6m] to the west, necessitating the alterations to stone-hole 6 in order to take a flat-bottomed, considerably shorter, megalith which may possibly have been originally intended to stand where stone 7 was actually erected.

In addition to this description is a listing of finds from stone-holes in the north-western sector (AKM 78510517) in which stone-hole 6 is listed in two parts: 'upper levels', which are noted as producing '5 sherds of late R.B. ware*',

'fragments of pig and ox* ('*presence probably due to late introduction during disturbance') and '2 flakes [flint]'. The 'lower levels' are noted as producing '2 sherds from E.B.A. vessel' , '2 pieces human skull, 1 worked cylindrical piece of bone, 1 worked [flint] nodule, 1 serrated [flint] flake, 1 [flint flake]' and 'charcoal from bottom of stonehole' (Figs 4 & 5).

Superficially the omission of the skull and bone object (which has now been identified as probably of antler; see Appendix 1 below for description and discussion of the group) from Keiller's description might seem to cast doubt on the reality of their association with the stone-hole, but an appreciation of Keiller's methods allows some confidence to be felt in the attribution. Keiller's method of composing his reports on the cuttings was to dictate, often late at night, a narrative account of the excavation, in which details were often left blank to be added later (and for some reports annotated drafts exist in which details have been added in manuscript). Additionally, Keiller on the whole appears to have paid more personal attention to the physical recording of features, and particularly to measurement and surveying, than to finds, although at the same time he appears to have ensured that his assistants were scrupulous in compiling full lists and catalogues of excavated material. In this light, the attribution of both the skull and the antler object, as well as the pottery, to the lower stone-hole seem compelling: left out of the narrative account of the trench perhaps simply by an omission of memory, but carefully recorded in the finds list by context.

The stone-hole is, as the description above makes clear, difficult to interpret, and Isobel Smith made the quite reasonable assumption that the excavator's textual description should be given primacy and so concluded that the bone object may have been from a disturbed context and did not illustrate it. Here we have concluded that in the case of objects the evidence of the finds catalogue should be allowed primacy. This leads to the further conclusion, given the date of the skull fragments, that although those, the

Fig. 4. The 'token' assemblage of pottery, antler object and skull fragments from stone-hole 41 (photo: David Wheatley)

lower stone-hole and been sealed beneath the newly erected or re-erected stone no earlier than the early centuries of the 2nd millennium BC.

In summary, although the collection of pot, antler object and human bone is not a primary association as a group, a reasonable interpretation would be that at the time when, perhaps because of a fall, stone 41 was re-erected, a small number of fragmentary objects were chosen from what appears to have been a disturbed Beaker-associated grave and placed beneath the re-erected stone as a 'token' burial. Perhaps this was done because the grave from which they originated had been deliberately placed close to the stone, although they could equally have been brought into the henge from a burial elsewhere. Because of the date from the skull fragments it is clear that the disturbed grave had been dug early in the 2nd millennium BC and although this date can only give a *terminus post quem* for the activity of stone raising, it seems very unlikely – given the general history of stone monuments in this country and the lack of any evidence to the contrary – that this could be later than the Early Bronze Age.

Discussion

The new dates from the ditch place the main henge earthwork at Avebury firmly within the mid 3rd millennium BC, and perhaps towards the end of the second quarter of that millennium. We know, however, that this replaced an earlier earthwork on much the same circuit (here styled Avebury 1). An earlier bank of chalk and turf, c.2.5m high and 5m wide, was observed during excavations by Henry Meux in 1894 and by Faith and Lance Vatcher at the Avebury School site in 1969 (Evans 1972, fig. 95; Pitts & Whittle 1992). Although it has not yet been established that this bank represents a complete circuit, its occurrence in two sectors seems to suggest that it does. The interval between the creation of Avebury 1 and the main earthwork visible today (Avebury 2) was sufficiently long for a distinct turfline to develop over the primary bank. The dating of the

bone object and the sherds were found not in their own primary context(s) (because they are fragmentary), they can only have entered the

Avebury 1 earthwork remains problematic. It would appear to seal a scatter of worked flint and earlier Neolithic bowl and Peterborough Ware pottery, pushing it into the late 4th millennium BC at the earliest (Smith 1965, 224: although insufficient detail exists relating to the distribution of this material, leaving the possibility that it lay under the Avebury 2 bank only). While currently unverifiable, it is tempting to place the Avebury 1 earthwork close to the beginning of the 3rd millennium BC, and therefore more or less contemporary with phase 1 of Stonehenge (Cleal et al. 1995). The matter may be resolved by a programme of coring through the henge bank, perhaps to take place in 2005, and the recovery of suitable samples from this (Mike Pitts pers. comm.).

In terms of the local sequence, the new dates for the Avebury 2 earthwork make it slightly later than the recently excavated enclosure in

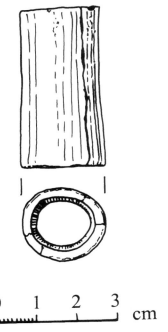

0   1   2   3   cm

Fig. 5. Antler object

Longstones Field, Beckhampton (Gillings et al. 2000, 2002), constructed around 2900-2600 cal BC, but perhaps marginally earlier than Silbury III at c.2500-2350 cal BC (Chadburn 2001), and the West Kennet palisade enclosures at c.2500-2200 cal BC (Whittle 1997). It is now possible to see the latest 4th millennium BC within the region (Whittle's phase D: 1993) as rather quiet in terms of monument construction, though not necessarily occupation. Avebury 1 and the Beckhampton enclosure, if placed in the first quarter of the 3rd millennium BC, then precede a period of very concentrated constructional activity in the middle of the millennium, beginning with Avebury 2 and the start of Silbury Hill, then the West Kennet palisades and perhaps Avebury avenues. There remain, however, many uncertainties. The West Kennet and Beckhampton Avenues are dated solely by their physical relationships to other sites and monuments, and no radiocarbon dates are available for the Sanctuary (Pitts 2001b). While it may be possible to envisage the Avebury 2 earthwork as contemporary with or slightly preceding the outer stone circle (perhaps best dated by HAR-10327; 2600-2000 cal BC: Pitts & Whittle 1992), our knowledge of the chronology of the inner stone settings at Avebury remains woefully inadequate. What we can say is that constructional activity at Avebury was protracted, spanning centuries rather than generations (see below).

Another implication of a mid 3rd millennium BC date for the Avebury 2 earthwork is that it can now be seen as broadly contemporary with the other Wessex 'henge enclosures' of Durrington Walls (Wainwright & Longworth 1971), Mount Pleasant (Wainwright 1979) and Marden (Wainwright 1971). While dates from the primary fills of these earthworks are few and old (in the sense of being obtained early in the history of radiocarbon dating), and further determinations on bone and antler would be desirable to refine the chronology of these sites, they do fall within a span of two or three centuries either side of 2500 BC (Harding 2003, table 1). There now exists the possibility that all four henge enclosures were constructed within the span of several generations of each other, with their appearance being stimulated by processes of inter-regional emulation and competition.

Of the fourth new Avebury date, while OxA-10109 cannot be used to date the original erection of stone 41, and by implication the construction of the outer circle, it does have some interesting implications. Not least, it provides further evidence of activity, including the reworking of stone settings, at Avebury during the established Early Bronze Age. Should this be seen as 'maintenance' – the re-setting of a fallen stone – or more 'meaningful' alteration? Whatever the case, it is certainly not unique. The socket for the Ring-Stone between the outer and southern inner circle also possessed a curious double base, inasmuch as the deep socket had been partially backfilled with sarsen and Lower Chalk and the stone set on this (Smith 1965, 202). Rather than a simple last-minute substitution of a smaller for a larger stone, this could be a much later re-setting, as with stone 41. Other stone settings may have been erected *de novo* during this period. This certainly seems to be the case with the 'stray' stone D within the southern inner circle. Sherds of Beaker were sealed beneath its clay packing, and Smith (1965, 227, 248) sees this as a late addition to the complex.

In only two other cases within the monument – stone 46 (the Swindon Stone) and its destroyed neighbour stone 45 – were Beaker sherds reported from features within the interior of the monument (Smith 1965, 226-7). Although these were from secondary contexts, at first sight they do at least seem suggestive of concentrated Beaker associated activity, but in both cases there is some doubt over the sherds. In the case of stone 46 the fabric of the rim is atypical for a Beaker, as it appears to include an organic additive, and the firing has left an unusually (for a Beaker) thin oxidised 'skin'. It seems at least possible that it is a later, possibly Anglo-Saxon,

sherd, which had become incorporated in the top of the prehistoric stone-hole filling (and there is one other occurrence of Anglo-Saxon pottery in this sector). In the case of the sherds from stone-hole 45, which is unquestionably disturbed, they are small and relatively undiagnostic; they could belong to either the Beaker tradition, or, conceivably be Grooved Ware or even Peterborough Ware. Although these therefore cast some doubt on the scale of Beaker associated activity within the north-west sector of the henge, there is no doubt about the activity at stone-hole 41 and there was in addition a single undisputed Beaker sherd, 'the only stray find of prehistoric pottery from the whole of the excavated areas within the Avebury monument' which was found in the field boundary bank near stone 46 (Smith 1965, 227, P347). It also seems more than coincidence that at two places within the henge – in the north-west Outer Circle between stones 41 and 46, and in the south-east sector in the area close to the Ring-Stone and stone-hole D – there should be evidence for: possible re-setting of stones (stone 41 and the Ring-Stone), Beaker pottery, and human remains (as, in addition to the skull fragments from stone-hole 41, a partially reconstructed skull and two rib fragments were found re-deposited in a medieval or post-medieval boundary ditch and could be Early Bronze Age). The south-east sector is also that part of the site with the only *in situ* burial from within the henge: that in the lower secondary silts of the ditch terminal at the southern entrance. Charcoal below this female skeleton was dated in the 1980s, giving a *terminus post quem* of 2350-1750 cal BC (HAR-10064; Pitts & Whittle 1992, 205). Beaker pottery and Collared Urn, as well as disarticulated bone, also occur at this relatively high level within the ditch (Gray 1935; Pollard & Reynolds 2002, 125-8).

That stones were being re-set and erected anew during the latest 3rd and early 2nd millennia BC at Avebury should occasion no surprise. Other stone structures were being constructed during this period, most notably the bluestone circle and horseshoe (phase 3v) and Z and Y Holes (phase 3vi) at Stonehenge (Cleal *et al.* 1995), assuming that the latter were intended to receive stones. Taking into account the evidence for further reworking of the stone settings and the scale of contemporary depositional activity discussed above, Avebury clearly continued to function as a major ceremonial focus in the region into the early 2nd millennium BC. It may perhaps be linked with a continuing tradition of associating burial with sarsen, as in the case of Beaker associated flat graves with sarsens, some of which are likely to be 2nd rather than 3rd millennium BC, as at Beckhampton (Cunnington 1926) and Winterbourne Monkton (Smith 1885, 85-6; Annable & Simpson 1964, 39); the primary, sarsen-associated Beaker period grave at West Overton G6b (Smith & Simpson 1966) may also be better seen as a flat grave rather than a barrow (*see* Cleal forthcoming for a discussion of these). As at Stonehenge, this occurred *alongside* the development of new traditions, and perhaps new ideologies, surrounding the commemoration of specific social personae, as exemplified by the appearance of adjacent round barrow cemeteries (Woodward & Woodward 1996).

Finally, in any consideration of the dating of Avebury it is worth passing comment on two radiocarbon dates which have so far excited no comment in the literature at all. Noted only as needing to be set aside as intrusive by Pitts and Whittle (1992), HAR-9696 (400 BC-150 cal AD) and HAR-10061 (770-390 cal BC), from, respectively charcoal in an ash layer in stone-hole 44 of the Outer Circle in the north-west sector, and charcoal from stakeholes on the edge of stone-hole 8 in the Outer Circle in the south-west sector, date to the Iron Age (or possibly to the Roman period in the case of HAR-9696). There is no context into which these may fitted in terms of 1st millennium BC activity around the henge, although early 1st millennium AD activity is suggested by the 'Aucissa' brooch and finds of Roman pottery from the henge ditch (Gray

1935, 156). The potential for Iron Age / Early Romano-British use of the henge to be investigated clearly exists, and has been highlighted in the *Avebury Research Agenda* (Corney & Walters 2001).

The new dates reported here go some way to further refining the chronology of prehistoric activity at the henge; and have raised interesting issues, particularly in relation to evidence for the reworking of megalithic settings. However, many questions remain, and future work must give priority to the dating of the Avebury 1 earthwork and, most critically, the complex internal stone settings. For this to happen new and reliable samples must be sought, and that will require additional excavation.

Acknowledgements

We wish to thank the SCARAB research centre at the University of Wales College, Newport for funding the new dates, and the Alexander Keiller Museum, Avebury, and the Wiltshire Heritage Museum, Devizes, for permission for samples to be taken. Stephanie Knight kindly provided the material identification of the antler object, and Dave Wheatley photographed the assemblage from stone-hole 41.

Appendix 1: finds from Stone-hole 41
[Figs. 4 & 5]

1. The antler object (1937 small find no. 'N.W. 1 Bone')
A slightly waisted hollow tube weighing 5.8g; it was initially identified as bone, but has since been suggested to be antler (Stephanie Knight pers. comm.). The length varies between 41-42mm; the external diameter is 20mm in one direction and 18mm in the other, giving a slightly oval cross-section. Much of the surface has been removed both on the interior and exterior, and both cut ends have also been smoothed. A high gloss varnish has been applied at some time to the exterior surface. The object appears to have been broken in two places and two broken

pieces re-joined to the remainder. There are no obvious signs of wear.

No direct parallels for this object in the Early Bronze Age have been identified in the literature, although bone toggles and rings are occasional accompaniments of Beaker and other Early Bronze Age burials. The objects with greatest similarity in terms of size are the dentated mounts (described in the literature as bone) from the Bush Barrow burial (Annable & Simpson 1964, 45, 99). These objects, which range around 40-50mm in overall length and around 20-25mm in width (measurements taken from drawings in Annable & Simpson 1964) are interpreted as having been slipped on to a wand or staff. In the case of the object from stone-hole 41 the interior diameter of 15mm in one direction and 12mm in the other does indicate that it could have fitted on a thin staff. Alternatively, its slightly waisted shape might suggest use as a bead, although the diameter seems large for that purpose. In this context, analogy might be sought among large bone beads, such as that associated with a Collared Urn from Llanabo, Gwynedd (Longworth 1984, pl. 89), and from early 2nd millennium BC levels within the ditch of the Mount Pleasant henge, Dorset (Wainwright 1979, 177, B2).

2. The pottery (1937 small find 'N.W. 4')

Two base angle sherds, now conjoined along what appears to be ancient break, were illustrated by Smith (1965, fig. 76, P348); both are plain and the base is slightly protruding. The fabric is soft (easily scratched with a fingernail), with a hackly fracture and contains moderate to dense grog (maximum dimension 7mm, most <3mm; sub-angular; it is difficult to establish frequency as it is difficult to distinguish from the matrix at X10 magnification, but is probably around 20-25% by surface area). Other non-plastics present are iron oxides as rare reddish lumps (<4mm maximum diameter; rounded) and as more frequent (perhaps c.3%) black and reddish grains (the former could also include glauconite which has a similar appearance);

there are also rare white brittle crystalline inclusions, one of 3mm maximum dimension, which may be calcite.

Both interior and exterior surfaces of the sherds are around Munsell 7.5 YR 6/6 (reddish yellow) and are in fair condition, showing little or no wear; the broken edges are fair, with only the sharp edges of the hackly fractures slightly worn.

Although undecorated this base fragment seems likely to belong to a slightly coarse Beaker. The fabric 'recipe' of mainly grog with some fe/gla and other non-additives is entirely typical, and although grog-tempered fabrics are found in both Late Neolithic Grooved Ware and non-Beaker Early Bronze Age ceramics (Collared Urns, etc) the former is usually less well-oxidised, and the latter often much coarser.

3. The skull fragments

Described simply as three small fragments of human skull by Smith (1965, 229). Two of the fragments are conjoined; it is not clear whether this was along an ancient or an excavation break. The conjoined fragments measure together approximately 60 x 60mm and the smaller 70 x 30mm; the latter has projecting pieces which are still quite sharp.

Summary

Although it is clear that the objects are not in their primary position, they would seem to have been placed in the stone-hole at no great time after either their original deposition or disturbance from their original place of deposition. The antler object is relatively fragile and unlikely to survive a long period of exposure. The sherds, in this soft fabric, would be expected to wear badly if subjected to trample or long exposure, and the condition of the skull fragments suggests a very short period of exposure.

Bibliography

Annable, F.K. & Simpson, D.D.A. 1964. *Guide Catalogue of the Neolithic and Bronze Age*

Collections in Devizes Museum. Devizes: WANHS

Bronk Ramsey, C. 2000. *OxCal (v3.5): a radiocarbon calibration and analysis programme*. Oxford: Oxford Radiocarbon Accelerator Unit

Chadburn, A. 2001. Progress at Silbury Hill. *Past* 39, 7-8

Cleal, R.M.J. Forthcoming. 'The small compass of a grave': Early Bronze Age burial in and around Avebury and the Marlborough Downs. In D. Field & G. Brown (eds), *The Avebury Landscape: the field archaeology of the Marlborough Downs*. Oxford: Oxbow Books/ English Heritage

Cleal, R., Walker, K. & Montague, R. 1995. *Stonehenge in its Landscape: Twentieth-century excavations*. London: English Heritage

Corney, M. & Walters, B. 2001. Romano-British. In A. Chadburn & M. Pomeroy-Kellinger (eds), *Archaeological Research Agenda for the Avebury World Heritage Site*, 68. Salisbury: AAHRG/Wessex Archaeology

Cunnington, M.E. 1926. Notes on recent prehistoric finds. *Wiltshire Archaeological & Natural History Magazine* 43, 395-400

Evans, J.G. 1972. *Land Snails in Archaeology*. London: Seminar Press

Gillings, M., Pollard, J. & Wheatley, D. 2000. The Beckhampton Avenue and a 'new' Neolithic enclosure near Avebury: an interim report on the 1999 excavations. *Wiltshire Archaeological & Natural History Magazine* 93, 1-8

Gillings, M., Pollard, J. & Wheatley, D. 2002. Excavations at the Beckhampton Enclosure, Avenue and Cove, Avebury: an interim report on the 2000 season. *Wiltshire Archaeological & Natural History Magazine* 95, 249-58

Gray, H.St.G. 1935. The Avebury excavations, 1908-1922. *Archaeologia* 84, 99-162

Harding, J. 2003. *Henge Monuments of the British Isles*. Stroud: Tempus

Longworth, I.H. 1984. *Collared Urns of the Bronze Age*. Cambridge: Cambridge University Press

Pitts, M. 2001a. *Hengeworld*. 2nd edition. London: Arrow Books

Pitts, M. 2001b. Excavating the Sanctuary: new investigations on Overton Hill, Avebury. *Wiltshire Archaeological & Natural History Magazine* 94, 1-23

Pitts, M. & Whittle, A. 1992. The development and date of Avebury. *Proceedings of the Prehistoric Society* 58, 203-12

Pollard, J. 2003. *Excavations at the Cove, Avebury, 2003: a preliminary report*. Unpublished report, University of Wales College, Newport

Pollard, J. & Reynolds, A. 1996. *Avebury: the biography of a landscape*. Stroud: Tempus

Smith, A.C. 1885. *A Guide to the British and Roman Antiquities of the North Wiltshire Downs*. Devizes: WANHS

Smith, I.F. 1965. *Windmill Hill and Avebury: excavations by Alexander Keiller, 1925-1939*. Oxford: Clarendon Press

Smith, I.F. & Simpson, D.D.A. 1966. Excavation of a round barrow on Overton Hill, north Wiltshire. *Proceedings of the Prehistoric Society* 32, 122-55

Wainwright, G.J. 1971. The excavation of a Late Neolithic enclosure at Marden, Wiltshire. *Antiquaries Journal* 51, 177-239

Wainwright, G.J. 1979. *Mount Pleasant, Dorset: excavations 1970-1971*. London: Society of Antiquaries of London

Wainwright, G.J. & Longworth, I.H. 1971. *Durrington Walls: excavations 1966-1968*. London: Society of Antiquaries of London

Whittle, A. 1993. The Neolithic of the Avebury area: sequence, environment, settlement and monuments. *Oxford Journal of Archaeology* 12, 29-53

Whittle, A. 1997. *Sacred Mound, Holy Rings. Silbury Hill and the West Kennet Palisade Enclosures: a Later Neolithic Complex in North Wiltshire*. Oxford: Oxbow Books

Woodward, A. & Woodward, P. 1996. The topography of some barrow cemeteries in Bronze Age Wessex. *Proceedings of the Prehistoric Society* 62, 275-91

East of Avebury: ancient fields in a local context

Peter Fowler

When Isobel Smith (1965) was writing of Windmill Hill, the ancient fields of her parish, in as much as they were known, were assumed to be of Early Iron Age or Romano-British date (VCH, 272-73). In the mid-1960s, Isobel herself participated as a site supervisor at the excavation of one site which, directed at answering questions about local ancient fields, provided key evidence for both revising the earlier part of that assumption while confirming the later one (Fowler 2000, xiii). Forty years on, we briefly reconsider these phenomena in the light of current perception, noting the revised chronology, now generally agreed, and looking more attentively at the morphology of field systems and their fields, and at the distribution of both. We look in particular at the pre-medieval fields on the west-facing slopes of the Marlborough Downs, west of the Ridgeway which itself forms the eastern boundary of the historic parish of Avebury.

The remains of what we now recognise as prehistoric fields were seen and mapped in the Avebury area by Smith (1885, Sections X and XI of the 'Great Map'), for example on Monkton and Abury (Avebury) Downs (see below for comment on both); though the whole of his discussion of 'lynchets' (1885, 26-27) is concerned not with the boundaries of early fields but with strip lynchets, here in use during the 2nd millennium AD even if their origins are earlier. The mid-20th century perception is conveniently summarised in VCH. One group of ancient fields (VCH, F. Field Systems, no. 15), 'surrounding Kennet Avenue', was tabulated as being entirely in Avebury parish, and four other groups (nos. 16-19) crossed parish boundaries from Avebury into the adjacent parishes of Bishops Cannings (no. 16: Horton Down), Cherhill (17: Cherhill Down-Knoll Down), West Overton (18: Overton Hill) and West Overton/Winterbourne Monkton (19: Avebury, Overton and Monkton Downs). Group 15 was deemed 'IAc or RB' but 16 was dismissed as 'medieval'; group 17 was dated as IAA and RB, 18 as IAA, and 19 as RB (for young readers, the 'c' and 'A' after the 'IA' refer to the then-current division of the Iron Age into A, B and C, respectively 'early', 'middle' and 'late', as stated but not explained in VCH, xviii: see Hawkes 1959).

Group 16 was of a 'very regular layout' (and implicitly demoted to 'medieval?' as a consequence). No associated evidence is noted of group 17, but both groups 18 and 19 were observed as 'cut across by the Ridgeway which could not then have been in use' (*sic* – see below). Of group 18 it was additionally noted that 'Some of the fields were planned to avoid the large bell-barrow Avebury 30', 'A magnificent example' with 'No record of excavation' (VCH, 208). It was also noted of group 19 that 'RB sherds have been found near the field system', no doubt a necessary record in Grinsellian mode but not necessarily of any chronological relevance whatsoever (but see below). Group 15 seems to have disappeared without further record and groups 16 and 17 require a separate paper. For reasons which become apparent below, we shall be looking in particular at groups 18 and 19, that is the continuous – as we now know – extent of pre-medieval fields stretching westwards off Overton Down across Avebury Down towards the henge and village.

The lynchets of so-called 'Celtic' fields supposedly of Iron Age date survived fragmentarily partly in grass on the west-facing slopes of the Marlborough Downs overlooking Avebury from the east. I began visiting the area regularly soon after VCH was published, and saw the field systems it tabulates just before they were flattened in the early 1960s as intensive arable farming extended from the permanent arable around Avebury itself up on to the hitherto grassy slopes. By the time I first flew over Avebury Down for archaeological air photographic purposes in the mid-1960s, earthwork remains had effectively disappeared but, in what is now a well-known paradox of crop-mark and soil-mark, in their destruction lay the recovery of their near-complete plan. Forty three years on from VCH 1957, thanks very much to the skills and kindness of what was still then the Royal Commission on the Historical Monuments of England, this author was able to publish at the very end of the 20th century two new authoritative maps showing the extent and much detail of the ancient fields east of Avebury (technically, east of northing 10 as far east as northing 16, and, from south to north, from grid

line 65 to 74: Fowler 2000, figs. 2.1, 15.3, (a) and (b); a simplified version of the map is in Fowler & Blackwell 2000, fig. 21). It may well be thought that there is little point in or need for authorial comment on such recent publications – though the maps are by no means identical - but, in particular, the relatively late arrival of fig. 15.3 in the development of Fowler 2000 meant that the privilege of including it was not complemented by appropriate discussion. This short essay recognises that deficiency with some brief comment in the light of the fieldwork and excavation on the adjacent Overton and Fyfield Downs, of relevant evidence from the Marlborough Downs in general (Gingell 1992, Brown *et al.* forthcoming), and of the recent discussion in the biography of the Avebury area (Pollard & Reynolds 2002).

VCH field group 18 equates with my groups 3 and, perhaps, 5, and VCH group 19 with my groups 1, 2, 4 and 6 (Fowler 2000, fig. 2.2). In both cases, I distinguished morphological and chronological distinctions within the VCH groups, based on the RCHME map and my own fieldwork and excavation. VCH group 18, Overton Hill, seems to refer principally to my group 3, almost entirely west of the Ridgeway. My group 5, immediately adjacent on the east and almost entirely within West Overton parish, I suggested was (early) Romano-British on the basis of the field system's relationship to the Roman road marking its southern edge and to two Romano-British settlements on its western (the 'Crawford complex') and eastern ('Headlands') edges. I noted that the system's axis was approximately 7 degrees west of north. Further, the system's fields are morphologically distinct, being long and rectangular (for details, here as elsewhere, see Fowler 2000 and related electronic archive with the excavation reports). At the system's northern end (my group 4), as VCH correctly notes of its group 18, the Ridgeway crosses it, so 'could not then have been in use' (the VCH shorthand seems to mean the opposite of what is stated). The Ridgeway did not exist on its present line, if at all, when my groups 5 and 4 were in use for arable, probably in the 1st and 2nd centuries AD.

VCH group 18 west of the Ridgeway is a distinct group, not only in relation to the Romano-British fields to its east but also in the wider context of ancient fields shown on figure 1 here. I recognised that by labelling it group 3 but that was merely because the fields were on the RCHME map; they lay outside the Overton/Fyfield study area that was then my concern and otherwise I barely noted them. The distinctive characteristic of the group is that it curves so markedly, from a SW/NE orientation at its northern end to a NW/SE orientation at its southern edge and indeed a W/E at its eastern edge if, as seems very likely, remnants of it cross under the Ridgeway to lie, invisibly, under 'Crawford's complex' and, visibly, north and south of it before being obliterated by the Romano-British cultivation of my group 5. This curvaceousness does not fit in at all with the three orientations I suggested for the ancient field systems at this south western corner of the Marlborough Downs as a whole (Fowler 2000, fig. 2.6); although it could fit in with all three (15½ degrees - ?early; 46 degrees - middle/late Bronze Age; 7 degrees - Romano-British). Perhaps it shows that too much stress on orientation can be misleading, since the shape of the system in this case is in large part – not entirely – topographically-influenced: it lies right on the corner of the downs and follows their contours around essentially from N/S to W/E.

Embedded in the system is the large surviving bell-barrow Avebury 30. I am not sure I would follow VCH in phrasing that relationship as 'avoidance' by the fields of the barrow; surely if, as seems likely, the barrow was already there when the field system was laid out, the fields 'respect' its presence. They also seem to respect most of the barrow group at the field system's south-western edge (my barrow group G), though it is not actually clear whether the barrows were there when the fields were laid out or whether the barrows had to be perched there, somewhat down-slope, because when a new cemetery came to be needed all the upper land was already in use. Personally, I favour the latter interpretation, not least because the barrow/fields relationship there seems to be so different from that with and around bell-barrow 30. In the latter case, regular blocks of fields on the north and south of the bell-barrow carefully acknowledge its existence at least, apparently using it as a marker with an axial boundary passing by on its north side roughly paralleled by similar axial boundaries c.110m distant to north and south. Indeed at the north, and very striking on air photographs with a vividness a map cannot convey, a neatly defined block of land, c.110m wide and c.245m long, is divided into five roughly equal fields some 50m wide. A similar block seems to lie on the south, and two further similar blocks adjacent to that just described lie further north. In other words, this is a field system with a strong internal structure, closely related to a pre-existing or contemporary funerary monument.

This structure runs right through the field system from the level of the system overall to individual field level. Immediately north of that third block on the north, for example, and some 665m north of bell-barrow 30, a single field approximately of the same size as those described (i.e. some 245m long by 50m wide) is itself subdivided into four roughly square plots. On balance, the most appropriate context for this system (my field group 3) would seem to be mid-2nd to mid-1st millennia BC, quite different from that immediately to its east (my group 5) but broadly contemporary with my group 6 across Overton Down only 1km to the east. Indeed, my groups 3 and 5 may well have been one field system before, after centuries of abandonment as arable, they were physically separated in the 1st century AD by the insertion of my group 5 over and between them.

VCH group 19, the main extent of ancient fields in Avebury parish, lies further north up the Ridgeway, embracing the whole of my groups 1 and 2 and parts of 4 and 6. It is possible, even probable, that the last, group 6 covering Overton

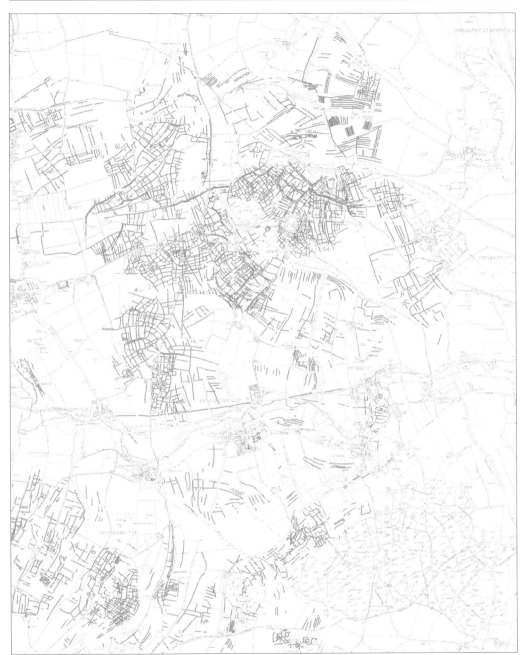

Fig. 1. Map of field systems in the Avebury area. (Reproduced by kind permission of Ordnance Survey © Crown Copyright NC/2004/31097)

Down, was eventually (by the late Bronze Age?) coterminous with groups 1 and 2 before being separated out by the insertion in the early centuries AD of group 4 (Fowler 2000, fig. 2.2). The important point here, however, is that our map (Fig. 1) shows that the relatively small area of fields depicted west of the Ridgeway and north of 'Green Street' (also labelled 'Herepath' as a misguided alternative) in Fowler 2000, figs. 2.1 and 2.6, is part of a much more extensive whole (as was apparent, though not commented on, in Fowler 2000, fig. 15.3 (a)). That map in fact extends further north, to northing 75, than our figure here which stops 2km further south; but the latter shows even more detail. We can see ancient fields typically high on Monkton Down, but of potentially considerable interest in hinting at both being on my '15½ degree axis', and therefore possibly 'early', and perhaps also earlier than a group of round barrows (my barrow group A). Fragmentary remains of these ancient fields descend westwards right off the downs and, as we can now see, close up against the eastern side of the village of Winterbourne Monkton itself. In this context, it is tempting to note an apparently analogous situation, though with even more fragmentary evidence, over the next 2km to the north towards Winterbourne Bassett where ancient fields also seem to have extended off the higher downs on to and across the flatter land of the Lower Chalk towards the Winterbourne stream. This is the important point, hinted at in earlier RCHM maps published in Fowler 2000, and here made explicit: that the ancient fields of Avebury were not limited to the higher ground on the east of the parish but, north of the henge and north of 'Green Street', occupied the lower, flatter land (almost) as far as the historical pattern of spring-line villages on the east bank of the Winterbourne.

They may even have occupied such land where the henge was subsequently built or occupied its interior after its delimitation. Six months after writing the previous paragraph, the author was privileged to hear a presentation by Martin Papworth (National Trust) about his geophysical survey in 2003 in the south-east and north-east quadrants of Avebury henge, and to receive a copy of his report (Papworth 2004). (Subsequent quotations in this paragraph are from that report. Numbers are those given to anomalies in that source. The following data are used with his permission; the comments are this author's.) In the context of an excavation proposal, resistivity and gradiometry were used primarily to locate and examine the nature of the sub-surface stones and stone-holes of the outer circle of now almost completely 'missing' mega-liths around the inner lip of the henge monement.

The survey additionally recorded 'Anomalies interpreted as... at least two phases of linear boundaries' (ibid., 2). Ten linear anomalies recorded in the NE quadrant are selected here as significant for present purposes (other linear anomalies there are ignored). Five linear anomalies were aligned NW-SE (nos. 70, 71, 72, 74, 75), four NE-SW (nos. 90-93) and one W-E (no. 76). They ranged from 10 to 70m long and 1 to 3-4m wide (though widths are only suggested in the text for three cases, nos. 90-92). Five are specifically suggested to be ditches (nos. 71-76) and the implication is that all are. Linear anomalies 71, 72 and 75 are roughly parallel with each other over a distance of some 130m and are respectively c.40m and c.60m apart. Anomaly 70 is one of the shortest lengths recorded (15m) and is only c.6m from anomaly 72 at its closest point but it could nevertheless be part of the same parallel land arrangement. It appears to cut circular feature 69, possibly a round barrow c.12 m in diameter. Linear anomalies 74 and 76 might also be part of the same arrangement but they are markedly more WNW-ESE in their alignment – hence Papworth's suggestion, presumably, that the system is of 'at least two phases'. Numbers 70, 72 and 74-76 are all overlain by a medieval boundary made up of linear anomalies 66-68.

A similar 'early' relationship with other structures is indicated at the north-eastern ends of the four NE-SW linear anomalies (nos. 90-93), fairly accurately at right angles to anomalies

70, 71, 72 and 75 but at an acute angle to numbers 74 and 76. This rectilinear relationship is best seen where the 70m long anomaly 71 crosses or is crossed at right angles by anomalies 92 and 93 c.20m apart. These NE-SW anomalies are also 'roughly parallel' over a distance of some 140m but, rather than lying beneath features, start close to, or even at (nos. 90, 91), the present inner lip of the henge ditch. The possibility that they may have been cut by that lip cannot be excluded, though presumably it is now some distance back from its original position. It is also conceivable that these linear features could be earlier than the stones: it is difficult to see how they could have been easily created once the stones were standing.

Papworth (2004, 18) suggested that linear anomalies 90-93 with 70-72 and 74-76 'may be evidence of field boundaries, possibly part of an early field system'. He concludes (ibid., 29):

A group of low resistance anomalies in the NE quadrant indicate by their common orientation that they may be part of an early allotment of land, perhaps part of a field system. The anomalies are aligned NW-SE and ignore the N-S alignments of the medieval banks and ditches... They are not visible on the ground and these anomalies are presumably ditches levelled by the medieval ploughing which is thought to have ceased within the henge within the later medieval period (Pollard and Reynolds 2002, 246). Traces of anomalies aligned NE-SW 90-93... suggest that the NE part of the henge was once divided into a rectilinear field system possibly prehistoric in origin.

Two points should nevertheless be noted: not a single example of an originally ditched prehistoric field was encountered during excavation of numerous field edges on Overton and Fyfield Downs (Fowler 2000); and the outlines of such fields depicted on the accompanying map here (Fig. 1) are almost exclusively derived from soil-marks of recently over-ploughed earthworks, not crop-marks of infilled ditches.

If the ditches within the NE quadrant of Avebury are indeed fragments of an ancient field system or systems, the fields would appear to have been of the order of 40-50m long and c.25-35m wide, assuming they were roughly rectangular as well as parallel. This is very similar to the dimensions of many fields on the downs to the east (Fig. 1) but a more specific analogy is provided by small clumps of small fields south of Green Street, 2km east of Avebury (SU 119703), and just south of the Avebury parish boundary with Winterbourne Monkton (SU 120714; both on Fowler 2000, fig. 2.1). An even more local context off the downs on the Lower Chalk plateau on which Avebury itself lies is provided by two further clusters of small fields. One is 2km north-east of Avebury at SU 115718 where there are both small enclosures roughly 40m square and ones very much of the size of the henge's examples at c.80 x 50m (Fowler 2000, fig. 2.1). The other is a kilometre west of those, immediately east of Winterbourne Monkton village at SU 105719 (Fig. 1; Fowler 2000, fig. 15.3(a) but not fig. 2.1).

Both clusters are aligned NW/SE-NE/SW like those inside the henge in general but with axes closer to the cardinal points. In that respect, these two particular clusters north and north east of Avebury are closer to the 15° (west of True North), and 'earliest', of the three alignments identified among the ancient field systems of the downs, while the putative field system inside the henge is closer to the commoner 46° (west of True North) axis. Accepting the existence of such axial distinctions and their possible chronological significance, it has been tentatively suggested that the earliest alignment may relate to a late Neolithic/EBA horizon and the main, truly NW-SE orientation to an MBA one (Fowler 2000, 25-27). Just west of Avebury, of course, across the Winterbourne, two main phases of ard-marks, and therefore in some sense of fields, were evidenced both before the construction of the South Street long barrow (c.3500-3000BC?), and therefore before the henge, and after the infilling of the barrow's southern ditch (c.2000BC?) (Ashbee *et al.* 1979).

This new evidence of a possible field system from within the henge emerges, then, in a reasonably documented local context of location, morphology and, at least relative, chronology. Three hypotheses arise from this re-enforcement of the observation *above* that the ancient fields of Avebury parish, well-known on the downs, also occupied the lower, flatter land (almost) as far as the historical pattern of spring-line villages on the east bank of the Winterbourne. In the first place, looking at the overall distribution on Fig. 1, and on the even more extensive coverage on Fowler 2000, fig. 15.3 (a) and (b), in general and largely irrespective of topography (and ignoring known or assumed medieval remains as on Fyfield and Wick Downs), the pattern of field systems does indeed seem to follow something akin to the three axial arrangements proposed in Fowler 2000, fig. 2.6. There is nothing new to say about the '7 degree axis', since no new examples are obvious: perhaps the ploughing up of new land in the 1st century AD was not as widespread on these Downs as I suggested might be the case (Fowler 2000, *passim*). In contrast, hints exist in the landscape as mapped, notably in peripheral areas as on Monkton Down and Manton Down (on the basis of which the idea was originally proposed), that fragments of the earliest field systems survive within, but particularly where not too affected by, later (but still prehistoric) land arrangements. Such appear to relate to axes some 15 degree west of True North but in any case nothing like as accentuated as the c.46 degree west of True North of the large extent of prehistoric field systems. This latter axis, impressive enough stretched across Overton and Fyfield Downs, can now be seen to extend right across at least some 40 sq. km of this south western corner of the Marlborough Downs, from Preshute Down in the north east to All Cannings Down in the south west (Fowler 2000, fig. 15.3). Maybe the arrangement is merely or primarily pragmatic, exposing as much of the field systems

to as much sun as possible; but even so, such consistency, even if it is rough and ready rather than measured with precision, commands respect now and implies then (?mid-2nd millennium BC onwards) if not political cohesion, at least some sort of unanimity of need.

A second hypothesis balances my bias so far in describing the phenomenon of ancient fields in and around Avebury parish as 'descending' on to the flatter land between downs and Winterbourne. Such a viewpoint reflects too many years up on the downs looking down into the valley. It may well have been in fact that, at least north of Avebury, in what are now the Winterbournes of Monkton and Basset, the earliest fields, and even their successors, were laid out from the stream eastwards towards the foot of the downs. Perhaps it was only then, all the lower land farmed and a need for agricultural produce still unfulfilled, that a new landscape was created as the local uplands were brought into cultivation. Such a model could well be a long time in developing (Smith 1984), even one to two millennia if we take into account the incontrovertible evidence for cultivation before the henge's bank and at South Street, before and after the construction of the long barrow (Ashbee *et al.* 1979). Probably the 'Beaker' cultivation over the top of the filled-in South Street long barrow ditch is the most relevant for present purposes, for a date around 2000BC could well be the sort of time when agricultural expansion across the Lower Chalk towards the downs might have begun. The Beaker burials on Overton Down (Site OD XI in Fowler 2000), almost certainly preceding fields, may well be relevant too.

My third hypothesis hinges around the caveat above expressed in the phrase 'north of the henge'. It is entered because, on present evidence (and discounting VCH's ancient field group 15 which is not recorded by RCHM) no traces of ancient fields as shown on Fig. 1 (and on Fowler 2000, fig. 15.3 (a)) north of Avebury lie to the south between the henge and the River

Kennet. The 'blank' area is quite striking, for across the Kennet the ground rises again to West and East Kennet long barrows which seem to mark its southern boundary (I stress on present air photographic evidence). South, west and east of them are large tracts of ancient fields, strikingly so, despite a heavy battering from modern agriculture, on All Cannings Down, Thorn Hill and Boreham Down. This distribution prompts the tentative thought that, possibly, some acknowledgement in the early centuries of the 2nd millennium BC was made by post-Neolithic farmers of former land-use in and around the 'sacred' area of the West Kennet Avenue and Silbury Hill. In the context of such an hypothesis, we can note that, in terms of evidence detectable by air photography, the next intrusion into this 'blank' landscape was not until the linear Romano-British settlement across the Winterbourne from Silbury Hill occupied a site beside the stream comparable to that, not of some other contemporary downland settlements in the area, but of the historic villages of the Winterbourne and Kennet valleys. The pattern of their distribution cries out for a village in that place between Avebury and West Kennet. It was there in the early centuries AD: what happened to it?

The ancient fields of Avebury and area are now, probably to a large extent, discovered and mapped. Doubtless further fragments of them will emerge and disappear as further air photography occurs but perhaps the basic distribution as described here will not change much. We may have recorded but we still have nearly everything to learn about chronology. This brief essay is itself based on an hypothesis about dating, itself based on a very small excavated sample of the whole (Gingell 1992, Fowler 2000). We simply do not know whether cultivation between Avebury and the scarp-foot to the east continued during the 1st millennia BC and AD, but it seems likely during at least the latter and was certainly so during the 2nd millennium AD. At the moment, however, it seems that, whatever the original dates of the

extents of ancient fields depicted on Fig. 1, the field systems on the downs lay uncultivated during the last centuries BC. Indeed, apart from brief and spatially limited episodes of cultivation in the 1st-2nd and 12th-early 14th centuries AD, much of the Marlborough Downs since c.500BC has been grass – 'old grassland' indeed, older far than the ken of many a nature conservationist. We know for certain that these downs were grazed by huge flocks of sheep in medieval times, a function that continued into the 20th century. But grass can support other animals too and – something I did not dare put into Fowler 2000 - prompted by horse skulls on my excavation (OD XI), really classy race-horses training on the downs today, and the obscure tradition, perhaps at least two or even three thousand years old, of chalk-cut equine hill-figures in the Avebury region, I have long wondered whether perhaps, between the later Bronze Age and the Roman conquest, the ancient fields east of Avebury became a landscape for breeding and training horses.

Bibliography

Ashbee, P., Smith, I. & Evans, J. 1979. Excavation of three long barrows near Avebury, Wiltshire. *Proceedings of the Prehistoric Society* 45, 207-300

Brown, G., Field, D. & McOmish, D. (eds) forthcoming. *The Avebury Landscape: aspects of the field archaeology of the Marlborough Downs*

Burl, A. 1979. *Prehistoric Avebury*. New Haven and London: Yale University Press

Fowler, P.J. 2000. *Landscape Plotted and Pieced. Landscape History and Local Archaeology in Fyfield and Overton, Wiltshire*. London: Society of Antiquaries, Research Report 64

Fowler, P. & Blackwell, I. 2000. *An English Countryside Explored. The Land of Lettice Sweetapple*. Stroud: Tempus

Gingell, C. 1992. *The Marlborough Downs: a later Bronze Age landscape and its origins*. Devizes: WANHS/Trust for Wessex Archaeology

Hawkes, C.F.C. 1959. The ABC of the British Iron

Age. *Antiquity* 33, 170-82

Malone, C. 1989. *English Heritage Book of Avebury*. London: English Heritage/ Batsford

Papworth, M. 2004. *Report on the Geophysical Survey of parts of the SE and NE quadrants of Avebury Henge: October-December 2003*. Avebury: National Trust

Pollard, J. & Reynolds, A. 2002. *Avebury: the biography of a landscape*. Stroud: Tempus

Smith, A.C. 1885. *Guide to the British and Roman Antiquities of the North Wiltshire Downs in a Hundred Square Miles round Abury*. Devizes: Wiltshire Archaeological & Natural History Society

Smith, I.F. 1965. *Windmill Hill and Avebury: excavations by Alexander Keiller, 1925-1939*. Oxford: Clarendon Press

Smith, R.W. 1984. The ecology of Neolithic farming systems as exemplified by the Avebury region of Wiltshire. *Proceedings of the Prehistoric Society* 50, 99-120

Ucko, P.J., Hunter, M., Clark, A.J. & David, A. 1991. *Avebury Reconsidered: from the 1660s to the 1990s*. London: Unwin Hyman

VCH = *Victoria County History: History of Wiltshire* 1.i 1957, London: Oxford University Press

Whittle, A. 1997. *Sacred Mound, Holy Rings. Silbury Hill and the West Kennet palisade enclosures: a Later Neolithic complex in north Wiltshire*. Oxford: Oxbow Books

The Destruction of the Avebury Monuments

Mark Gillings, Rick Peterson & Joshua Pollard

Isobel Smith opened her definitive account of Alexander Keiller's excavations at Avebury with a discussion of the 'History of the Monuments' and 'Dilapidations' of the stone settings and earthwork (Smith 1965, 175-82). Her account of stone burial and breaking during the medieval and early post-medieval periods outlines a now familiar sequence. Beginning in the early 14th century, and possibly at the behest of the church, a number of stones were deliberately toppled and carefully buried in specially dug pits. A subsequent phase of more active destruction began in the later 17th century when numerous standing stones within the henge monument were broken-up through fire-setting in order to provide building material for the growing village: its houses, ancillary buildings and boundary walls. Although this activity appears to have peaked in the two decades either side of 1700, stone destruction continued until the early 19th century, the last recorded act taking place around 1829 when gunpowder was used to remove a stone deemed to be stubbornly blocking the entrance to a rick-yard (Smith 1965, 183).

A detailed investigation into the destruction of the Avebury stones was not part of Keiller's original remit; nor really that of Isobel's 1965 report, though the latter presents much detailed information on the process. In fact, until recently there has been a tendency to treat stone destruction as an unfortunate disturbance, or an act of vandalism that serves as a hindrance to our understanding of the prehistoric fabric of the monument. However, the status of these destruction events has become more important in recent years as the result of a developing interest in historical archaeology in general (e.g. Johnson 1996, Funari et al. 1999) and in early post-medieval Avebury in particular (e.g. Ucko et al. 1991, Gillings & Pollard forthcoming). It is becoming apparent that the destruction features (stone burials and destruction pits) are important in their own right, both as crucial remains of a key episode in the ongoing life of the monument, and as evidence of a fascinating historically-specific process. This in itself resonates with a current interest in the 'afterlife of monuments' (Bradley 1993, chapter 6; 2002).

We are fortunate that the main period of destruction during the late 17th and early 18th centuries coincided with the realisation of Avebury's status as an antiquity and the first concerted campaigns of antiquarian recording by John Aubrey and William Stukeley. They recorded the prehistoric fabric of the monument as it was slowly being dismantled around them (Aubrey 1980, Stukeley 1743). Add to this the physical evidence for these destruction episodes as recorded during excavations by Keiller and others, and we are in the enviable position of having both contemporary observation and archaeological record, perhaps making Avebury unique among British megalithic monuments in terms of the wealth of extant detail on its destruction.[1]

However, the accounts presented by early antiquaries have tended to dominate our understanding of the destruction process. They themselves are almost exclusively based upon Stukeley's records, which in turn are based largely upon oral testimonies. As Ucko et al. have convincingly and elegantly illustrated (1991, 182), Stukeley's records of the stone destruction cannot be regarded as wholly authoritative, being riddled with internal contradictions and inconsistencies. As a result, many key questions – such as *'when did it start?'*, *'how was the process organized?'* and *'what were the key motivations for stone breaking?'* – remain poorly addressed.

Drawing primarily upon the results of recent excavations and documentary research, we here present some further thoughts on the process of post-medieval stone destruction at Avebury.[2] This will involve a careful look at the technologies of stone destruction and the dating of the destruction events, along with a detailed examination of the reasons why such a tradition should develop. As will become clear, whilst undoubtedly comfortable, the accepted view of a coherent, tidy 'episode', pitting the forces of commerce against the solidity of stone and rationality of enlightened scholarship, masks a much more complex, muddled and intriguing situation. Stone breaking involved a variety of technical responses and underlying rationales, and was intimately bound up with contemporary perceptions of antiquity and the value of ancient monuments, economics, local politics and religious conflict.

Living with the Stones

Living in early post-medieval Avebury involved living with stone. Houses, barns, pastures, orchards and roads were interspersed among the megaliths of the Neolithic henge. In the fields beyond were the remains of the West Kennet and Beckhampton Avenues, earlier chambered tombs, and natural spreads of uncleared sarsen stretching along valley bottoms. Both Aubrey and Stukeley commented on the diverse ways in which the inhabitants of Avebury made active use of the stones of the monument. Aubrey, for example, claimed that one of the stones had been converted into a pigsty or cattle stall, whilst Stukeley records a fallen stone of the northern inner circle being regularly employed as a fishslab during market day (Ucko et al. 1991, 177). In addition, the excavations of Keiller in Avebury and along the West Kennet Avenue showed how medieval and later field boundaries were aligned upon the sarsens, effectively using them as boundary markers (Keiller & Piggott 1936, 421, fig 2; Stone 102 – unpublished notebooks in Alexander Keiller Museum). In this sense, stones were as much affordances as hindrances, and their destruction should not be taken as axiomatic.

Stone burning and breaking: new and old evidence reviewed

There was some *ad hoc* destruction of stones as and when they fell down, what we might think of as 'monumental windfall'. Aubrey records a stone at the start of the West Kennet Avenue falling in 1684 and breaking into two or three pieces (Aubrey 1980, 37). Stukeley in turn records how a large stone in the northern entrance that fell within the lifetime of Reuben Horsall, the parish clerk, was subsequently broken up by the villagers through the use of wooden wedges (Stukeley 1743, 22, 24).

In these cases we are dealing with largely pragmatic acts. Stones fell and were *then* broken. However, what sets the destruction episodes so

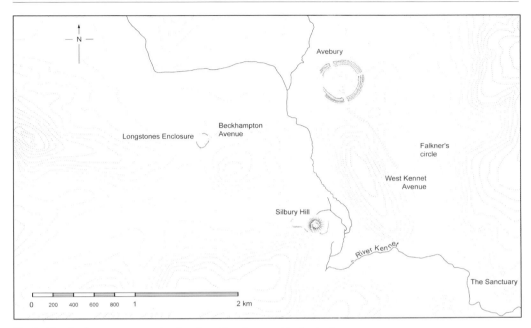

Fig. 1. The Avebury monuments, showing sites discussed in the text

vividly recorded by Stukeley apart from the above is *intent*. In the latter, stones were deliberately and systematically destroyed. This was not restricted to recently fallen stones or those lying recumbent: standing stones were deliberately pulled down to facilitate destruction, and even stones that had previously been buried were dug up and destroyed. In the context of Avebury, details of these different modes of destruction are given in Isobel's report (Smith 1965, 180ff).

Evidence for many of these practices was also revealed during recent excavations along the Beckhampton Avenue to the west of Avebury (Gillings *et al.* 2000, 2002) and at the Falkner's Circle to the south. Both monuments are part of the later Neolithic complex, and had suffered extensive damage from stone breaking during the early post-medieval period (Fig. 1).

The Beckhampton Avenue

A 150m length of the Beckhampton Avenue in Longstones Field, Beckhampton – including its

original terminal and the Longstones Cove – was investigated during 1999 and 2000 (Fig. 2). The excavations revealed 13 stone settings, two of which had been dismantled in prehistory (L12 and 13). Illustrative of the range of techniques later used to 'clear' megalithic settings, three of the stones were fully buried in specially dug pits (L2, 5 and 6), two partially buried (L3 and 8), and seven destroyed through fire-setting (L1, 4, 7, 8, 11, 15 and 16: including one of the previously buried megaliths, L8). Here the Avenue ran through open fields during the late medieval and early post-medieval periods; traces of ridge-and-furrow being encountered in all trenches.

Following a familiar pattern, the stone burials appear to represent the earliest 'destruction' features (Fig. 3). Their character was identical to that described by Smith for excavated stone burials at Avebury and on the West Kennet Avenue (1965, 177): the stones lay snugly in carefully dug pits which had been backfilled with

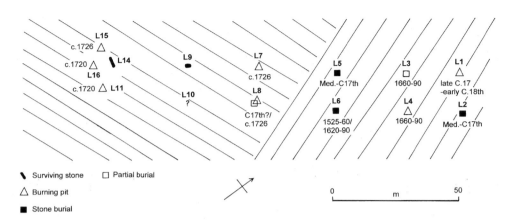

Fig. 2. Longstones Field, Beckhampton, showing distribution of stone burials and burning pits along with the dates of their enactment. Traces of ridge-and-furrow are also shown in order to illustrate the lack of correlation between the axes of medieval/early post-medieval cultivation and extant megalithic settings

chalk rubble, much compacted at the top. The detail of the process of overthrow and burial still remains unclear. Either standing stones were supported by timber props while a burial pit was being dug (at Beckhampton cutting into the socket itself), then the stone was toppled in; or the stone was first overthrown, its outline marked out on the ground, the stone dragged to one side, a pit dug and then the stone pushed in. While at first sight appearing unnecessarily complicated, the latter would be less dangerous, alleviate the problem of mis-fall, explain why the shape and size of the burial pits conforms so closely to that of the stones, and account for the skewed angles at which the stones often seem to lie in relation to the socket (i.e. the bases of the stones are often not adjacent to the sockets).

On analogy with similar stone burials at Avebury, dated through ceramic and artefactual evidence to the early 14th century (Jope 1999, 67), it was expected that the Beckhampton burials would also be medieval. However, a radiocarbon date on a chopped cattle rib from the clean chalk backfill of the burial pit for L6 produced a range which spanned the 16th and 17th centuries AD, with a 41.6% probability of

the true date falling within the span 1620-90. There are no archaeological grounds for dismissing this date, even though it implies a much longer and more episodic history of stone burial within the complex than has previously been envisaged. It should perhaps occasion no surprise. In his *Abury*, Stukeley talked of stone burial in terms that implied memory of the practice had survived into the early 18th century (Stukeley 1743, 29-30). Such oral testimonies are unlikely to have lasted beyond a handful of generations, and could even record relatively recent events. In fact, the occasional burial of stones continued up until the early 20th century, though here driven by an ethos of preservation rather than riddance. The latest recorded burial is that of stone 63b of the West Kennet Avenue, buried in order to preserve it from agricultural improvements during the winter of 1921-2 (Smith 1965, 207n), and excavated in the summer of 2002 (Fig. 4).

Two of the Beckhampton stones (L3 and 8) were subject to partial burial; a practice also recorded at Avebury (e.g. stones 41 and 42 in the north-west sector: Smith 1965, 188). In both instances the pits for these were rather more

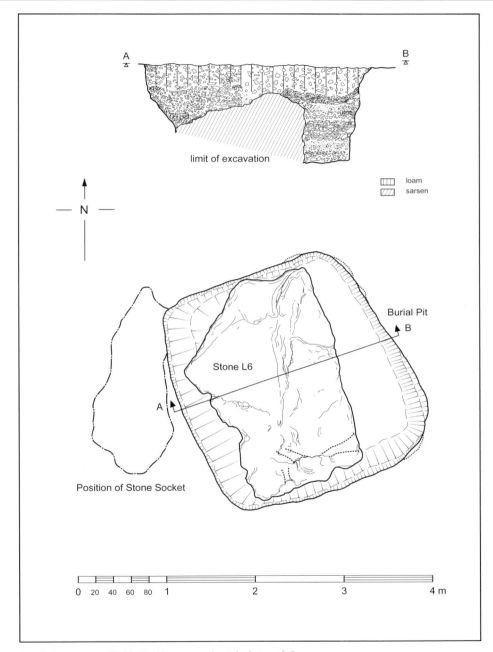

Fig. 3. Longstones Field, Beckhampton: burial of stone L6

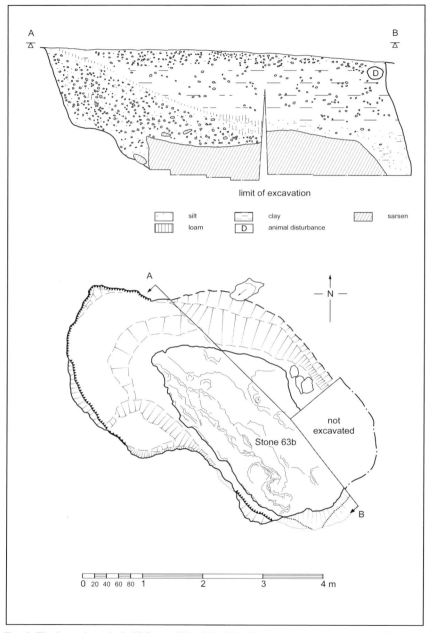

Fig. 4. The latest burial of all? Stone 63b of the West Kennet Avenue, buried in 1921-2 and excavated in 2002

irregular than those associated with conventional stone burials, though deeper and more uniform than burning pits. Neither contained a stone, demonstrating subsequent removal, which could only have been facilitated had the buried megaliths remained visible, projecting above the level of the contemporary ground surface. In the case of L8 the stone was dug out during the early 18th century and destroyed through fire-setting, providing a *terminus ante quem* for the burial itself. Sherds of blue-and-white transfer printed pottery and Pearlware from the upper fill of the pit for L3 indicate that the removal of this stone is likely to post-date 1800. Given the absence of burning deposits and stone debris, in this instance the stone was probably removed as part of agricultural clearance and dragged off to the field edge.

Of the burning pits, six were of a 'conventional' format, that is dug into the chalk in an expedient manner with sides and bases left uneven. Oval in plan, they ranged in maximum dimension from 1.8m (L7) to 5.8m (L11), and were up to 0.95m deep. Their size was influenced both by the dimensions of the stone and the depth of ploughsoil through which the pits were cut – in this instance note has to be taken of the undulating ground surface provided by overlying ridge-and-furrow. The basal fills comprised extensive spreads of flaked and burnt sarsen within a matrix of burnt straw and charcoal. Features of conchoidal fracture on the sarsen fragments (including large bulbs of percussion) demonstrate *in situ* trimming of fractured blocks, achieved with consummate skill. The destruction pit for one of the larger stones, L11 (forming the central element of the original Avenue terminal), was cut from the south sloping down towards, and directly up to, the base of the stone (Fig. 5). The wedge-shaped profile seems designed to facilitate the removal of broken stone, while the clear irregularity in the base of the cut could either reflect the employment of a rather *ad hoc* digging strategy, or a much more deliberate attempt to ensure a flow of air beneath the stone once firing had begun.

In all instances these destruction deposits were sealed by layers of ploughsoil containing sherds of medieval and early post-medieval pottery, occasional iron fragments and pieces of clay pipe. These upper fills seem to have formed slowly, perhaps as the result of repeated episodes of ploughing, since the charcoal-rich soil in L1 and L4 was 'washed' from around the sarsen fragments, only surviving underneath them. Dating for the destruction is provided by fragments of late 17th and early 18th century clay pipe from the burning deposits, along with a copper-alloy button of the same period.

These pits are the product of a stone breaking technology that utilised a combination of heat and percussion. The essence of the process was described by Aubrey in the later 17th century, when it appears to have already been an established methodology:

> I have verbum Sacerdotis for it, that these mighty stones (as hard as marble) may be broken in what part of them you please; without any great trouble: Sc. Make a fire on that […] line of the stone where you would have it crack; and after the stone is well heated, draw over a line with cold water, & immediately give a knock with a Smyths sledge, and it will break like the Collets at the Glass house. (Aubrey 1980, 38)

This was further elaborated by Stukeley in the 1720s, drawing upon both local testimony and perhaps first-hand observation (implied by his famous 'atto de fe' drawings: Smith 1965, pl. XXVII). First, a pit was dug against the stone while the latter was supported by substantial timber props. Prior to toppling, large chunks of stone were placed in the pit to support the sarsen when it fell, thus creating an airway beneath it. Often the sheer bulk of the falling sarsen was sufficient to cause these supporting stones to break and shatter. Straw was placed in the base of the pit, the props taken away, the stone pushed in and the fuel ignited. The application of water and the sledge followed a sufficient period of heating (Stukeley 1743, 15-16). Needless to say, the work was both hazardous and labour intensive.

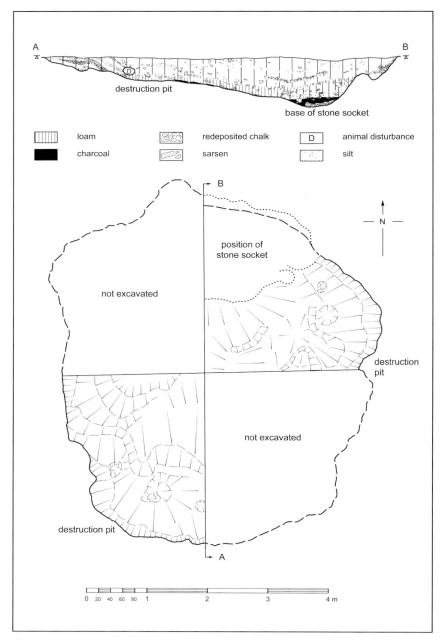

Fig. 5. Longstones Field, Beckhampton: early 18th century destruction pit of stone L11

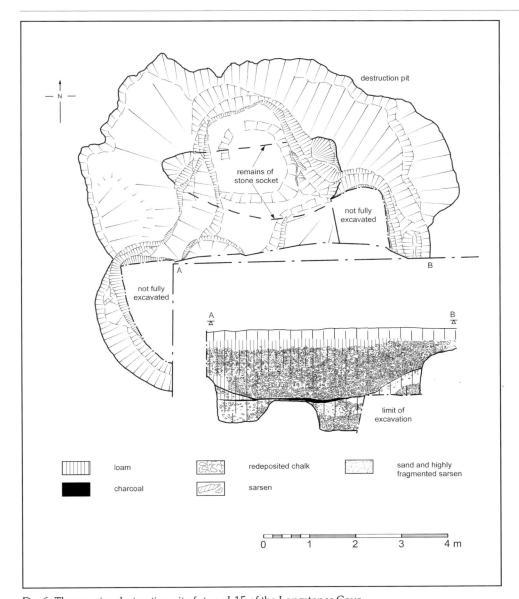

Fig. 6. The massive destruction pit of stone L15 of the Longstones Cove

In a number of respects, the archaeological evidence from Longstones Field conforms to Stukeley's account: the pits were dug against the stones, smaller sarsen boulder 'supports' were occasionally found on the bases of the pits (i.e. that for L16), and straw was the predominant fuel. Metal fittings from some of the pits could even derive from recycled structural timbers used as props. However, both here and at the Falkner's Circle (see below) more variability can be found in the process than is implied by the antiquarian accounts.

In contrast to these simple burning pits, the destruction features relating to the north-west stone of the Cove (L15) were quite different (Fig. 6). Perhaps weighing in the order of 50 tonnes, this stone had fallen at an early date, maybe even by the Roman period. Lying recumbent, it posed particular problems for the stone-breakers, who needed to create a sufficient space under the stone in order to pack straw and other fuel for the fire-setting and provide a free flow of oxygen. An elaborate, ingenious and rather dangerous solution was adopted, which involved sinking shafts around the fallen stone and then mining underneath, leaving the stone supported on un-dug spurs of chalk. Essentially, the pit became a furnace with the stone as its 'lid'. The result was a massive multi-lobate pit over 6.5m across, formed by an interconnecting arrange-ment of three deep sub-rectangular pits linked by a shallower central section. Each pit was itself in the order of 2.5-3.0m across and up to 2.1m deep. In order to maximise the surface area of the fire, the deeper pits were partially backfilled up to the level of the central section, thus creating an even artificial base on which fuel for the burning could be spread. In this instance the destruction feature was just too large to leave open, so following the burning of the stone the pit was backfilled with chalk rubble. A slight hollow remained, but this soon filled with ploughsoil washed in from the sides.

A similar approach was used to break-up the Obelisk in the centre of the inner southern circle at Avebury. This was also a massive recumbent block which posed equal difficulties to the stone-breakers. Smith records that 'a series of pits... had been scooped out under the prostrate stone in order to insert straw for the heating' (1965, 198); the result being a multi-lobate destruction pit c.6 x 4m across, though lacking the depth, coherence and engineering seen at the Beckhampton Cove.

What remains so striking is how patchy and seemingly unsystematic the whole destruction process was, involving varying strategies of burial, partial burial and burning that spanned at least 50 years, if not a few centuries. At the end of this two stones were still left standing. However, taking radiocarbon and artefactual evidence together, and irrespective of the specific response to individual stones, there is a hint of sequence. Within the investigated area of Longstones Field the stones in the eastern half were tackled first. These include the burials and partial burials (perhaps as late as the 17th century), and two destruction pits dated by associated clay pipes to c.1660-90. The largest stones of the Cove and the penultimate pair of the Avenue were left until the 1720s when they were broken up soon before, perhaps during, and after Stukeley's visits (i.e. around the period 1720-30). The sequence could be read as a westerly progression. Alternatively, it may reflect the materialisation of developing technique, confidence and audacity as increasingly massive sarsen blocks were sought and attacked; though it should be noted that the equally bulky third stone of the Cove at Avebury was broken up as early as 1713 (Stukeley 1743, tab. I).

The motivations behind different strategies of 'riddance' are likely to have been manifold, and in a cultivated area such as this perhaps linked to decisions on the part of individual strip owners to either retain or remove stones. Those broken-up through fire-setting were destined to become building material,[3] although the motivation to do this may have been influenced by other agendas (see below). Contrary to common assumption, the stones themselves need not have been viewed as an impediment to cultivation, as witnessed by the laying out of ridge-and-furrow across the stone circle at Long Meg and Her Daughters, Cumbria, in a manner which seems oblivious to the presence of the stones (Soffe & Clare 1988). In this context, it is interesting to note that at Beckhampton the axes of cultivation, which pre-dated the stone destruction pits at least, bear no relation to the position of the Avenue and Cove.

Falkner's Circle

Work on the Falkner's Circle – a small late Neolithic setting of 12 stones 800m to the south-east of Avebury – undertaken during 2002 revealed four stone positions making up the southern and eastern arc of the circle (Fig. 7). Two of these were marked by sockets (F.3 and 8) into which sarsen debris had been pushed. These were seemingly related to depressions seen by the Devizes antiquary Mr Falkner in 1840 (Long 1858, 345-6), implying the former presence of shallow destruction pits wholly or largely cut into the topsoil. However, on the southern side deeper destruction pits survived, one (F.7) associated with a socket. Surviving as a shallow oval scoop, this was similar to the smaller examples excavated on the Beck-hampton Avenue. The second (F.6) was of a very different nature, being some 3.6m wide and 0.9m deep. The pit base and sides were extensively fire-reddened, in some places turning the clayey sub-soil into brick-like lumps. Both the depth of the pit and its dished base suggest that it was cut *around* rather than *against* a standing stone, largely obliterating the socket in the

process. It certainly represents a more tidy technique than the usual practice of digging an extensive pit adjacent to a megalith that conformed to the vertical shape and size of the stone. However, the evidence for two separate firing episodes suggests it may not have been as efficient in distributing heat along the stone. As well as differences in form, there was also a difference in the fuel utilised. In contrast to the pits at Avebury and Beckhampton, here oak roundwood was used as the principal fuel for the firing (Ruth Young pers. comm.).

Radiocarbon dates on charcoal strongly suggests that the burning associated with pit F.6 occurred during the main phase of stone breaking between the 17th and early 19th centuries. Those for F.7 have proved more of a surprise, spanning the early 15th to late 17th centuries with the probability weighted towards the earlier part of that range. Pre-dating by a reasonable margin the recorded destructions at Avebury itself – but perhaps not far removed from Aubrey's account of stone breaking – the latter dates are contemporary with, or even earlier than, that obtained for the burial of L6 at

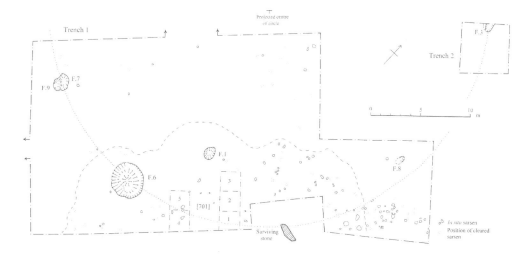

Fig. 7. Falkner's Circle: plan of features revealed during the 2002 excavation

Beckhampton. It is difficult to avoid the implication that traditions of burial and burning were, for a time, coeval.

Variation in the practice of stone breaking within Avebury

The variety of technological practices associated with stone breaking revealed by recent excavations on the Beckhampton Avenue and at the Falkner's Circle can also be found within Avebury itself (Smith 1965, 195ff). The settings of the southern inner circle perhaps provide the clearest illustration. Of the stones of the inner circle proper investigated by Keiller in 1939 (stones 101-109) three had been destroyed by fire: 104, 107 and 108. While employing a broadly similar methodology, in each case the burning pits displayed different characteristics. Pits were dug up against the outer faces of stones 104 and 107; that of the former being larger and more irregular than the latter, even though the stones must have been of comparable size. However, in the case of 108, a large, irregular pit was dug around the base of the stone leaving it more or less unsupported immediately prior to toppling (information from excavation records in Alexander Keiller Museum).

Of the smaller internal settings adjacent to the Obelisk, stone *i* was found to have been buried before being discovered and burned, perhaps around 1700-1710 (Smith 1965, 199). In keeping with the surviving stones of this setting and the overall size of the burial pit, this does not appear to have been a particularly large sarsen. However, to facilitate the burning of this stone a complex procedure had been adopted. It appears that a cavity some 0.34m deep was dug beneath the stone as it lay in its burial pit, its bulk left supported on undug spurs of chalk. This void was then filled with straw and the stone burned. It is interesting to note that this approach mirrors that taken with the recumbent Beckhampton Cove stone described above, and with the Obelisk itself. In contrast to the elaborate and carefully planned furnace constructed to destroy stone *i*, stones *ix*, *x* and *xi* were burned in a single

communal burning pit centred upon stone *x*. This appears to have been an entirely pragmatic act. Whilst digging the burning pit for stone *x* the burial pit for *ix* was discovered and the stone dug out and burned in the existing pit. Stone *xi* was discovered likewise. If this was not variation enough, a final stone setting, stone *xii*, appears to have been broken-up *in situ* using direct fracture instead of fire. This was suggested by the complete absence of any burning debris and a spread of 87 pieces of fractured sarsen covering an area of 2.5 x 1.5m to the south of the stone socket (Keiller, unpublished notebooks). Far from forming a single coherent practice, it is clear from the destruction features within this relatively restricted area of the henge that a number of distinct strategies of stone breaking were employed. A summary of this variation in practice across the Avebury monuments is given in Tables 1-3.

Why were stones broken-up?

Breaking sarsens through fire-setting was clearly a massive undertaking. It was also expensive, involving large amounts of labour and materials. Indeed, the notorious stone-breaker Tom Robinson confessed to Stukeley that a stone burning could cost anywhere between 30 and 60 shillings, and noted that two stones had cost £8 to destroy (Stukeley 1743, 15-16, 25).

Stukeley famously claimed that the chief motivation for stone destruction was a 'covetousness of the little area of ground, each stood on' (Stukeley 1743, 15). This implies that it was land that was important rather than the stone itself. We have already seen that this desire to obtain further small parcels of land is unlikely to provide a motivation for the removal of settings within cultivated areas, where the laying out of ridge-and-furrow more or less ignored the presence of stones. Furthermore, inside the henge standing stones often served a useful function as boundary markers in the organisation of garden plots and orchards. Stukeley's explanation also fails to explain why

	Burial	Partial burial	Removal	Fire-setting	Cold splitting
Avebury	•	•	•	•	•
West Kennet Avenue	•	-	•	•	•
Beckhampton Avenue	•	•	•	•	-
Falkner's Circle	-	-	-	•	-
The Sanctuary	-	-	•	-	-

Table 1. Techniques of stone destruction or removal employed in the early post-medieval period (c.1600-1830)

Nature of destruction	Dating	Selected Examples
Rough, shallow pit dug adjacent to stone	Generally mid 17th to early 18th century c.1470-1640 at Falkner's Circle (radiocarbon)	Various at Avebury; West Kennet Avenue; Beckhampton Avenue; Falkner's Circle
Rough shallow pit dug around stone	Clay pipe c.1660-90 (Beckhampton)	Avebury 108; Beckhampton Avenue L4
Deep, well-cut pit dug around stone	c.1650-1680 (radiocarbon)	Falkner's Circle F.6
Stone dug out of burial pit and dragged onto existing pyre	c.1700-1710 (Stukeley)	Avebury ix, xi
Stone burned in burial pit through excavation of a furnace beneath it	c.1700-1710? (Stukeley)	Avebury i
Stone levered out and burnt in burial pit	Post-1724 (Stukeley)	Beckhampton Avenue L8
Furnace dug beneath recumbent stone	Post-1724 (Stukeley)	Beckhampton Cove L15
Burning scoops dug around recumbent stone	Post-1723 (Stukeley)	Avebury Obelisk

Table 2. Summary of stone burning features encountered among the Avebury monuments

Mode of destruction	Selected Examples
Direct fracture of *in situ* or fallen stone	Avebury xii; West Kennet Avenue 20a; 22a
Burning using straw	All Avebury and Beckhampton Avenue
Burning using wood	Falkner's Circle
Toppling and wholesale relocation of suitable stones	Stones from the Beckhampton Avenue use to create a bridge over the Winterbourne in 1701 (Burl 1979, 46). The Sanctuary

Table 3. Techniques of stone breaking

breaking rather than burial should be the preferred strategy of riddance. Added to this, archaeological evidence clearly contradicts his statement. Within the henge the majority of destruction pits were left open once stones had been removed (Smith 1965, 180; Ucko et al. 1990, 181). The recovery of horse bones from the upper fills of the multiple burning pit near the Obelisk suggests it had been left open and subsequently used as a convenient receptacle for the dumping of refuse from the adjacent tanner's yard. Smith and Cunnington's excavation of the site of the Obelisk showed the pit had been left open to act as a repository for broken bottles from the nearby inn (Smith 1867, 212). Stukeley talked of 'nettles and weeds growing up' in the places where stones had been removed (1743, 22), and many destruction pits remain visible today as hollows (e.g. in the northern inner circle: Ucko et al. 1991, pl. 67). If this was merely clearance for horticulture or agriculture then why was the debris left littered around and the holes left to accumulate nettles and rubbish?

One popular explanation for the spate of stone destructions links it to a general boom in building within the village during the late 17th and early 18th centuries (e.g. Malone 1980, 121-2; Ucko et al. 1990, 166). Whilst stone destruction was undoubtedly linked to the creation of building material, as testified by the numerous sarsen-built cottages, barns and walls within and around Avebury, Stukeley noted in detail the cons of such a strategy:

> They have sometimes us'd of these stones for building houses; but say, they may have them cheaper, in more manageable pieces, from the gray weathers. One of these stones will build an ordinary house; yet the stone being a kind of marble, or rather granite, is always moist and dewy in winter, which proves damp and unwholesome, and rots the furniture. (Stukeley 1743, 16)

In the face of such apparently contradictory evidence it is hard to claim a single, all-encompassing rationale for these acts of stone breaking. We feel the motivation for these practices may be more complex than previously envisaged, and that it is necessary to look to the social and religious context of everyday life in early post-medieval Avebury for a clearer understanding.

William Stukeley and the stone breakers: the political and religious context of stone destruction
Stukeley's account of this destruction process has been used, particularly by Burl (1979, 30-56), to add to our archaeological understanding of the stone burning. However, there are problems with Stukeley's evidence and, as we have already seen, it should not be accepted uncritically as eyewitness testimony. These prob-lems can be highlighted by comparing Stukeley's field notes, written in the 1720s, with his published account in *Abury: A Temple of the British Druids* (Stukeley 1743). The first of these questions concerns who precisely was responsible for organising the destruction. Six men are listed in *Abury* as stonebreakers: 'Tom Robinson the Herostratus of Abury' (Stukeley 1743, 15), 'farmer Green', 'John Fowler' (Stukeley 1743, 24) 'Walter Stretch' (Stukeley 1743, 25), farmer Griffin (Stukeley 1743, 31), and Richard Fowler (Stukeley 1743, 35). He refers to them collectively as 'miserable farmers' (Stukeley 1743, 37) and says that 'the cuvetous farmer and grazier have conspired to abolish this most magnificent monument' (Stukeley 1743, 30).

Most of these men are also attested in other contemporary records, several of them belonging to families who had been living in the area for at least two hundred years by this date. The Griffins (or Griffens) were tenants of Sir Richard Holford and his descendents (WRO 184/4). John Griffin entered into a tenancy with Sir Richard Holford in 1703 (WRO 184/4) and was presumably the 'farmer Griffin' Stukeley refers to. John Griffin also owned some land in Avebury (WRO 184/4: WRO 435/24) as did Walter Stretch (WRO 212A/36/1 No.1), although by 1725 Stretch was dead and the land was in the hands of his son George. Stukeley's field notes give us further background detail about these people. Richard Fowler was the landlord of the Hare and Hounds Alehouse on the Bath Road (Bodl. MS Gough Maps 231 f244v). Walter Stretch was landlord of the Catherine Wheel on Green Street in Avebury (Bodl. MS Eng. Misc. c. 323 p129). John Griffin lived in what is now Trusloe Manor farm (Bodl. MS Gough Maps 231 f243v). Green is referred to as having a house in Beckhampton (Bodl. MS Eng. Misc. c. 323 p.129) and he may be the Mr Richard Green mentioned in a survey document of 1714 (WRO 184/4) as holding part of Silbury meadow.

Stukeley's field notes from the 1720s list other people who were involved in the process of stone destruction apart from the six 'miserable farmers' he blamed in 1743. 'Mr Smith a lawyer in W. Kennet lives in monument yard and desires to take away the stones of S long barrow [West Kennet long barrow] to make a bridge' (Bodl. MS Gough Maps 231 f9); 'Mr Boak plow^d up overton Hill [the Sanctuary] tho' land is Mr Saunders late Mr Tuckers.' (Bodl. MS Gough Maps 231 f25 v); and concerning Millbarrow 'the late parsone of the Town [Winterbourne Monkton] took one of the finest stones & made a tomb of it for himself.' (Bodl. MS Gough Maps 231 f237). What distinguishes these stone-breakers seems to be their social class. With the possible exception of Green, none of the men listed in print by Stukeley seem to have been categorised at the time as gentlemen: no contemporary record of John Griffin, Thomas Robinson, Walter Stretch, John or Richard Fowler refers to them as 'Esquire', or gives them the title 'Mr'. This contrasts with the three gentlemen in Stukeley's field notes, who seem to have been ignored in the final account of destruction perpetrated by 'miserable farmers'.[4]

It is also possible that Stukeley may have exaggerated Thomas Robinson's role as a leader of the stone destruction. Robinson is mentioned in several places in the surviving field notes: Stukeley painted a pen and wash portrait of him on the 26 July 1722 (Bodl. MS Gough Maps 231

f 241). In a note made in 1722 Stukeley recorded:

> ...since then [1694] *Tho. Robinson* has been a terrible Mallet, tho' he ownd to us two of them cost £8 breaking, & upon our remonstrances has promisd to spare all those that are standing in his ground. (Bodl. MS Eng. Misc. c. 323 p.129)

Stukeley was clearly relying on oral testimony here, probably from Robinson himself. When he began to prepare his draft versions of the plan of Avebury from 1722 onwards he labelled a group of nine or ten stones in the south-east quadrant as demolished or taken away around 1700 and in around half the surviving drafts he names Thomas Robinson as the demolisher of these stones. Despite the apparently clear nature of this information it is probably wrong. Ucko *et al* (1991, 210-11) have established, building on the discovery by Lukis (1881, 153), that these stones had been buried rather than burnt or removed, and that the stones in question were almost certainly buried before John Aubrey made his plan of Avebury in 1663. It is clear that Stukeley's personal relationship with Robinson worsened during the 1720s. The portrait painted on the 26th of July 1722 was originally labelled with Robinson's name and the date. Subsequently Stukeley added the epithet 'Ierostratus', a reference to Herostratus, recorded by Strabo as the destroyer of the temple of Artemis in Ephesus, and added the phrases 'Stone-Killer' and 'got his wife (an old woman above 50) with child' (Bodl. MS Gough Maps 231 f241). An engraving of this portrait was used as part of the tailpiece for chapter 10 of *Abury* (Stukeley 1743, 53) in which Robinson's features were so demonised as to be almost unrecognisable (Fig. 8).

The reference to Herostratus brings us to the most obvious omission in Stukeley's lists of stone-breakers. Caleb Baily, owner of the nearby manor of Berwick Basset, does not appear in either Stukeley's field notes or in the published *Abury*. Baily was buying land in Avebury during the early 1720s and the Society of Antiquaries held him responsible for much of the stone breaking (Law 1969, 104-5). They used the same Classical analogy to refer to him as 'an Herostratian', commissioned Sir Allan Ramsey to attack him in verse, and wrote to him asking him to stop breaking stones. Ramsey's poetic assault was stopped when Baily wrote to the Society expressing 'real penitence' for his actions and, presumably, stopped stone breaking. Stukeley had been a leading member of the Society of

Fig. 8. The face of stone breaking: Stukeley's original 1722 portrait of Thomas Robinson, the 'Herostratus of Avebury' (Bodleian Library, University of Oxford, Gough Maps 231, fol. 241r), and the demonised engraved version published in his *Abury* of 1743

Antiquaries and he must have known about Baily's actions. Although Stukeley left London at the end of that year (Haycock 2002, 189), he was still involved with the Society in 1725 when Sir John Clerk wrote to Ramsey about Caleb Baily. It is likely that the slightly obscure analogy with Herostratus had a common origin when used by Stukeley about Robinson and the Society about Baily.

Stukeley's published account of the stone breaking seems to minimise the involvement of the local minor gentry, to present a picture of destruction planned and organised by yeoman farmers. This was probably a conscious strategy to contrast ignorant destruction with an educated appreciation of the monument. For example, Sir Richard Holford's modifications of the henge bank were described very differently to the actions of the stone-breakers, being presented not as destruction but as restoration:

> All the way from the north round the top of the vallum on the other side of the ditch was leveld by Sr Richd Holford whos name ought ever to be mentiond with honor & his memory dear to Antiquarians for his great care in preserving these glorious remains. (Bodl. MS Eng. Misc. c. 323 p.120)

Stukeley's attitude to Ralph Stawell's destruction of the western bank to build the great barn is part of this trend, as the act of destruction is passed over in the text of *Abury* without comment (Stukeley 1743, 27). There is also the question of the destruction of the south-western bank between 1721 and 1724. Stukeley recorded this change in his field drawings without making any surviving notes as to who carried out the work and why.

By the time he came to publish *Abury*, it seems that a personal dislike of Thomas Robinson led Stukeley to exaggerate his role in the destruction. Perhaps most importantly, there was a common factor linking many of the stone-breakers, both gentlemen and yeoman, which Stukeley either concealed, or was never aware of. This was their religious affiliation. John Griffin

and his father Peter (Dunscombe 1998, 6-7: Reeves 1956, 107n), Thomas Robinson (Dunscombe 1998, 7) and Caleb Baily (Reeves 1956, 123) were all involved in the early nonconformist church. Burl (1979, 46) clearly considered the idea that there was a religious dimension to the early modern stone destruction at Avebury, and made the pertinent suggestion that the use of sarsen derived from the destruction of stones of the southern circle in building the chapel may have had a symbolic dimension. It is this religious context that we would like to explore further.

Placing the Avebury stone-breaking within the history of later 17th and early 18th century religious dissent and Whig politics allows us to make sense both of the motives of the stone-breakers and of those, like Stukeley and the parish clerk Ruben Horsall, who opposed them. The conflict between the established Anglican church and protestant nonconforming sects had its origins in the early part of the 17th century (the discussion in this paragraph follows particularly Sharpe 2000, especially 350-7). At this date the general debate within the Church of England about the proper nature of protestant worship could be characterised as being between 'Puritan' and 'Laudian' clerics. The Puritans were concerned to simplify religious ritual and establish a worship of God free of idolatry. This simplified religion was to be reinforced with a personal reading and under-standing of the Bible. Laudian churchmen regarded themselves, and the English church in general, as heirs of an historic compromise whereby Elizabeth I had preserved the essential and traditional forms of worship but had rescued them from the despotic influence of the Pope. The forms and rituals attacked by the Puritans were regarded by Laudians as essential to the stability of the church and the state, and they feared that too open a religion would lead to the collapse of both into a morass of conflicting heresies. Both sides shared several key beliefs which served to make the conflict more intense. Both groups were driven by a paranoid fear of Catholic conspiracy, and both believed that their opponents were either the servants or the stooges of Rome. Even more damagingly, neither side gave much credence to the idea of a private conscience. If the nation was to be saved then the national religion must conform to God's will. Dissenters from this religion enjoyed the benefits of God's grace without contributing to the earning of that grace and were a burden on the state.

All of these issues were intensified by the nature of the settlement which followed the restoration of the monarchy in 1660 (Harris 1993, 7-8: 40-1). After the period of Puritan ascendancy during the Commonwealth, the Cavalier parliament reintroduced a strongly Laudian, or High Anglican, church along with savage penalties for nonconformity. In 1662 parliament passed the Act of Uniformity which required all ministers and teachers of the church to testify adherence to the Authorized version of the Bible and the Book of Common prayer in order not to be deprived of their livings (Harris 1993, 40-1). Many Puritan clerics refused to testify. In Wiltshire alone sixty ministers were deprived of their livings at this date, around half of whom remained in the county preaching to like-minded members of their former con-gregations (Reeves 1956, 104). Several of these men, including John Baker of Chisledon, Thomas Rashley of Salisbury and John Row were active in Avebury and Berwick Bassett (Reeves 1956, 105), and the permanent nonconformist chapel in the village probably grew from these beginnings (Dunscombe 1998, 6). The degree of persecution of these dissenting ministers and new churches varied during the rest of the 17th century, depending on both local factors and national politics (Harris 1993, 45). A number of pieces of legislation were passed in this period. Some of these (Harris 1993, 39, 56) were designed to prevent dissenters and Catholics holding public office but others (Harris 1993, 41) specifically banned nonconformist meetings, and were intended to completely destroy the dissenting churches.

These acts, and their impact on early nonconformist churches, formed part of a three-sided political struggle in later 17th century England (see particularly Harris 1993, 7-40). On the one hand there were the Tories, High Anglican churchmen and the aristocracy, broadly similar in outlook and membership to the Laudian interest of the early 17th century. They were committed to ritualistic forms of worship, one national church and the upholding of the royal prerogative, linking the state, church and crown together against the menace of Catholicism. Opposing the Tories in parliament were the Whigs, who were in favour of simpler forms of worship, were prepared to tolerate at least the more moderate dissenting churches, and who were highly concerned about the Catholic sympathies of the court and so inclined to look for limits on Royal power. This group included those landed gentlemen who had previously supported the Commonwealth regime. The third party in this struggle was the king and his court. Despite the theoretical link between the Tories and the crown, Charles II had a distinct political agenda of his own, primarily concerned with securing the royal succession to his Catholic brother James. In pursuit of this aim Charles also made several attempts to increase religious toleration, particularly of the Catholic church.

These tensions ultimately led to the exclusion crisis of 1679-81. In an atmosphere of increased anti-Catholic paranoia following the fraudulent revelations by Titus Oates of a 'Popish Plot' to take over England (Harris 1993, 52), parliament introduced a number of bills designed to exclude James from the succession. The crisis ended in 1681 when Charles refused to recall parliament, beginning a period of complete Tory political dominance which lasted until the early years of James II's reign (Harris 1993, 80-1, 117-21). The 1680s were a particularly onerous time for the dissenting churches, in the aftermath of various Whig plots against James, the anti-nonconformist legislation was enforced savagely (Harris 1993, 119-21). In 1687 James attempted to revive his brother's policy of promoting religious toleration by issuing a Declaration of Indulgence which suspended all the penal laws and Test Acts (Harris 1993, 126-8). This had two effects. First, an Anglican campaign of civil disobedience against religious toleration, primarily, but not exclusively, directed at Catholics. The Declaration of Indulgence also brought the Tories into a general parliamentary movement to bring pressure on James II. This pressure was ultimately to lead to the accession of William and Mary in 1689 but the key factor which led to James' downfall was that he had alienated the Tory Anglicans. The settlement which led to the handover of power in 1689 was a compromise, but one dominated by Tory concerns and ultimately more favourable to Anglicanism than dissent (Harris 1993, 128-40).

In Avebury these political battles were played out, as everywhere, within the context of specific local loyalties. The dissenting church was relatively strong within the village community: in 1676 there were at least 25 nonconformists in the parish (Reeves 1956, 107n) and by 1715 the congregation had risen to around 130 (Dunscombe 1998, 8). They were also supported to a certain extent by the Whig sympathies of some local landowners. Sir Edward Baynton, who had briefly held Avebury Manor under the Commonwealth (Freeman 1983, 91), continued to own land in Avebury Trusloe and was a prominent Whig and local JP. Baynton's support was limited by his concern for his own position as he had repeatedly been in trouble in the 1660s for his involvement in radical Whig politics. Indeed, he was forced by political pressure to take a part in the particularly savage persecution led by John Eyre in the Warminster and Devizes divisions after the second Conventicle act of 1670 (Norrey 1988, 807). From 1696 onwards Caleb Baily, who was also a JP, held the nearby Berwick Basset manor (Law 1969, 104). Baily's support for the nonconformist churches led to him leaving a bequest in his will in 1749 to establish a fund for the assistance of people 'who shall preach or study to be fit to preach to congregations of Presbyterian, Baptist or Independent denominations' (Reeves 1956, 123).

The Tories were also represented in Avebury, but several factors seem to have weakened their influence. Avebury manor was mainly held in the later 17th century by the Stawell family. Sir John Stawell bought the manor in 1640 and, apart from a brief period during the Commonwealth, his family held it until 1696 (Freeman 1983, 91). However, Avebury was peripheral to the bulk of the Stawell lands, which were in Somerset (Underdown 1985, 155-6). Sir Richard Holford, who bought the manor in 1696 and whose family held it until the early 19th century, did apparently use Avebury manor as his main family residence. Despite this, the Holfords were still absent in London or elsewhere for large parts of the year during the early 18th century (WRO 184/4). It is noticeable that when Stukeley reported evidence from members of the Holford family about the former state of Avebury he gained that information at meetings in London rather than in the village (Bodl. MS Gough Maps 231 f9, for example). The position of the Anglican church in early 18th-century Avebury was not helped by a long and bitter dispute between the Holford family and the incumbent, the Reverend John White. This began in 1696 and some sort of settlement was first reached in October 1701. However, the extensive collection of papers relating to the matter in the Swindon and Wiltshire Record Office (WRO184/4) seems to indicate that the arguments continued into the 1740s. The Holfords were supported in their legal arguments by repeated depositions from their nonconformist tenants Peter and John Griffin.

So, despite persecution from national and local government, the congregation of the late 17th-century dissenting church in Avebury could take comfort from at least tacit support from some of the neighbouring gentry and the divisions in the local Anglican establishment. These conditions probably helped the church to grow and perhaps provided the space for a politically motivated outbreak of stone destruction which probably began during the 1690s. The destruction had its origins in one aspect of the early 17th-century dispute between Puritan and Laudian clerics in the Church of England. This centred around the issuing in 1618 of the 'Book of Sports' by the court (Marcus 1994, 153). The book attempted to define a series of recreations which would be legal on the Sabbath and was regarded by contemporaries and near-contemporaries as a major part of the political conflict which led to the Civil War (Davies 1992, 203; Sharpe 2000, 355; Stukeley 1742, 17).

Marcus (1994, 153-4) links the 'Book of Sports' with the defence of the Anglican parish by the re-assertion of the right of people to have dancing, athletics, May-games, Whitson Ales and Morris dancing against Puritanism. During the Civil War and after this became a mark of a 'specifically Stuart and Anglican' (Marcus 1994, 153) outlook. Laudian priests went out of their way to revive these customs in the 1630s and 40s (Marcus 1994, 154) and they were subsequently banned by the Long Parliament (Harris 1993, 44). Maypoles in particular were used in the 1660s as part of a symbolic rejection of the Puritan past. Harris quotes Anthony Wood's account of the many maypoles set up in Oxford in May 1660, 'set up on purpose to vex the Presbyterians and Independents' (Wood, in Harris 1993, 44). Keiller's excavations in the centre of the southern inner circle at Avebury discovered a number of early modern postholes which were identified as marking the site of the village maypole (Smith 1965, 191, 204n). If this suggestion is true it means that the early meeting houses in the village, which seem to have been in Green Lane even before the construction of the current chapel around 1707 (Dunscombe 1998, 7), would have been sited right next to the maypoles and stones used by the Anglicans as part of their celebration of the High Church vision of the parish. As the Anglican establishment was actively involved with the persecution of dissent throughout the later 17th century it is not hard to see how this situation

Fig. 9. The confrontation of faiths: the re-erected stones of the inner setting within the southern inner circle at Avebury with the nonconformist chapel in the background

may have led to a politically motivated assault on the stones as symbols of the Anglican parish. In this context, it is interesting to note that some of the earliest dates given by Stukeley for stone removal relate to megaliths adjacent to the chapel (Stukeley 1743, tab. I; Ucko et al. 1991, pls 32-40) (Fig. 9).

Other events may have contributed to the identification of prehistoric monuments with the Anglican parish. The earliest detailed record of Avebury was made by a royalist, John Aubrey, who first saw the site in 1649 (Ucko et al 1991, 14). In August 1663 Aubrey and Sir Walter Charleton persuaded Charles II, the Duke of York and Sir Robert Moray to visit Avebury, after a discussion at court about the site (Ucko et al 1991, 25). The royal party visited Avebury and walked to the top of Silbury Hill and Charles commanded Aubrey to write an account of the monument (Aubrey 1980, 21-2). Memory of this visit remained strong in Avebury: it was recorded by Pepys on his visit in 1668 and in more detail by Stukeley in the 1720s (Ucko et al 1991, 26). Stukeley recorded how Charles was remembered as having ridden into the yard of the Catherine Wheel to view the Cove and that Charles, the Duke of York and the Duke of

Monmouth were supposed to have ridden up Silbury Hill (Stukeley 1743, 23, 43). Stukeley also provides an account of popular festivities on church feast days directly linked to the Avebury monuments:

> The country people have an anniversary meeting on the top of *Silbury-hill* on every *palm-sunday*, when they make merry with cakes, figs, sugar and water fetch'd from the *swallow-head*, or spring of the *Kennet*. (Stukeley 1743, 43-4)

Stukeley's own political and religious opinions have been dealt with in studies by Piggott (1985) and Haycock (2002). Both present him as a latitudinarian member of the Church of England, that is, one of an increasing minority of clergymen tolerant of dissent. Haycock in particular has examined the development of Stukeley's religious ideas and their impact on his archaeological writings. He sees Stukeley's latitudinarianism, in the context of early 18th-century debates about science and religion, as a position which gave him the freedom to speculate and publish on religious matters. Haycock interprets Stukeley's writings as belonging together as an enquiry about the roots of religion. This project seems to have been aimed at refuting the views of those men, such as Newton and William Whiston, who had developed a Newtonian view of religion which denied the Trinity (Haycock 2002, 188). Haycock's interpretation of Stukeley's work as a defence of the doctrine of the Trinity is fundamentally correct, but both he and Piggott (1985) may have overemphasised Stukeley's commitment to a latitudinarian position. Stukeley was certainly a moderate Whig in politics, although he was not above allying himself with local Tories in Boston in an attempt to build his medical practice (Haycock 2002, 46). Stukeley quoted with approval his own father's tolerance of dissent (Bodl. MS Eng. Misc. c. 533 f6v) but some of his later writings show that he, at least in print, adhered strongly to the importance of a national rather than a private conscience. His

later writings also show a distinct hostility to the structure of religious worship under the Commonwealth. In a sermon in the Palace of Westminster on the anniversary of the execution of Charles I he characterised the Commonwealth church as resembling the captivity of the Jews in Babylon (Stukeley 1742, 4).

If we accept Stukeley's evidence, then the burning of the Avebury stones did not begin until the persecution of the nonconformists was waning in the 1690s. A number of different motivations may have led to the stone breaking and economic considerations may have played a part. However the subconscious or conscious association of the stones with the Anglican parish may have reinforced the will to remove inconvenient stones. There are a number of possible ways in which we might imagine the dissenters' faith influencing their actions. We might imagine that the stone burning began as an explicitly political act by dissenters using their new freedoms to gain a measure of revenge for the indignities of the later 17th century. Alternatively the primary motive for the destruction may have been economic but local Anglican opposition may have politicised it. The fact that everyone Stukeley records as opposing the stone-breaking locally was either a member of the gentry or directly connected with the Anglican church – particularly Ruben Horsal, Sir Richard Holford, and Charles Tooker – may have given dissenting stone-breakers more incentive to continue. Whatever the motivation, it remains the case that by the 1720s Stukeley either failed to perceive or did not record any religious or political dimension to the stone burning. This may mean that by this date any political influences were either subconscious or belonged to an earlier phase of destruction. However, we know that Stukeley gave only a partial account of the stone destruction he witnessed, and it may be that he deliberately did not record this aspect.

The stone breaking seems to have begun in Avebury itself around the 1690s and at least part of the direction and organisation of this phase of destruction came from the nonconformist villagers. Stone breaking seems to have been going on both around the chapel in the henge and on the Beckhampton Avenue on the Griffins' land, although individual stones elsewhere in the complex were also broken. It is not clear whether the large-scale stone breaking stopped as a result of the representations of Stukeley and Ruben Horsal or whether the changing political climate of the 1720s removed the ideological urge to destroy the stones. Some piecemeal removal of stones continued into the 19th and 20th centuries (Smith 1965, 183-5, 207n) but there were no more sustained campaigns to remove entire portions of the monument.

Conclusion

A combination of new archaeological and historical research has demonstrated a greater complexity to the story of the destruction of Avebury's megalithic monuments than was previously envisaged. Our work suggests that both the chronology of different technologies of stone 'riddance' and the motivations that lay behind them require more critical investigation.

In relation to issues of chronology, while the traditional account of stone burial followed by a phase of stone breaking still holds true at a general level, these techniques are not as neatly separated in time as was thought. The evidence from the Beckhampton Avenue shows stone burial to be a long-lived practice, beginning in the 14th century and continuing, perhaps on a more episodic basis, into the 16th or 17th century. Although a religious imperative probably lies in its origins as a practice (as detailed in Smith 1965, 179-80), once established as a recognised technology for removing stones it had the potential to be employed in a variety of circumstances.

Stone breaking through fire-setting, while at its peak during the latest 17th and early 18th centuries, now looks to have a longer ancestry. Radiocarbon dates from the Falkner's Circle could push this practice back as early as the 15th

or 16th century, although probably not for Avebury itself. Cold-cutting techniques might also have been employed at this date. In this context, note should taken of the use of dressed sarsen in the 15th century rebuilding of the southern aisle of Avebury church (Freeman 1983, 103). Whether these stones were fire-set or split cold, from megalithic settings or 'natural' sarsens, is difficult to tell, but they do illustrate the breaking up of sarsen for use in high status buildings during the late medieval period.

If, as now seems likely, the practices of burial, partial burial and fire-setting of megaliths overlapped for a period during the 16th and/or 17th century, we are still left unclear as to why stone-breaking should eventually become the preferred technology. Undoubtedly, a demand for building stone has a part to play in this, but the realisation that the practice was also influenced by political and religious agendas stresses the danger of making recourse to purely pragmatic and mercantile explanations. Like any form of technology, stone breaking was embedded within contemporary social and cultural values. The 17th and 18th centuries represented a period of considerable social and ideological transformation, which has been represented by some as marking the shift from a medieval to a 'Georgian' mindset (Deetz 1996). Johnson (1996) has characterised these changes as revolving around concepts of order, closure and commodification, and operating at several levels from the individual body to the landscape. Underpinning a 'rationalisation' of the agricultural landscape, as promoted by contemporary treatise on farming and estate management, were ideas surrounding the ordering of an unruly nature through processes such as enclosure (Johnson 1996, 72, 87), and of the moral and aesthetic 'improvement' inherent in these laboured practices. One wonders whether Avebury's dissenting stone breakers viewed their work as contributing to such an 'improved' social and physical landscape – clearing the land, but also removing stones tainted by traditional superstition and associated in their minds with the dubious nature of Anglican values. Such work also facilitated a transformation in the nature of these stones, from the material remains of an ungodly past into commodities in the making. The circumspect and careful treatment implied by earlier traditions of burial suggests that while the medieval mind had attached an almost inalienable quality to them, this was gradually eroded from the Tudor period onwards.

Although fire-setting was potentially more expensive and certainly involved greater risk than cold-working, it may have become the preferred technology of the stone breakers because of its highly visible nature, and because of the metaphoric connections that it could draw upon. Fire-setting of the larger stones must have provided a very public spectacle, especially when undertaken close to houses within the village. Its enactment would surely have recalled in people's minds the kinds of public bonfires popular during the period. Could the use of fire have been viewed as symbolically cleansing and perhaps apotropaic, in the same way that the common practice of lighting midsummer fires was intended to ward off evil and provide protection and blessing (Hutton 1996, 320-1)? Was the burning of ungodly stones linked in the minds of nonconformists to the burning of papal or devil effigies as a part of Gunpowder Treason Day celebrations? These are just speculations, but they illustrate the potential cultural complexity of what, at first sight, might appear a relatively pragmatic process. Of course there remain many ambiguities, and the archaeological evidence reminds us just how episodic, piecemeal and generally 'messy' the destruction of Avebury's megalithic monuments was.

We hope that Isobel will forgive this excursion into historical archaeology within a volume ostensibly dedicated to Neolithic and Bronze Age topics; but for her it is a matter that is, quite literally, close to home.

Acknowledgements

We would like to acknowledge the generous support of the Arts and Humanities Research Board in funding the fieldwork and historical research upon which much of this paper is based. It is not uncommon for a process of 'intellectual convergence' to occur in work of this kind, and we wish to point out that Brian Edwards discovered the same connection between the stone-breakers and nonconformity quite independently. Ros Cleal at the Alexander Keiller Museum in Avebury, the staff of the Swindon and Wiltshire Record Office in Trowbridge and the Bodleian Library in Oxford provided access to archive material in their care. Thanks are also due to Madeleine Gray for advice on early modern religious history. Finally, without Isobel's magisterial 1965 report the direction for this research would never have existed.

Notes

1. Comparable strategies of stone burial and stone breaking are attested archaeologically at the Devil's Quoits henge monument, Stanton Harcourt, Oxfordshire (Barclay et al. 1995). However, this monument lacks the wealth of antiquarian record on stone destruction found at Avebury, as well as being much smaller in scale.
2. We do not cover the issue of stone burial during the medieval period, which has recently been reviewed elsewhere (Jope 1999).
3. Stukeley records two of the Cove stones (the south-eastern and south-western) being broken-up by Richard Fowler and others in order to provide building material for a local inn (the present day Wagon and Horses) (Stukeley 1743, 35-6; Bodl. MS Gough Maps 231 42).
4. Burl (1979, 49) following Stukeley (1743, 17) lists a Mr Ayloff as a stone-breaker but it is clear from the context of Stukeley's reference that in this case he is giving an example of the hardness and size of natural sarsen and that Ayloff had nothing to do with the destruction of Avebury sarsens.

Bibliography

Aubrey, J. 1980. *Monumenta Britannica*. Eds J. Fowles & R. Legg. Sherbourne: Dorset Publishing Company

Barclay, A., Gray, M. & Lambrick, G. 1995. *Excavations at the Devil's Quoits, Stanton Harcourt, Oxfordshire, 1972-3 and 1988*. Oxford: Oxford Archaeological Unit

Bradley, R. 1993. *Altering the Earth: the origins of monuments in Britain and Continental Europe*. Edinburgh: Society of Antiquaries of Scotland

Bradley, R. 2002. *The Past in Prehistoric Societies*. London: Routledge

Burl, A. 1979. *Prehistoric Avebury*. New Haven & London: Yale University Press

Davies, J. 1992. *The Caroline Captivity of the Church: Charles I and the remoulding of Anglicanism*. Oxford: Oxford University Press

Deetz, J. 1996. *In Small Things Forgotten: an archaeology of early American life*. 2nd edition. New York: Anchor

Dunscombe, H. 1998. *Avebury, a five mile chapel: the story of three hundred years of life and worship in a congregational country Chapel*. Avebury: Avebury Chapel

Freeman, J. 1983. Avebury. In D.A. Crowley (ed), *A History of Wiltshire (VCH)*, Vol 12. Oxford: Oxford University Press

Funari, P.P.A., Hall, M. & Jones, S. (eds) 1999. *Historical Archaeology: back from the edge*. London: Routledge

Gillings, M. & Pollard, J. forthcoming. *Avebury*. London: Duckworth

Gillings, M., Pollard, J. & Wheatley, D. 2000. The Beckhampton Avenue and a 'new' Neolithic enclosure near Avebury: an interim report on the 1999 excavations. *Wiltshire Archaeological & Natural History Magazine* 93, 1-8

Gillings, M., Pollard, J. & Wheatley, D. 2002. Excavations at the Beckhampton Enclosure, Avenue and Cove, Avebury: an interim report on the 2000 season. *Wiltshire Archaeological & Natural History Magazine* 95, 249-58

Harris, T. 1993. *Politics under the Later Stuarts: party conflict in a divided society 1660-1715*. Harlow: Longmans

Haycock, D.B. 2002. *William Stukeley: science, religion and archaeology in eighteenth century England*. Woodbridge: Boydell Press

Hutton, R. 1996. *The Stations of the Sun: a history of the ritual year in Britain*. Oxford: Oxford University Press

Johnson, M. 1996. *An Archaeology of Capitalism*. Oxford: Blackwell

Jope, E.M. 1999. The Saxon and Medieval pottery

from Alexander Keiller's excavations at Avebury. *Wiltshire Archaeological & Natural History Magazine* 92, 60-91

Keiller, A. & Piggott, S. 1936. The West Kennet Avenue, Avebury: excavations 1934-5. *Antiquity* 10, 417-27

Law, A. 1969. Caleb Baily, the demolisher. *Wiltshire Archaeological & Natural History Magazine* 64, 100-6

Long, W. 1858. Abury. *Wiltshire Archaeological & Natural History Magazine* 4, 309-63

Lukis, W.C. 1881. Report on the prehistoric monuments of Stonehenge and Avebury. *Proceedings of the Society of Antiquaries of London* (2nd ser) 9, 141-57

Marcus, L.S. 1994. Politics and pastoral: writing the court on the countryside. In K. Sharpe & P. Lake (eds), *Culture and politics in early Stuart England*. London: Macmillan

Norrey, P.J. 1988. The Restoration regime in action: the relationship between central and local government in Dorest, Somerset and Wiltshire. *Historical Journal* 31, 789-12

Piggott, S. 1985. *William Stukeley: an eighteenth century antiquary*. New York: Thames & Hudson

Reeves, M.E. 1956. Protestant nonconformity. In R.B. Pugh & E. Crittall (eds), *A History of Wiltshire (VCH)*. Vol 3, 99-149. London: Oxford University Press

Sharpe, K. 2000. *Remapping Early Modern England: the culture of seventeenth century politics*. Cambridge: Cambridge University Press

Smith, A.C. 1867. Excavations at Avebury. *Wiltshire Archaeological & Natural History Magazine* 10, 209-16

Smith, I.F. 1965. *Windmill Hill and Avebury: excavations by Alexander Keiller 1925-1939*. Oxford: Clarendon Press

Soffe, G. & Clare, T. 1988. New evidence of ritual monuments at Long Meg and Her Daughters, Cumbria. *Antiquity* 62, 552-7

Stukeley, W. 1742. *A sermon preached before the honourable House of Commons at St. Margaret's, Westminster; on the 30th day of January, 1741-2. Being the anniversary of the martyrdom of King Charles I*. London: T. Cooper

Stukeley, W. 1743. *Abury, a temple of the British druids, with some others described*. London: W Stukeley

Ucko, P.J., Hunter, M., Clark, A.J. & David, A. 1991. *Avebury Reconsidered: from the 1660s to the 1990s*. London: Unwin Hyman

Underdown, D. 1985. *Revel, Riot and Rebellion: popular politics and culture in England 1603 - 1660*. Oxford: Clarendon Press

Whittle, A. 1994. Excavations at Millbarrow Neolithic chambered tomb, Winterbourne Monkton, North Wiltshire. *Wiltshire Archaeological & Natural History Magazine* 87, 1-53

The Dating and Diversity of the Earliest Ceramics of Wessex and South-west England

Rosamund M.J. Cleal

Introduction

Isobel Smith's doctoral thesis, 'The decorative art of Neolithic ceramics in south-eastern England and its relations' (1956), is a work which, although unpublished, has exercised a profound influence on the analysis of Neolithic pottery for nearly half a century and remains highly influential. It examined the ceramics of the whole Neolithic period and facilitated, in particular, the analysis of the large causewayed enclosure assemblages which have been examined since (and not least by Isobel Smith herself). In one respect – that of chronology - however, the passing of years has radically changed the picture, and it is perhaps timely both to attempt a brief review of the current situation regarding dating of earlier Neolithic ceramics and to examine their nature, in at least one area – largely outside that examined in Smith 1956 - and to offer it to Isobel as a small token of regard for her contribution to a field of study in which I have found so much pleasure and in which I, like many others, look to her as one of its greatest practitioners.

Reviewing the earliest Neolithic ceramics

The great change in ceramic chronology during the last fifty or so years has been, of course, occasioned by the development of, and changes in, radiocarbon dating over that time. It is salutary now to study Stuart Piggott's chronological chart in *Neolithic Cultures of the British Isles* (1954) and realise that the whole of the Neolithic period was thought to lie between c.2000 BC and about 1500 BC (1954, fold-out facing p.380). Once radiocarbon dating became well-established it very soon became apparent that the chronology had to be extended by about a thousand years, giving, by the 1960s and 1970s, a Neolithic period extending from about 3300 to c.1800 uncalibrated radiocarbon years BC. It was in this context that Smith published a highly influential paper synthesising knowledge of the Neolithic period to that date and introducing the term 'Grimston/Lyles Hill Series' (Smith 1974, 108) to encompass both carinated bowls and S-profiled bowls (the latter the former Heslerton Ware which had then recently been merged with the

Grimston carinated bowls by Terry Manby (Smith 1974 282, n24).

In 1988, and still using the relatively short chronology of radiocarbon years, Andrew Herne published a wide ranging paper examining the Grimston/Lyles Hill series, 'A time and a place for the Grimston Bowl'. Herne opens this paper with his definition of his new term 'Carinated Bowl':

> a class of high quality undecorated open carinated vessels, unless this is stated otherwise. They are characterised by an angular bipartite profile and are distinguished from a category of 'Shouldered Bowls' in which the carination defines an upright shoulder on the upper part of the vessel. (Herne 1988, 9)

Later in the same paper he adds to this by returning to the definition of the classic Grimston Bowl as first defined by Piggott (1954, 114), describing it as: 'of fine fabric and finish, with an open and shallow profile, marked carination and a simple everted and beaded rim. The overall impression is of a bipartite bowl, the lower part of the vessel sharply differentiated from the upper part, with the carination often low on the body' (Herne *op cit.* 15). Later still, however, he notes that the Sweet Track (Somerset) vessels show that 'An upright profile is a characteristic local feature', so including upright forms in the definition. His main points are that 'the initial horizon for the British and Irish Neolithic can be recognised by the common presence across a range of related contexts of the fine Carinated Bowl as typified by Hanging Grimston' (*op. cit.* 16) and that in particular the S-profiled bowls and 'shouldered bowls' (i.e. those having high carinations) with developed rims typical of the Broome Heath assemblage, which had become associated with the Grimston/Lyles Hill Series in the archaeological literature, were not part of the earliest ceramic repertoire (*op cit.* 15). His argument hinged largely on the dating of Broome Heath and he rejected, quite understandably, the earlier dates from that site (*op cit.* 14). Herne's re-examination of the earlier ceramics of the British Neolithic led him to

formulate a model which characterized the ceramics of the British Isles as developing from the 'simple to complex, from the universal to the particular' (*op. cit.* 23). In interpretation he suggests that this is a 'direct consequence of wider everyday use of pottery in order to fulfill a wider range of functional requirements in the middle Neolithic.' and that 'a partition and differentiation in the social contexts of ceramic use may have material expression through stylistic differentiation of individual vessels and ceramic suites' (ibid.).

The effect of Herne's review, which remains current, is best exemplified by Alex Gibson's summary of the earliest pottery in the British Isles in his recent volume *Prehistoric Pottery in Britain and Ireland* (2002). There, Gibson illustrates a range of classic Carinated Bowls (*op. cit.* fig. 34) and describes the uniformity of shape and fabric characteristic of them. These are followed in the chronology of the earlier Neolithic, he explains, from 'sometime before 3600 BC' by more diverse forms. He cites the south-west as having a well-defined regional style and specialist manufacture in the tradition of simple open and shouldered bowls found at sites such as Carn Brea, Cornwall, made from gabbroic clay (*op cit.* 72). He accepts this as emerging in the early 4th millennium cal BC on the basis of radiocarbon dates from Carn Brea and continuing into the middle of the millennium at sites such as Windmill Hill, Wiltshire (*op. cit.* 72). In other areas a wide range of vessels develops around 3600 BC, including shouldered forms, open and closed bowls, slack shoulders and S-shaped forms, much of which has been recovered from causewayed enclosure ditches. It is at this time too that decorated pottery is found in many areas and in many forms, which Gibson briefly reviews (*op cit.* 72-74).

This broad model, of generally early carinated forms developing, late in the first half of the 4th millennium cal BC, into a wide range of forms and styles, including decorated styles, is so self-evidently largely grounded in fact that without startling discoveries it is not likely to be refuted, but there is some scope, I think, for refining it before it becomes entrenched as an orthodoxy, and in particular there is scope to examine the apparent dominance of the Carinated Bowl. I am not concerned here to undertake a full-scale critique of Herne's paper, not least because of its impressive breadth, but there a number of points which seem worth examining. In the following pages I will argue that although there is quite clearly an early preference for carinated forms, Herne's paper, and its subsequent interpretation, is leading to a situation in which resemblance to a Carinated Bowl 'norm' is emphasised while dissimilarities are paid little attention. I will argue that the very existence of the model of the Carinated Bowl (and previous writers' Grimston Bowl) is helping to create this and that efforts have to be made to recognise and differentiate diversity of form within this broad early tradition. I want in this paper to concentrate on Wessex and the south-west, not only because it is the area I know best, but because it is an area Herne found difficult to accommodate in his model, is explicitly mentioned by Gibson, and is still proving problematic in ceramic terms.

Chronology

With so few extant earlier Neolithic radiocarbon dates associated with pottery available for Wessex and the south-west, even for causewayed enclosures, it is not possible to undertake a thorough review of Neolithic ceramic chronology in the region, although with a major programme of radiocarbon dating of causewayed enclosures beginning as I write (by Alasdair Whittle, Alex Bayliss, Frances Healy and others) there is hope for a more refined chronology, at least for those ceramic assemblages, in the future. Fig. 1 lists existing dates for causewayed enclosures at Hembury (Devon), Whitesheet, Knap Hill (both in Wiltshire) and for the hilltop (or 'tor') enclosures at Helman Tor and Carn Brea (both in Cornwall)[1]. Windmill Hill (Wiltshire) has a large number of dates, but of the six dates for primary fill

(including those 'under primary fill' – i.e. directly on ditch base) all but two have the earlier end of the 95% confidence range in the mid-37th century (3650/3640 cal BC) and the two remaining have it at 3700 cal BC. The earlier end of the 68% confidence ranges at Windmill Hill are all between 3640 and 3610 cal BC (Whittle *et al.* 1999, table 52). The recent extensive dating programme of dating the Hambledon Hill (Dorset) enclosures is discussed in detail in this volume (Healy). No activity at Hambledon associated with the enclosures dates to before the 37th century cal BC (Healy expresses it as 300 – 400 years of activity pre-3300 BC). Maiden Castle primary dates, which appear to indicate an early inception for that enclosure, are shown separately, in Fig. 2, as these are particularly interesting, having been dated relatively recently and are discussed separately, below (and in Appendix 1), where an interpretation differing from that of the excavator is offered.

With the exception of Hembury (and excluding for the moment Maiden Castle) none of the calibrated dates for causewayed enclosures in the south-west need suggest that they began to be constructed before about 3650 cal BC. A single date for Carn Brea extends its range substantially earlier than this at 95% confidence (BM-825, 3950-3650 cal BC with 95% confidence, 3940-3860 (22.2%) or 3810-3700 (46%; see Appendix 1 for discussion of context)) but this was obtained from 'block' oak charcoal (Mercer 1981, 42) suggesting that it was heartwood and therefore possibly as much as 300-400 years older than the event it has been interpreted as dating. The remaining two dates suggest a firmly post-3650 cal BC occupation for the enclosure, and as they too are apparently on oak heartwood it is possible that much of the use of the site considerably post-dates 3650 cal BC.

Helman Tor also has produced one substantially pre-3650 cal BC date (HAR-8818 4880 ± 120 BP) from a post-hole. This is a date on smallwood (Mercer 1997, 21) but has a large error margin. At 95% confidence it can only be dated to 3950 – 3350 cal BC and at 68% 3900 –

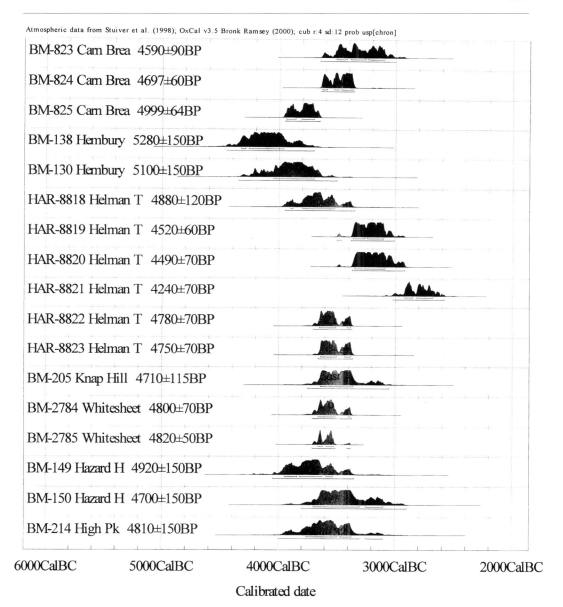

Atmospheric data from Stuiver et al. (1998); OxCal v3.5 Bronk Ramsey (2000); cub r:4 sd:12 prob usp[chron]

BM-823 Carn Brea 4590±90BP

BM-824 Carn Brea 4697±60BP

BM-825 Carn Brea 4999±64BP

BM-138 Hembury 5280±150BP

BM-130 Hembury 5100±150BP

HAR-8818 Helman T 4880±120BP

HAR-8819 Helman T 4520±60BP

HAR-8820 Helman T 4490±70BP

HAR-8821 Helman T 4240±70BP

HAR-8822 Helman T 4780±70BP

HAR-8823 Helman T 4750±70BP

BM-205 Knap Hill 4710±115BP

BM-2784 Whitesheet 4800±70BP

BM-2785 Whitesheet 4820±50BP

BM-149 Hazard H 4920±150BP

BM-150 Hazard H 4700±150BP

BM-214 High Pk 4810±150BP

6000CalBC   5000CalBC   4000CalBC   3000CalBC   2000CalBC

Calibrated date

Fig. 1. Radiocarbon dates from causewayed and 'tor' enclosures in the south-west and from High Peak and Hazard Hill

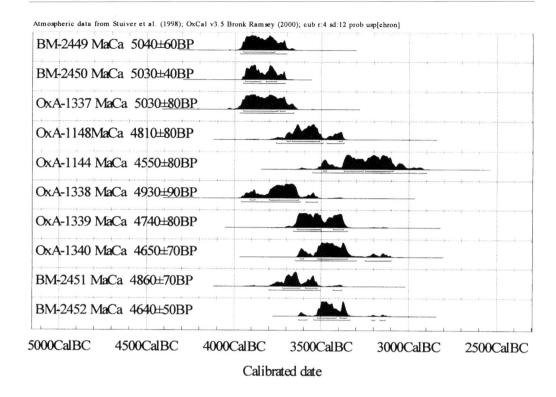

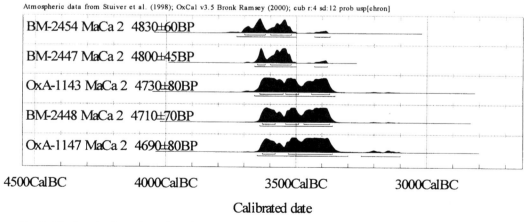

Fig. 2. Maiden Castle: radiocarbon dates from (a - top) primary contexts and (b) secondary contexts in the causewayed enclosure ditches

3520 BC (and even at 66.8% can only be narrowed to 3800 – 3520 cal BC), allowing a possibility that the charcoal dates to post-3650 cal BC. (See Appendix 1 for a description of the Helman Tor dates and their contexts.) Although this date appears to allow that a pre-37th century inception to South-Western Style assemblages may be represented here, a single date from a site at which the excavator acknowledges that there are problems in interpreting the dates (Mercer 1997, 22-23) seems very little to build on.

Hembury remains the enclosure with the earliest dates in the region, but the possibility of oak heartwood having been used and the large error term means that it must be regarded as virtually undated until the new programme is forthcoming. Maiden Castle, however, is a different matter, having been a relatively recent excavation (1986). The excavator argues for the digging of the enclosure ditch at an early date, some time between 3900 and 3700 cal BC (Sharples & Clark 1991, 105 'a') and possibly around 3800 BC (Sharples 1991, 253) principally on the grounds of dates from charcoal and one from animal bone in the primary filling of the Inner Ditch (Sharples & Clark 1991, 104, Table 8: BM-2449 and BM-2450 (charcoal) and OxA-1337 (bone)) (Fig. 2a). It is possible to argue, however, on the grounds of the published evidence, that the construction of the enclosure may not pre-date by many years the deposition of the midden material on top of the primary chalk rubble filling (Fig. 2b), which gives a date of around 3700 cal BC at the earliest (see Appendix 1 for details).

If it seems reasonable, on present evidence, to assume that it is unlikely that the south-west enclosures at least will emerge as pre-37th century after the forthcoming dating programme, it is also interesting to note that a similar date for inception may apply to at least one other monument type of the 4th millennium: cursus monuments, but that these both appear to post-date another: long burial mounds, both chambered and unchambered. The dating of

cursus monuments has been reviewed recently by Alistair Barclay and Alex Bayliss (1999) who conclude on the basis of a wide range of radiocarbon dates that 'the construction of cursus monuments seems to belong to the second half of the 4th millennium cal BC. On the evidence of the monuments for which we currently have absolute dating, this period was between *3640-3380 cal BC (95% confidence)* and *cal BC 3260-2920 (95% confidence). (op. cit.* 25). Long barrows, although also awaiting the results of a dating programme (Southern British Early Neolithic barrows and bones project), seem to show an earlier inception, although some at least of the very early dates have now been discounted. Schulting has recently published new dates for Lambourn long barrow (in Berkshire), which was formerly one of the earliest dated monuments in Britain (dated by Gx-1178 5365±180 BP) along with a more general reappraisal of the evidence for the earliest Neolithic. An antler pick lying on the ditch floor at Lambourn is now dated to 4870 ± 45 BP (OxA-7692; 3765-3535 at 95% confidence) and is supported by another two dates on human bone, averaging to 3760-3645 cal BC (Schulting 2000, 28). Schulting argues that similar circumstances may apply to the 'early' dates for Horslip and Fussell's Lodge long barrows (both in Wiltshire; the latter including 'Decorated' vessels (Whittle 1977, 94, fig. 15)). A re-evaluation of the pottery associated with these must await the publication of the full results of the dating programme. Although Schulting allows that 'it may be premature to discount the possibility of a pre-5200 BP Neolithic presence' (*op. cit.* 30) he also describes the 'emerging view of the British Early Neolithic as a relatively late phenomenon, with few or no acceptable (i.e. from clear Neolithic contexts on short-lived materials, and with standard errors of 100 years or less) dates prior to 5200/5100 BP (c. 4000 cal BC)' (Schulting 2000, 29).

On present evidence, then, it seems a reasonable assumption to take the causewayed and 'tor' enclosures, and the pottery associated with them, as a mid-4th millennium cal BC phenomenon. It removes, however, from the south-west, the early appearance of carinated bowls of the South-Western/Hembury tradition. Other sites such as Hazard Hill and High Peak, both in Devon and with Gabbroic Ware, are no assistance in identifying early ceramics, having dates with large error terms and calibrated ranges. What then remains as the earliest pottery and is it all the Carinated Bowl of Herne? In Wessex and the south-west, as elsewhere, there is very little pottery dated by association with radiocarbon dates for the early to mid-4th millennium cal BC. What there is, however, does include the most closely dated early Neolithic ceramics in the British Isles, those from the Sweet Track, Somerset.

Pottery from the Sweet Track

(See Appendix 1 for descriptions of context and for references; see Fig. 5 for redrawn pottery at a common scale with pottery from other sites; see Appendix 2 for explanation of terms used in Figs. 4 and 5.)

Since the publication of the Sweet Track dendrochronological dating which showed the Track to have been built of wood felled largely in 3807/3806 BC (Coles & Coles 1990), the handful of Neolithic vessels associated with it have been recognised as the most closely dated Neolithic vessels in the British Isles, but there has been surprisingly little discussion of how the collection compares with other early pottery. Ian Kinnes, in his report on the Drove Site vessel (see Fig. 5), noted the classic Grimston Bowl type profile and the generally eastern distribution of this type, and noted too that the variation in profile between the bowl S6 and the vessel from the Drove Site was particularly important given the precise chronology applying to the Sweet Track (Kinnes 1979, 52). Of the same vessels Herne noted only that while there was some variation in profile, 'an upright profile is a characteristic feature' and that the whole Sweet Track collection was 'markedly similar in fabric,

finish, and form' (Herne 1988, 17). A degree of variation was identified, therefore, but regarded as very limited. Two factors, however, may be militating against highlighting variation within this collection: one is an undoubted similarity, as described, in finish and fabric as well as of form. The second, however, is a more general problem in that the literature of ceramics of this period largely lacks a language to describe subtle variation in form, a function of the relative neglect of form for the earlier Neolithic period which I have highlighted in an earlier paper (Cleal 1992). Ian Kinnes, for example, refers to the bowl S6 (Fig. 5) as 'shouldered' (Kinnes 1979, 52) in a use of that term related to that of Herne, who uses it to include carinated vessels other than Carinated Bowls, as when he writes that 'the shouldered bowls from Broome Heath have a dominant emphasis on the upper part of the body, the carination is invariably high on the body and is only part of a stylistic and functional complex of shoulder/neck/rim' (Herne 1988, 15). This presumably applies, although he does not cite examples, to vessels such as Broome Heath P350 and P351 (Wainwright 1972, fig. 25) or to the Broome Heath vessel illustrated here, Fig. 5, and are forms he is identifying as later than the classic Carinated Bowls and part of a middle Neolithic assemblage (op. cit. 16). In the case of the Sweet Track vessel S6 it is arguable that it is not a carinated vessel at all, if a true carination is understood as marking a change in angle of the body wall (it is, after all, a term derived from the Latin for 'keel') and not just a superficial emphasis on part of the profile such as by pinching or pushing it out to raise an angle or building it up by adding clay.

There has always been a reluctance to use named types for earlier Neolithic ceramics, largely on the understandable argument that in a society in which pottery production is on a local and probably household level it is not appropriate to identify widespread types in the way that later pottery styles are often identified. However, because the Carinated Bowl has been so identified, and does seem to reflect a real preference for carination in the early part of the Neolithic, it has come to dominate the study of earlier Neolithic ceramics. In order to counteract this I would like to demonstrate that there are other forms which occur at this early date, which are not all of the classic Carinated Bowl form. (It would also undoubtedly help lessen confusion were some other term to be found to distinguish the pottery of the *middle* Neolithic, other than the general 'Neolithic Bowl' which at present tends to be used for anything which is not classifiable as Carinated Bowl, but that is outside the scope of this article.) To help focus on diversity of form at this unarguably early date – i.e. at exactly that period dominated by the Carinated Bowl in Herne's argument – we can turn to the detail of the Sweet Track collection. In it we can, arguably, find at least three types, including Herne's Carinated Bowl, which we can name to enable us to distinguish them:

Classic Carinated Bowl (Fig. 5)
Firstly, there are quite classic examples of Herne's 'true' Carinated Bowl, typified by Hanging Grimston (Herne 1988, 15 -16) with a sharp shoulder (i.e. with a true change in angle of the body wall), neutral or open form, a rolled-over rim, a fine finish and the carination low on the body.

Pseudo-Carinated Bowl (Fig. 5)
In this vessel, S6, Kinnes's 'shouldered bowl' although not matching the sharpness of a 'true' carination, the shoulder appears from the illustration to have more of an 'angle' than is usual in round-shouldered vessels, a distinction not at present having a name. Because it seems clear that some sort of angle was intended, on an essentially bag-shaped vessel, I suggest 'pseudo-carinated', the name implying that an impression of actual or near carination was 'meant' by the potter but that it is different from the profile created by a change in angle of the pot wall. Later, in enclosure assemblages, this form may recur, with the impression of carination there created by a 'girth cordon' (e.g. Smith 1981, fig 72).

Deep-bodied Carinated Bowl (Fig. 5)
The Sweet Track vessel E3, although incomplete, shows enough profile to indicate that it is a distinctly deep-bodied form with a shallow, concave neck beneath a rolled over rim. The concave neck, rolled-over-rim and carination clearly indicate that it belongs with the more typical bowl, but the depth of the body cannot be ignored: not only does it completely change the balance (literally and aesthetically) from the 'classic' Carinated Bowl form, it may well indicate a difference in function. It is interesting to note that it is this proportion of body and neck – that is, a relatively shallow neck – which becomes common in the causewayed enclosure assemblages of the mid-late 4th millennium cal BC. It is also directly comparable to the shallow-necked vessels at Broome Heath noted above and cited by Herne as not belonging to the Carinated Bowl 'horizon' (compare Fig. 5 E3 and the vessel illustrated from Broome Heath in the same figure which probably dates to the mid-4th millennium cal BC).

No other groups in the south-west or Wessex have such close dating as the Sweet Track vessels, but I want now to examine three groups in which the forms suggest the possibility of early dates for deposition, with varying degrees of support for this from associated radiocarbon dates.

Coneybury Anomaly, Amesbury Wiltshire

(See Appendix 1 for details of context)
Coneybury Anomaly is anomalous in more ways than intended when it was named by its excavator Julian Richards from its appearance on a geophysical survey plot, and indeed Isobel Smith commented on the untypical (for the south-west) nature of the ceramics in a verbal comment to this writer (cited in Cleal 1990, 54). Although its dating is based on only one radio-carbon determination, on animal bone, that date has a 94.5% probability of being before the date taken here as the upper limit of earlier pottery:

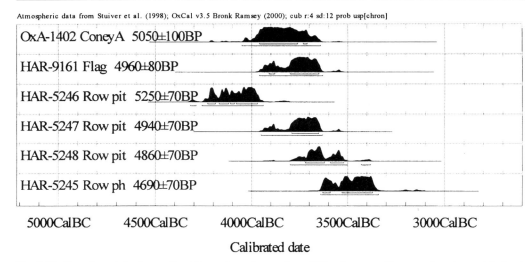

Atmospheric data from Stuiver et al. (1998); OxCal v3.5 Bronk Ramsey (2000); cub r:4 sd:12 prob usp[chron]

OxA-1402 ConeyA 5050±100BP

HAR-9161 Flag 4960±80BP

HAR-5246 Row pit 5250±70BP

HAR-5247 Row pit 4940±70BP

HAR-5248 Row pit 4860±70BP

HAR-5245 Row ph 4690±70BP

5000CalBC   4500CalBC   4000CalBC   3500CalBC   3000CalBC

Calibrated date

Fig. 3. Radiocarbon dates from pits at Coneybury Anomaly and Flagstones and from a pit and a post-hole at Rowden

i.e. 3650 cal BC (Fig. 3) . This is enough to warrant treating this group as among the earliest dated pottery in the British Isles, but it includes very different forms to those represented at the Sweet Track, 70 km due west of Coneybury.

Among the forty or so vessels represented in the Coneybury Anomaly assemblage (and assigning sherds to separate vessels was very difficult because of the similarity of fabric and finish so this should be treated as an approximate number) are forms which could be termed (see Fig. 4 for the most reconstructable vessels, redrawn):

Classic Carinated Open Bowl (Cleal 1990, P1); Simple Open Bowl (op.cit. P2); Inflected Neutral Bowl (see Appendix 2 for definition of Inflected) (op. cit. P4); Simple Neutral Bowl; Inflected Closed Round-bodied Bowl (or Jar, the depth being unknown) (op. cit. P7); Inflected Neutral Round-bodied Bowl (P6); as well as simple Cups (conventionally vessels with mouth diameters of 120mm or less). This variety of course is in great contrast to the Sweet Track assemblage, and, in addition to the number of forms present, particularly those other than carinated, there is

also a single instance of a lug on the closed vessel P7. The assemblage is even more anomalous in terms of fabric and finish, in that even the Carinated Bowl P1 is not in the fine fabric described as a common feature of the classic Carinated Bowl in general, nor of the generally fine quality of the Sweet Track vessels. Even the redrawn and much reduced illustrations here (Figs 4 and 5) illustrate the difference, showing the Coneybury Anomaly vessels to be thicker than those from the Sweet Track, illustrated at the same scale. Having recently, though briefly, re-examined the Coneybury Anomaly pottery (mainly to check that the illustrated scale is correct because of the apparent thickness of the vessel wall in P1) the general coarseness and thickness of the pottery is striking. Another feature, which unforgivably is not in the original report (this writer's omission), is that the lug on P7 appears to have been broken and worn in antiquity, a fact which accords with the degree of curation attested by the mending hole on another vessel, P20 (not the same vessel as the lugged vessel) (Cleal 1990, 30, P20 being of unknown form but possibly carinated as it has a slightly concave neck). Two sherds, possibly from one vessel, have pre-firing holes which may be decoration, and I discussed a small number of other sherds which had surface features which possibly could be interpreted as decoration (*op. cit.* 53). In conclusion then, the Anomaly dates to an early period – and possibly a very early period - within the Neolithic; exhibits an unusually wide range of forms; shows other anomalous features, including a lug and possible decoration and has been subjected to wear and a degree of curation. Whether the difference is chronological, a function of the use to which the ceramics were being put, or an indication that geographical differences were already emerging, it is unarguable that the Coneybury Anomaly pottery differs markedly from the Sweet Track collection. It shows considerable similarity, however, to a pit group from a pit pre-dating an enclosure at Flagstones, Dorchester, Dorset, which is also of potentially early 4th millennium cal BC date.

Flagstones, Dorchester, Dorset

(See Appendix 1 for details)
Flagstones is better known for its middle Neolithic enclosure which shares some features with the primary enclosure at Stonehenge (Stonehenge 1, Cleal *et al.* 1995) but a number of cut features close to the ditch appear to be of much earlier date. In particular, two pits, 221 and 274, which were both near-circular, with sloping sides and flat bottoms, contained earlier Neolithic pottery and other artefacts (Healy 1997, 30). Only material from one of the pits, charcoal from 221, has been radiocarbon dated, to 3960-3630 BC (95.4% probability; Fig. 3), the charcoal being noted in the publication as oak (*op.cit.*, Table 1). The majority of the pottery came from the undated pit, 274, 25m from pit 221, but the pottery was similar in both form and fabric, and, importantly, at least one rim sherd from 274 was identified as likely to have come from a vessel represented by other rim sherds in 221 (Cleal 1997, 95, fig. 64). I noted of the pottery from the pits that 'The assemblage is

homogeneous, and may well represent a short period of manufacture and use' (Cleal 1997, 88). That being so, and while accepting that the association between the dated charcoal and some of the pottery render this less certainly early than Coneybury Anomaly, it is worth considering as a potentially pre-3650 BC group (and one for which there is the possibility of further determinations). Within this group (taking the two pits as one group), the following forms can be defined (Fig. 4):

Classic Carinated Neutral Bowl (the vessel probably represented in both pits), *Inflected Neutral Bowl* and *Simple Neutral or Closed Bowl* (rim of uncertain angle). A feature of the pottery from the group is the occurrence of lugs: four occurred within pit 274, two of which almost certainly belong to a single vessel, the other two to two different vessels. All are oval and horizontally applied, and two (the pair) vertically perforated. Fabrics were very restricted, comprising a flint-tempered fabric and a shelly fabric.

The final group I wish to consider is the least firmly dated to before 3650 cal BC, but is included here because its forms seem to have something in common with, particularly, the Sweet Track pottery; as with Flagstones, there appears to be potential for further determinations. This group is from Rowden in southern Dorset.

Rowden, Winterbourne Stepleton, Dorset

(Fig. 4; see Appendix 1 for details of context).
The group from pit 327, a feature discovered fortuitously during the excavation of a Middle Bronze Age settlement, has, like Flagstones, a potentially early date and an interesting, and also anomalous assemblage. Rowden's dates (Woodward 1991, 54), all on oak charcoal (not specified as small or twiggy wood, so could included heartwood) span a wide range, from 4320-3940 BC (95.4% probability for HAR-

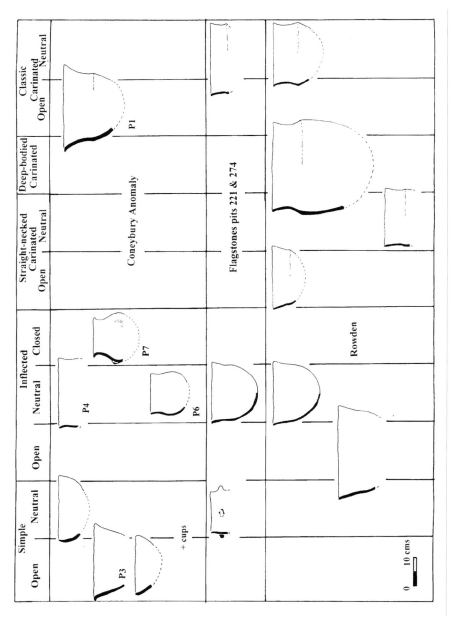

Fig. 4. Pottery from Coneybury Anomaly, Flagstones and Rowden (Illustrations after (illustrator where identifiable): Read in Cleal 1990 (Coneybury Anomaly); James in Cleal 1997 (Flagstones), Read in Woodward 1991 (Rowden)

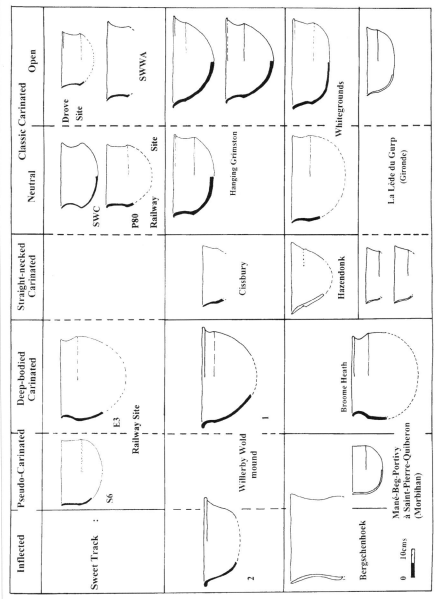

Fig. 5. Pottery from the Sweet Track and other British and Continental contexts (see Appendices 2 &3 for definition of terms). Illustrations after Boddington in Wainwright 1972 (Broome Heath), M.W.S. in Brewster 1992 (Whitegrounds), Manby 1963 (Willerby Wold), L'Helgouach 1965 (Mané-Beg-Portivy), Louwe Kooijmans 1976 (Bergschenhoek and Hazendonk), Newbigin 1937 (Hanging Grimston), Smith 1976 (Sweet Track, Railway Site), Dean in Kinnes 1979 (Sweet Track, Drove Site), Coles and Orme 1984 (Sweet Track SWC and SWWA), Roussot-Larroque 1995 (La Lède du Gurp), Barber et al. 1999 (Cissbury)

5246), from charcoal relatively high in the filling, to 3800-3380 (95.4% probability for HAR-5348) for charcoal on the bottom of the pit. The former would seem better rejected, both as being likely to be in a secondary position in the pit and derived from earlier material (albeit showing, interestingly, activity which could have taken place around the turn of the 5th millennium cal BC, although the heartwood effect could of course place this later) while the latter date *could* indicate pre-3650 BC activity (a 46.8% probability of the date lying between 3720 and 3620 BC). Although this is approaching the 'causewayed enclosure' period, the assemblage is not similar to that from, for instance, the nearby site of Maiden Castle.

The assemblage is a relatively uniform one largely of carinated forms, but within this, as within the other groups considered here, there is variety, in this case including forms which may be termed (Fig. 4):

Classic Carinated Neutral Bowl (Davies *et al.* 1991, fig. 52:4 and possibly 5*), Deep-bodied Carinated Neutral Bowl, Inflected Neutral Bowl,* all already identified elsewhere, and the novel: *Straight-necked Carinated Open Bowl, Straight-necked Carinated Neutral Bowl,* and *Inflected Open Bowl.* There appears to be a preference for straight necks and simple rather than rolled-over rims (although the *Classic Carinated Neutral Bowl* has a rolled-over rim) and there is a notable absence of cups. The fabrics are largely shelly, with some sandy fabrics (Davies *et al.* 1991, 98). When I commented on this group, from drawings, for the publication, I noted its dissimilarity from Maiden Castle (*ibid.*).

These three groups, while all are potentially of the first half of the 4th millennium cal BC, are less firmly placed pre-3650 cal BC than the Sweet Track, largely because of the potential of heartwood effect; all, however, have some potential for further dating, and, although including many carinated vessesl, also display a reasonable proportion of non-Classic Carinated Bowl forms. These groups have been highlighted because of their dates, but other groups occur both within and outside Wessex and the south-west which have no dating evidence at present. Pits at Roughridge Hill, near Devizes, Wiltshire, fall into this group, and include one very large feature apparently with carinated vessels, excavated by Edwina Proudfoot and currently being prepared for publication (note in *Wiltshire Archaeological & Natural History Magazine* 60 (1965, 133)). A collection of apparently associated carinated vessels, also including non-classic Carinated Bowl forms, was recovered from what appears to have been the infill of a naturally occurring shaft at Cannon Hill, Maidenhead, Berkshire (Bradley *et al.* 1975-76); here, although there is an early radiocarbon date the association between the pottery and the dated material is too tenuous because of the nature of both the wood and the context, for this to be useful. This occurrence of fairly large groups of vessels, often including large or very large individual vessels associated with smaller bowls and sometimes cups, with other artefacts and ecofacts in large features often with charcoal-rich fills begs the question of whether, if they are all early, they may represent particularly important places in the landscape, well before the appearance of those humanly-constructed important places: causewayed enclosures. Such locations may include prominent places, suggested by the low ridge setting of Coneybury Anomaly; places of passage, such as a passage up from the Vale of Pewsey to the chalk downs in the case of Roughridge Hill; or where a ready-made opening in the earth made it unnecessary to dig a pit for chthonic ritual (Cannon Hill). Apart from these, however, there are also many other pits which, in contrast, contain Neolithic pottery comparable to that from causewayed and 'tor' enclosures and potentially therefore of post-3650 cal BC date. Until further well-associated dates are obtained it will be impossible to further the interpretation of the ceramics from these features or to determine the social context in which they were created.

A critical look at the Carinated Bowl

It has not been my intention here to offer a wide ranging review of Neolithic ceramics and such a review is also hampered by the at present uncertain chronology. All I have attempted to do, by focussing on a number of small assemblages which certainly (Sweet Track), probably (Coneybury Anomaly) or possibly (Flagstones, Rowden) belong to a period considerably earlier than the postulated 'enclosure horizon' of the 37th century cal BC or later, is to suggest that even on present evidence the situation is more complex than the currently accepted Herne 'model' (that is, of the earliest British ceramics being almost exclusively of Carinated Bowl and in turn being superseded by the varied and often decorated ceramics of the middle Neolithic). The ceramics I have chosen to highlight here could be dismissed as differing only in detail from the established Carinated Bowl type, but I would argue that in a ceramic tradition or traditions with an essentially limited repertoire slight apparent differences in detail are highly important and are not the random product of individual invention or poor technique on the part of potters. Focussing on the fine detail may lead to a greater understanding of the nature of early ceramic manufacture and use, and of the relations of its makers with the world outside our own islands.

It is perhaps also pertinent at this point to consider an even more basic issue – the nature of stylistic variation and the creation of categories. John Barrett has made an important contribution to the debate around categorisation in direct application to the Middle Bronze Age ceramics of Cranborne Chase (Barrett 1991), where he distinguishes between the identification of the pottery form as 'cultural norm', in the cultural historical sense, and in contrast of pottery form as a prototypical core at the heart of a category (op. cit. 204). Whereas classification identifying 'cultural norms' tends to interpret these virtually as 'given' and views them as static

in the social context in which they occur and often as imposed from outside, in the identification of categories, in contrast, the prototypical core may be recognised as continually constructed and renegotiated through social practice. Barrett writes: 'They [prototypes] may be constructed with contrasting reference to other prototypical categories, and around them may extend a wide gradation of family resemblances which are accepted as belonging to this category' (ibid.). Barrett refers to Miller's influential (1985) work on the pottery of central India, in which he notes that 'variability should not be viewed as a mere side-effect of the inaccuracy of representation of material form, but as an essential property of categories' and, later, that he has shown variability to 'represent a necessary property of categories, permitting the maintenance of structure in the face of heterogeneity of context and practice' (Miller op. cit. 202). While not suggesting that Herne intended to imply a normative or cultural historical meaning to his identification of the category 'Carinated Bowl' – his acknowledgement of Barrett quite clearly suggests that he did not - the rigidity of his definition and, particularly, the way it has been used since has led to it acquiring such a meaning. There is a difference between, on the one hand, acknowledging that an early Neolithic potter did not work in a vacuum and must have had some idea of what constituted an appropriate and useful pot for a particular context, and, on the other, of assuming that a potter would be intent on producing a vessel as close as possible to a specific and unchanging form which is therefore liable to be interpreted today as a cultural marker or 'norm', in this case for the earliest Neolithic in the British Isles. When Herne writes, for example, of an assemblage from Llandegai in which rims are slightly more developed than usual, 'similarities are perhaps best emphasised over differences' (Herne 1988, 18), he is encouraging a view of the Carinated Bowl as unchanging and any differences between vessels as minor and meaningless. In the Barrett or

Miller view, above, such variation may not only be seen as intrinsic to the form, but may be demonstrating how that form was being constructed (in the conceptual rather than the technological sense) by its makers and users in different contexts. In his final paragraphs, however, Herne does stress that the Carinated Bowl has to be seen as intrinsic to those social practices which define the very early Neolithic and that in those social practices lay its meaning. Although quite rightly stressing that a pottery form should not be divorced from its social context, the emphasis he places on identifying practices of an earliest Neolithic phase with a *single* form seems to have led to a current situation in which indicators of greater variability are played down, while it is in fact in such variation that clues to social practice may lie.

Up to this point in the paper I have concentrated on drawing attention to the possibility (or, in the case of the Sweet Track, the firmly dated presence) of forms other than the Carinated Bowl at an early date. I would like now to turn the argument in another direction, for the purpose of strengthening the argument that although carination is prototypical for the earliest Neolithic, Carinated Bowl is not, by examining the dating evidence for some of the classic Carinated Bowls cited by Herne, and also by examining the distinction he makes between Carinated and Shouldered Bowls, which he argues is chronological. As I stated at the outset this cannot be a full critique of Herne 1988, but one or two points are easily made.

Fig. 5, of redrawn vessels largely from the first half of the 4th millennium cal BC, shows an apparently coherent formal group to the right of the matrix, showing that it is indeed possible to pick out classic 'Carinated Bowls' in widespread 4th millennium cal BC assemblages (although even these demonstrate some degree of variation, particularly between Neutral and Open forms, which does not appear to be regional). It is much more difficult, however, to argue that this is a coherent early 'horizon' as the

'classic' Carinated Bowls to the right of the table are not on present evidence datable either to a well-defined 'horizon' nor are they particularly early. Critical to Herne's definition is the pottery from Hanging Grimston (Barrow 110 in Mortimer 1905, 102-5) and similar sites in Yorkshire. Most of these, however, have virtually no reliable or relevant dates, or are dated only broadly to the first half of the 4th millennium cal BC, that is, no earlier than the more varied Sweet Track, Coneybury Anomaly, Flagstones and Rowden assemblages examined above. At Whitegrounds, an oval barrow (Brewster 1992), for example, which has one of the most firmly associated dates for classic Carinated Bowls - as it is on articulated human bone associated with the pottery - the date range is similar to that of the Coneybury Anomaly (3970-3530 at 95% confidence, 3910 – 3640 at 68% (HAR-5580 4950±90 BP, Brewster 1992, 19, 28) compared with 4050 – 3640 and 3960 – 3710 cal BC on bone from Coneybury Anomaly). None of the other dates considered by Herne are more reliable or well-defined than this (1988, 19) and because of heartwood effect and lack of firm association with the pottery do nothing to confirm his predicated early horizon. Willerby Wold long barrow, however, is even more interesting, despite the fact that Herne states that there is no association between the pottery and the two radiocarbon dates associated with the construction (Herne 1988, 19; BM-189 4960±150 BC, BM-188 4900±150 BC, Manby 1967). Here, Herne identifies only 'shouldered plain-ware bowls' (Herne 1988, 19) and comments that they are unrelated to the dates for the primary structure as they came from secondary contexts in front of the mound. Although the report is slightly ambiguous, it seems reasonably clear that the pottery noted as from the 'occupation deposit', which is illustrated here in Fig. 5, is from within the mound, while a separate scatter lay to the east (in Manby's (1963) fig. 7 two groups are distinguished, five vessels from the 'occupation debris' and three from 'east of the mound', the latter being outside the mound and not part of it). The excavator noted that the 'occupation deposit' material had been 'deliberately included in the mound at this point when it was being constructed' and a photograph of pottery sherds in the mound would seem to confirm this stratigraphic position (Manby 1963, 183-4, 187-9 (pottery report), pl. XXII). Although the dates were obtained from large timber associated with the crematorium beneath the mound and do nothing better than suggest a date probably in the first half of the 4th millennium cal BC for the construction, this is a highly important context in terms of the Carinated Bowl horizon because in Herne's appraisal of the ceramics from the Yorkshire long barrows no pottery other than Carinated Bowl could be found pre-dating the mounds. 'There are consistent patterns and trends in the evidence. Carinated Bowls where present are associated with primary use and primary phases of these monuments. C14 dates where applicable are universally early' writes Herne (1988, 19). If my interpretation of the Willerby Wold report is correct, and with a critical viewing of the dates, neither of those statements can stand: the deposition of pottery Herne classifies as 'shouldered' is provided with a *terminus ante quem* by a mound, when in his terms it should, because it is not Carinated Bowl, be later than the mound, and the dates may, because of potential heartwood effect, considerably pre-date the activity they have been taken to date, which may not therefore necessarily be particularly early.

Willerby Wold, therefore, also highlights what is evident from Fig. 5 and the Sweet Track assemblage: which is that the distinction Herne makes between Carinated Bowl and 'shouldered bowl' is not supportable as being a typological distinction which reflects a real difference in date. In the terms of this article the short-necked bowl with a carination noted as shouldered at Willerby Wold (Willerby Wold 1 in Fig. 5), and which in Herne's terms should be late, appears to be an Open version of the Deep-Bodied Carinated form, and the other Willerby

Wold vessel illustrated in Fig. 5 is Inflected (or possibly Simple with an out-turned rim, the published drawing shows a variable profile). They certainly do not fulfill Herne's strict Carinated Bowl criteria, but they may be seen now as perfectly acceptable as reasonably early and of lying within the looser 'family' of carinated vessels *and* the range of other forms being identified here as current in the early 4th millennium cal BC.

It is not only in the key area of Yorkshire that some doubt can be cast on the reality of this Carinated Bowl Horizon. In Wales too, although much early pottery is undoubtedly carinated, clear evidence of an easily distinguished, early horizon of Carinated Bowl seems to be elusive. Rick Peterson's immensely useful work (2003) identifies a small number of sites at which early radiocarbon dates are in reasonably reliable association with pottery, as well as some with activity but no pottery (*op.cit.* figs. 4.3-4.6). Some of the earliest pottery, however, such as that from Trefignath, for example, includes vessels which are highly unlikely to have been even carinated, and certainly not Carinated Bowls (e.g. Peterson *op. cit.* 5.7 TfH, L and M). The same is true at Gwernvale, where what appears to be a thumb-groove pot (i.e. with a shallow groove just below the rim on an otherwise simple form) occurs among otherwise carinated (including Classic Carinated Bowl) pottery in Phase 1 (pre-mound) contexts, (Peterson 2003, gv1, fig. 7.5). At others, such as the Breiddin, Classic Carinated Bowl is present but with no evidence that it is particularly early (Peterson 2003, 77; Peterson phases it as Early Neolithic Phase 1, (2003, 91-2, tables), presumably on form as there was no dating evidence at all, which illustrates how influential the idea of the earliness of Carinated Bowl has been). Overall, Peterson's survey illustrates more the serious lack of reliable associations between radiocarbon dates and pottery in the first half of the 4th millennium cal BC than offers evidence for the primacy of Carinated Bowl.

Summary

In Gibson's useful summary he notes that 'sometime before 3600 BC' (Gibson 2002, 70) more diverse forms began to enter the record, eventually going on to develop into the enormously varied 'middle Neolithic' ceramic assemblage. Although broadly correct, on the evidence marshalled here, I would argue that the following is a more accurate representation of the situation:

• that the 'horizon' of classic Carinated Bowl as defined by Herne is an archaeological construct which is misleading us as to the nature of the earliest pottery of much of England and Wales.

• that carination, however, *was* the 'core' feature of a category 'pot' which was the preference among early users of ceramics, for most – but not all – contexts and uses. That is, that the majority were carinated in some way, but were not all of the Classic Carinated Bowl form, which should focus our attention and interest particularly on the minority which were not carinated at all.

• although there was certainly some variation within these earlier ceramics before c. 3650 cal BC the majority of the development of the rich variety of 'middle Neolithic' pottery did *not* precede the development of causewayed enclosures by a large margin but was more or less concomitant with it. If there is a 'horizon' of rapid change and development to be identified anywhere in the 4th millennium cal BC it is here, in the 37th – 36th centuries BC.

• that pit groups in particular may be reflecting some early pattern of use, current in the first half of the 4th millennium cal BC and which was in some way superseded by the gatherings at causewayed enclosures.

If the development of the rich range of 'middle' Neolithic styles *was* relatively fast, say in a few generations from not much before 3650 BC,

then the role of the causewayed enclosures in the genesis and encouragement of that development would have to be acknowledged. One feature which gives a hint that some radical change happened around this time is that there is no evidence of which I am aware that Gabbroic Ware appear earlier than around the same time as the appearance of the causewayed and 'tor' enclosures, and that the earliest of those were not strikingly early (if the reassessment of the Carn Brea dates presented here (Appendix 1) is accepted). The occurrence of this true 'Ware' (i.e. style and fabric indicating a common source) is such a striking novelty that it suggests, if the dating is correct, a sizeable shift in the way society was organised at around this time which would be entirely in accord with the appearance of the enclosures.

A ceramic-friendly chronology for the Neolithic?

This focus on chronology raises a more general question of how pottery, if it could be better dated, would influence our understanding of the development of the Neolithic. At present there is not even a consensus on the terminology for describing the Neolithic period as a whole. There are two common usages, both of which are applied to the ceramics: some writers prefer a bipartite division into 'earlier' and 'later' Neolithic, the division occurring at around 3000 BC; others use a tripartite division into Early (c. 4000 BC to, variously, anything from c.3600 - c. 3300 BC), Middle (variously c. 3600 - 3300 to 3000, or 2900/2800 BC) and Late. In terms of the ceramic styles, round-based bowl is confined to 'Earlier' or is 'Early' to 'Middle'; Peterborough Ware and some other impressed wares are found largely in 'Earlier' but extend into 'Later', or, to use the tripartite division, begin towards the end of 'Early' flourish in 'Middle' and go out of use in 'Late'; and Carinated Bowls belong entirely to 'Earlier', or largely to 'Early' with some survival into 'Middle'. If this demonstrates anything it is that the current chronologies do not allow a fine enough resolution to take account of even the existing ceramic chronology, and certainly not enough to allow for any refinement for that chronology. An exception to this is Rick Peterson's work on Welsh Neolithic ceramics (2003), in which he defines four Neolithic phases, with some sub-divisions for areas within Wales, but this is too recent to yet have had much impact. Although the research for the present paper and formulation of a four phase 'earlier' Neolithic, below, predated my reading of Peterson, the regional chronologies defined by Peterson for Wales (2003, 133) are not radically different from those proposed here for Wessex and the south-west, although he suggests one phase, 3800 – 3400 cal BC, where I suggest two, the difference probably being due to the absence of a causewayed enclosure 'horizon' in Wales. Using the little information gathered here it is perhaps possible to offer a potential regional chronology for Wessex and the south-west. This could comprise:

Earliest or Contact Neolithic (c. ?4100 – 3850 BC) This may have been virtually aceramic and is attested mainly by interventions in the environment which are often difficult to distinguish as Neolithic. This could include for instance, the episode of clearance indicated by the age of the mature oaks used in the construction of the Sweet Track, about 150 years before the Track was built (Coles & Coles 1990, 217), or the pig femur from the Down Farm (Dorset) shaft (Allen and Green 1998, 32; OxA-7981 5250 ± 50 BP.) Outside the region, to the west, Peterson's extremely useful plot of 140 Neolithic radiocarbon dates shows only eight to have most of their probability distributions falling before 3800 cal BC, and these include some with very large ranges which also include a reasonable probability that the true dates lie post-3800 cal BC (Peterson 2003, 167-81). On this evidence it is difficult to conclude other than that some 'Neolithic' practices were introduced and were being practised at the very beginning of the 4th millennium cal BC (and probably in the

late 5th millennium cal BC), before the earliest evidence for the making and using of ceramics. The term 'Contact' Neolithic, expresses both its earliness and the fact that whatever the nature of the transition and the contribution of existing population as against incoming population was, there seems likely to have been contact of some sort between the two.

Early or Developing Neolithic (say c. 3850 – 3650 cal BC) Ceramics of this phase are largely carinated, but, probably right from the beginning – as argued above - other forms were used alongside these, principally inflected forms and cups and small bowls, nor were the carinated forms exclusively the Classic Carinated Bowl. By 3800 cal BC, as demonstrated by the Sweet Track, an early stage of woodland management, exploitation of the Levels, ceramics, polished exotic axes and flint axes were all current, in what could be termed the earliest phase of the Neolithic to have most of the features we recognise as typical of the period. Some of the earliest long mounds may belong here, although the dating is uncertain, and there are as yet no convincingly early mounds quite this early in the south-west. From elsewhere in the country there is some evidence that flint mines may belong to this early phase, or even to the previous 'Contact' Neolithic, but dating is still uncertain and the identification of an axe from the Sweet Track as being a flint mine product (Coles & Coles 190, 218) is now regarded as uncertain (Barber *et al.* 1999, 69, fig. 5.13). Chambered and unchambered long mounds certainly began within this phase, as at Hazleton, which appears likely to have been constructed between c. 3780 – 3640 cal BC (Saville 1990, 239).

'High' or Developed Neolithic (c. 3650 – 3350 BC): this is the phase with features of the 'classic' earlier part of the Neolithic most fully developed: causewayed and 'tor' enclosures emerge here, joining long barrows, and ceramics; it also includes the origins of Peterborough Ware as

part of a widespread developing pattern of impressed wares.

Middle Neolithic : 3350 – 3000/2950 cal BC: in ceramic terms this is the period in which the Peterborough tradition is fully developed and in which the bowl styles of the mid- late 4th millennium BC go out of use.

Subsequent phases belong outside the bounds of this paper.

Looking outwards

So far in this paper I have concentrated on the nature of ceramics in south-west England and Wessex in the centuries before 3650 cal BC, that is, before the tentatively identified 'enclosure horizon', a period of intense change and development associated with the development of causewayed and 'tor' enclosures. In these early centuries of the Neolithic, I have argued, there was a general preference for carination but this was neither exclusive nor confined to the classic Carinated Bowl. These early developments, however, cannot be viewed in isolation. Continental ceramics have been scrutinised by hopeful British archaeologists since at least the early 20th century for signs of having been the 'source' of the British Neolithic, though never with convincing success. For some years the perceived slowness of the Mesolithic-Neolithic transition, encouraged by some very early 'Neolithic' dates such as those from Ballynagilly, which have since been rejected, led to a view that the transition was likely to have involved diverse sources for material culture and social practice and to have taken place over such a long period that contacts with the Continent could have varied, over a long period, and be difficult to identify. With the increasingly short transition which seems to be emerging, it seems worth reviewing the possibilities for evidence of contact. A wide ranging review of Continental and British ceramics, however, which as far as I am aware has not been undertaken since the

widespread adoption of the calibrated chronology, is far outside the scope of this paper and this writer, but I will offer a few very brief and non-systematic comments.

The geographical areas in which convincing antecedents for the ceramics of the British Neolithic have been repeatedly sought – naturally enough, given their geographical proximity - are those lying along the Atlantic, Channel, and North Sea coasts of Atlantic Europe from the Netherlands to the Atlantic coast of France. One of the areas with the most convincing parallels in Europe for aspects of the British Neolithic is the Netherlands, along with neighbouring areas, where discoveries over the past thirty years have led – in the recognition of the Michelsberg-related 'Hazendonk' pottery – to the identification of a style with some similarity to British earlier Neolithic ceramics. L.P. Louwe Koojimans, in his 1976 discussion of Hazendonk and nearby sites, commented that Hazendonk suggested that 'the Michelsberg province north of the Ardennes had similar connections with Grimston-Lyles Hill, as Hembury had with the Chasséen of western France' (1976, 265-6). Louwe Koojimans made clear, however, that he was not arguing simply that 'Grimston-Lyles Hill is a Belgian Michelsberg extension, nor the reverse' but only that there was some convincing evidence for contact having occurred between the two at around 5150 BP (i.e around the turn of the 5th – 4th millennia cal BC). The range of Michelsburg forms overall (i.e. not just the tangential Hazendonk related pottery), however, does not show striking similarity to British forms, not even with the greater variety of British forms postulated here as probably current in 3850 – 3650 cal BC. The true 'tulip' beaker, which is the classic form of the Belgian Michelsberg, for instance (Scollar 1959, 55, fig. 1: type 4a), is not found in British assemblages, and only the less characteristic carinated bowl type 4f (ibid.) shows really close parallels in early southern British ceramics.

In the pottery of Hazendonk and other Swifterbant sites the closest parallels with early southern British ceramics, identified in the 1970s and 1980s, were between vessels which here would be classified as shouldered (in Herne's terms or Deep-bodied Carinated here) and Inflected bowls of just those types which Herne rejected as belonging to his earliest 'horizon'. Although a short necked, deep bodied form has been identified in this paper as among the certainly earliest pottery in the south-west and Wessex (i.e. at the Sweet Track), short-necked, rather shallow carinated and Inflected bowls do not appear to become common until a later period in the 4th millennium cal BC at sites such as Broome Heath and it is these forms which also seem to occur in a number of assemblages in the Netherlands. Parallels were drawn, for instance, using sites such as Het Vormer (Louwe Koojimans 1980) with what was then believed to be some of the earliest pottery in the British Isles (e.g. Louwe Koojimans 1976, 272, n162 cites Wainwright 1972 (Broome Heath) P300, P308 and 375, which are Inflected Bowls), although Loouwe Koojimans also noted the lack of counterparts in the Netherlands for the 'wide carinated bowl' (*op. cit.* 272). Louwe Koojimans (*op.cit.* 204), however, also argued for a re-examination of the Broome Heath dates eight years before Herne's reassessment of the chronology, pointing out that the Grimston/Lyles Hill Series as then postulated was of an unreasonable duration (Louwe Koojimans 1980, 204). In the same paper he suggested that 'the British forms [of carinated bowls] are ancestral to the continental ones, in view of the isolated situation of the Dutch carinated bowl province' and that therefore some other source had to be looked to for the British form (ibid.). In the calibrated chronology, and with Broome Heath rejected as Grimston/ Lyles Hill and placed with the broader variety of the causewayed enclosure assemblages in the mid-4th millennium cal BC, developments on both sides of the North Sea of short-necked carinated bowls, alongside inflected forms, in the Netherlands and in Britain may well be seen as related, but as part of a phase of increasing variety and development in ceramics which goes with widespread social change in the mid-4th

millennium cal BC and not related directly to the earlier preference for carination in the British Isles. It seems to suggest that there may have been increasingly strong contact between the British Isles and areas of the Continent well on into the 4th millennium cal BC, as suggested by the enclosures themselves, and which may also be suggested by ceramics further south.

That there are certainly some points of similarity, however, between even the early pottery of the late 5th/early 4th millennium cal BC either side of the southern North Sea is indisputable and worth illustrating. Fig. 5 shows two vessels from Hazendonk and Bergschenhoek, the former showing the straight neck characteristic of a minority of Hazendonk vessels and not dissimilar to straight neck forms at Cissbury and Rowden (Fig. 4), while the Bergschenhoek vessel in comparison with inflected vessels from all three pit groups illustrates the occurrence of that feature on both sides of the southern North Sea at a potentially early date. (The stratigraphic position of the straight-necked vessel illustrated from Hazendonk has been queried, but Raemaekers in a recent article accepts it as probably belonging to Hazendonk 2; 1999, 69.) Bergschenhoek is suggested by Raemaekers (1999, fig. 3.37) as likely to date to the second half of the 5th millennium cal BC and Hazendonk 1 and 2 to the very early 4th millennium cal BC (*ibid.*). Radiocarbon dates for Hazendonk 2 are very similar to that from Coneybury Anomaly (Lanting and van der Plicht 1999/2000, 57). Raemaekers places both Hazendonk 1 and 2, and Bergschenhoek in the middle Swifterbant culture, ending at around 3800/3900 cal BC (1999, 108). The pottery of the Swifterbant is largely 'S-shaped' (inflected), although some vessels 'show a pronounced neck-shoulder transition or a pronounced transition at the point of maximum circumference' (Raemakers 1999, 108) (that is, they are carinated), among these latter are vessels such the straight-necked form illustrated in Fig. 5 and discussed above. The illustrated bowl from the Cissbury flint mines, of this form (Barber *et al.* 1999, 69), cited above, is of unknown date within the 4th millennium cal BC (calibrated dates quoted in Barber *et al* 1999, 81-2, cover the whole of the millennium) so gives no assistance in pinning down when this feature, if it is representative of external contacts, may have been current.

To the south, and as other writers have long ago pointed out, the French Chasséen contains some features strikingly similar to British early Neolithic ceramics, although alongside forms, such as *vase-support*, which never occur in the British Isles. Indeed, in the discussion of Dutch carinated vessels by Louwe Koojimans cited above (1980), the possibility that they are related to the Chasseén is raised, since it extends as far north as Jonquieres, but he also notes a geographical separation between the two areas by one in which carination was not used and in which other forms dominated (*op. cit.* 203). As noted above, Whittle has summarised the archaeological interest in the Chasseén (1977, 180-2), but both Whittle and Louwe Koojimans were writing in relation to the South –Western / Hembury Style. If, as seems possible, many of the forms of that style, such as the more elaborate lugs and many of the simple, bag-shaped pots, may belong to the 'explosion' in form of the postulated 'enclosure' horizon, this raises the possibility that those similarities attest to continued, or renewed, or more intense contact between coastal regions of the southern North Sea/Channel/Atlantic coast in what has been termed here the 'High' or Developed Neolithic', just as similarities between Dutch assemblages of Hazendonk 2 and Broome Heath, say, may relate not so much to very early contact, but rather to ongoing or intensifying relationships across the southern North Sea in the same period. Even so, and even allowing for a general paucity of very convincing parallels for exactly the forms of the earliest Neolithic of the British Isles, it is still noticeable that there are some. The form of the Sweet Track 'pseudo-carinated' bowl, for example, is strikingly similar

to the Breton example illustrated in Fig. 5 from Mané-beg-Portivy (L'Helgouach 1965, 95) and likely to date to the late 5th or early 4th millennium cal BC (Patton 1993, 75, fig. 4.3a). Even as far south as the Gironde, in the first half of the 4th millennium cal BC, strikingly similar bowls to the Classic Carinated Bowl occur as at La Lède du Gurp (Grayan-et-l'Hôpital, Gironde; Roussot-Larroque 1995, 82, fig. 5) illustrated in Fig. 5. These are associated with a radiocarbon date not dissimilar to that for Coneybury Anomaly (Gif-5464 5020±150 BP on charcoal, compared with 5050±100 BP, OxA-1402 for Coneybury Anomaly, on bone), although the quality of the association appears to have been questionable (*ibid.*). That examples even as remote as this may represent real contact – of some sort, direct or indirect – is suggested, for example, by the occurrence of the jadeite axe of possibly Alpine origin (Patton 1993, 20), probably to be seen as coming to the British Isles via Brittany, which was also found associated with the Sweet Track and attests to long distance contacts by at least 3800 cal BC.

It is apparent even from the most superficial consideration of the Continental evidence, as here, that at present the dating of the early part of the British Neolithic, and of the immediately preceding and contemporary periods in neighbouring areas of the Continent, is too imprecise to establish primacy of particular styles between areas which appear to show similarities. It does seem likely, however, that there was a certain amount of shared experience and practice in pottery-making, although even in cases where some similarity in form is discernible, technology may appear very different, as is the case between the commonly grog-tempered Dutch ceramics (Raemaekers 1999, 108) and the predominantly non-grog-tempered British earlier Neolithic pottery (although see Darvill, this volume for a focus on grog). How this experience was shared, and why, in some cases, it appears closer in ceramics than in other media, particularly lithics, is an interesting question, perhaps to be related to the identities of potters. It seems unarguable that knowledge travelled more widely than individual vessels, judging by the lack of clearly 'intrusive' pots until at least the appearance of Gabbroic Ware in non-gabbroic areas (which seems unlikely to much, if at all, pre-date 3650 cal BC). As it is difficult, in non-literate societies, to pass technical knowledge other than by one practitioner teaching another, it seems at least possible that the craft may have been gender-related and the transmission of knowledge related to social practices which regulated marriage, or the formation of familial ties, and through which potters came to move more frequently and further than those working in other media, such as stone.

This paper has largely been an exercise in kite-flying and it may be that future work, and particularly the completion in the near future of the large-scale radiocarbon dating projects currently underway, brings the kite crashing to the ground, but I hope that a few points may have been usefully made. In particular I hope that this examination of the ceramics of the earlier part of the 4th millennium cal BC, even in such a limited way, raises the possibility of a more interesting 'ceramic' earlier Neolithic than that dominated by the Carinated Bowl. Although the 'breaks' in Herne's 'horizon' seem small, I would suggest that once diversity is acknowledged and the dominance of the Carinated Bowl examined in a more systematic and wide-ranging way than I have been able to do here, the chinks will widen. In particular, I feel that there is potential in other small pits groups, as yet undated, for further work and definition of early ceramics, and only with a more refined chronology will it be feasible to look more closely at what these apparently isolated pit groups represent in terms of social context. Isobel Smith herself drew attention to a number of pit groups in her contribution to the 1964 article 'New Neolithic Sites in Dorset and Bedfordshire' (Field *et al.* 1964). It is possible, for instance, that if early, mid- and late 4th millennium cal BC pit groups could be distinguished, differences in

likely function would emerge between them, perhaps reflecting differences in role between those pre-dating causewayed enclosures and those contemporary with them. As suggested earlier, the former may represent some of the social practices, such as those requiring meetings or gatherings, which later featured in the enclosures. In the 'enclosure horizon' too – if indeed that is what the dating programme produces – there is much to investigate. If some of the Continental contacts identified in the Netherlands and with the Chasseén do hold good as the chronology on both sides of the water is refined, then perhaps other features of the middle part of the 4th millennium cal BC could be examined more closely. It could be suggested, for instance, that the inception of finger-decoration on pottery, which appears in the mid-4th millennium cal BC, largely on eastern Decorated Bowl pottery and in the Peterborough tradition, might be traced to a period of intensified contact around the mid-millennium with, say, the Netherlands, where finger-decoration is a feature of Hazendonk 3 (Louwe Kooijmans 1976, fig. 14). In this case perhaps traditions of lithic manufacture may have been more mobile too, as it is at this stage that the first British transverse arrowheads, associated with Peterborough Ware, appear, and this type is also characteristic of the Chasseén.

It is very appropriate, I think, to have ended this article by discussing the excitement and potential of pottery from Neolithic pit groups and causewayed enclosures, for this is, more than perhaps any other of the fields in which she has worked, Isobel Smith's territory. Isobel's work stands beacon-like in the study of ceramics, as in Neolithic studies in general, and I hope she will feel that, reflected by this paper and the others in this volume, her contribution to this area of scholarship is widely recognised and appreciated.

Notes

1. All calibrations have been carried out using OxCal V. 3.5

Appendix 1

The Sweet Track (published in the *Somerset Levels Papers* series, see specific references below)
The Sweet Track was a plank walk 1800m long linking areas of high ground across a swamp. Dendrochronology has dated the felling of the majority of the timbers to the winter of 3807/ 3806 BC and the construction therefore probably to 3806 BC. The Sweet Track was preceded by the Post Track, which includes timbers felled some thirty years earlier. The Sweet Track is likely to have been usable only for about ten years (Coles & Coles 1990, 218), so giving a date of around 3800 BC for the deposition of the pottery found alongside or within the track. In all, about 10-15 pots are represented by sherds, all fine, with thin walls (*ibid.*) The pottery reports referred to in the figures are the Drove Site by Ian Kinnes (1979), the Railway Site by Isobel Smith (1976) and sites SWC and SWWA (Coles & Orme 1984). A recent article by Bond (2003) has reviewed the context of the pottery and argued for purposeful discard rather than casual loss as the mode of deposition for many of the vessels (*op. cit.* 23).

Coneybury Anomaly, Amesbury, Wiltshire
(Richards 1990; pottery by Cleal)
This pit, an apparently isolated feature on a low hill *c.* 1km from Stonehenge, was 1.25m deep from the present chalk surface and about 1.9m in diameter. The primary fill was only about 0.2m deep on excavation, but appears to have been highly organic and may originally have filled the pit to a much greater depth. Major assemblages of pottery, animal bone and worked flint were recovered. A high charcoal content (including oak, hazel and *Rosaceae* sp. (cherry/blackthorn and hawthorn/rowan/ whitebeam) show that it may have been burnt (Richards 1990, 40-2). One radiocarbon date derived from animal bone was obtained from the primary fill: OxA 5050±100, calibrating to 4050 – 3640 at 94.5%

probability, 3960 – 3760 at 65.3%, 3730 – 3710 at 2.9%.; cattle and roe deer dominated the animal bone assemblage; pig, red deer and beaver occurred in small numbers and a fish vertebra was a good match for brown trout (Maltby 1990).

There is no published evidence for the radiocarbon date having been obtained from articulated bone and at the time of the submission of the sample this is unlikely to have been a consideration. All the artefactual and ecofactual evidence, however, points to the material in the pit having derived from a fairly short period of use and discard and there is therefore a reasonably strong association between the radiocarbon date and the use and deposition of the pottery.

Flagstones, Dorchester, Dorset (Healy 1997, pottery report by Cleal)
This site is best known for the substantial enclosure with segmented ditch dating to the late 4th millennium cal BC, but two pits containing Neolithic pottery certainly predated this, and a number of other features probably did also. Pit 221 showed an uncertain relationship with a segment of the enclosure and a disturbed upper filling, suggesting that it was probably a partially silted feature when the ditch segment was dug. The pit was just under 2m in diameter and between 0.5 and 0.8m deep (one part being markedly deeper than the rest). The bottom of the pit was stained black and the basal layer also was black with charcoal and ash, with burnt chalk and burnt bone. The radiocarbon determination was on charcoal from this layer; it is noted as oak (Healy 1997, 38) and there is no charcoal report for the site. Dr M. Allen, however, has provided further details from his own doctoral research, in which he noted the presence of at least some small twiggy material, including probably *Pomoideae* (?*Crataegus* or *Prunus* thorn), *Corylus* and ?*Fraxinus* (identifications by J. Ede); this suggests that it could prove possible to obtain further, more reliable, dates.

The other pit, 274, was 24m to the north-east of 221 and showed no relationship with the enclosure ditch; it was just over 1m in diameter and 0.35m deep; there was no primary fill, the whole fill being a stone-free silty clay loam. Most of the pottery (224 sherds) came from this pit, with only 28 from pit 221 (almost all of them from the basal layer). There was a small quantity of animal bone, and worked flint (Healy 1997, 30). Pit 274 produced sherds belonging to at least ten vessels and pit 221 a minimum of three (although one at least may have been represented in both) (Cleal 1997, 89).

Rowden, Winterbourne Stepleton, Dorset (Woodward 1991, pottery by P. Woodward) Two Neolithic features produced radiocarbon dates here, one of which was associated with a sizeable ceramic assemblage; one of the dates, however, was published incorrectly as is shown in the published report by comparison of the uncalibrated dates with the calibrations given (Fig. 3, here, uses the dates as given in 'Archaeological Site Index to Radiocarbon Dates from Britain and Ireland', see entry for Helman Tor, below). The two features were found during the excavation of a Middle Bronze Age structure and comprised a pit, 327, approximately 2m in diameter and 1m deep, with, next to it and cutting its upper fills, a steep-sided feature 0.7m deep with a post-pipe (Woodward 1991, 43).

Pit 327 had an ashy and charcoal rich lower fill, the charcoal being mostly oak and hazel; there is no information given as to the exact nature of the charcoal used for the determination. The pit also produced, apart from the pottery, large quantities of lithic waste, carbonised grain and animal bone. No vessel estimate is given for the pottery, but seven vessels are illustrated. (Woodward, 1991, 98).

Carn Brea, Illogan, Cornwall (Mercer 1981; pottery by Isobel Smith) This site produced a number of radiocarbon dates from a 'tor' enclosure. BM-825 from Site D is the only date which could date some of the ceramics to before 3650 cal BC. This was on 'block charcoal' (oak) (Mercer 1981, 42) and calibrates to 3950 – 3650 (95.4%) or 3940 – 3860 (22.2%) or 3810-3700 (46.0%) cal BC. The charcoal was from a feature, F63, which may have formed part of a structure which appeared to respect the enclosure wall (ibid.) There is also a date (BM-824) from a deposit in Area E which also contained an open bowl with trumpet lug, but descriptions of the charcoal as including at least one substantial block (Mercer 1981, 61-2) means that the date for this classic South-western form cannot be narrowed beyond the second half of the 4th millennium cal BC. Two other dates (Fig. 1) suggest occupation later than the middle of the 4th millennium cal BC.

Helman Tor, Lostwithiel, Cornwall (Mercer 1997; pottery by Isobel Smith) The six radiocarbon dates from this site, a 'tor' enclosure, which were all on smallwood but include some from bulked samples, present a confusing picture of the chronology of the site and are discussed at some length by the excavator (Mercer 1997, 21-4). The confusion is increased by one date certainly being incorrectly published (as indicated by excavator's comments not being in agreement with the dates in the published table (HAR-8822 and 8823). Both are shown in Fig. 1 as they are listed in the 'Archaeological site Index to Radiocarbon Dates from Britain and Ireland' (http://ads.ahds.ac.uk/ catalogue/specColl/c14_cba/results.cfm). Two dates from a hearth, F103 (HAR-8822 and HAR-8823) which cut through the main midden deposit which contained most of the pottery suggest that the midden could have been forming by the 37th century cal BC, or possibly even earlier, although the midden deposit itself produced a much later date (HAR-8819) which the excavator suggests indicates the continued accumulation of material on the top of the midden subsequent to the cutting of F103 into part of it. The single much earlier date, for F59 (HAR-8818) would suggest a pre-3650 cal BC date for activity, and was obtained from charcoal from a posthole or post-pit (*op. cit.* 20, 22) which was close to, and appeared to form part of the same occupation as, the feature which produced HAR-8820 but which appears not to have contained any pottery. The pre-3650 cal BC date (HAR-8818) has no stratigraphic association with the midden deposit containing most of the pottery. The midden itself is problematic; it could be dated by the relatively late date (HAR-8819), but the indistinguishable dates from hearth 103 must, it seems provide a *terminus ante quem* for at least the early stages of ceramic deposition in the midden, suggesting that it began no later than the 37th century cal BC.

Maiden Castle

As noted in the text, above, an early dating for the construction of the Maiden Castle enclosure depends largely on dates from the Inner Ditch, but the situation in the Outer Ditch is also important. This has produced two early dates (BM-2451, OxA-1338) from disarticulated human bone and slightly later dates (OxA-1339-40, BM-2452) from animal bone. Here Sharples and Clark (1991, 105) argue that the human bones may have been old when they entered the ditch leaving the possibility that the ditch is truly dated, by the animal bones, to post-3640 cal BC (at one sigma; *op cit.* Table 8) . This argument, however, can be applied equally to the Inner Ditch *contra* Sharples and Clark. In this alternative interpretation the charcoal can be dismissed as possibly including heartwood (as they acknowledge, *op. cit.* 104) and the animal bone rejected as potentially belonging to earlier activity (like the human bone cited by Sharples and Clark *op cit* 105, as a possibility in the case of the Outer Ditch.). Although the animal bone from the Inner Ditch is noted as not showing signs of 'prolonged exposure' (Sharples & Clark 1991, 104), and therefore possibly not old when it entered the ditch, incorporation in a midden might have protected it (and the human bones in the Outer Ditch are not cited as worn in order for

it to be argued *there* by Sharples and Clarke that they are *redeposited*). The date for the construction of the Inner Ditch could then be taken as preceding the articulated human burial in the upper primary filling (which has a date (OxA-1148) of 3670 – 3510 at 61.5% probability or 3760 – 3370 at 95.4%) by only as many years as is usual in the formation of primary fillings on the bases of chalk-cut ditches, that is, perhaps no more than 25 years and possibly as little as ten (e.g. Bell *et al.* 1996 figs 4.4 and 5.3 showing accumulation of primary fill in Overton Down Experimental earthwork in 1968 and 1976). This depends, however, on the stratigraphic context of the burial, that is, whether it was cut from a much higher level or not. Although it is described as 'inserted' into the primary fill the section shows no cut (*op. cit.* 51, fig. 51) and it is later interpreted as a 'late insertion in the primary fills which might immediately precede the deposition of the midden layers' (Sharples & Clark *op. cit.* 104); even this still places it immediately following the completion of the primary filling process and with no evidence for a long hiatus between that and the midden deposition, *contra* the suggestion in Sharples and Clarke (105 a – b) that there was a difference of decades or even centuries between the two. (The remaining primary date in Fig. 2a, OxA-1144, is regarded by the authors as simply unacceptable as far too late; *op. cit.* 104.) The fairly coherent dates for the 'secondary midden layers', rich in pottery and other artefacts (Sharples 1991, 51), following closely on the formation of the primary filling, suggest a date of not much before 3700 cal BC for the foundation of the causewayed enclosure at Maiden Castle and quite possibly within or later than the 37th century cal BC.

Appendix 2: Definitions

The terms used in Figs. 4-5 and in the text are largely self-explanatory. Some, however, do require further explanation.

'Open', 'Neutral' and 'Closed'

These terms are used in a similar way to that of Whittle (1977, 77) and others, that is, that in 'Open' the greatest diameter is normally at the mouth, in 'Neutral' the diameter at the mouth and around mid-height are approximately the same, and in 'Closed' that of the body exceeds that of the mouth. Applying this over many years, however, has convinced me that it is not as easy to apply in practice as in theory because in many cases the difference may be small and therefore while the mouth may technically be greater than the body diameter it is not a difference the eye would pick up readily in life. To counteract this I worked from vessels which appeared unequivocally 'open' and 'closed' and calculated the mouth diameter as a percentage of the maximum body diameter (i.e. by dividing the mouth diameter by the maximum body diameter). Vessels with mouths between 90% and 110% of body diameter appear essentially neutral forms, those greater than 110% are fairly obviously open, and those less than 90%, closed. This can be applied to reductions without calculating the actual size, as the proportions remain constant. The main point of this in this context has been to highlight the fact that upright necks (i.e. Neutral forms) are not a regional preference but are widespread.

'Inflected'

This term is borrowed from Anna O. Shepard (1954) and refers to vessels without a sharp change in profile (i.e. a carination) in which there is a change in direction of a tangent run up or down the profile of the pot (i.e. a tangent on the lower body might move clockwise as it moved up the profile but then switch to anti-clockwise as it ran up the upper body). This is easily established from profile drawings, but there is scope for alternative interpretations in the treatment of the rim. Where a tangent would only switch direction immediately below the rim I have not generally classed the vessel as Inflected – interpreting it as essentially an uninflected form with an out-turned rim; this is illustrated, for example, by P3 from Coneybury Anomaly, which I have classed as Simple rather than Inflected (Fig. 4). I originally adopted the term along with others from Anna Shepard in my 1992 paper, but this was unnecessarily complex, and Julian Thomas has made a more practical use of the term (1999, 102-4).

Appendix 3: Mouth diameter as % of maximum body diameter for illustrated vessels

Fig. 4 – Coneybury Anomaly: ('P' nos are publication illustration numbers): Carinated Open (P1) (130%), Inflected Closed P7) 80%, Inflected Neutral (upper vessel, PP4 100%, lower vessel (P8) 93%;

Flagstones: Inflected Neutral 110%; Carinated Neutral 102%;

Rowden: Carinated Neutral 102%, Carinated Deep-bodied 95%; Carinated Straight-necked Neutral 102%, Open 115%; Inflected Open 116%, Neutral 109%

Fig. 5: Classic Carinated Open: Drove site 111%; SWWA 115% ; Whitegrounds 114%; Hanging Grimston 116%; (upper), 114% (lower); La Lède du Gurp 112%

Classic Carinated Neutral: SWC 100%; Whitegrounds 102%; Hanging Grimston 105%, Railway Site 100%

Straight-necked Carinated: Cissbury 113%; Hazendonk 124%; La Lède du Gurp 114% and 117%.

Deep-bodied Carinated (Open and Neutral, both in the column): Sweet Track 93%; Willerby Wold 111%; Broome Heath 93%

Pseudo-carinated: Sweet Track and Mané-beg-Portivy 100% Inflected: Bergschenhoek 100%

Acknowledgements

I would particularly like to thank my co-editor, Josh Pollard, for his helpful comments on the paper and for his patience, and Mike Allen for so promptly supplying information.

Bibliography

Allen, M. & Green, M. 1998. The Fir Tree Field shaft; the date and archaeological and palaeo-environmental potential of a chalk swallowhole feature. *Proceedings of the Dorset Natural History and Archaeological Society* 120, 25-38

Barber, M., Field, D. & Topping, P. 1999. *The Neolithic Flint Mines of England* English Heritage

Barclay, A. & Bayliss, A. 1999. Cursus monuments and the radiocarbon problem. In A. Barclay and J. Harding *Pathways and Ceremonies. The cursus monuments of Britain and Ireland*, 11-29. Oxford: Oxbow Books

Barrett, J. 1991. Bronze Age pottery and the problem of classification. In J. Barrett, R. Bradley & M. Hall *Papers on the prehistoric archaeology of Cranborne Chase*, 201-30. Oxbow Monograph 11

Bell, M., Fowler, P.J. & Hillson, S.W 1996. *The Experimental Earthwork Project 1960-1992.* York: Council for British Archaeology Research Report 100

Bond, C. 2003. The coming of the earlier Neolithic, pottery and people in the Somerset Levels. In A. Gibson (ed.) *Prehistoric Pottery. People, pattern and purpose*, 1-57. Prehistoric Ceramics Research Group Occasional Paper No. 4, British Archaeological Reports International Series 1156

Bradley, R., Over, L., Startin, D.W.A. & Weng, R. 1975-6. The excavation of a Neolithic site at Cannon Hill, Maidenhead, Berkshire, 1974-75. *Berkshire Archaeological Journal* 68, 5-19

Brewster, T. 1992. *The excavation of Whitegrounds barrow, Burythorpe.* 2nd edition, Wintringham, Yorkshire: John Gett Publications

Cleal, R.M.J. 1990. The prehistoric pottery [Coneybury Anomaly]. In J.Richards, *The Stonehenge Environs Project*, 45-57. English Heritage Archaeological Reports No. 16

Cleal, R.M.J. 1992. Significant form: ceramic styles in the earlier Neolithic of Southern England. In N. Sharples & A. Sheridan (eds) *Vessels for the Ancestors*, 286-304. Edinburgh: Edinburgh University Press

Cleal, R.M.J. 1997. Earlier Prehistoric pottery. In R. Smith, F. Healy, M. Allen, E. Morris, I. Barnes and P. Woodward, *Excavations Along the Route*

of the Dorchester By-pass, Dorset, 1986-8, 86-102. Wessex Archaeology Report No. 11

Cleal, R.M.J., Walker, K. & Montague, R. 1995. *Stonehenge in its Landscape: twentieth century excavations.* English Heritage Archaeological Reports 10

Coles, J. & Coles, B. 1990. Part II: the Sweet Track date, 216-219, in J. Hillman, C. Groves, D. Brown, M. Baillie, J. Coles & B. Coles, Dendrochronology of the English Neolithic. *Antiquity* 64, 210-20

Coles, J. M. & Orme, B.J. 1984. Ten excavations along the Sweet Track (3200bc). *Somerset Levels Papers 10*, 5-45

Davies, S., Woodward, P. & Ellison, A. 1991. The pottery. In P. Woodward *The South Dorset Ridgeway. Survey and excavations 1977-84*, 96-101. Dorset Natural History and Archaeological Society Monograph Series Number 8

Field, N., Matthews, C. & Smith, I.F. 1964. New Neolithic sites in Dorset and Bedfordshire, with a note on the distribution of neolithic storage pits in Britain. *Proceedings of the Prehistoric Society* 30, 352-81

Gibson, A. 2002. *Prehistoric Pottery in Britain and Ireland.* Stroud: Tempus

Harding P 1990. Lithics [Coneybury Anomaly]. In J.Richards, *The Stonehenge Environs Project*, 43-5. English Heritage Archaeological Reports No. 16

Healy, F. 1997. Site 3. Flagstones. In R. Smith, F. Healy, M. Allen, E. Morris, I. Barnes & P. Woodward *Excavations Along the Route of the Dorchester By-pass, Dorset, 1986-8*, 27-48. Wessex Archaeology Report No. 11

Herne, A. 1988. A time and a place for the Grimston Bowl. In J.C. Barrett & I.A.Kinnes (eds) *The Archaeology of Context in the Neolithic and Bronze Age. Recent trends*, 9-29. Sheffield: Department of Archaeology & Prehistory, University of Sheffield

Hillman, J., Groves, C., Brown, D., Baillie, M., Coles, J. & Coles, B. 1990. Dendrochronology of the English Neolithic. *Antiquity* 64, 210-20

Kinnes, I. 1979. Description of the Neolithic bowl. *Somerset Levels Papers* 5, 52, 54

Lanting, J.N. & van der Plicht, J. 1999/2000. De ^{14}C-chronologie van de Nederlandse pre- en protohistorie III: Neolithicum. *Palaeohistoria* 41/42

L'Helgouach, J. 1965. *Les Sépultures Mégalithiques en Armorique*. Travaux du Laboratoire d'Anthropologie de l'Université de Rennes I

Louwe Kooijmans, L.P. 1976. Local developments in a borderland. A survey of the Neolithic at the Lower Rhine. *Oudheidkundige Mededelingen* 57, 227-97

Louwe Kooijmans, L.P. 1980. De midden-Neolithische vondstgroep van Het Vormer bij Wijchen en het cultuurpatroon rond de zuidelijke Noordzee circa 3000 v. Chr. *Oudheidkundige Mededelingen* 61, 113-208

Maltby, M. 1990. Animal bones [Coneybury Anomaly]. In J.Richards, *The Stonehenge Environs Project*, 57-61. English Heritage Archaeological Reports No. 16

Manby, T.G. 1963. The excavation of the Willerby Wold long barrow, East Riding of Yorkshire, England. *Proceedings of the Prehistoric Society* 29, 173-205

Manby, T. 1967 Radiocarbon dates for Willerby Wold long barrow. *Antiquity* 41, 306-7

Mercer, R. 1981. Excavations at Carn Brea, Illogan, Cornwall, 1970-73. *Cornish Archaeology* 20, 1-204

Mercer, R. 1997. The excavation of a Neolithic enclosure complex at Helman Tor, Lostwithiel, Cornwall. *Cornish Archaeology* 36, 5-63

Miller, D. 1985. *Artefacts as Categories*. Cambridge: Cambridge University Press

Mortimer, J.R. 1905. *Forty Years Researches in British and Saxon Burial Mounds of East Yorkshire*. London: A. Brown and Sons

Newbigin, N. 1937. The Neolithic pottery of Yorkshire. *Proceedings of the Prehistoric Society* 3(2), 189-216

Patton, M. 1993. *Statements in Stone. Monuments and Society in Neolithic Brittany*. London: Routledge

Peterson, R. 2003. *Neolithic Pottery from Wales*. Oxford: British Archaeological Reports British Series 344

Piggott, S. 1954. *Neolithic Cultures of the British Isles*. Cambridge: Cambridge University Press

Raemaekers, D.C.M. 1991. *The Articulation of a 'New Neolithic'*. Archaeological Studies Leiden University. Leiden: Faculty of Archaeology, University of Leiden

Richards, J. 1990. *The Stonehenge Environs Project*. English Heritage Archaeological Report No. 16

Roussot-Larroque, J. 1995. La sequence Neolithique de La Lède Du Gurp et sa chronologie. *Actes du 20ème colloque interrégional sur la Néolithique*. Revue Archéologique de l'Oest, supplément no. 7, 75-87

Saville, A. 1990. *Hazleton North: the excavation of a Neolithic long cairn of the Cotswold-Severn Group*. London: English Heritage

Scollar, I. 1959. Regional groups in the Michelsburg Culture. *Proceedings of the Prehistoric Society* 25, 52-134

Schulting, R. 2000. New AMS dates from the Lambourn long barrow and the question of the earliest Neolithic in southern England. *Oxford Journal of Archaeology* 19(1), 25-35

Sharples, N. 1991. *Maiden Castle. Excavations and field survey 1985-1986*. English Heritage Archaeological Report No. 19

Sharples, N. & Clark, A. 1991. Interpretation [Radiocarbon dates]. In N. Sharples *Maiden Castle. Excavations and field survey 1985-1986*, 104-5. English Heritage Archaeological Report No. 19

Shepard, A. O. 1956. *Ceramics for the Archaeologist*. Washington DC: Carnegie Institute Publication 609

Smith, C. A. & Lynch, F. 1987. *Trefignath and Din Dryfol. The excavation of two megalithic tombs in Anglesey*. Cambrian Archaeological Association

Smith, I.F. 1956. The decorative art of Neolithic ceramics in south-eastern England and its relations. Unpublished Ph.D. thesis London: Institute of Archaeology

Smith, I.F. 1974. The neolithic. In C. Renfrew (ed.) *British Prehistory*, 100-36. London: Duckworth

Smith, I. F. 1976. The pottery, 63-64, in J.M. Coles & B.J. Orme, The Sweet Track, Railway Site. *Somerset Levels Papers* 2, 34-65

Smith, I. F. 1981. The Neolithic pottery, 161-185, in R. Mercer, Excavations at Carn Brea, Illogan, Cornwall, 1970-73. *Cornish Archaeology* 20, 1-204

Thomas, J. 1999. *Understanding the Neolithic*. London: Routledge

Wainwright, G.J. 1972. The excavation of a Neolithic settlement on Broome Heath, Ditchingham, Norfolk, England. *Proceedings of the Prehistoric Society* 38, 1-97

Whittle, A.W.R. 1977. *The Earlier Neolithic of Southern England and its Continental*

Background. Oxford: British Archaeological Reports International Series 35

Whittle, A.W.R., Pollard, J. & Grigson, C. 1999. *Harmony of Symbols. The Windmill Hill causewayed enclosure, Wiltshire*. Oxford:

Oxbow Books

Woodward, P. 1991. *The South Dorset Ridgeway. Survey and excavations 1977-84*. Dorset Natural History & Archaeological Society Monograph Series No. 8

Soft-rock and Organic Tempering in British Neolithic Pottery

Timothy Darvill

One of the great achievements of Isobel Smith's monumental report on the 1925-9 excavations at Windmill Hill, Wiltshire (Smith 1965), was her study of the substantial pottery assemblage and the use of conclusions from it to inform wider discussions about the overall purpose and use of the site. Developing work first set out in her doctoral thesis (Smith 1956), sadly never published but much referred to, Isobel cross-correlated traditional studies of vessel form with the analysis of fabric, production techniques and decoration in a way that set new standards for the treatment of ceramic assemblages from prehistoric sites. Central to her approach was the investigation of fabric groups, and their potential sources, especially the application of results from the thin-sectioning carried out by Henry Hodges at the Institute of Archaeology in London (Hodges 1962; Cornwall & Hodges 1964; Hodges in Smith 1965, 43-4).

Among the more curious features of the Windmill Hill assemblage revealed by Isobel's work was a fundamental binary division between what, in broad terms, may be referred to as hard-rock tempered wares and those with soft-rock and organic tempering. At the time, relatively little was made of this distinction and its possible significance, but while working with Isobel in the early 1980s on the Neolithic pottery assemblages from Hambledon Hill, Dorset, Hazleton North, Gloucestershire, and several other sites beside, the widespread occurrence of soft-rock and organic tempered wares became apparent to us as a matter clearly deserving further research. This contribution to a *festschrift* in her honour arises from correspondence on the matter over the last twenty years or so, and fondly remembered discussions about Neolithic pottery over tea and biscuits around the hearth of her cottage in Avebury. Much of the original data presented here derives from the analysis of assemblages undertaken during the preparation of my doctoral thesis (Darvill 1983), a piece of work that benefited greatly from Isobel's kindly advice and encouragement.

My aim here is simply to draw attention to the question of hard and soft materials in Neolithic ceramics, to examine a small selection of 4th and 3rd millennium BC ceramic assemblages in terms of the range of tempering agents represented, and to review briefly a few possible interpretations and implications. As a starting point for this discussion I would like to turn to the type-site for so many aspects of Neolithic studies: Windmill Hill, on the chalk downland of northern Wiltshire. Here, successive episodes of excavation in 1922-3, 1925-9, 1937-8, 1957-58, 1959-60 and 1988 (Smith 1965; Whittle *et al.* 1999) brought to light the largest assemblage of Neolithic pottery currently available from the British Isles.

Hard and soft tempering in the Windmill Hill assemblage

Analysis of the 4th millennium BC pottery from the 1925-9 excavations at Windmill Hill – the eponymous Windmill Hill Ware – revealed that about 69 per cent of the assemblage contained fragments of what may be described as 'hard rock' either naturally within the original raw clay (clasts) or introduced as additives (tempering).

Principal amongst these clasts and tempering agents were flint, sand, quartz, and crushed igneous rock (Smith 1965, 45; Fig. 1A). A similar proportion of the pottery found during the 1988 excavations (71 per cent) may be classified as containing hard-rock clasts or tempering (Zienkiewicz in Whittle 1999, 258-69). Most of these vessels were locally made, but about 1 per cent of the overall assemblage contain igneous rock fragments that have been traced to a source area on the Lizard Peninsula of Cornwall some 280km distant to the southwest (Peacock 1969). The remainder of the assemblage, about 30 per cent, contained fragments of what may loosely be described as 'soft-rock', again present either as naturally occurring clasts or added tempering. In addition, a little less than 1 per cent of vessels had been tempered with finely chopped organic vegetable matter of some kind that had burnt out

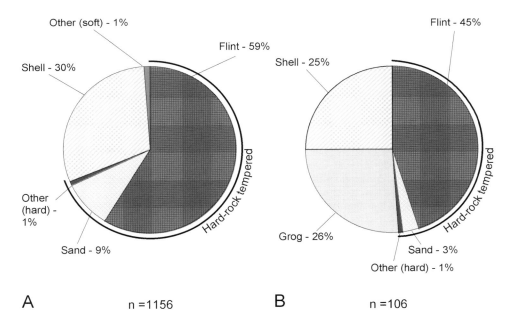

A   n = 1156   B   n = 106

Fig. 1. Pie charts summarizing the composition of ceramic assemblages from Windmill Hill, Wiltshire. A – Fourth millennium BC (early and middle Neolithic). B – Third millennium BC pottery (later Neolithic). Based on data from Smith 1965, fig. 11 and 73-80

on firing to leave distinctive voids within the core of the fabric and on the vessel surfaces. Principal amongst the soft-rock fragments recorded were fossil shell, oolitic limestone, chalk, molluscan shell and grog (broken pottery). In marked contrast to the hard-rock tempered vessels, only a small amount of the soft-rock tempered wares were strictly local (perhaps 2 per cent overall). The rest was probably made using materials derived either from the Corallian limestone beds perhaps 12-15km west of Windmill Hill (cf. Darvill in Evans & Smith 1983) and/or from the Great Oolite and Forest Marble beds in the Frome/Bath region about 30km distant to the west (Cornwall & Hodges 1964, 32; Smith 1965, 46). Significantly, these soft-rock tempered vessels at Windmill Hill tended to be more commonly decorated (24 per cent of vessels as against 14 per cent of hard-rock tempered wares: Smith 1965, 50), and mainly occurred as open carinated and cordoned bowls or as pots/jars in which the height of the vessel exceeds the maximum diameter.

Turning to the ceramics of the 3rd millennium BC at Windmill Hill – culturally speaking, Peterborough series and Grooved Ware – a similar pattern can be seen even though the total size of the assemblage is markedly smaller (Fig. 1B). Overall, pottery containing fragments of hard rock account for about 48 per cent of the assemblage, although classification is less straightforward because the deliberate addition of tempering agents is common and highly variable so that yellow quartz, sand, and flint are represented in various combinations, often with grog as well (see also Hamilton in Whittle et al. 1999, 292-3). No gabbroic pottery is represented amongst the 3rd millennium BC assemblage. About 25 per cent of the assemblage contains fragments of soft-rock, mainly fossil shell and/or ooliths. No vesicular pottery suggestive of organic tempering is represented. There are, however, slight variations between the recognized ceramic traditions of the later Neolithic in terms of the preferences for flint tempering or grog tempering

as a hard-rock additive even through the overall balance is fairly constant. The makers of Ebbsfleet Wares, for example, favoured flint tempering over grog, while the makers of Grooved Ware favoured grog over flint.

Function and meaning

It has long been recognized that the fabric used in the manufacture of a pottery vessel is closely related to its physical properties (strength, texture and refractive capabilities). The incorporation of non-plastic elements within the basic clay matrix, whether naturally as part of the clay or by adding selected materials, is an important facet of fabric construction and widely seen as a cultural choice. Indeed, the fact that assemblages almost always contain a range of different fabrics only serves to emphasize the potential significance behind the deliberate selection, combination and manipulation of raw materials. So, might there be, at a broad level, any significance to the observed differences between pots with hard rock as part of the fabric and those with soft rock or organic tempering? Traditionally, attention has focused on the relationships between raw materials and the processes of manufacture. Anna Shepard, for example, stressed the way in which non-plastic elements of a ceramic fabric served to reduce shrinkage during firing (1956, 56) and such matters have also been considered by Hodges (1964, 25), Gibson (2002, 37-9) and Henderson (2000, 129-30). Emphasizing the relationships between materials and technology, and privileging the role of the potter, seems attractive from the modern western perspective, but is it appropriate to less centrally organized modes of production, for example what David Peacock (1981) defined as 'household' or 'domestic' industries? For while the production process may well have been important to the potter, far more significant to everyone else would be the suitability of a vessel for its intended use and the various and perhaps multiple meanings that might attach to the materials used in its manufacture, and its form, colour, decoration, and overall appearance.

In simple functional terms the refractive properties and inherent strength of vessels manufactured in fabrics containing pieces of hard rock makes them well-suited to the demands of cooking pots for use on open fires and as robust everyday domestic wares used for preparing and serving food. Hard and dense inclusions such as flint and quartz mean that vessels containing these materials have a high resistance to thermal shock both during firing and for subsequent uses (Howard 1981; Braun 1983). Moreover, the stone serves to conduct heat through the wall of the vessel thus ensuring that both the surrounding clay matrix and also anything inside the pot would be heated quickly and fairly evenly. Hard-rock additives also serve to reduce the porosity of the vessel wall and thus promote the retention of liquids. By contrast, vessels containing fragments of soft rock within their fabric would, in general, be quite unsuitable for cooking and use over open fires as limestone and chalk have little resistance to thermal shock and have a tendency to disintegrate, spall, or explode when exposed to rapid heating and/or temperatures above about 450°C. Calcareous materials are not especially good conductors of heat, although experimental work in the United States suggests that calcium-carbonate-rich tempering agents create a strong ceramic composite and tend to expand and contract at more or less the same rate as the clay body (Hoard *et al.* 1995, 825). Soft-rock tempered wares and vesicular organic tempered fabrics do, however, tend to be porous and have a cooling effect on liquids kept within them. This is one of their main attractions and can be used to advantage for the storage of cold water, blood, or milk because evaporation from the outer surface of the vessel serves to slow-down the rate at which the contents of the vessel warms-up to match the surrounding air temperature.

Beyond simple function, colour and an understanding of the material forming the fabric of the vessel may also be significant in the construction and use of pottery in terms of the symbolic meanings imbued in a particular vessel. The extensive use of recycled pottery in the form of grog during the later Neolithic especially may somehow represent wider life-cycles involving birth and death, a possibility noted by Allen (1991) in relation to middle Bronze Age funerary vessels from a cremation cemetery at Long Bennington, Lincolnshire. Likewise, Gibson (1995) has noted the abundant use of highly visible white quartz in Mortlake wares in Wales. This, he suggests, is linked to the wider symbolic meanings of quartz amongst Neolithic communities in the west of England, well exemplified by the use of quartz pebbles and boulders in ceremonial contexts and perhaps somehow associated with the souls of the ancestors (Darvill 2002). Multiple meanings may indeed attach not only to the pot as a pot but also to the materials forming the pot and by association the things inside. As containers, and also as crucibles for the transformation of foodstuffs and liquids from one state to another (raw to cooked; sour to sweet; milk to yogurt; mash to beer, etc.), pots may have been conceived as dynamic agents in everyday existence and even having a 'life' of their own.

Taken together, functional and symbolic characteristics may suggest differences in the use and meaning of vessels containing hard rock as against those containing soft rock or organic tempering. Provisionally, these vessels containing soft rock or having a vesicular fabric may be seen as relevant to the storage of temperature-sensitive liquids such as milk or blood, while at the same time reflecting a range of symbolic meanings that, at present, are hard to fathom.

Residue analysis and the study of lipids preserved in vessel walls potentially provides another way of investigating these issues further, but to date attention has focused mainly on identifying modes of vessel use and dietary habits (e.g. Dudd & Evershed 1999). There has been little attempt to correlate the findings with variables such as the fabric, form, decorative scheme, or the colour of the vessels sampled.

Moreover, the potential of the approach to address detailed contextual and interpretative issues is naturally limited by difficulties arising from uncertainties over the intensity and frequency of use needed to create the various chemical signatures associated with particular activities and the exact nature of the matter from which the lipids and proteinaceous components derived. It is, however, an important area for future research as the results of work on material from the Walton Basin, discussed below, clearly show.

Soft-rock and organic tempered wares beyond Windmill Hill

Not all ceramic assemblages of the 4th and 3rd millennia BC include fabrics that contain soft rock or organic materials,[1] although vessels in such fabrics are fairly widespread at least amongst larger assemblages. A broad picture is provided by Ros Cleal's study of Neolithic pottery fabrics in Wessex. This showed that amongst the 27 assemblages examined the pattern at Windmill is also reflected at other sites. In all, 55 per cent of early and middle Neolithic vessels contained crushed flint and a further 9 per cent contained flint and sand. Sand alone was present in about 8 per cent of fabrics, mainly small vessels. The remainder (about 29 per cent) mainly contained fossil shell tempering (Cleal 1995, 187). In the later Neolithic the range of fabrics diversified with flint typical of Peterborough Series wares while grog played a more important role in Grooved Ware. Fossil shell was typically present in about 30 per cent of vessels in all later Neolithic traditions, except amongst Mortlake Wares where just 10 per cent of recorded vessels in the study had this tempering (Cleal 1995, 188).

Fossil shell of various kinds is probably the most well-represented form of soft-rock tempering amongst Neolithic assemblages. Fourth millennium BC pottery from the Abingdon causewayed enclosure, Oxfordshire, fell into two main groups on the basis of its visible features: a stone-tempered sandy ware with mainly flint tempering that accounted for about 5 per cent of the assemblage; and a shell-tempered ware which petrological studies suggested may derive from the local Kimmeridge clays accounted for 95 per cent of assemblage (Avery 1982, 27-8). Fossil shell tempered wares, not all derived from the same source, have been recorded in different concentrations at many sites, including Robin Hood's Ball (c.15%; Thomas 1964, 14), Maiden Castle, Dorset (c.40%; Cleal in Sharples 1991, 171), Hurst Fen, Suffolk (3.5%; Clark 1960, 228), and the Whiteleaf Barrow, Buckinghamshire (c. 50%; Smith in Scott 1954, 221), among numerous others.

Soft rock components of Neolithic pottery fabrics are not confined to fossil shell, ooliths, and grog; several other kinds of soft-rock and organic tempering tempering have been noted, some of them fairly exotic. As long ago as the late 1920s the presence of oyster shell was noted in Grooved Ware from Woodhenge, Wiltshire (Davy in Cunnington 1929, 75). More recently further cases have been confirmed through a study of sherds from three separate assemblages from around Amesbury, Wiltshire. This work showed that all the sherds examined contained marine oyster shell rather than fossil shell; such shells must ultimately have come from the coast, at least 50km distant (Cleal et al. 1994). Whether the shell arrived in the Stonehenge / Woodhenge / Amesbury area in ready-made pottery, as raw materials for potting, or as foodstuff which contributed discarded material for potters to utilize is not known. It is possible, of course, that oysters played some kind of special role in one or more ceremonies in the area and that remains from the event were physically embodied into pottery as a reminder of the event: a materiality of memory. However, the incidence of marine shells in Grooved Ware is not confined to central southern England; oyster and mussel shells, for example, have also been recognized in a substantial assemblage from Redgate Hill, Hunstanton, Norfolk (Cleal in Bradley et al. 1993, 40).

Earlier in date are the remains of a decorated open bowl from a small heath in the south quarry at the Hazleton North long barrow, Gloucestershire (Darvill & Smith 1990, 146). Probably placed into the heath after the ashes had cooled, this vessel had a very soft crumbly fabric tempered with fragments of limestone and a liberal scatter of bone. Made from locally available materials (clay and limestone), an examination of two fragments of the bone by Don Brothwell suggested that one was certainly and the other probably of animal origin. Other cases of bone being used as tempering in British Neolithic pottery have been noted at Robin Hood's Ball, Wiltshire (Thomas 1964, 14), Avebury, Wiltshire (Gray 1935, 138, note 1), and The Breiddin, Powys (Darvill in Musson 1991, Microfiche 3: 13.1, Fabric 3), but many more no doubt await identification. In Ireland, similarly constituted pottery has been observed at Tomb 27, Carrowmore, Co. Sligo (Cleary 1984, 73); Creevykeel, Co. Sligo (Hulthén 1984, 208); and amongst Beaker Ware from The Grange Stone Circle, Lough Gur, Co. Limerick (Cleary 1984). Crushed burnt bone was also used in creating the white in-fill used on comb-impressed Beaker pottery in Scotland (Clarke 1970, 10). Further afield, bone has been identified as a tempering agent in 4th and 3rd millennium BC ceramics around Telemark and Vestfold in Norway (Cleary 1984; Hulthén 1981), among the Kesseleyk ceramics of the Netherlands (Cleary 1984; Modderman 1981), in Belgium (Cleary 1984; Hulthén 1984, 208), and in northern France (Cleary 1984; Constantin and Courtois 1980). Hulthén has argued that the inclusion of bone has a strengthening effect on ceramic wares, producing stronger and lighter vessels (1984, 208). Why exactly bone was used in the British cases though, many of which are closely associated with funerary monuments, is far from clear as the pottery is generally weak and crumbly. On balance, some kind of symbolic significance that included, perhaps, the perpetuation of memories or the capture and embodiment in physical form of

some real or imagined spirit or energy seems most likely.

The pan-European interest in bone-tempered wares can be mirrored in the distribution of organic tempered pottery. Here, chopped plant material (typically straw) or dung was added to the clay while it was being prepared, and would have remained a visible element of the fabric up until the dried vessel was fired. During firing the organic elements of such vessels would burn out to leave small angular voids in the baked fabric. Hulthén (1977, 49) has discussed some of the continental potting traditions that include organic-tempered wares, the earliest of which can be found among the *Linearbandkeramic* assemblages of the late 6th and 5th millennia BC (Tringham 1971, 121). At Olszanica in southwest Poland, for example, detailed studies of the ceramic fabrics of an LBK settlement of the 5th millennium BC showed that 12.5 per cent of coarsewares contained only organic tempering, while about the same again contained organic matter as one element of a more mixed range of tempering agents. By contrast, none of the finewares were organic tempered (Milisauskas 1986, 18-20). In Britain, the organic-tempered wares of 4th millennium BC date from Windmill Hill have already been noted, and other broadly contemporary assemblages where they are present include: Fengate, Cambridgeshire (100%; Pryor 1974, 8); Etton, Cambridgeshire (?%; Kinnes in Pryor 1998, 161); Robin Hood's Ball, Wiltshire (1.7%; Thomas 1964, 14); Hambledon Hill, Dorset (1.4%; Darvill forthcoming); Maiden Castle, Dorset (c.3%; Cleal in Sharples 1991, 171); and perhaps Abingdon, Oxfordshire, where a few dark corky sherds are dismissed as cases where the shell tempering has eroded out may well be from vessels that once had an organic temper (Avery 1982, 27-8).

Recognizing bone-tempered and organic-tempered pottery in the west of Britain is complicated by the impact on ceramic assemblages of post-depositional changes, particularly the weathering out of soft-rock tempering. It is thus common to recognize what is frequently referred to as 'vesicular pottery' as a cover-term for fabrics that were either: organic tempered; bone tempered but from which the bone has since dissolved; or tempered with a calcareous rock that been dissolved away. Differentiating between these options is extremely difficult, even when thin sections are

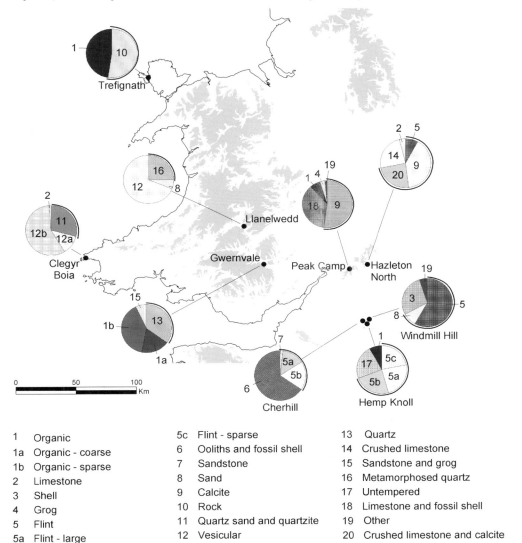

Fig. 2. Fabric composition spectra for selected ceramic assemblages of 4th millennium BC date in the mid-west of England and Wales. Sources: various

1	Organic	5c	Flint - sparse	13 Quartz
1a	Organic - coarse	6	Ooliths and fossil shell	14 Crushed limestone
1b	Organic - sparse	7	Sandstone	15 Sandstone and grog
2	Limestone	8	Sand	16 Metamorphosed quartz
3	Shell	9	Calcite	17 Untempered
4	Grog	10	Rock	18 Limestone and fossil shell
5	Flint	11	Quartz sand and quartzite	19 Other
5a	Flint - large	12	Vesicular	20 Crushed limestone and calcite
5b	Flint - small	12a	Vesicular - coarse	

available, but of course all of them fall into the general category of soft-rock and organic-tempered wares suggested here. Most important, as in southern England, these fabrics with soft-rock and organic tempering can be distinguished from fabrics containing fragments of hard-rocks, usually igneous or metamorphic rock.

Soft-rock and organic tempering in time and space: a case study from the west of England and Wales

In broad terms, the mid-west of England and Wales can be sub-divided into three main geo-topographic or environmental zones (Fig. 2): the downlands of north Wessex and the Cotswolds; the hill and vale country of the Severn Valley and Welsh Marches; and the uplands of the far west with their mountainous core and low-lying coastal fringe. Each of these areas has yielded ceramic assemblages of 4th and 3rd millennia BC date, a selection of which have been examined and the fabrics represented classified according to the nature and frequency of visible inclusions (clasts and added temper). Representative examples of some assemblages have been thin-sectioned (Darvill 1983, 552-62).

Figure 2 shows in graphical form the composition of nine assemblages of 4th millennium BC date across the mid-west of England and Wales. Most derive from settlement sites and include vessels of different forms and sizes. What is clear, however, is a general trend in which the proportion of soft-rock and organic tempered wares increases westwards. In the far east, on the chalk downlands of Wessex, only around 30 per cent of vessels are typically made in fabrics containing soft rock or organic materials. Further west, around the fringes of the downlands and across onto the Cotswolds the percentage of soft-rock and organic tempered wares increases to 50 per cent or more, as for example at Cherhill, Hazleton North, Peak Camp, and Gwernvale. In the far west two out of the three assemblages examined contain more

than 60 per cent of vessels with fabrics containing soft-rock or organic tempering, for example Clegyr Boia and Llanelwedd. The one slight exception is Trefignath where about 45 per cent of the 21 recorded vessels contained organic tempering (Jenkins in Smith 1987, 60-73).

Such a pattern is counter-intuitive because in an essentially mountainous region where hard igneous and metamorphic rock-types predominate amongst surface exposures one would expect to find a strong representation of such rocks in the pottery fabrics. But this is not so. In the east, flint dominates the hard-rock used, in the Cotswolds calcite is common, while in the west various kinds of quartzite predominate. Interestingly, all three kinds of rock expand upon heating at about the same rate as most good potting clays. Amongst soft-rock and organic tempered wares shell is most common in the east, while organic tempered fabrics are well represented further west. In the case of pottery from the pre-cairn settlement at Gwernvale, Powys, organic wares in Fabric 2 (coarse) and Fabric 3 (fine) represented 7 per cent and 69 per cent respectively (total 76 per cent) of the assemblage (Darvill 1984, 110-13). Interestingly, these fabrics were less dominant in the later assemblages connected with the use of the long barrow and its eventual blocking-up (Fig. 3).

Figure 4 shows in graphical form the composition of nine assemblages of 3rd millennium BC date scattered through the study area. Here, however, patterning is far less clear than for the earlier assemblages. In the far east of the region, the assemblage from the Avenue Occupation Site near Avebury contains almost exclusively hard-rock tempered wares, whereas at nearby Windmill Hill only about a half of vessels are hard-rock tempered, a situation broadly mirrored at Cherhill. In the same area, but not shown on Figure 4, the Grooved Ware from the West Kennet palisaded enclosures mostly seems to have been grog tempered with lesser amounts of other inclusions such as flint, shell, and sand (Hamilton in Whittle 1997, 93).

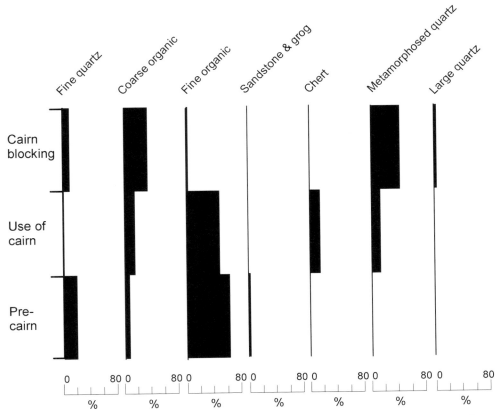

Fig. 3. Changes in fabric representation through three successive phases of activity at Gwernvale, Powys. Based on Darvill 1984, 112

On the eastern fringes of the Cotswolds, the assemblages from Roughground Farm and Partridges Pit (both of which contain some Beaker wares) show very small hard-rock tempered components compared with the range of soft-rock tempered wares, and at Cam in the Severn Valley immediately west of the Cotswolds most of the 20 or so vessels are limestone tempered with only a small number having additional visible fragments of quartz. At Trelystan Long Mountain overlooking the upper Severn Valley near Welshpool, all of the assemblage has grog tempering, but about 50

per cent also contains fragments of sandstone (Darvill in Britnell 1982, 192-5). The most westerly assemblages, Ogmore (Gibson 1998) and Llanilar (Darvill in Briggs 1997, 34-6), both contain only hard-rock tempered wares. This is perhaps the most marked contrast with the earlier 4th millennium BC traditions.

Not examined as part of the original study forming the core data mapped here are the assemblages from various sites in the Walton Basin recovered during excavations in 1993-7. As might be expected from its position in the central Marches, both the Peterborough Ware

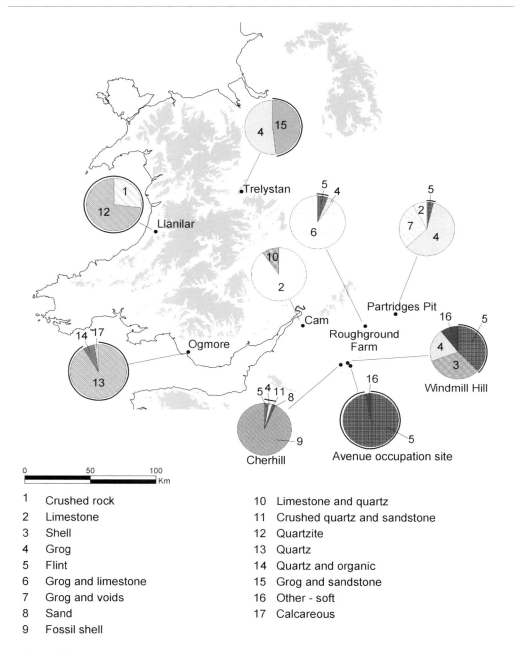

1   Crushed rock
2   Limestone
3   Shell
4   Grog
5   Flint
6   Grog and limestone
7   Grog and voids
8   Sand
9   Fossil shell
10 Limestone and quartz
11 Crushed quartz and sandstone
12 Quartzite
13 Quartz
14 Quartz and organic
15 Grog and sandstone
16 Other - soft
17 Calcareous

Fig. 4. Fabric composition spectra for selected ceramic assemblages of 3rd millennium BC date in the mid-west of England and Wales. Sources: various

and the Grooved Ware assemblages from this work were dominated by hard-rock tempered wares that included fragments of siltstone, sandstone, quartzite/mica schist, and several types of igneous rock. Only three Grooved Ware vessels (c.2% of the Grooved Ware assemblage), all from Upper Ninepence, had a soft 'corky' vesicular fabric resulting from soft-rock tempering weathering out of the sherds (Jenkins & Williams 1999). Analysis of a sample of 17 sherds revealed lipid residues on ten of them, of which the Peterborough Wares correlated well with modern reference fats from ruminants (cow and sheep) while the Grooved Ware correlated with non-ruminants (pig). Of the seven samples with very little or no lipid residues, one was a sherd from a Grooved Ware vessel in the vesicular fabric (Dudd & Evershed 1999).

Clearly, potting traditions and the preferred choices of fabric changed over time. As a working hypothesis it may be suggested that the soft-rock and organic tempered wares of the 4th millennium BC may be related to the production and storage of milk, and that the distribution of such wares broadly reflects local variations in subsistence economy with a greater emphasis on pastoralism in upland areas and the hill and vale country of the Welsh Marches (and see Webley 1976). Extensive scientific analysis of lipid residues is needed to confirm this, but there is some supporting evidence for the proposition in the faunal assemblages from sites with high levels of soft-rock and organic-tempered wares. At Gwernvale, Powys, for example, 76 per cent of the pottery from the pre-long barrow settlement had organic tempering, while 65 per cent of the animal bones in the same layers were cattle (O'Connor in Britnell 1984, 153). At Hazleton North, Gloucestershire, about 52 per cent of the pottery from the pre-long barrow settlement contained soft-rock tempering, while 33 per cent of the large mammal bones from the same deposits were of cattle (Levitan in Saville 1990, 200). Similarly, at Windmill Hill where 30 per cent of the vessels in the early phases had soft-rock or organic

tempering, about 40 per cent of the animal bones were cattle (Smith 1965, 143).

Elements of this pattern continued through into the 3rd millennium BC, but an increase of pigs in place of cattle may, in practical terms, require different demands for pottery (Thomas 1991). Moreover, at this time ceramic vessels had perhaps taken on additional meanings that emphasized important and central symbolic roles in ceremony and ritual. Barclay (1999, 12) observes, for example, that in the upper Thames Valley Grooved Ware in the Woodlands and Clacton sub-styles is of open-tub form and predominantly shell-tempered, whereas examples of the bucket-shaped vessels of the Durrington Walls sub-style tend to be grog tempered, the choice of temper he argues being deliberate and not simply the result of local availability of resources. Taking the interpretation of meaning rather further, Hamilton and Whittle (1999, 45) use ethnographic evidence to illustrate how specific pots were used to communicate with and attract ancestors to meals, to hold the souls of the living and the dead, to contain or protect against known spirits, or to mark achieved social *persona*. Any of these could underlie the meanings that later Neolithic people derived from seeing and using their ceramic vessels.

Conclusions

Distinctions between fabrics containing fragments of hard rock and those with soft rock or organic materials can be seen in many, but not all, pottery assemblages of the 4th and 3rd millennia BC in Britain. More work is needed to evaluate the links between these broad groups and the forms and styles of vessels represented, and the analysis of any residues remaining in a range of soft-rock and organic tempered wares would be useful too. Here, it is shown that the range of organic and calcareous materials used to produce these soft-rock and organic tempered wares is considerable and includes: chalk, fossil shell, limestone, ooliths, marine shell, mollusca shell, bone, chaff, and other kinds of vegetable matter.[2] From the 4th millennium BC, domestic assemblages in the mid-west of England and Wales show some regional variations in the representation of these soft-rock and organic tempered wares. Assemblages with the greatest proportion of soft-rock and organic tempered wares occur in the upland and hill and vale country and can tentatively be linked to the storage of milk or animal products for which such vessels would be ideal. Soft-rock and organic tempered wares were sometimes deposited in ceremonial contexts, and these tend to include exotic materials in terms of the soft inclusions within the fabric. During the 3rd millennium BC changes in the subsistence base perhaps meant that the symbolic aspects of pottery were more widely emphasized, and it is notable that assemblages are far more variable in the proportions of fabrics containing fragments of soft-rock as against hard-rock. Again, further work is needed on the exact nature of the vessels represented in these contrasting fabric types.

Acknowledgements

I would like to thank all the excavators of Neolithic sites whose pottery I was able to view and study and the many museum curators and assistants who made available pottery collections in their care for me to examine and record. Vanessa Constant prepared the figures for this paper.

Notes

1. In particular, assemblages from Scotland and the southwest peninsula of England seem to be dominated by hard-rock tempered pottery with very little else.
2. Mention may also be made of the cereal grains and other seeds/fruits noted in the fabric of Neolithic ceramics (Helbaek 1952, 196-203). Although generally considered accidental inclusions it is possible that some were deliberately incorporated within clay being prepared for pot-making in order to provide an additional layer of meaning or significance to the vessel.

Bibliography

Allen, C.S.M. 1991. Thin sections of Bronze Age pottery from the east Midlands of England. In A. Middleton & I.C. Freestone (eds), *Recent Developments in Ceramic Petrology*, 1-15. London: British Museum Occasional Paper 81

Avery, M. 1982. The Neolithic causewayed enclosure, Abingdon. In H.J. Case & A.W.R. Whittle (eds), *Settlement Patterns in the Oxford Region: excavations at the Abingdon causewayed enclosure and other sites*, 10-49. London: Council for British Archaeology Research Report 44

Barclay, A. 1999. Grooved Ware from the Upper Thames Region. In R. Cleal & A. MacSween (eds), *Grooved Ware in Britain and Ireland*, 9-22. Oxford: Oxbow Books / Neolithic Studies Group Seminar Papers 3

Bradley, R., Chowne, P., Cleal, R.M.J., Healy, F. & Kinnes, I. 1993. *Excavations at Redgate Hill, Hunstanton, Norfolk, and at Tattershall Thorpe, Lincolnshire.* Norwich: East Anglian Archaeology Report 57

Braun, D.P. 1983. Pots as tools. In J.A. Moore & A.S. Keene (eds), *Archaeological Hammers and Theories*, 107-34. New York: Academic Press

Briggs, C.S. 1997. A Neolithic and early Bronze Age settlement and burial complex at Llanilar, Ceredigion. *Archaeologia Cambrensis* 146, 13-59

Britnell, W. 1982. The excavation of two round barrows at Trelystan, Powys. *Proceedings of the Prehistoric Society* 48, 133-201

Britnell, W. 1984. The Gwernvale long cairn, Crickhowell, Brecknock. In W.J. Britnell & H.N. Savory (eds), *Gwernvale and Penywyrlod: Two Neolithic long cairns in the Black Mountains of Brecknock*, 43-154. Cardiff: Cambrian Archaeological Association Monograph 4

Clark, J.G.D. 1960. Excavations at the Neolithic site of Hurst Fen, Mildenhall, Suffolk. *Proceedings of the Prehistoric Society* 26, 202-45

Clarke, D.L. 1970. *Beaker Pottery of Great Britain and Ireland.* Cambridge: Cambridge University Press

Cleal, R.M.J. 1995. Pottery fabrics in Wessex in the fourth and second millennia BC. In I. Kinnes & G. Varndell (eds), *'Unbaked urns of rudely shape'. Essays on British and Irish Pottery for Ian Longworth*, 185-94. Oxford: Oxbow Monograph 55

Cleal, R.M.J., Cooper, J. & Williams, D. 1994. Shells and sherds: identification of inclusions in Grooved Ware, with associated radiocarbon dates, from Amesbury, Wiltshire. *Proceedings of the Prehistoric Society* 60, 445-8

Cleary, R.M. 1984. Bone tempered Beaker potsherds. *Journal of Irish Archaeology* 2, 73-5

Constantin, C. & Courtois, L. 1980. Utilization d'os comme dégraissant dans certaines poteries néolithiques. In E.A. Slater & J.O. Tate (eds), *Proceedings of the 16th International Symposium on Archaeometry and Archaeological Prospection*, 195-216. Edinburgh: National Museum of Antiquaries of Scotland

Cornwall, I.W. & Hodges, H.W.M. 1964. Thin sections of British Neolithic pottery: Windmill Hill – a test site. *Bulletin of the Institute of Archaeology* 4, 29-33

Cunnington, M.E. 1929. *Woodhenge.* Devizes: Simpson

Darvill, T.C. 1983. *The Neolithic of Wales and the mid-west of England: a systemic analysis of social change through the application of Action Theory.* Southampton: Southampton University, unpublished PhD thesis

Darvill, T.C. 1984. A study of the Neolithic pottery fabrics from Gwernvale. In W.J. Britnell & H.N. Savory (eds), *Gwernvale and Penywyrlod: Two Neolithic long cairns in the Black Mountains of Brecknock*, 110-113. Cardiff: Cambrian Archaeological Association Monograph 4

Darvill, T. 2002. White on Blonde: quartz pebbles and the use of quartz at Neolithic monuments in the Isle of Man and beyond. In A. Jones & G. MacGregor (eds), *Colouring the Past. The significance of colour in archaeological research*, 73-92 Oxford: Berg

Darvill, T. forthcoming. A petrological analysis of the ceramic fabrics represented amongst the Neolithic pottery from Hambledon Hill, Dorset. In R. Mercer & F. Healy, *Hambledon Hill, Dorset, England. Excavation and survey of a Neolithic monument complex and its surrounding landscape.* London: English Heritage

Darvill, T.C. & Smith, I.F. 1990. The prehistoric pottery. In A Saville, *Hazleton North. The excavation of a Neolithic long cairn of the Cotswold-Severn group*, 141-152. London: English Heritage / HBMCE Archaeological Report 13

Dudd, S.N. & Evershed, R.P. 1999. The organic residue analysis of the Neolithic pottery. In A. Gibson, *The Walton Basin Project: Excavation and survey in a prehistoric landscape 1993-7*, 112-120. York: Council for British Archaeology Research Report 118

Evans, J.G. & Smith, I.F. 1983. Excavations at Cherhill, North Wiltshire, 1967. *Proceedings of the Prehistoric Society* 49, 43-117

Gibson, A. 1995. First impressions: a review of Peterborough Ware in Wales. In I. Kinnes & G. Varndell (eds), *'Unbaked urns of rudely shape'. Essays on British and Irish Pottery for Ian Longworth*, 23-40. Oxford: Oxbow Monograph 55

Gibson, A. 1998. Neolithic pottery from Ogmore, Glamorgan. *Archaeologia Cambrensis* 147, 56-67

Gibson, A. 2002. *Prehistoric Pottery in Britain and Ireland.* Stroud: Tempus

Gray, H.St.G, 1935. The Avebury excavations, 1908-1922. *Archaeologia* 84, 99-162

Halbaek, H. 1952. Early crops in southern England. *Proceedings of the Prehistoric Society* 18, 194-233

Hamilton, M. & Whittle, A. 1999. Grooved Ware of the Avebury area: styles, contexts and meanings. In R. Cleal & A. MacSween (eds), *Grooved Ware in Britain and Ireland*, 36-47. Oxford: Oxbow Books / Neolithic Studies Group Seminar Papers 3

Henderson, J. 2000. *The Science and Archaeology of Materials. An investigation of inorganic materials.* London: Routledge

Hoard, R.J., O'Brien, M.J., Khorasgany, M.G. & Gopalaratnam, V.S. 1995. A materials-science approach to understanding limestone-tempered pottery from the midwestern United States. *Journal of Archaeological Science* 22, 823-32

Hodges, H.W.M. 1962. Thin sections of prehistoric pottery: an empirical study. *Bulletin of the Institute of Archaeology* 3, 58-68

Hodges, H.W.M. 1964. *Artefacts.* London: John Baker

Howard, H. 1981. In the wake of distribution: towards an integrated approach to ceramic studies in prehistoric Britain. In H. Howard & E.L. Morris (eds), *Production and Distribution: a ceramic viewpoint*, 1-30. Oxford: British Archaeological Reports International Series 120

Hulthén, B. 1977. *On ceramic technology during*

the Scanian Neolithic and Bronze Age. Stockholm: Institute of Archaeology at the University of Stockholm Theses and Papers in North-European Archaeology 6

Hulthén, B. 1981. *Porous Neolithic Ceramics*. Oslo: Oldsaksamlingens Årsbok

Hulthén, B. 1984. The Carrowmore pottery: a technological study. In G. Burenhult, *The Archaeology of Carrowmore*, 202-9. Stockholm: Institute of Archaeology at the University of Stockholm Theses and Papers in North-European Archaeology 14

Jenkins, D. & Williams, J. 1999. Thin section analysis of pottery from Upper Ninepence. In A. Gibson, *The Walton Basin Project: Excavation and survey in a prehistoric landscape 1993-7*, 120-25. York: Council for British Archaeology Research Report 118

Milisauskas, S. 1986. *Early Neolithic Settlement and society at Olszanica*. Ann Arbor: Memoirs of the Museum of Anthropology, University of Michigan 19

Modderman, P.J.R. 1981. Céramique du Limbourg: Rhénanie-Westphalie, Pays-Bas, Hesbaye. *Helinium* 21, 140-60

Musson, C.R. 1991. *The Breiddin Hillfort. A later prehistoric settlement in the Welsh Marches*. London: Council for British Archaeology Research Report 76

Peacock, D.P.S. 1969. Neolithic pottery production in Cornwall. *Antiquity* 43, 145-9

Peacock, D.P.S. 1981. Archaeology, ethnology and ceramic production. In H. Howard & E.L. Morris (eds), *Production and Distribution: a ceramic viewpoint*, 187-94. Oxford: British Archaeological Reports International Series 120

Pryor, F. 1974. *Excavation at Fengate, Peterborough, England: the first report*. Toronto: Royal Ontario Museum Archaeology Monograph 3

Pryor, F. 1998. *Etton. Excavations at a Neolithic causewayed enclosure near Maxey, Cambridgeshire, 1982-7*. London: English Heritage Archaeological Report 18.

Saville, A. 1990. *Hazleton North. The excavation of a Neolithic long cairn of the Cotswold-Severn group*. London: English Heritage HBMCE Archaeological report 13

Scott, L. 1954. Excavation of a Neolithic barrow in Whiteleaf Hill, Bucks. *Proceedings of the Prehistoric Society* 20, 212-30

Sharples, N.M. 1991. *Maiden Castle. Excavations and field survey 1985-6*. London: English Heritage HBMCE Archaeological Report 19

Shepard, A.O. 1956. *Ceramics for the Archaeologist*. Washington DC: Carnegie Institution of Washington Publication 609

Smith, C.A. 1987. Trefignath. In C.A. Smith & F.M. Lynch, *Trefignath and Din Dryfol. The excavation of two megalithic tombs in Anglesey*, 1-88. Cardiff: Cambrian Archaeological Association Monograph 3

Smith, I.F. 1956. *The Decorative Art of Neolithic Ceramics in South Eastern England and its Relations*. London: Institute of Archaeology, University of London unpublished PhD thesis

Smith, I.F. 1965. *Windmill Hill and Avebury. Excavations by Alexander Keiller 1925-1939*. Oxford: Clarendon Press

Thomas, N. 1964. The Neolithic causewayed camp at Robin Hood's Ball, Shrewton, *Wiltshire Archaeological & Natural History Magazine* 59, 1-27

Thomas, J. 1991. *Rethinking the Neolithic*. Cambridge: Cambridge University Press

Tringham, R. 1971. *Hunter, Fishers and Farmers of Eastern Europe, 6000-3000 BC*. London: Hutchinson

Webley, D. 1976. How the west was won – prehistoric land use in the southern Marches. In G. Boon & J.M. Lewis (eds), *Welsh Antiquity*, 19-35. Cardiff: National Museum of Wales

Whittle, A. 1997. *Sacred Mound, Holy Rings. Silbury Hill and the West Kennet palisaded enclosures: a later Neolithic complex in north Wiltshire*. Oxford: Oxbow Monograph 74

Whittle, A., Pollard, J., & Grigson, C. 1999. *The Harmony of Symbols. The Windmill Hill causewayed enclosure, Wiltshire*. Oxford: Oxbow Books

Making an Impression: Beaker combs

D.D.A. Simpson

Impressed comb decoration is considered to be one of the most distinctive features of Bell Beaker pottery and is found throughout Central, Western and West Mediterranean Europe. In Britain, at least, Greenwell was the first antiquary to mention the use of a specific tool to decorate Beakers in discussing the ornament on a vessel from Rudstone, East Riding of Yorkshire (1876, 255). The actual tools used to produce such ornament are remarkably scarce, most notably in the British Isles.

The site which has so far produced the most examples of such tools is the multi-period sand dune settlement at Northton, Isle of Harris, in the Outer Hebrides. This is a coastal site situated on the extreme south-western tip of the island and consisted of eight occupation horizons, dating from the Mesolithic to the Iron Age, separated by layers of sterile wind blown sand (Simpson 1976, Simpson et al. forthcoming). Two distinct Beaker horizons occurred above an earlier Neolithic level and produced some 3400 sherds representing a minimum of 210 vessels. In addition, large quantities of food remains, both terrestrial and marine, were recovered and a series of bone and antler tools, among which were three bone combs, while a fourth came

from the preceding Neolithic level, almost certainly moved downwards by the activities of burrowing animals. All four combs were made from flat bones such as mammalian ribs or scapulae. Each was triangular in shape, worked to a point at the apex with the broad end having a series of small fine teeth, some of which were broken or abraded due to wear (Fig. 1.1-4). Two of the combs had drilled perforations toward the narrow ends which may have been used for suspension. All of the surfaces were smooth and polished due to wear. It would be reasonable to assume that the Northton combs were used to impress pottery to produce the characteristic dentated ornament and the pointed end the much more common incised decoration (Fig. 2). In spite of the fact that fabric analysis suggests that the clay used in potting was of local origin, plasticine impressions made with all four combs (Fig. 3) could not be matched on any of the comb ornamented Beaker sherds from the site nor on the single example from the Neolithic level.

Somewhat similar impressions on the Northton Beakers were produced using shells although such decoration tends to be more lopsided. Again experiments using the serrated

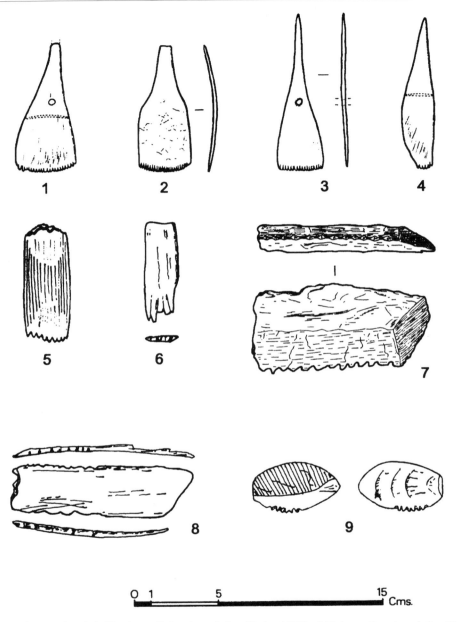

Fig 1. Beaker combs: 1-4, Northton; 5 Gwithian (after Clarke 1970); 6 Bishops Cannings (after Gingell 1992); 7 Crig-a-Minnis (after Christie 1960); 8 Dean Bottom (after Cleal 1992); 9 flint comb (after Young 1950)

edges of shells impressed into plasticine indicate that two species were employed, the limpet (*patella vulgata* Fig. 4.1) and the cockle (*cerastoderma edule* Fig. 4.2), the latter producing more 'comb-like' impressions. Both can be matched among a small number of Beaker sherds from both levels.

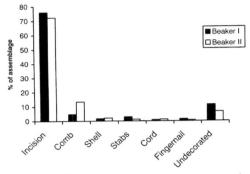

Fig. 2. Northton: frequency of decorative techniques on pottery from both Beaker levels

The closest parallel for the Northton combs is an example from the multi-period sand dune settlement at Gwithian, Cornwall. The nine teeth were worked on the end of a portion of mammalian rib bone (Fig. 1.5). This comb cited and illustrated by Clarke (1970, 10, fig. l.6) comes not from the Beaker and Earlier Bronze Age site, XV, but from site X (Megaw 1976, 62, fig. 4.6, 12). On the other hand, in layer 7 of site XV was found a slate comb (unpublished) capable of producing the broad toothed hyphenated ornament exhibited by pottery from the same layer. A further parallel, again made from a rib bone, comes from Bishops Cannings Down, Wiltshire (Gingell 1992, 115, fig. 83.1) (Fig. l.6). The excavations revealed the overlapping ground plans of two post-built round houses associated with pottery in the Deverel Rimbury tradition. There were also 10 weathered sherds of Beaker pottery recovered from the excavations and a test pit and it is presumed that the comb belongs to this phase of activity on the site.

A comb of a rather different character comes from Dean Bottom, Wiltshire (Cleal 1992, 111-4) in what was interpreted as a re-used Beaker storage pit (Fig. 1.8). In addition to 18 other pieces of worked bone and antler it also contained 271 sherds of Beaker pottery of Clarke's Wessex/Middle Rhine group, 40% of which was decorated with comb impressions. The comb, apparently incomplete, was made from a large ungulate split rib with teeth cut along both edges showing traces of use wear. In spite of the internal homogeneity of the assemblage and the possibility that most of the pottery was made from local clay sources, plasticine impressions made from both sides of the comb made it clear from the spacing and pattern of variation of the teeth that the Dean Bottom comb was not employed in the decoration of the pottery from the pit with which it was associated.

Possible combs of a different character were excavated at Lakenheath, Suffolk (Briscoe

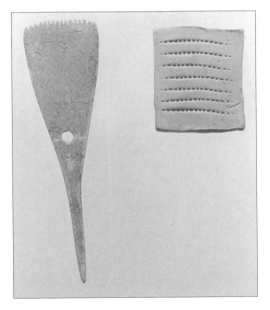

Fig. 3. Northton bone comb and plasticine impression

Fig. 4. Impressions made in plasticine with limpet (1) and cockle (2) shells and Beaker sherds showing similar impressions

1960). Here a small black pit contained over 200 sherds of Beaker and Rusticated ware and fragments of animal bone and teeth, the latter molars or pre-molars of bovine type, with one horse incisor. It was suggested that some of the teeth fragments had a series of notches cut in the dentine and produced the impressed decoration found on the sherds of a giant Beaker from the pit. A series of experiments were carried out to demonstrate this hypothesis. The results of the experiment indicated that the dentine core of the roots rather than the enamel could be scratched with the sharp edge of a flint flake to produce a notched tool. Further experiments were conducted using the thin edge of a mammalian rib bone (species not stated) producing a coarser but longer tool. Such an artefact was not represented among the material. Earlier speculations on the nature of the tools used to produce hyphenated ornament had been published by Ward (1902, 1916). In describing a Beaker from a cist burial at Cwm Car Farm, he suggested that the decoration had been produced by impressing a comb into the unfired clay (1902, 26), whereas a second Beaker from a pit at St. Fagans he suggested was impressed with a notched plate of bone, wood or other hard substance convexly curved or possibly forming the periphery of a disc, the impressions being produced by a rolling motion (Fig. 5). Ward (1916) also recovered Beaker pottery during his excavation of the chambered tomb of St. Nicholas, better known as Tinkinswood. Four

Fig. 5. Suggested tool used to decorate a Beaker from St. Fagans Glamorgan (after Ward 1918)

sherds of comb-impressed sherds of Beaker pottery came from the same vessel, two from the chamber and a further two just outside. In his original report he published the sherds as part of a bowl-shaped vessel, their true nature being first recognised by Piggott (1931, 136). Ward suggested that the decoration had been produced using the notched edge of a thin stamp of bone or wood. In studying the impressions on the Tinkinswood Beaker he was able to demonstrate they were made from the same portion of the stamp and not from a cog wheel or roulette. Comparable experiments were conducted using the articular ends of bird or small mammal bones to reproduce impressions found on later Neolithic pottery (Liddell 1929). A final possible bone comb is mentioned by Ward:

> Mr. Wright informs me that there is in the Joslin Collection, Colchester Museum, a toothed instrument made from the shoulder blade of some animal. Its thin edge, about 3 in. long, is serrated like a saw and the serrations are about the size of those of a rather coarse Joiners saw. He suggests that it was a potters tool for producing dotted lines like those on prehistoric Beakers. (1918, 45, note 1)

This object can no longer be located in Colchester Museum.

The slate comb from Gwithian mentioned above has a possible parallel from a Bronze Age barrow context. Crig-a-Minnis, Cornwall, was a causewayed ditched mound covering two Trevisker-style urns decorated with plaited cord impressions (Christie 1960). A saw-toothed object of grey-green puckered slate of local origin, broken at one end, was found in the ditch north of the causeway. The teeth were quite fresh and since the slate is quite soft it can never have suffered much use against a resistant surface (Fig. 1.7). It was interpreted as a tool to decorate pottery although no such pottery was found on the site.

The frequency of comb impressions in Britain and much of continental Europe suggested to Cleal (1992, 111) that the scarcity of bone combs indicates that such tools were made from other materials. Experiments using a replica of the Dean Bottom comb demonstrated that it abraded rapidly, ultimately giving uneven impressions after continual use. Wooden combs were suggested as the preferred material. On the other hand, experiments conducted by Young (1950), regrettably not discussed in detail, using bone and wooden combs immediately ruled out the latter as they tended to 'pull' on the clay. He suggested that a notched flint blade provided a more convincing and durable implement and compared impressions on the Beaker from Beckhampton, Wiltshire, with notched impressions made with an experimental flint tool (Fig. 1.9).

Clarke (1970, 432), in his study of Beaker pottery from Britain and Ireland was able to record in 104 cases the length of the comb used to decorate the vessels with reasonable accuracy. These varied from 10-54mm long with the majority (70%) falling between 30-42mm. The Northton, Gwithian and Bishops Cannings tools are at the lower end of this scale while the Dean Bottom example fits the mean.

Rare examples of comb impressions are found on Neolithic pottery. The sherd from Northton has already been mentioned and a second Hebridean example comes from the settlement on Eilean an Tighe, North Uist (Scott 1950, fig. 7, no. Z7). Possible comb ornament has also been recognised on Peterborough pottery (Gibson 2001, 59, fig. 3.5), but the bulk of the evidence suggests that this technique appears as a major component in pottery decoration with the introduction of Beakers into Britain and Ireland, a legacy which was maintained in Primary Series Collared Urns, usually employing a point toothed comb, but a much coarser comb is also known (Longworth 1984, 8). In continental Europe the technique has a much more ancient ancestry.

In northern Europe bone combs have been recorded from TRB contexts in Denmark (Glob 1944) and north Germany (Sprockoff 1938, Struve 1955). These include tools with teeth

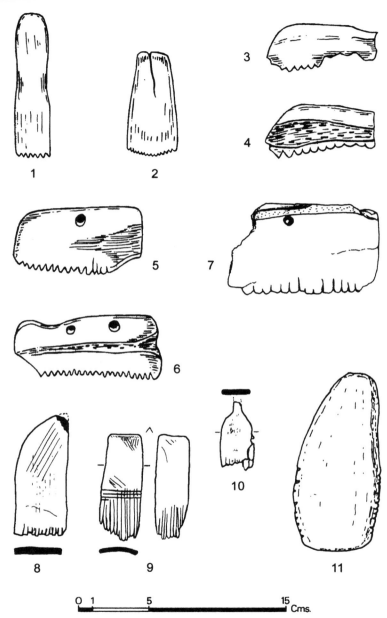

Fig. 6. Beaker combs: 1 Felsted, Germany (after Sprockhoff 1938); 2 Jutland (after Glob 1944); 3-4 Erfurt, Germany (after Sprockhoff 1938); 5-6.Cueva de Ameyago, Spain (after Castillo 1928); 7-10 around Tagus Estuary, Portugal (after Harrison 1977); 11 Dar-es-Soltan, Morocco (after Jodin 1954)

worked on the end of a mammalian rib bone and other examples with teeth executed along the length of the bone (Fig. 6.l-4). To the writer's knowledge there are no combs from Bell Beaker contexts in north/central Europe. Again in south-western Europe combs were used to decorate Early Neolithic Cave Culture pottery in Spain and Portugal, not by impressing the tool into the clay, but by drawing it across the surface to produce an undulating or wavy pattern, the ultimate inspiration for such decoration being the Cardial Ware associated with the first agri-culturists in the central and west Mediterranean (Savory 1968, 69, fig. 19g). The tradition of comb ornament continued into Millaran and Vila Nova de San Pedro contexts and such decoration was applied not only to pottery but was frequently used to decorate clay loom weights in VNSP assemblages (Harrison 1977, 47), and combs exist for this period (Fig. 6.7-10) and into the succeeding Beaker phase. Two bone combs were recovered from the Ameyugo Cave, Burgos province (Castillo 1928, 55) (Fig. 6.5-6). Little experimental work has been carried out on the tools used in decorating European Beakers. The exception is the work of Jodin (1954) on the material from Dar-es-Soltan, Morocco. This was an occupied cave site; the horizon which produced Beaker pottery was described as a 'kitchen midden' with numerous marine shells and animal bones. In this deposit was an almost complete Palmella Beaker and a further 28 sherds all decorated with comb impressions. What was described in the original report as a bone amulet (Ruhlman 1951), Jodin suggested was a tool used to produce dentated ornament (Fig. 6.11) on Beaker pottery and demonstrated this possibility by making im-pressions on wax with the bone, similar, but not identical, to those found on the pottery from the cave deposit.

It is a great pleasure to offer this brief paper in Isobel's honour with grateful thanks for long ago happy and stimulating days in Wiltshire and instilling in me an understanding of earlier prehistoric pottery – I hope a little of her know-ledge has rubbed off.

Bibliography

Briscoe, G. 1960. Giant Beaker and Rusticated Ware from Lakenheath, Suffolk and repro-duction of ornament. *Proceedings of the Cambridge Antiquarian Society* 53, 1-7

Castillo Yurrita, A. del. 1928. *La Culture del Vaso Canpaniform Sue Origen y Extension en Europe.* Barcelona

Christie, P.M. 1960. Crig-a-Minnis: a Bronze Age barrow at Liskey, Perranzbuloe, Cornwall. *Proceedings of the Prehistoric Society* 26, 76-97

Clarke, D.L. 1970. *Beaker Pottery of Great Britain and Ireland.* Cambridge: Cambridge University Press

Cleal, R. 1992. The Dean bottom assemblage. In C. Gingell, *The Marlborough Downs: a later Bronze Age landscape and its origins*, 111-4. Devizes: Wiltshire Archaeological & Natural History Society

Glob, P.V. 1944. *Studier over men Jyske Enkelgravskultur. Aarboger For Nordisk Oldkyndighed.* Og Historie, 1-283

Gibson, A. 2001. Neolithic pottery from Ogmore, Glamorgan. *Archaeologia Cambrensis* 147, 56-67

Gingell, C. 1992. *The Marlborough Downs: a later Bronze Age landscape and its origins.* Devizes: Wiltshire Archaeological & Natural History Society

Greenwell, W. 1876. *British Barrows.* Oxford: Clarendon Press

Harrison, R.J. 1977. *The Bell Beaker Cultures of Spain and Portugal.* Cambridge (MA): American School of Prehistoric Research, Peabody Museum, Harvard University

Jodin, A. 1954. La ceramique campaniform de Dar-es-Soltan. *Bulletin de la Société Préhist-orique Francaise* 54, 44-8

Liddell, D.M. 1929. New light on an old problem. *Antiquity* 3, 283-91

Longworth, I.H. 1984. *Collared Urns of the Bronze Age.* Cambridge: Cambridge University Press

Megaw, J.V.S. 1976. Gwithian, Cornwall: some notes on the evidence for neolithic and bronze age settlement. In C. Burgess & R. Miket (eds), *Settlement and Economy in the third and second millennium BC*, 51-79. Oxford: British Archaeological Reports

Piggott, S. 1931. Neolithic pottery of the British Isles. *Archaeological Journal* 88, 67-158

Ruhlman, A. 1951. La Grotte Préhistorique de Dar-es-Soltan. *Collection Hesperis* XI.

Savory, H.N, 1968. *Spain and Portugal*. London: Thames & Hudson.

Scott, W.L. 1950. Eilean an Tighe: a pottery workshop of the second millennium BC. *Proceedings of the Society of Antiquaries of Scotland* 85, 1-37

Simpson, D.D.A. 1976. The Later Neolithic and Beaker Settlement of Northton Isle of Harris. In C.B. Burgess & R. Miket (eds), *Settlement and Economy in the third and second millennia BC*, 221-231. Oxford: British Archaeological Reports

Simpson, D.D.A., Murphy, E.M. & Gregory, R.A. forthcoming. *Excavations at Northton Isle of Harris*

Sprockhoff, E. 1938. Die Nordische Megalithkultur. *Handbuch der Urgesichte Deutschland 3*

Struve, K.W. 1955. *Pie Einzelgraberkultur in Schleswig Holstein und ihr kontintentalen Beziehungen*

Ward, J. 1902. Prehistoric interments near Cardiff. *Archaeologia Cambrensis* 2, 25-33

Ward. J. 1916. The St. Nicholas chambered tumulus Glamorgan II. *Archaeologia Camb-rensis* 116, 239-94

Ward, J. 1918. Some prehistoric sepulchral remains near Pendine, Carmarthenshire. *Archaeologia Cambrensis* 18, 35-79

Young, W.E.V. 1950. A Beaker interment at Beckhampton. *Wiltshire Archaeological & Natural History Magazine* 53, 311-27

Texture and Asymmetry in Later Prehistoric Lithics, and their Relevance to Environmental Archaeology

J.G. Evans

In considering the theoretical basis of this contribution, I am reminded of a remark of an American behaviourist psychologist reported by Terry Eagleton (1996, 140) in his book *Literary Theory: an introduction*: 'The trouble with Freud's work is that it just isn't testicle'. In environmental archaeology, many of our ideas are not testable, especially in terms of how materials, environments and ideas were drawn into past human lives, yet I believe, following the post-processualist – and specifically interpretive – mode of theory (e.g. Shanks & Hodder 1995), that this is one of the ways in which environmental archaeology should currently be played out (Evans 2003). Nor is the reference to Freud himself unrelated since the unconscious, the way we use it in the structuring of our lives, and especially in how we create futures with reference to the past are significantly developed through the concept of the *chaîne opératoire*. My aim here is to discuss such modes of behaviour through an exploration of the relationships between small lithic debitage and people. As an environmental archaeologist, I am interested in lithics because in some areas such material is widespread, abundant and extremely visual, and thus constitutes a significant part of the human environment. I was aware of this early on in my archaeological career, working on excavations under Isobel Smith around Avebury and also on the scarp of the Chiltern Hills near my home where I often collected flints off the fields. Flints can give significant visual texture to the land, especially where it is cultivated; the land immediately to the north of the West Kennet Long Barrow, where I spent many weeks on the excavation of a round barrow under Isobel's direction, is a case in point. Yet flints do not seem to have been much brought into considerations of the prehistoric environment as a medium of social expression as suggested for material culture in the post-processualist paradigm (Shanks & Tilley 1987, ch. 4), and this is as much a deficiency in the archaeological world as a whole as in environmental archaeology specifically.

Lithics as sociality

For example, in the southern Hebrides Mesolithic project at Bolsay Farm, Islay, flints are not seen as having been actively emplaced or even actively used in social lives, but instead as relating to raw functional considerations, for example of knapping and dumping of debitage in relation to the siting of a spring, or in manufacture and repair and as the discard of composite tools (Mithen *et al.* 2000). Similarly, at Staosnaig on Colonsay as part of the same project, reasons for core abandonment are seen in terms of functionalist considerations alone, like size, flaws and specific technical features, and not in terms of their visuality in social expression (Mithen & Finlay 2000). On the other side of the Atlantic, a whole book on lithic debitage with 16 authors fails to address the interpretive or post-processual paradigm at all (Andrefsky 2001). Indeed, one of the main protagonists of practice in lithic debitage studies advocates a distinction between objective recording and interpretation in behavioural terms (Sullivan 2001, 205): '...the time is long overdue to scrutinize the usefulness of the widely held assumption that analytical units should carry meaning'; and '...strong inferences about debitage assemblage origins can be developed with interpretation-neutral units of analysis'.

Yet for at least 15 years, workers have been discussing the symbolism inherent in stone use, and it is worth citing the work of Paul Taçon (1991) in Arnhem Land in this respect. Importantly, in the world of social agency, it is not just the tools and their manufacturing stages along *chaînes opératoires* but also the debris of cores, flakes and other miscellaneous debitage which are relevant. In this view, terms associated with flint working, like 'debitage', 'core' and 'blank' are only relevant in specific technological contexts; in that these materials have a use in the construction and reproduction of social lives, their understanding by archaeologists as 'waste' is erroneous. Equally, if we view cores and other debitage as actively mediatory in social worlds after their final working, the very concept of 'abandonment' becomes redundant.

Take the example of cores in the British Mesolithic and earlier Neolithic (Figs 1 & 2). It is usual that these are worked around only a part of their periphery as in the case of the platform cores described by Clark (1955, 7; 1960, 216)

from eastern England and as quantified for the Hebridean Mesolithic (Finlay *et al.* 2000, 560). To me these differences look like a way in which the knapper is expressing him- or herself through different styles of symmetry. They remind me of the ideas of Erving Goffman (1969, ch. 3) about back and front regions of presentation, one surface, the back, having some cortex and natural frost weathering, old flake scars partially truncated by core rejuvenation or in the course of later flaking and fresher scars, the other, the front, presenting finely worked parallel blade facets. And like Goffman's fronts and backs, meaning depends on social context. Thus the backs as just described may lack striking platforms and inverse bulbs of percussion, yet they can have deeper meaning as expressed in their more complex surfaces and different levels of time (Fig. 1, nos. 2 & 3), while the fronts as the latest stage of reduction with their fresh and complete flutings are of much simpler importance. Fronts and backs can well be reversed, yet in our perception of the fronts we often illustrate just the fluted surfaces. As an extension of this idea – the idea that there is greater meaning in a surface that has a longer history – there are situations where old patinated cores and larger pieces of flint have later been found and re-worked, as with an assemblage from a Bronze Age ring-ditch at Barleycroft Farm, Needingworth, Cambridgeshire, where Neolithic pieces were reworked on a fair scale, perhaps as a way of creating connections to an ancestral past (Josh Pollard pers. comm.). Again the concept of 'abandonment' seems irrelevant.

These asymmetries take on more significance when we remember that they are encompassed in a wider range of materialities and greater scales. Long barrows and chambered tombs, for example, embed a nested series of asymmetries from the very local, seen in the sidedness of their construction, as at South Street (Ashbee *et al.* 1979), in their stone textures as in several Pembrokeshire and Galloway sites, like Cairnholy (Cummings 2002), and in their siting at significant soil boundaries (Whittle *et al.*

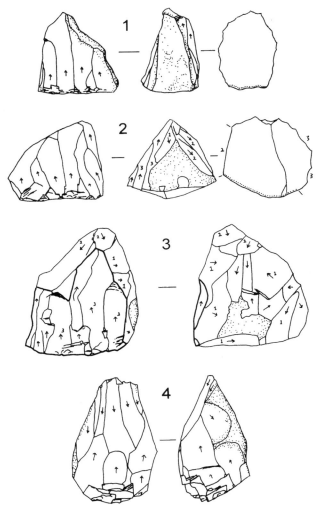

1993: 230), to the wider setting in relation to views (Cummings *et al.* 2002). For the Mesolithic, we can point to the siting of shell middens at precise textural boundaries of turf and storm beach (Mellars 1987), and of flint-working sites at the edge of tufa or peat, in all of which a symbolic contrast of stability and instability may be being referenced rather than the functional relationship to ecotones so usually invoked. Some shell middens contain hand bones (Pollard 1996), a clear index of sidedness. It may even be that the asymmetries of the flint cores are a means of enhancing these wider, landscape, asymmetries, and one of the ways this may work is through gender. Some shell middens are associated with burials where there is a contrast in diet as shown by isotope analysis, with women taking more land-based foods than men (Schulting & Richards 2001). Perhaps these dietary opposites, the asymmetries of siting and their enhancement with the cores constitute a schema whereby women symbolically express their gender.

Returning to the lithics, as a consequence of this discussion, the term '*reduction* sequence' as applied to the removal of flakes, blades and rejuvenation pieces from a core

Fig. 1. Mesolithic flint cores [1]. 1, Bossington, Hants; single-platform blade core. 2, Bossington, Hants; single-platform core, with one subsidiary platform, relating to episode 2; in the left view, all scars relate to episode 3; the scars of episode 2 have inverse bulbs; the single scar of episode 1, the earliest, is incomplete, and the striking platform has been removed. 3, Bossington, Hants; 3-platform core; scars of episode 1 lack striking platform or bulbar scars; scars of episode 2 are complete and derive from two opposite, subsidiary, platforms at the apex of the core; the scars of the latest removals, 3, are mostly for blades and are enclosed in the heavy black line. 4, Fullerton, Hants; opposite-platform core, one platform for blades, at the top, the other for flakes, at the bottom; the blade removals are neater than those of the flakes with their heavy stepping, yet in terms of social content, the latter have greater intensity of information and meaning

should only be used in a technological context. A core may be reduced in mass, but at the same time much debitage, tools and, in these and in the process of their production, opportunities for social engagement are created, so in terms of socialities it is very much a '*construction sequence*'. Indeed, I would question whether there is such a thing as a pure technological context at all.

All is not doom and gloom by a long chalk. Work on localised deposits is couched in terms of the active role of flints in social lives, as with regard to artefacts in the establishment of status (Edmonds 2001, 14-17) and of structured deposition of debris in causewayed camps (Whittle *et al.* 1999), while Humphrey and Young (1999) have looked at impoverishment in Later Bronze Age and Iron Age flint-working as a response to the replacement of the finer flintwork of earlier times by other media of social expression. The ideas in the last paper are exceptionally interesting and might also explain the shift from Mesolithic/Early Neolithic to Late Neolithic/Bronze Age core technology in Britain as discussed by Isobel Smith (1965) in her work on Windmill Hill and further quantified by Pitts (1978). Belatedly I have read the contribution by James Conolly (1996) on the Çatal Höyük lithics. I have illustrated two Bronze Age cores (Fig. 2, nos 6 & 7) and also a rather poor example of a Mesolithic core (Fig. 2, no. 5); intuitively, these are technically inferior to the fluted 'fronts' of the Mesolithic cores (Fig. 1) yet is there not the same amount of social information in the two groups? I would see such differences of style as an integral part of, rather than a passive response to, shifting styles in other media of expression.

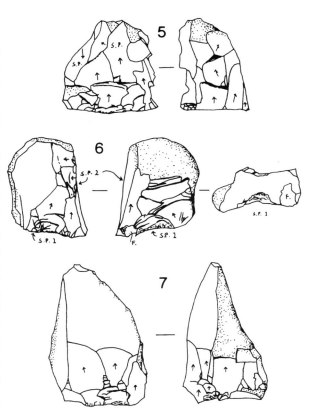

Fig. 2. Flint cores. 5, Mesolithic from Fullerton, Hants; single-platform core of inferior quality, with two subsidiary striking-platforms, S.P.; the strong step and hinge fractures indicate significant use which, in view of the abundant flint on the site and other well-worked cores (e.g. Fig. 1, no. 4), can hardly be functional and is probably of a more expressive nature. 6 and 7, Later Neolithic or Bronze Age cores from the Hartshill Barrow (WO-G.19), West Overton, Wilts (unpublished excavations of G. Swanton, illustrated by permission); the middle view is at 180 degrees to the left view; both these cores, like no. 5 from Fullerton, lack distinctive back and front areas. F. = fault in the flint

Talk of style is interesting, and again the discussion can be widened, as Josh Pollard has reminded me:

> During the later Neolithic there seems to be a number of styles in operation, blade-working as at West Kennet palisades (Whittle 1997), the creation of 'Levallois' flakes for fancy knives and arrowheads, and, alongside these, more 'mundane' broad-flake production. It may be that the more elaborate and fancy styles of working have an association with activities at monuments, where there was a greater need to display and reaffirm different kinds of social identity.

Another possibility for the cores is that the finer blade cores with their expressive fluting and asymmetry of style are the product of a more settled way of life than those of less symmetrical form which perhaps relate to more transient communities. I come to this again through the ideas of Goffman (1969) and my own observations on houses in student areas of Cardiff where, in the latter, the contrast between the squalid backs and elegant fronts of the permanent Victorian style breaks down in the transience of their university role (Fig. 3). On the other hand, and somewhat in opposition to this, there is the possibility that, as with the use of the Levallois technique in the Middle Palaeolithic (Gamble 1999, 242), the more far-travelled materials were subject to the more refined techniques.

Lithics on the land: *chaînes opératoires*

Environmental archaeologists, as Terry O'Connor and I explained a few years ago (Evans & O'Connor 1999, ch. 9), are particularly interested in debitage because it is widely distributed on the land, yet there has not been the same understanding of this context in terms of social meaning as there has been for more localised deposits. Surveys see flint distributions in terms of settlements, off-site activities like transhumance and lithic procurement, and

manuring (e.g. Richards 1990; Woodward 1991; Schofield *et al.* 1999). There is no sense of lithics being employed in entexturing the land for the specific purposes of exploring social lives. This is what environmental archaeology needs to address (Evans 2003, ch. 6).

Fig. 3. The breakdown of distinctive fronts (upper) and backs (lower) of student houses in the Cathays area of Cardiff

At the same time, we should not separate local depositions and widespread distributions as two distinct modes, because they are intimately associated as *chaînes opératoires* in which meaning is lodged in the entire sequence (Moore 1986; Dobres 2000). A part of the establishment of meaning through social agency is in the temporal dimension; engagements with individual slices of technology or environment always refer to the past and take place in anticipation of the future. People plug into particular stages as a means of establishing particular social conditions but each stage is not autonomous; like a single note or chord in a musical piece it takes meaning from what went before and in the anticipation of what is to come. Moreover, the narrow concept of the *chaîne opératoire* beginning with the acquisition and testing of raw material and ending with the retouching of blanks (e.g. Finlay *et al.* 2000) cannot be sustained. The various stages are established in people's minds and social needs long before any physical engagement with the lithics takes place, while the so-called debitage or waste materials and their discard can be engaged with on the land for years or centuries. People may visit an area with their animals at particular times of the year and at the same time engage in the working of stone. This may have happened in the Tarragona region of north-east Spain where most waste from cores was tertiary and away from habitations, in contrast to the high density of tools in the home-range (Schofield *et al.* 1999). What is not pointed out in this work is that the marking of the land with flints can have had an active influence in its identification or at least in some kind of engagement for the people who used it for grazing their animals. Once more we see how the concept of 'abandonment' is only relevant in the context of specific parts of the *chaînes opératoires* connected with tool manufacture; in regard to social lives debitage is not debitage and it is never abandoned.

Environment must be thought of as not just the physical environment but any mediatory influence in the workings of social agency. It includes ideas, ideologies and individuals themselves. In the knapping of flint and the engagement with tools and debris, the individual is creating and engaging with the physical environment but at the same time is a part of that environment in that he or she is developing his/her social life in relation to it. Different levels of history and past engagements are known about and explored, such as the use of flint in learning and apprenticeship, the danger of flint to children and animals if left lying around in large quantities, and a knowledge of deeper history of past uses, for example through an understanding of the sequence of flake scars on cores (see especially Fig. 1, nos. 3 & 6). Often it is the older cores that display the greater amount of historical information, although this does not always apply, as with Norwegian bipolar cores where the final form is more similar whatever the starting point – pebbles, single-platform cores, slender cylindrical cores, or fragments of large robust blades – than are the younger phases of working (Ballin 1999). Past articulations of gender and power relationships in the household and in disposal are established through these deeper meanings of time and allow an immediate significance to be established and placed on flints (e.g. Moore 1986). Importantly, meaning is established not passively by mapping action onto flints as if they were some kind of textual signifier but through engagement with meaning in the first place. For example, apprenticeship can be explored through practice in the skills of flint-knapping and is an important part of a person's cognitive training but this is only successful if it is done through an exploration of sociality – either of one's self or with others – yet this has been missed in certain studies of the cognitive school (e.g. Karlin & Julien 1994). Cognitive archaeology *sensu* Renfrew and Zubrow (1994) is not an alternative to post-processualist or an agency-centred archaeology but a part of it; cognition, like memory, can only be brought into being through social action.

Surveys

This is clearly relevant to flints in the landscape and surveys. Since meaning may originate in localised contexts, the evidence from field survey cannot be interpreted in isolation. Beyond the use of flint in settlements and its primary disposal around them, there is further connotation in the use of flint in structured depositions in ditches and pits. In these, its annotatory role is soon hidden from view but retained at least in some sectors of the community in the meaning it gives to these features. But active deposition and engagement with debris applies not only to these localised associations, but also to the widespread distribution of these materials on the land as identified in field surveys. Here, flint comes to reside through its disposal, its incorporation as manure, and its deliberate strewing as an entexturing medium; middening can be a deliberate strategy to make visible traces of former occupation; or, some flint may derive from primary working on the land away from the settlements. So there can be considerable complexity to the origins and meaning of lithics on the surface of the land. Yet this should not detract us from looking for interpretations which can be quite simple, in that this complexity of origins can have been itself understood as a holism through which people in the past took understanding, just as we do in our taphonomic analyses today. It can even have been that there was widespread manipulation of flint distrib-utions as a means of socialising the environment – adding to them, removing from them, or modifying them with flints of particular style. Look at some of the very large areas of contrast in flint density in the Stonehenge survey and the sharp boundaries between them, such as that to the south of the Normanton Down barrows (Richards 1990, fig. 10), and take these in combination with the nearby stripping of turves over several hectares to make round barrows as described by Woodward (2000, 52). Perhaps these two features are functionally related. Concepts of taphonomy may be attractive to the environmental reductionist but in terms of past meaning and engagement they are redundant.

Conclusions

The widespread and dense distribution of flint in the landscape, its durability and, in this, its record of history, made it a powerful tool in social reproduction. Significant and sharp differences in density on a local and regional scale, for example in relation to soil build up or erosion and geology, allowed for a diversity of engagements. Meaning can have been en-hanced in the way particular types of debitage were used in particular contexts. Asymmetrical Mesolithic blade cores from river valleys in central southern England, some of which I have already discussed, were deployed precisely at the junction of valley side and floodplain as if their opposing sides were a metaphor of this land divide. But it was the social world and its development that provided the structure through which these properties brought into being the *chaîne opératoire* as a distinctive feature of flint technology. Social agency can involve single individuals coming to terms with their selves; it can involve two or more people exploring specific or opposing interests; and it can be about identities of much bigger groups of entire peoples. Agency is not, as is often thought, the idiosyncratic interventions of single individuals but the mediation through the environment of socialities at any scale. This is realised in the use of flint in various walks of life and its potential for use by everybody in one way or another. Young men can have established prowess in working flint, as suggested in the concentrations of hammer-stones and freshly worked cores in specific areas around Stonehenge (Richards 1990) and Maiden Castle (Sharples 1991); individuals may have collected flints from the fields and piled them at their edges as a means of creating in themselves a sense of well-being, as seen in the small cairns and associated cremations at Winterbourne Steepleton on the

Dorset Ridgeway (Woodward 1991, fig. 34); women may have cleared the land and constructed banks at their edges as a means of formalising the land or perhaps of domesticating it in the oppressiveness of a dominant male order, as Seremetakis (1991) describes of women in Inner Mani; settlements can have been established where flint was abundant as a specific means of intensifying social relations or opposing others elsewhere, with areas rich in flint being actively sought out for such a purpose; equally, areas of poor quality flint, such as plateau deposits, may have been deliberately engaged with to establish a specific meaning, perhaps through the subtle colour differences so vividly described by Kendall (1922) for north Wiltshire, as may areas where lithic resources were being reduced by environmental change like sea-level rise. Importantly, the use of flint in these ways does not negate its more functional or practical uses. It may be that such uses in the social domain worked through the unconscious, and in this respect it is interesting that neo-Freudian (e.g. Lacanian) psychotherapy sees the unconscious as coming into being as a series of chains of transference through social engagement (Eagleton 1996, 142-50).

It is no accident that the concept of the *chaîne opératoire* originated in flint technology, even though this was founded in the concept of a deeper transformatory process of nature to culture and developed out of ideas of Marcel Mauss in the 1920s (Schlanger 1994) who saw quite clearly the socially mediatory origins of such engagements. It is just unfortunate that such meanings have, until recently (e.g. Dobres 2000; Edmonds 2001; Humphreys & Young 1999), been lost. Flintworking was exceptionally suited to the establishment of socialities. It was a medium like writing, used variously in different styles and genres, but overall it gave the stamp of super-sociality to certain prehistoric societies, just like writing gives the stamp of literacy to ours, and out of which more monumental styles of symbolism emerged.

Note

1. In Figs 1 and 2, the left view is the latest area of removals, the middle or right view one of earlier, less patterned, removals and/or cortex (the latter stippled) at 90 degrees to the left view and turned clockwise (except Fig. 2, no. 6). In 1 and 2, the right view is of the main striking platform, shown at the base in the other two views; stippled area is cortex. Numbers on the scars refer to the order of removals, earliest 1, latest 3. The drawings were not done photogrammetrically but with setsquare and calipers and are designed to show life histories. Scale is 50% actual size.

Acknowledgements

I thank Nyree Finlay and Elizabeth Walker for help with literature and Josh Pollard for his valuable ideas and comments. The work on Bossington and Hartshill is progressing, but I take this opportunity to thank the land owners, John Fairey and Gill Swanton, for their continuing support.

Bibliography

Andrefsky, W. (ed.) 2001. *Lithic Debitage: context, form and meaning*. Salt Lake City: University of Utah Press

Ashbee, P., Smith, I.F. & Evans, J.G. 1979. Excavation of three long barrows near Avebury, Wiltshire. *Proceedings of the Prehistoric Society* 45, 207-300

Ballin, T.B. 1999. Bipolar cores in southern Norway: classification, chronology and geography. *Lithics* 20, 13-22

Clark, J.G.D. 1955. A microlithic industry from the Cambridgeshire fenland and other industries of Sauveterrian affinities from Britain. *Proceedings of the Prehistoric Society* 21, 3-20

Clark, J.G.D. 1960. Excavations at the Neolithic site at Hurst Fen, Mildenhall, Suffolk. *Proceedings of the Prehistoric Society* 26, 202-45

Conolly, J. 1996. Chapter 10: The knapped stone. In I. Hodder (ed), *On the surface: Çatalhöyük 1993-95*, 173-98. Cambridge & Ankara: McDonald Institute for Archaeological Research & British Institute of Archaeology at Ankara

Cummings, V. 2002. Experiencing texture and transformation in the British Neolithic. *Oxford Journal of Archaeology* 21, 249-61

Cummings, V., Jones, A. & Watson, A. 2002.

Divided places: phenomenology and asymmetry in the monuments of the Black Mountains, south-east Wales. *Cambridge Archaeological Journal* 12, 57-70

Dobres, M.-A. 2000. *Technology and Social Agency.* Oxford: Blackwell

Eagleton, T. 1996. *Literary Theory: an introduction.* Oxford: Blackwell

Edmonds, M. 2001. *Stone Tools and Society: working stone in Neolithic and Bronze Age Britain.* London & New York: Routledge

Evans, J. & O'Connor, T. 1999. *Environmental Archaeology: principles and methods.* Stroud: Sutton

Evans, J.G. 2003. *Environmental Archaeology and the Social Order.* London: Routledge

Finlay, N., Finlayson, B. & Mithen, S. 2000. Chapter 8.3. The primary technology: its character and inter-site variability. In S. Mithen (ed.), *Hunter-gatherer Landscape Archaeology: the southern Hebrides Mesolithic project, 1988–98*, 553-69. Cambridge: McDonald Inst-itute for Archaeological Research

Gamble, C. 1999. *The Palaeolithic Settlement of Europe.* Cambridge: Cambridge University Press

Goffman, E. 1969. *The Presentation of Self in Everyday Life.* Harmondsworth: Penguin Books

Humphrey, J. & Young, R. 1999. Flint use in later Bronze Age and Iron Age England – still a fiction? *Lithics* 20, 57-61

Karlin, C. & Julien, M. 1994. Prehistoric technology: a cognitive science? In C. Renfrew & E.B.W. Zubrow (eds), *The Ancient Mind: elements of cognitive archaeology*, 152-64. Cambridge: Cambridge University Press

Kendall, H.G.O. 1922. Scraper-core industries in north Wilts. *Proceedings of the Prehistoric Society of East Anglia* 3, 515-41

Mellars, P. 1987. *Excavations on Oronsay: prehistoric human ecology on a small island.* Edinburgh: Edinburgh University Press

Mithen, S., Lake, M. & Finlay, N. 2000. Chapter 4.10. Bolsay Farm, Islay: area excavation. In S. Mithen (ed.), *Hunter-gatherer Landscape Archaeology: the southern Hebrides Mesolithic project, 1988–98*, 291-328. Cambridge: McDonald Institute for Archaeological Research

Mithen, S. & Finlay, N. 2000. Chapter 5.2. Staosnaig, Colonsay: excavations 1989–1995. In S. Mithen (ed.), *Hunter-gatherer Landscape Archaeology: the southern Hebrides Mesolithic project, 1988–98*, 359-441. Cambridge: McDonald Institute for Archaeological Research

Moore, H.L. 1986. *Space, Text and Gender: an anthropological study of the Marakwet of Kenya.* Cambridge: Cambridge University Press

Pitts, M.W. 1978. On the shape of waste flakes as an index of technological change in lithic industries. *Journal of Archaeological Science* 5, 17-37

Pollard, T. 1996. Time and tide: coastal environ-ments, cosmology and ritual practice in early prehistoric Scotland. In T. Pollard and A. Morrison (eds), *The Early Prehistory of Scotland*, 198-210. Edinburgh: Edinburgh University Press

Renfrew, C. & Zubrow, E.B.W. (eds) 1994. *The Ancient Mind: elements of cognitive archaeo-logy.* Cambridge: Cambridge University Press

Richards, J. 1990. *The Stonehenge Environs Project.* London: English Heritage

Schlanger, N. 1994. Mindful technology: unleashing the *chaîne opératoire* for an arch-aeology of the mind. In C. Renfrew & E.B.W. Zubrow (eds), *The Ancient Mind: elements of cognitive archaeology*, 143-51. Cambridge: Cambridge University Press

Schofield, J., Millett, M., Keay, S. & Carreté, J.-M. 1999. Prehistoric settlement in the Tarragona region of north-east Spain: results from the Ager Tarraconensis survey. *Lithics* 20, 33-47

Schulting, R.J. & Richards, M.P. 2001. Dating women and becoming farmers: new palaeo-dietary and AMS dating evidence from the Breton Mesolithic cemeteries of Téviec and Hoëdic. *Journal of Anthropological Archaeo-logy* 20, 314-44

Seremetakis, N. 1991. *The Last Word: women, death and divination in Inner Mani.* Chicago: University of Chicago Press

Shanks, M. & Hodder, I. 1995. Processual, post-processual and interpretive archaeology. In I. Hodder, M. Shanks, A. Alexandri, V. Buchli, J. Carman, J. Last & G. Lucas (eds), *Interpreting Archaeology: finding meaning in the past*, 3-29. London: Routledge

Shanks, M. & Tilley, C. 1987. *Social Theory and Archaeology.* Cambridge: Polity Press

Sharples, N.M. 1991. *Maiden Castle: excavation and field survey 1985–6.* London: English Heritage

Smith, I.F. 1965. *Windmill Hill and Avebury: excavations by Alexander Keiller, 1925–1939*. Oxford: Clarendon Press

Sullivan, A.P. 2001. Holme's principle and beyond: the case for renewing Americanist debitage analysis. In W. Andrefsky (ed.), *Lithic Debitage: context, form and meaning*, 192-206. Salt Lake City: University of Utah Press

Taçon, P. 1991. The power of stone: symbolic aspects of stone use and tool development in Western Arnhem Land, Australia. *Antiquity* 65, 192-207

Whittle, A. 1997. *Sacred Mound, Holy Rings. Silbury Hill and the West Kennet palisade enclosures: a Later Neolithic complex in north Wiltshire*. Oxford: Oxbow

Whittle, A., Pollard, J. & Grigson, C. 1999. *The Harmony of Symbols: the Windmill Hill causewayed enclosure, Wiltshire*. Oxford: Oxbow Books

Whittle, A.W.R., Rouse, A.J. & Evans, J.G. 1993. A Neolithic downland monument in its environment: excavations at Easton Down long barrow, Bishops Cannings, north Wiltshire. *Proceedings of the Prehistoric Society* 59, 197-240

Woodward, A. 2000. *British Barrows: a matter of life and death*. Stroud: Tempus

Woodward, P.J. 1991. *The South Dorset Ridgeway: survey and excavations 1977-84*. Dorchester: Dorset Natural History & Archaeological Society

A Polished Flint Axehead from near Hayscastle, Pembrokeshire, Wales, and its Typological Context

Alan Saville

The exceptional polished flint axehead published here (Figs. 1-3) is one of the prehistoric gems in the collection of Tenby Museum (registration number TENBM: 1983: 2066), where it has been since 1881 when it was presented by the Revd D. Bateman. Bateman had been given the axehead some time after 1840 by Mrs Skreel, widow of the finder Mr Skreel, who had, according to museum records, found it that year 'in a turf moor near New House Farm, Hayscastle, north-east of Newgale'. An alternative provenance from 'a bog on Plumstone Mountain' was given by Laws (1888, 17). Plumstone Mountain is actually east of Newgale (at NGR c.SM 915 233), while Hayscastle is north-east of Newgale (at c.SM 897 256). New House Farm itself is at Pont-yr-hafod, immediately north-east of Hayscastle (at c.SM 905 263). In the absence of any more specific clue to the actual findspot, somewhere within walking distance of Pont-yr-hafod is the best guess for where Mr Skreel found this axehead. Nevertheless, it seems appropriate to retain Hayscastle for the axehead's conventional geographic designation as per the museum records.

The first notice of the axehead seems to have been by Laws (1888, 17), who described it as 'a very beautiful axe, of chert, which has acquired a rich golden hue either from peat water, or iron, since it was made'. In his booklet on the prehistoric collections of Tenby Museum, Leach (1918, 6) described this axehead as follows:

> A very beautiful axe of polished flint, taken from a peat bog near St Davids [Case 12], illustrates the wonderful skill attained by prehistoric workers in flint. It could not have been made in this county. Possibly it came from south-eastern England, if not from a source outside the British Isles.

In the second edition of this booklet (1931) the reference to '... outside the British Isles' was deleted. An undated sheet of museum documentation on the axehead, which was originally classified as 'A10 (Hayscastle)', says:

> This axe must have been made in SE England or in the Continent: flint of similar quality and zonal markings abounds in the Thames Valley at Swanscombe below Dartford. Many of the well-known Early Palaeolithic hand-axes and flakes [Clactonian and Acheulian] found in the Swanscombe High Terrace gravels were made of such banded flints.

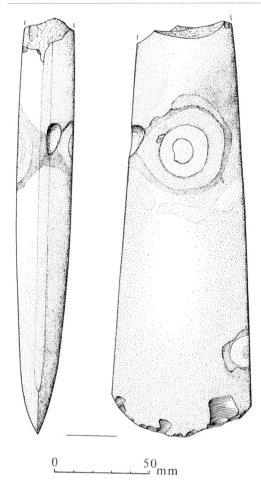

0   50
└─────┴─────┴─────┘ mm

Fig. 1. Hayscastle flint axehead: line drawing by
Marion O'Neil (after a sketch by Alan Saville)

The documentation sheet also, percipiently
(see below), cites a parallel for the axehead in an
example (AF62) published with an illustration
in the catalogue of the National Museum of
Antiquities of Scotland (Anon 1892). This is one
of the well-known pair of flint axeheads (the
'Smerrick hoard') found near Enzie in former
Banffshire, north-east Scotland (Anon 1882, fig.
2; cf. Clarke et al. 1985, 253-4 & fig. 5.10).

The axehead does not appear to have
attracted any further attention until it was mentioned by Pitts (1996, 342) and a photograph of
it, grouped together with three other axeheads,
was published by Children and Nash (1997, pl.
2). Since 1998 the axehead has again been on
permanent display in Tenby Museum.

The Hayscastle axehead (Figs. 1-3)

This is a flint axehead of refined form with a
high-gloss surface finish, damaged at the cutting
edge and broken at the butt. Most of the damage
at the cutting edge is ancient and the same
colour as the body of the axehead, though two
chips expose the interior mid-grey flint, as does
the more recent break and flaked edge at the
butt. These break and flake surfaces at the butt
are slightly corticated, however, so are not
entirely modern.

The immediately striking element about the
appearance of the axehead is produced by the
banding within the flint, which results in
concentric sub-circular ring-features on both
faces, most pronounced towards the butt end,
and to a lesser extent towards the cutting edge.
Both these features are also visible on the
respective side of the axehead to which they are
adjacent. The overall surface colours – yellow,
orange, brown, grey – result from variable
staining, possibly within peat, and are
generally lighter on the face with the paper
label (Fig. 2). The condition of the surface is
now less than perfect; there are several 'potlid'
flake scars and the original high gloss has dulled
somewhat.

There are other surface pits and striations
visible under magnification, some of which, but
definitely not all, may relate to the pre-polish
grinding. Nevertheless, it is clear that originally
this was a superb piece, with no trace of the
preparatory flaking remaining visible on what
was macroscopically a flawless polished
surface.

The current maximum length is 231mm, the
maximum breadth (at the cutting edge) is 72mm,

and the maximum thickness is 30mm. The weight is 650 grams. Both of the convergent lateral edges are virtually straight. The side facets are marked, extremely well-prepared, and run the whole length of the axehead. These facets are slightly bevelled or convex rather than being perfectly flat, and their edge angles only approach sharpness at one point towards the butt on the shorter side. The maximum width of the side facets is 5mm. The cross-section is a flattened oval and the refinement of the axehead is indicated by the thickness:length ratio (1:7.7), which would of course have been even more pronounced when the axehead was complete.

More subjectively, the axehead when tapped has the 'ring of fine china' which characterizes slender, 'refined' flint axeheads (as it does those of jadeite).

Something of the museum history of the object is indicated by the adhering circular paper label, marked 'A10' in black ink, with 'TENBM:1983:2066' added subsequently and then lacquered. On the broken butt end 'P90' is written in black ink, which relates to cataloguing of the axehead in the county-by-county petrological survey lists, the 'P' standing for Pembrokeshire (Houlder 1988).

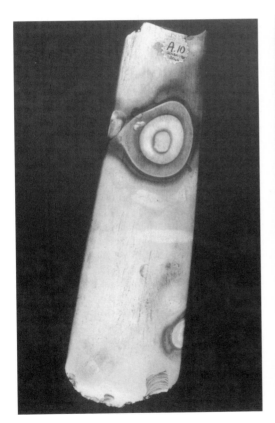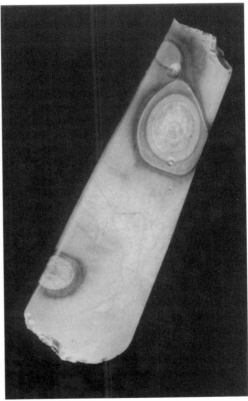

Figs. 2-3. Photographs of the Hayscastle axehead at Tenby Museum, showing both faces

Discussion

The Hayscastle axehead belongs to an increasingly well-recognized sub-group of British Neolithic flint axeheads with all-over polish and high gloss, the other characteristics of which are a symmetrical form, near-straight convergent edges, side facets, a semi-circular butt, and an absence of traces of the original flaking. They tend to be of above average length (often above 200mm), slender and highly refined, as shown by the thickness:length ratio, and using flint which is distinctive by virtue of fossil inclusions, unusual colour, or, more particularly, variegated colour in mottled or banded form. The type has recently been reviewed by Sheridan (1992, 209) and Saville (1999) when publishing new finds of Scottish examples. These axeheads are inter-preted as high-status, prestige artefacts, never intended to be hafted as functional axes, but perhaps used ceremonially in some way, vener-ated, and/or involved in complex gift exchange.

As the writer of the Tenby Museum docu-mentation sheet recognized, a close match in terms of overall character and raw material for the Hayscastle axehead is with the smaller of the two axeheads in the 'Smerrick hoard' from north-east Scotland (see above). It is indeed in Scotland that what might usefully be called the Smerrick type of polished flint axehead is best attested, with 11 examples from predominantly east-coast findspots (Saville 1999, illus 2).

Since publishing the example from Bolshan Hill (Saville 1999), the present author has been investigating the occurrence of definite and related instances throughout the UK. There are several findspots in England, which by and large reinforce the predominantly eastern distribution of the type. These include the well-known examples from Helpringham, Lincolnshire (Moore 1979, 85-6) and Kentford, Suffolk (Edwardson 1962).

The Hayscastle axehead appears to be the only example of this type so far known from Wales, and is thus an anomalous, far-flung,

westerly outlier to the current distribution. There are, however, no grounds for doubting its general provenance in Pembrokeshire, and, especially given the early date of the find, there is little reason to suspect it could be a modern loss of a discovery originally made elsewhere.

Perhaps more relevant than its westerly location is the situation of the findspot only seven or so kilometres (less than five miles) from the present coast, a locational characteristic it shares with most of the Scottish examples. Any significance to be drawn from this distribution is not straightforward, but, since the raw material is clearly not local to Wales any more than it is to Scotland, it can perhaps be suggested that these axeheads may normally have arrived by sea.

Origin of the raw material is obviously the key to understanding more about this group of axeheads, but no resolution of this issue has been reached. Leach's (1918) speculation about a foreign source is of interest, and perhaps more feasible than the suggestion about south-east England, since nothing quite similar occurs at Swanscombe or the Thames Valley, and since there is no south-eastern concentration of this axehead type to suggest a centre of production.

I have discussed elsewhere (Saville 1999) the similarity of the kind of banded raw material used for axeheads like that from Hayscastle with flint found in Denmark and commonly used for axeheads there in the Neolithic period (Vang Petersen 1999, 22-23). I also considered the problems posed by the fact that the otherwise most comparable class of so-called thin-butted axeheads found in Denmark and adjacent areas is typologically distinct from the Smerrick-type axeheads in normally having much more pronounced side facets, giving a less lenticular, more sub-rectangular cross-section (Stafford 1999, 44-50). Nevertheless, one is left with the fact that axeheads like some of those in the famous hoard of thin-butted axeheads from Hagelbjerggård, Jutland (Nielsen 1977, fig. 36), provide the best raw material and general size/shape analogues for the Smerrick type. Despite the infrequency of any other recognizable

Neolithic imports from Scandinavia, an origin for the raw material for these axeheads in the banded flint of Denmark still seems possible (Saville 1999).

If this is so, and no convincing alternative source for the raw material has yet been suggested, there seems little doubt that axeheads of Smerrick type would have, simply by virtue of their exotic raw material, a high prestige value (Taffinder 1998). Add to this the impact of the sheer size of these axeheads and the quality of their exquisite surface finish, then their symbolic characteristics are likely to have been consid-erable. Whatever its precise origin, the Hayscastle axehead would have been fantastic-ally alien in Neolithic Wales and hence likely to have been an item of significant socio-economic and/or socio-political power. In fact it would seem reasonable to categorize the Hayscastle and other Smerrick-type axeheads as classic hypertrophic items, which in a Neolithic context would be '... rare, demand a high degree of manufacturing skill and a large investment in time, and... made of raw materials to which there is limited access' (Olausson 1997, 270).

The implications of this for assessment of social organization in Neolithic Pembrokeshire, as elsewhere in Britain where such axeheads are found, remain to be addressed. Implicit in current conceptualizations of Neolithic society, however, is the supposition that Smerrick-type axeheads, like other 'exotics', indicate the existence of elites or 'aggrandizers' (Olausson 2000, 122). The rationale for this rests upon the assumption that these axeheads would be universally desired and that elites would control their acquisition within a prestige-goods social system, thereby reinforcing the social power of those elites. One of the many outstanding questions begged by this scenario, if it is true that these axeheads were coming from Scandinavia, would be the mechanism by which their importation was secured, and whether the impetus for that mechanism lay in Britain or abroad.

Acknowledgements

I am grateful to Nicholas Moore for initially drawing my attention to the illustration of this axehead in Children and Nash (1997) and for further helpful advice. When I visited Tenby Museum in 2001 I was given every assistance by the hospitable staff to facilitate my study of the axehead, and I thank Sally Goodyear in particular for her help in many ways. The photographs were taken for me by a local professional photographer, Gareth Davis, and I am grateful to Joyce Smith of NMS Photography for help with reproducing them here. Marion O'Neil turned my crude pencil sketch into the finished drawing shown in Fig.1. My travel and accommodation expenses when visiting Tenby were covered by an award from the Friends of the National Museums of Scotland.

It is a pleasure to dedicate this note to Isobel Smith in view of her career-long interest in Neolithic flint and stone tools, and to be able to acknowledge my personal indebtedness to her, initially for the example and inspiration provided by her seminal book on Windmill Hill, then subsequently for the direct help and friendly guidance and encourage-ment she has given me in prehistoric studies.

Bibliography

Anon. 1882. List of the articles acquired by the Purchase Committee. *Proceedings of the Society of Antiquaries of Scotland* 16 (1881–82), 407-417

Anon. 1892. *Catalogue of the National Museum of Antiquities of Scotland*. Edinburgh: Society of Antiquaries of Scotland

Children, G. & Nash, G. 1997. *The Anthropology of Landscape: a Guide to Neolithic Sites in Cardiganshire, Carmarthenshire and Pembrokeshire*. Little Logaston: Logaston Press

Clarke, D.V., Cowie, T.G. & Foxon, A. 1985. *Symbols of Power at the Time of Stonehenge*. Edinburgh: HMSO

Edwardson, A.R. 1962. Two Neolithic axes from Suffolk. *Proceedings of the Suffolk Institute of Archaeology* 29(2), 216

Houlder, C.H. 1988. The petrological identification of stone implements from Wales. In T.H.McK. Clough & W.A. Cummins (eds), *Stone Axe Studies, Volume 2*, 133-136. London: Council for British Archaeology

Laws, E. 1888. *The History of Little England Beyond*

Wales. London: George Bell & Sons

Leach, A.L. 1918. *Some Prehistoric Remains in the Tenby Museum*. Tenby

Moore, C.N. 1979. Stone axes from the East Midlands. In T.H.McK. Clough & W.A. Cummins (eds), *Stone Axe Studies*, 82-89. London: Council for British Archaeology

Nielsen, P.O. 1977. Die Flintbeile der frühen Trichterbecherkultur in Dänemark. *Acta Archaeologica* 48, 61-138

Olausson, D. 1997. Craft specialization as an agent of social power in the south Scandinavian Neolithic. In R. Schild & Z. Sulgostowska (eds), *Man and Flint*, 269-277. Warsaw: Institute of Archaeology and Ethnology, Polish Academy of Sciences

Olausson, D. 2000. Talking axes, social daggers. In D. Olausson & H. Vandkilde (eds), *Form, Function and Context*, 121-133. Stockholm: Almquist & Wiksell International (Acta Archaeologica Lundensia Series in 8⁰, No.31)

Pitts, M. 1996. The stone axe in Neolithic Britain.

Proceedings of the Prehistoric Society 62, 311-371

Saville, A. 1999. An exceptional polished flint axehead from Bolshan Hill, near Montrose, Angus. *Tayside & Fife Archaeological Journal* 5, 1-6

Sheridan, A. 1992. Scottish stone axeheads: some new work and recent discoveries. In N. Sharples & A. Sheridan (eds), *Vessels for the Ancestors: Essays on the Neolithic of Britain and Ireland in Honour of Audrey Henshall*, 194-212. Edinburgh: Edinburgh University Press

Stafford, M. 1999. *From Forager to Farmer in Flint. A Lithic Analysis of the Prehistoric Transition to Agriculture in Southern Scandinavia*. Aarhus: Aarhus University Press

Taffinder, J. 1998. *The Allure of the Exotic: The Social Use of Non-Local Raw Materials during the Stone Age in Sweden*. Uppsala: Department of Archaeology and Ancient History, Uppsala University (=*Aun* 25)

Vang Petersen, P. 1999. *Flint fra Danmarks Oldtid* (2nd edn). København: Høst & Søn

Isobel Foster Smith: a bibliography

Compiled by Alan Saville

Note: This bibliography aims to include all of Isobel Smith's major works. It also attempts to include her shorter notes, reviews, and specialist finds contributions, but the latter are so numerous that many may regrettably have escaped the compiler's attention. Deliberately excluded are the many instances where Isobel Smith's advice and comments on finds are noted by the authors of excavation reports but not specifically itemized. I am very grateful to Frances Healy for assistance with some of the following references.

1954
(with V.G. Childe) The excavation of a Neolithic barrow on Whiteleaf Hill, Bucks. *Proceedings of the Prehistoric Society* 20 (1954), 212-30

(with S.H. Warren) Neolithic pottery from the submerged land-surface of the Essex coast. *Annual Report of the University of London Institute of Archaeology* 10 (1954), 26-33

1955
Late Beaker pottery from the Lyonesse surface and the date of the transgression. *Annual Report of the University of London Institute of Archaeology* 11 (1955), 29-42

Bibliography of the publications of Professor V Gordon Childe. *Proceedings of the Prehistoric Society* 21 (1955), 295-304

1956
The Decorative Art of Neolithic Ceramics in South-East England and its Relations. Unpublished PhD thesis, University of London Institute of Archaeology

(with J.J. Butler) Razors, urns, and the British Middle Bronze Age. *Annual Report of the University of London Institute of Archaeology* 12 (1956), 20-52

1958
The 1957–8 excavations at Windmill Hill. *Antiquity* 32 (1958), 268-9

1959
Excavations at Windmill Hill, Avebury, Wilts., 1957–58. *Wiltshire Archaeological & Natural History Magazine* 57 (1959), 149-62

Windmill Hill and Avebury: a Short Account of the Excavations, 1925-1939. London: The Clover Press

1960
Museum acquisitions: macehead and axes. *Wiltshire Archaeological & Natural History Magazine* 57 (1960), 400-2

Radiocarbon dates from Windmill Hill. *Antiquity* 34 (1960), 212-13

(with P. Ashbee) The Windmill Hill long barrow. *Antiquity* 34 (1960), 297-9

(with S.S. Frere) The pottery. In J.H. Money, Excavations at High Rocks, Tunbridge Wells, 1954–1956. *Sussex Archaeological Collections* 98 (1960), 207-11

1961
An essay towards the reformation of the British Bronze Age. *Helinium* 1.2 (1961), 97-118

Review of P. Ashbee, 'The Bronze Age Round Barrow in Britain'. *Antiquaries Journal* 41 (1961), 243-4

1962
The pottery and flints. In P.A. Rahtz, Farncombe Down barrow, Berkshire. *Berkshire Archaeological Journal* 60 (1962), 13-19

The pottery. In J F Dyer, Neolithic and Bronze Age sites at Barton Hill Farm, Bedfordshire. *Bedfordshire Archaeological Journal* 1 (1962), 14-19

1963
Review of S. Piggott, 'The West Kennet long barrow, excavations 1955–56'. *Wiltshire Archaeological & Natural History Magazine* 58 (1963), 462-4

Appendix B. Notes on the flints from Rag Copse barrow. In G.M. Knocker, Excavation of a round barrow in Rag Copse, near Hurstbourne Tarrant, Hants. *Proceedings of the Hampshire Field Club* 22.3 (1963), 141-3

Transversely sharpened axe from Cornwall. *Proceedings of the Prehistoric Society* 29 (1963), 429

1964
Avebury: the northern inner circle. *Wiltshire Archaeological & Natural History Magazine* 59 (1964), 181

(with D.D.A. Simpson) A leatherworker's grave from North Wiltshire. *Antiquity* 38 (1964), 57-61

(with N.H. Field & C.L. Matthews) New Neolithic sites in Dorset and Bedfordshire, with a note on the distribution of Neolithic storage-pits in Britain. *Proceedings of the Prehistoric Society* 30 (1964), 352-81

(with D.D.A. Simpson) Excavation of three Roman tombs and a prehistoric pit on Overton Down. *Wiltshire Archaeological & Natural History Magazine* 59 (1964), 68-85

(with J.J. Wymer) The Treacher collection of prehistoric artefacts from Marlow. *Records of Buckinghamshire* 17.4 (1964), 286-300

Review of S. Piggott (ed), 'The Prehistoric Peoples of Scotland'. *Antiquaries Journal* 44 (1964), 67

1965
Windmill Hill and Avebury: excavations by Alexander Keiller, 1925-1939. Oxford: Clarendon Press

Excavation of a bell barrow, Avebury G.55. *Wiltshire Archaeological & Natural History Magazine* 60 (1965), 24-46

Neolithic pottery from Rybury Camp. *Wiltshire Archaeological & Natural History Magazine* 60 (1965), 127

Windmill Hill ware and Beaker ware. In G. Connah, Excavations at Knap Hill, Alton Priors, 1961. *Wiltshire Archaeological & Natural History Magazine* 60 (1965), 11-14

[Note on the Bronze Age pot] In H.C. Bowen & P.J. Fowler, A Bronze Age pit near Jenner's Firs, Upavon. *Wiltshire Archaeological & Natural History Magazine* 60 (1965), 128-9

1966

Pottery from the Lambourn long barrow. In J.J. Wymer, Excavations of the Lambourn long barrow, 1964. *Berkshire Archaeological Journal* 62 (1965–66), 10-14

Windmill Hill and its implications. *Palaeohistoria* 12 (1966), 469-81

(with D.D.A. Simpson) Excavation of a round barrow on Overton Hill, north Wiltshire, England. *Proceedings of the Prehistoric Society* 32 (1966), 122-55

Description and catalogue of the Neolithic and Bronze Age pottery. In P. Ashbee, The Fussell's Lodge long barrow excavations, 1957. *Archaeologia* 100, 18-23

Neolithic finds. In S.H.M. Pollard, Neolithic and Dark Age settlements on High Peak, Sidmouth, Devon. *Proceedings of the Devon Archaeological & Exploration Society* 23 (1966), 44-52

Worked flints from Old Burrow and Martinhoe. In A. Fox & W.L.D. Ravenhill, Early Roman outposts on the North Devon coast, Old Burrow and Martinhoe. *Proceedings of the Devon Archaeological & Exploration Society* 24 (1966), 36-7

(with P. Ashbee) The date of the Windmill Hill long barrow. *Antiquity* 40 (1966), 299

[Western Neolithic vessel.] In J.H. Barrett, Tom Tivey's Hole rock shelter, near Leighton, Somerset. *Proceedings of the University of Bristol Spelaeological Society* 11.1 (1965–1966) 18

1967

Pottery and flints from sites A, B, C, D, and M. In A. Oswald (ed), Excavations for the Avon/Severn

Research Committee at Barford, Warwickshire. *Transactions of Birmingham & Warwickshire Archaeological Society* 83 (1966–67), 33-7

Pottery from site E. In A. Oswald (ed), Excavations for the Avon/Severn Research Committee at Barford, Warwickshire. *Transactions of Birmingham & Warwickshire Archaeological Society* 83 (1966–67), 45-6

Report on the pottery. In P.M. Christie, A barrow-cemetery of the second millennium B.C. in Wiltshire, England. *Proceedings of the Prehistoric Society* 33 (1967), 350-53

Finds. In S.H.M. Pollard, Seven prehistoric sites near Honiton, Devon. Part I. A Beaker flint ring and 3 flint cairns. *Proceedings of the Devon Archaeological & Exploration Society* 25 (1967), 27-8 & 36

The Beaker pottery from site OD XI. In P.J. Fowler, The archaeology of Fyfield and Overton Downs, Wiltshire (third interim report). *Wiltshire Archaeological & Natural History Magazine* 62 (1967), 30-1

1968

Report on Late Neolithic pits at Cam, Gloucestershire. *Transactions of the Bristol & Gloucestershire Archaeological Society* 87 (1968), 14-28

(with J.G. Evans) Excavation of two long barrows in North Wiltshire. *Antiquity* 42 (1968), 138-42

Review of P.J. Fowler, 'Wessex'. *Wiltshire Archaeological & Natural History Magazine* 63 (1968), 127

The pottery. In R. Sanford, Excavation at Church Street, Twickenham. *Borough of Twickenham Local History Society Paper* 12

1969

A flint axe from Bere Regis. *Proceedings of the*

Dorset Archaeological & Natural History Society 91 (1969), 174

Prehistoric pottery from Baston Manor, Hayes. *Kent Archaeological Review* 18, 30-31

Flint tools. In S.H.M. Pollard & P.M.G. Russell, Excavation of a Round Barrow 248b, Upton Pyne, Exeter. *Proceedings of the Devon Archaeological Society* 27 (1969), 69-70

1970
Pottery. In P.M. Christie, A round barrow on Greenland Farm, Winterbourne Stoke. *Wiltshire Archaeological & Natural History Magazine* 65B (1970), 69

Review of P. Ashbee, 'The Earthen Long Barrow in Britain'. *Wiltshire Archaeological & Natural History Magazine* 65B (1970), 223

1971
Causewayed enclosures. In D.D.A. Simpson (ed), *Economy and settlement in Neolithic and Bronze Age Britain and Europe*, 89-112. Leicester: Leicester University Press

1972
Ring-ditches in eastern and central Gloucestershire. In P.J. Fowler (ed), *Archaeology and the Landscape: Essays for L.V. Grinsell*, 157-67. London: John Baker

(with E.D. Evens & F.S. Wallis) The petrological identification of stone implements from southwestern England: fifth report of the subcommittee of the South-Western Federation of Museums and Art Galleries. *Proceedings of the Prehistoric Society* 38 (1972), 235-75

Flints from Nanstallon. In A. Fox & W. Ravenhill, The Roman fort at Nanstallon, Cornwall. *Britannia* 3 (1972), 108

1973
Prehistory. In C. & A.M. Hadfield (eds), *The*

Cotswolds: a New Study, 76-84. Newton Abbot: David & Charles

Review of G.J. Wainwright & I.H. Longworth, 'Durrington Walls: Excavations 1966–68'. *Wiltshire Archaeological & Natural History Magazine* 68 (1973), 152-3

The prehistoric pottery [from site 1, Baston Manor, Hayes]. In B.J. Philp, *Excavations in West Kent 1960–1970*, 9-14. Dover: Kent Archaeological Rescue Unit (Research Report 2)

1974
The Neolithic pottery. In F. Pryor, *Excavation at Fengate, Peterborough, England: the first report*, 31-3. Toronto: Royal Ontario Museum Archaeology Monograph 3

The jet bead from Fengate, 1972. In F. Pryor, *Excavation at Fengate, Peterborough, England: the first report*, 40-42. Toronto: Royal Ontario Museum Archaeology Monograph 3

The Neolithic. In C. Renfrew (ed), *British Prehistory: a New Outline*, 100-36. London: Duckworth

A stone axe from Huish. *Wiltshire Archaeological & Natural History Magazine* 69 (1974), 173

The pottery. In A.B. Page, The excavation of a round barrow at West Meon Hut, Hampshire. *Rescue Archaeology in Hampshire* 2, 26

1975
(with B. Philp) A new Neolithic site at Cheriton, Folkstone. *Kent Archaeological Review* 42, 42-5

Neolithic pottery. In K. Jarvis & V. Maxfield, The excavation of a first-century Roman farmstead and a Late Neolithic settlement, Topsham, Devon. *Proceedings of the Devon Archaeological Society* 33 (1975), 249-51

1976
The pottery. In J.M. Coles & B.J. Orme, The

Sweet Track, Railway site. *Somerset Levels Papers* 2 (1976), 63-4

(with H.C. Bowen, B. Eagles, *et al.*) *Ancient and Historical Monuments in the County of Gloucester, Volume One: Iron Age and Romano-British monuments in the Gloucestershire Cotswolds*. London: HMSO (Royal Commission on Historical Monuments, England)

Pottery discussion. In C.L. Matthews, *Occupation sites on a Chiltern Ridge*, 9-11. Oxford: British Archaeological Reports (British Series 29)

1977
(with H.C. Bowen) Sarsen stones in Wessex: the Society's first investigations in the evolution of the landscape project. *Antiquaries Journal* 57.2 (1977), 185-96

Pottery and flint industry. In J.D. Ogilvie, The Stourmouth–Adisham water-main trench. *Archaeologia Cantiana* 93 (1977), 97-101

1978
Review of J. Guilaine (ed), 'La Préhistoire Française. Tome II. Les Civilisations Néolithiques et Prothistoriques de la France'. *Antiquaries Journal* 58 (1978), 170-71

1979
Long barrows in Hampshire and the Isle of Wight. London: HMSO (Royal Commission on Historical Monuments, England)

The chronology of British stone implements. In T.H.McK. Clough & W.A. Cummins (eds), *Stone Axe Studies*, 13–22. London: Council for British Archaeology (Research Report 23)

Pottery report. In A. Saville, Further excavations at Nympsfield chambered tomb, Gloucestershire, 1974. *Proceedings of the Prehistoric Society* 45 (1979), 76-7

(with P. Ashbee and J.G. Evans) Excavations of three long barrows near Avebury, Wiltshire. *Proceedings of the Prehistoric Society* 45 (1979), 207-300

(with D.J. Bonney) *Stonehenge and its Environs: Monuments and Land Use*. Edinburgh: Edinburgh University Press (for the Royal Commission on Historical Monuments, England)

1981
Stone artefacts. In R.J. Mercer, Excavations at Carn Brea, Illogan, Cornwall, 1970–73 – a Neolithic fortified complex of the third millennium bc. *Cornish Archaeology* 20 (1981), 153-60

The Neolithic pottery. In R.J. Mercer, Excavations at Carn Brea, Illogan, Cornwall, 1970–73 – a Neolithic fortified complex of the third millennium bc. *Cornish Archaeology* 20 (1981), 161-85

The earlier prehistoric pottery. In R.J. Silvester, Excavations at Honeyditches Roman villa, Seaton, in 1978. *Proceedings of the Devon Archaeological Society* 39, 57-9

(with M. Guido) Figsbury Rings: a reconsideration of the inner enclosure. *Wiltshire Archaeological & Natural History Magazine* 76 (1981), 21-5

1982
Pottery. In P.J. Fasham, The excavation of four ring-ditches in central Hampshire. *Proceedings of the Hampshire Field Club Archaeological Society* 38 (1982), 22 & fiche

1983
(with J G Evans) Excavations at Cherhill, North Wiltshire, 1967. *Proceedings of the Prehistoric Society* 49 (1983), 43-117

1985
(with S.J. Shennan & F. Healy) The excavation of a ring-ditch at Tye Field, Lawford, Essex. *Archaeological Journal* 142 (1985), 150-215

(with C. Grigson) Neolithic pottery and the

horncore of an aurochs (*Bos primigenius*) from Corhampton, Hampshire. *Proceedings of the Hampshire Field Club Archaeological Society* 41 (1985), 63-8

[observations on Millbarrow] In C.T. Barker, The long mounds of the Avebury region. *Wiltshire Archaeological & Natural History Magazine* 79 (1985), 15-16

1987
Neolithic pottery. In H.R. Hurst, D.L. Dartnall & C. Fisher, Excavations at Box Roman Villa, 1967–8. *Wiltshire Archaeological & Natural History Magazine* 81 (1987), 44

The Neolithic and Bronze Age pottery. In C.S. Green, *Excavations at Poundbury, Vol.1*, 114-17. Dorchester: Dorset Natural History & Archaeological Society (Monograph Series No.7)

1988
(with R.V. Davis & H. Howard) The petrological identification of stone implements from south-west England: sixth report. In T.H.McK. Clough & W.A. Cummins (eds), *Stone Axe Studies: Volume Two*, 14-20. London: Council for British Archaeology (Research Report 67)

1989
Ring-ditches. In T.C. Darvill & L.V. Grinsell, Gloucestershire barrows: supplement 1961–1988. *Transactions of the Bristol & Gloucestershire Archaeological Society* 107 (1989), 84-96

1990
(with T.C. Darvill) The prehistoric pottery. In A.

Saville, *Hazleton North, Gloucestershire, 1979–82: the Excavation of a Neolithic Long Cairn of the Cotswold-Severn Group*, 141-52. London: English Heritage (Archaeological Report No.13)

1991
Round barrows Wilsford cum Lake G51–G54: excavations by Ernest Greenfield in 1958. *Wiltshire Archaeological & Natural History Magazine* 84 (1991), 11-39

1993
Review of C. Gingell, 'The Marlborough Downs: a Later Bronze Age Landscape and its Origins'. *Wiltshire Archaeological & Natural History Magazine* 86 (1993), 168-70

Neolithic pottery. In A. Hannan, Excavations at Tewkesbury, 1972-74. *Transactions of the Bristol & Gloucestershire Archaeological Society* 111 (1993), 46

1997
The Neolithic pottery. In R. Mercer, The excavation of a Neolithic enclosure complex at Helman Tor, Lostwithiel, Cornwall. *Cornish Archaeology* 36 (1997), 29-37

Forthcoming
The pottery from the hilltop excavations of 1974-82, and stone axes. In R.J. Mercer & F. Healy, *Hambledon Hill, Dorset, England. Excavation and Survey of a Neolithic Monument Complex and its Surrounding Landscape*. English Heritage

Index

This is primarily an index of names, places and sites. Certain categories of material culture are included where considered appropriate, but the listing is by no means exhaustive. Note, 'Neolithic' and 'Bronze Age' are not included as categories. Page references in italics refer to figures.